ENERGY AND STRUCTURE

*A Theory of Social Power*

*Man's power over Nature turns out to be a power
exercised by some men over other men with Nature
as its instrument.*
C. S. Lewis

# Energy and Structure

## A Theory of Social Power

By RICHARD NEWBOLD ADAMS

UNIVERSITY OF TEXAS PRESS, AUSTIN AND LONDON

Library of Congress Cataloging in Publication Data

Adams, Richard Newbold, 1924–
  Energy and structure.
  Bibliography: p.
  Includes index.
  1. Power (Social sciences) 2. Social structure.
3. Man—Influence on nature. I. Title.
HM136.A23        301.15′5        74–19392
ISBN 0–292–72012–2 (cloth)
ISBN 0–292–72013–0 (paper)

FOR
LESLIE A. WHITE
AND
BETTY HANNSTEIN ADAMS

# CONTENTS

## TABLES

# FIGURES

# PREFACE

The discipline of anthropology has tried, at least in its western branch, to concern itself with man as a whole, as a biological, ecological, cultural, social being, to be seen throughout the entire course of his evolution and history. In this unity there has been both strength and weakness. Certainly of benefit is the fact that it recalls its practitioners' attention from time to time to the object of their dedication, the whole man, the whole species, even though each scholar in his own right must specialize on a geographical region, a historical period, a biological component, a cultural facet, or a particular problem. Even though the solid foundation of knowledge rests on these microscopic foci, the anthropologist is called upon to redirect his consideration to the larger problem to see what implications there may be for mankind. On the negative side, this concern with the whole has turned some anthropologists into intellectual vagabonds, moving from one area and topic to another, picking up concepts and insights from a German physicist, a Japanese novelist, a Brazilian explorer, an African curer, or a Melanesian Big Man. These roving reporters gain in human insight, but eclecticism, even when systematic, seldom results in sound theoretical formulations. In the following, I try to follow the first course, to bring my attention to a general problem that was stimulated by some specific area of investigation to which I was earlier dedicated.

The subject of this essay, social power, has not been in the classic catalogue of anthropological topics. In approaching it I have looked to other disciplines; but, if I know my nonanthropologist colleagues, I will be criticized for borrowing too little rather than too much. The central core and central theoretical products, for better or for worse, were derived principally from my concerns with typically anthropological materials. Although I have been much interested in the power structures of contemporary complex societies and intend to continue to direct attention to them in the future, the basic problem that led me to social power was the question of how societies of more classical anthropological concern were related to the larger world society. My interest was born specifically of witnessing the collapse of the Guatemalan Revolution in 1954 and the effects of events of the previous and subsequent years on that population. Power as a central concept emerged from the fact that in the middle of the twentieth century, whether one was an anthropologist working in a modern university or a village Indian trying to identify and solve his problems in a Central American nation, there were complicated and essentially similar determinants that gripped the actor and forced him to accept alternatives that were far removed from his desires.

It is not only in anthropology that social power has received little attention; it has been underplayed in all of western social science. Of course, its invocation has become a litany in political analysis, but the term *power* is mentioned far more often in the titles of such books than in their indices. I have overtly borrowed little, because so many of the studies have moved so little beyond metaphor, and I do not believe that we can even begin to grasp the nature of a phenomenon until we can dignify it with its own existence.

While I have overtly borrowed little, I am also acutely aware that, taken separately, there is little that is original in this essay. I do believe that, in a subject so close to man, most insights I am likely to have will have earlier occurred to others, especially among those who have dedicated themselves to thinking through those parts of the problem dealt with here. So my intellectual indebtedness is far more extensive than I can indicate or than I am even aware.

The concept of energy, which will prove to be so central to the present work, was introduced into contemporary anthropology literature by Leslie White in his now classic paper, "Energy and the Evolution of Culture" (1943). It was not seriously used as a variable in theory or research until almost two decades later, when it was brought in as part of an empirical concern with energy consumption in the expanding interest in ecology (see Rappaport 1968). My own interest in the subject evolved from undergraduate courses I had with White and led to a series of four papers prepared between 1959 and 1962. I did not seek publication of these works, since I felt that I did not sufficiently command the physical aspect of the problem, but I was sufficiently convinced of certain of the theoretical aspects that I did include some propositions derived therefrom in one article (1962). Today the widespread concern with the role of energy in the future of man is making the entire subject more palatable to many who at an earlier date refused to take it seriously. Nearly thirty years after White's article, professional disinterest in the subject is still evident, however: ". . . to predict directionality to any one part is ultimately impossible because of the enormous number of unknowable factors (which are changing) and which all provide the basis for the ultimate direction of change. Possibly we can be global and say the ultimate direction is entropic, while negentropic for us for the nonce, but this really doesn't say much" (R. Cohen 1972).[1] I hope the present essay will suggest that there is something that can be said, and that it isn't "negentropic for the nonce."[2]

My efforts to comprehend power have led me to a typical scholarly bias: I think that it is an extremely important topic. I see it (as will become evident to the reader who continues) as a part of the process of man's adaptation to the physical world, particularly concerning his relations to the social world around him. To understand it, we need to stand equally in the realm of the "materialistic" and in that of "mentalistic structures." Power rests in the conjunction of what the individual perceives of his own internal being, what he perceives in the world about him, and how he relates these perceptions to establish his relations with other human beings.

The work is basically rationalistic in its methodology, a mode that will leave many anthropologists quite unimpressed. It has been, however, derived from ideas that were constructed to make

[1] Reprinted from *American Anthropologist*, vol. 74, no. 6 (1972), by permission of the American Anthropological Association.

[2] A work that originally appeared in German in 1970 but only came to my attention through its Spanish version during the copy editing of the present work is Hass 1972. While initially treating the same over-all problem, I cannot see that the two efforts parallel each other, or even pose the problems in the same terms.

sense out of assorted but related field materials concerning Latin
America. There is no pretense here of presenting the materials in
a manner that can lead to ready testing, and that will probably dis-
tress fewer social scientists, for there are, as Jack Gibbs has pointed
out, few social-science theories that are seriously subject to that
treatment anyway. But, in the present case, I have found that the
construction of concepts and a series of related theoretical propositions, such as compose this essay, is for the moment a job in itself
and has to come before the propositions can be formulated in a
more rigorous manner.

Working from a series of basic concepts such as appear in Part
One permits one to move in a number of directions. I could, for
example, undertake a detailed analysis of a specific contemporary
or historical case, both to demonstrate and to develop further the
entire set of constructs. Or I could analyze the power theories of
several other scholars or historical figures, to see into the nature of
their construction, as well as, again, to continue the development
of the present one. However, in these choices one's own predilec-
tions are paramount, and I have preferred to examine in more detail the metatheory that lay behind the work (Part Two) and to
apply the concepts to an analysis of the evolution of power to see
if they serve to clarify more classic anthropological materials (Part
Three). The volume is, then, in my view very much an anthropological product; and, while I obviously hope that it will be of use
far beyond that field, that is where it started.

Although it is explicit in Part Two, it is probably worth noting
at the outset that my position in the present essay is monistic; I
assume the world is best explained ultimately in terms that will be
meaningful within scientific discourse; yet I have to resort methodologically to a dualism—a thing many people do as easily as they
think thoughts, or eat nutrients, but without caring one way or
another. But I do care, because what is serviceable as a methodological device confines the theory somewhat, making some rather
popular kinds of questions meaningless (such as whether ideas
cause behavior, or the reverse); and I think this is all to the good.
Nevertheless, this device is unlikely to find friends among the more
staunchly materialist or idealist readers.

The essay consists of three parts. The first evolved out of problems that I encountered when I was working in Guatemala in the early 1950's and found that the theoretical and conceptual materials I had carried with me from my university education were quite inadequate to the task of understanding what was going on about me. What with one thing and another, it was not until late in the 1950's that I first began worrying about the subject of energy and prepared some four papers that I presented at professional meetings at that time but left unpublished. On the basis of those, I started a research project in Guatemala to calculate the actual energy flow within a small community, but that enterprise fortunately floundered; I say fortunately, for, in retrospect, it was methodologically unsound and theoretically immature. Nonetheless, the experience did permit me to clarify the concept of power and to publish in 1966 the first effort in that direction, a paper that had been presented some three years earlier. That, in turn, provided the basis for a more general research project on Guatemala, the major results of which appeared in a volume published in 1970 (R. N. Adams 1970*a*). That research, however, was not specifically directed at elaborating theory; rather, it was designed to force dealing with materials of considerably more complexity than those I had dealt with previously.

During a year and a half in Argentina as a Ford Foundation adviser and as an associate of the Instituto Torcuato Di Tella, I presented a series of three lectures at the Natural History Museum of the University of La Plata. These formed the first effort to move beyond the basic concepts that had directly been clarified in the 1970 volume. This was followed by a course in the graduate anthropology program of the Federal University of Rio de Janeiro in the spring of 1970. The same seminar saw annual expansion in Austin in subsequent years and is currently still being taught, subject to annual shaking up and revisions. The preparation of this book, then, marks the bringing together of some of the materials of the course, with supplements that the occasion permits me to prepare.

Parts Two and Three began as a few pages on the evolution of power in an early draft of Part One, but were not developed fully until the summer of 1973, under support from the Institute of Latin American Studies of the University of Texas, and the first months of 1974, under a Guggenheim Fellowship and the University of Texas University Research Institute.

If I were to characterize the three parts in general terms, Part One is fundamentally conceptual, Part Two moves back and forth between theory and metatheory, and Part Three is theoretical. Readers may find their own interests better served by beginning with one rather than another of the parts; the only danger in not starting at the beginning is that I use a series of terms in very specific ways, and it is quite possible to read Part Three and wholly misunderstand it unless the concepts set forth in Part One are well in hand. Part Two poses less of a trap in this respect.

# ACKNOWLEDGMENTS

There are two reasons I have been somewhat nervous about candidly listing people to whom I am aware of indebtedness. The first is that it is clear that one cannot remember all the influences, and the omission of names is both misleading and unfair to some who may have been of considerable importance. The second is that on one occasion when I did list a friend and former colleague (with the usual disclaimer of responsibility, etc.) he shot back a letter saying he did not regard it to be an honor, and he wanted his name excised from the list. So with some trepidation I do want to acknowledge my indebtedness to those who have aided me intellectually and practically, whether innocent of intent or not, in the preparation of this book, and to free them of any guilt or responsibility for the product.

For criticism on portions of the manuscript in one or another of its avatars: Richard and Louise Bauman, James Bill, Harley Browning, Ira Buchler, Shane and Martha Davies, Francisco Delich, Jack Gibbs, John Higley, Friedrich Katz, Olga Linares, Margaret Mead, Richard P. Schaedel, and Joel Sherzer.

For criticism and discussion in the seminars given on these materials: Sandra Broyles, Denis Cabra, Wilma Geneletti, Beatriz Heredia, Roberta Katz, James Thomas, Steven Neuse, Marianne Schmink, Walter Smith, Thomas Sonandres, Gilberto Velho, Yvonne Velho, and Stanley Verhoeven.

For help in preparing the various drafts of the manuscript both for student use and for press: Juanita McBride, Betsy Parrish, Lili Quan, Carole Smith, and Rebecca González.

For institutional support in various phases and stages of the development of the work: Michigan State University; the University of California at Berkeley; Universidad Nacional de La Plata and

Dr. Alberto Rex González; Instituto Torcuato Di Tella and Ing. Enrique Oteiza and Dr. Roberto Cortés Conde; the Ford Foundation and Drs. Reynolds Carlson and Kalman Silvert; the Federal University of Rio de Janeiro and Drs. Roberto Cardoso de Oliveira and Roberto Da Matta; Wenner-Gren Foundation for Anthropological Research and Ms. Lita Osmundsen; the John Simon Guggenheim Memorial Foundation; and the Universidad Ibero-americana and Drs. Angel Palerm and Arturo Warman. At the University of Texas at Austin, there have been the Institute of Latin American Studies and Dr. William Glade; the Population Research Center and Dr. Harley Browning; the College of Social and Behavioral Sciences and Dean James McKie; the Department of Anthropology and Dr. Jeremiah Epstein; and the University Research Institute and Drs. Austin Gleason and Alejandro Portes.

# PART ONE

## The Nature of Power

# 1. INTRODUCTION

*Power* is a subject common to all the social sciences. The term has received the greatest attention from political scientists and sociologists, many of the former holding that it is the central subject of their discipline, although despairing of bringing it under intellectual harness. Perhaps no other subject matter in the social sciences so subtly exposes the intellectual, ethnocentric, personal, and political biases of the analyst. Moreover, the term *power* has been used with such a range of meanings that serious pursuit of its varieties would soon become an intellectual history of a wide area of social thought. Nevertheless, a work that pretends to any novelty whatsoever should be placed in the context of its predecessors. This is particularly important in discussing power, since almost everything that can be said on the matter has at least been intimated by better heads than mine. I will here look primarily at a few of the more recent authors that have been important channels through which the present generation of students has formed its images of power. I will attempt, not to present their ideas as wholes, but to identify elements that have been important in the thinking of others, particularly as they collectively cast light on the general problem.

Although it will shortly be obvious, I should make it explicit that the term *power* or *social power* is used throughout this essay in a sense quite apart from its physical usage as the rate of doing work or the rate of energy flow. Since social power is directly dependent on energy forms and flows, some confusion may be caused if the reader does not accept this arbitrary usage from the outset.

NOTE. An earlier version of Part One appeared in Spanish as "El poder: Sus condiciones, evolución y estrategia," in *Estudios Sociales Centroamericanos*, no. 4 (January–April 1973), pp. 64–141 (San José, Costa Rica: Editorial Universitaria Centroamericana).

It can be argued that we should not appropriate the term; but it can equally be argued that the physical usage is an appropriation.

Perhaps the most influential theorist in contemporary social science in matters of power is Max Weber. Weber's concept of power will be found at the base of much subsequent thinking of many sociologists, political scientists, and anthropologists:[1] "Power (*Macht*) is the probability that one actor within a social relationship will be in a position to carry out his own will despite resistance, regardless of the basis on which the probability rests."[2]

There are elements here that are central to almost any analytical concept of social power: that it is a relationship; that any statement of the outcome of its exercise must be couched in terms of probability; and that almost anything may serve as a basis of power. However, the definition has one serious liability that makes it impossible and confusing to use in the present context: it can deal only with *relative* power differentials, that is, the will of one party against relative resistance. This relativity makes difficult the comparison of cultures and societies of different places and in different epochs. An evolutionary approach necessitates concepts that will be durable when applied comparatively. To hold that power exercise is merely a differential within a specific relational system may help to understand that particular event, but it is confounding when

[1] Among those within the Weberian traditions are R. H. Tawney (1931), H. Goldhammer and E. Shils (1939), Harold Lasswell and Abraham Kaplan (1950), Robert Dahl (1957), Peter M. Blau (1964), Bertrand Russell (1938), Herbert Simon (1957), and Talcott Parsons (1954). A recent work that professes to follow the Weberian tradition is Gerhard Lenski's (1966, p. 44). I find, however, that Lenski's handling of many problems is extremely close to mine, even though he has tended to focus in a slightly different direction. I can only conclude that he did not take Weber's explicit definition that seriously.

[2] Max Weber 1964, p. 152. (First published in German in 1922; reprinted from *The Theory of Social and Economic Organization*, translated by A. M. Henderson and Talcott Parsons, by permission of Macmillan Publishing Co. Copyright 1947 by Oxford University Press, New York, Inc.) I cannot embark on a serious examination of what Weber really intended. There is much to suggest that his followers have severely misread him. But a man's influence, for better or worse, is seldom congruent with his intent, and we must here note the effect, not the motives. Reinhard Bendix felt that, as a general statement, the "term has no scientific utility" (1960, p. 294). He implies, however, that the differentiation between a "constellation of interests" and "established authority" makes it more effective. I fail to see that it does.

we move to another place and time, and compare one event with another. A comparison requires not merely that we know that there is a differential in each, but also (*a*) that the differential be described in terms of a set of elements that can be used as reference points in both situations, and (*b*) that the measurement or quantification used be in terms that can be cross-culturally meaningful.

Another influential effort is that of Harold Lasswell and Abraham Kaplan. It is not possible to explicate this work briefly, because it is based on a series of interdependent definitions. Central for these authors are the following: "Power is participation in the making of decisions"; "A decision is a policy involving severe sanctions (deprivations)"; "A sanction is conduct in response to an act—that is expected to modify future acts in the direction of conformity . . ."; "Most specifically, however, power is regarded as a sub-class under the more inclusive category of influence."[3] While the Lasswell and Kaplan treatment is impressive for its apparent formality and systematic definitions, it leaves us with the same Weberian relativity, allowing us no basis of comparison from one situation to another. Nevertheless, Lasswell and Kaplan contribute a good many useful concepts to the literature, not the least of which is the emphasis on decision-making as a central feature of the power process.

A rather different approach, and one with which the present work is more in accord, is suggested by Robert Bierstedt's definition: "Power is the ability to employ force."[4] While almost all students of power agree that the use of coercion or force is often an element, most reject using it as a central feature. Crucial in Bierstedt's notion, however, is the idea that the ability to use force lies behind the use of power, not that force is always exercised. Morton H. Fried tends to follow in this line too: "Power is the ability to channel the behavior of others by threat or use of sanctions."[5] Edmund R. Leach (after making much of an inferior notion of power as being something that only officeholders have)

3 Harold Lasswell and Abraham Kaplan 1950, pp. 75, 74, 48, 77. Reprinted from *Power and Society* by permission of Yale University Press.

4 Bierstedt 1950, p. 733.

5 Morton H. Fried 1967, p. 13. Reprinted from *The Evolution of Political Society: An Essay in Political Anthropology*, copyright © 1967 by Random House, Inc., by permission of Random House.

notes that, "In the last analysis, the power relations in any society must be based upon the control of real goods and the primary sources of production, but this Marxist generalization does not carry us very far. The way in which particular goods and services are evaluated one against another is a cultural phenomenon which cannot be deduced from first principles."[6] In spite of Leach's doubts, his "Marxist generalization" does in fact carry us a good deal further than does Weberian relativism (against which few have ventured to criticize the "first principles"—perhaps because they are too generalized and vague to bring meaningfully into discussion).

F. G. Bailey carries this position further in his discussion of politics: "Through political activity a man achieves command over resources, or power over men, or both these things. . . . Society is an area (or !field!) in which men compete for prizes; to control one another; to achieve command over property and resources . . . and, negatively, to avoid being controlled by others and to retain such resources as they already possess. . . . In enquiring why men abandon one kind of allegiance and prefer another, one needs to ask of every incident: Whose was the profit?"[7] Although Bailey emphasizes that his description is specifically of political activities, about " 'political entrepreneurs,' not about everyone" (p. 257), I find much the same concept to be useful more broadly. Ralph Nicholas uses a very similar concept: " 'Power' is control over resources, whether human or material . . . No assumption need be made about what a political actor seeks power for; control over material resources and men may be used to attain a great variety of personal objectives."[8]

Georges Balandier takes what initially appears to be a rather distinctive approach: ". . . power may be defined, for every society, as resulting from the need to struggle against the entropy that threatens it with disorder." "Although power obeys internal deter-

[6] Leach 1965, p. 141. Reprinted from *Political Systems of Highland Burma* by permission of the Athlone Press of the University of London. See also p. 10.

[7] F. G. Bailey 1960, pp. 10–11. Reprinted from *Tribe, Caste and Nation* by permission of Manchester University Press.

[8] Nicholas 1966, p. 52. Reprinted from *Political Anthropology*, ed. Marc J. Swartz, Victor W. Turner, and Arthur Tuden, by permission of Aldine Publishing Co.

minisms that reveal it as a necessity to which every society is subjected, it seems none the less to result from an external necessity.
Each society is in relation with the world outside itself . . . Power
. . . is reinforced under the pressure of external dangers—real or
supposed."[9] Of particular note in Balandier's treatment is the fact
that power is seen not merely as the individualistic exercise of
pressure or force by one actor against another, but rather as a
necessary (and therefore presumably in some sense a constructive)
device for the maintenance of society against pressures of disorder
and chaos. Balandier really does not provide us with a definition,
but he sees power as relating a society to its total environment
through the process of constantly trying to evade disorder, to reform the environment and the society itself in order to keep it in
operating condition. Perhaps it is a Gallic talent to see to the heart
of things and then to present them as a mystery. Balandier certainly sees into the central issues in posing power against entropy;
but his discussion is so metaphorical and removed from the nitty-
gritty of energy flow and loss that it is difficult to build on it.

It would not be proper, even in a review as summary as this, to
fail to mention Marx in his own right. He presents a problem, however, because on the one hand much of the burden of his work has
to do with power, and many of his basic concepts have been incorporated in the work of others with little or no direct reference.
Certainly that is the case in the present work.[10] On the other hand,
Marx also discussed a concept of "social power" that is essentially
that on which the present work is based:

In exchange value, the social relations of individuals have become
transformed into social connections of material things; personal power
has changed into material power. The less social power the means of
exchange possess and the closer they are still connected with the nature

---

[9] Georges Balandier 1970, p. 36. Reprinted from *Political Anthropology*, trans.
A. M. Sheridan Smith, copyright © 1970 by Random House, Inc., by permission
of Random House.

[10] My familiarity with Marx is still largely episodic, and I found *Die Grundrisse* only recently. I am wholly conscious that Marx, in many of his aspects,
has had an indirect (and probably strong) influence on the present work through
the general intellectual channels of our society. I cannot, with any honesty,
however, attribute much that is specific in the present work directly to a
familiarity with his work.

of the direct product of labor and the immediate needs of those exchanging, the greater must be the power of the community to bind the individuals together: the patriarchal relationship, the ancient communities, feudalism and the guild system. Each individual possesses social power in the form of a material object. If the object is deprived of its social power then this power must be exercised by people over people.[11]

I would interpret this passage, in its context, to mean that Marx had a concept of power, but that it was a fairly auxiliary notion to his more principal foci. In this passage, he speaks of "personal power," "material power," "social power," "power of the community," and "power . . . exercised by people over people." Basically what I call *power* in general, or *social power* to distinguish it from the physical or engineering usage, is contained in his "social power." However, I would include all of his usages in my general sense. There is an important divergence, therefore, as Marx would hold that what I am calling power really only comes into being when relationships over commodities take precedence over relations between people. He might find my usage acceptable, but only in the more advanced societies, where money and exchange value have brought about the alienation of the producer from his product and where, therefore, "Each individual possesses social power in the form of a material object." My usage would probably be unacceptable, however, because I insist that it is this very quality that makes the concept useful for analyses of *all* societies, from the most primitive to the most contemporary. Marx draws what is for him a crucial dichotomy with the advent of exchange value; for me it is an important event and distinction, but no more crucial than many other elements that emerge in the course of the evolution of power. What enables me to take a different view is that I include all energetic forms and processes in my notion of "the material," whereas he directs his attention toward natural resources and artifacts in the more traditional use of those terms.

The present work has evolved from a few basic sources. First are the evolutionary theory of Leslie A. White[12] and the fundamental writings of Alfred Lotka on the processes of energy and their re-

[11] Marx 1971, pp. 66–67. Reprinted from *The Grundrisse*, ed. and trans. David McLellan, by permission of Harper and Row.
[12] White 1959 and, more specifically, 1943.

lation to natural selection and evolution.[13] A very central notion
was provided by Theodore Newcomb in a lecture that I attended
as an undergraduate: that all relations between individuals exist
about something: for every $A$ and $B$, there must be an $X$. Beyond
this, the work of evolutionarily inclined anthropologists and
ecologists of the naturalistic tradition has been most influential,
while the work of political scientists and sociologists I confess to
have provided substantive rather than theoretical insights.[14]

Finally, for those with a philosophic bent, perhaps it will help
to set the ground for what follows if I suggest that we are working
in terms of a fundamental monism, but that, because of the complexity of our materials, we are forced to set up the concepts and
theory *as if* they were dualistic. While I am personally satisfied
that the substance of our concern is an energetic and ordered nature, whether manifest in the volcanic movements of mountains or
in the nervous action of a brain wave, much of this ordered nature
is unavailable for our direct observation. Moreover, whether we like
it or not, we must deal with it in terms of the limited capacities of
our own brains. Consequently, our treatment deals with the environment of energy forms and flows *as if* we had some real possibility of knowledge of it; and it deals with the rationality, cognition, and evaluations of the human mind *as if* our descriptions of
these activities concerned some reality beyond our own private,
mental constructs. I will return to this in Part Two of the essay.

## 2. BASIC ELEMENTS

Power is that aspect of social relations that marks the relative
equality of the actors or operating units; it is derived from the

---

[13] Lotka 1921, 1922*a*, 1922*b*, 1925, 1945.

[14] Two recent sociological essays stand close in their definitions to the position
taken here, but I have had difficulty in utilizing them directly: Burns and
Cooper (1971) and Bannester (1969). Conversations with Burns have proved

relative control by each actor or unit over elements of the environment of concern to the participants. It is therefore a socio-psychological phenomenon, whereas control is a physical phenomenon. The process of power is readily identifiable in the subhuman past. Power lies in the dominance and leadership of one animal over others and in the relative controls that the various members of a band individually and collectively exercise over their environments. As with all things, however, when we shift our attention from the subhuman to the human, the ability to symbolize, to structure an environment with meaning, significance, and values, throws the entire operation into a different dimension. As with all living things, man's survival depends on a continuing control over the environment. As distinct from that of other species, the evolution of man's control has led to an ability to endow elements of the habitat with arbitrary meanings, to change a mineral to a tool, to make a dead organism into a bone weapon or a skin house, to convert a handful of seeds into a field of grain or fossilized organic matter into rocket fuel. The combination of the ability to invent new symbols, *culture*, and the ability to elaborate the physical skills and forms, *technology*, has provided man with an increasingly successful control, which is extremely complex and becomes more complex as culture advances. There are, however, some fairly obvious indices that give us some notion of the progress that man has made in this ever-widening control.

One is the mere increase in the amount and varieties of the environment exploited and destroyed by man in the course of his occupation. This can be portrayed in terms of the amount of territory used to live on, the amount and variety of plant and animal life harvested and slaughtered, the amount of petroleum extracted and expended, and so forth. While hard to convert to common measurements,[15] this does give unquestionable evidence of quantitative change. A second index is the number and variety of social relationships. As man controls his environment more effectively, a necessary corollary is that his society grows in size and he neces-

---

stimulating. The definition by Harris (1971, p. 649) also is very similar, but I cannot see that Harris has developed the notion theoretically.

[15] It may be that power, as defined here, can never be converted to measurement, that conceptually its utility lies in serving as a construct. See Gibbs 1972.

sarily specializes, and specific relations become multiplied and
ramified. As his abilities grow, so does the complexity of his society.
A problem with this index is that it removes attention from the
environment, and I suspect that this readiness to treat social relationships apart from their environment is responsible for making
some otherwise distinguished efforts in sociology and political science both confusing and of limited utility.[16]

A third way to get an index of control over the environment is
to follow Leslie White's lead and use the amount of energy harnessed per capita per year by a society as a measure.[17] Since in its
strictest sense everything in the environment is a form of energy,
control over elements of the environment should theoretically be
measurable in terms of energy, or energy flow. Of course, some
energy forms are more important—those specifically related to the
subsistence of the society, the basic resources, the means of produc-

[16] Whether Max Weber intended it or not, I am not certain, but it is quite
clear that some of his major interpreters have read him this way. Reinhard
Bendix posed, as a kind of formula to characterize Weber's thought in this
connection, that ". . . any behavior, always had two related attributes: men in
society are oriented towards each other (even when they are alone), *and* they
are oriented towards norms (even when these are inarticulate)" (1960, pp. 290–
291). I hope that it will become clear that the formula being used in the present
work will contrast: norms are among the devices used by men in society when
orienting themselves to each other with respect to energy forms and flows.

Aside from calling attention to the far-reaching mischief of Weber's "definition," I do not want to waste the reader's time in arguing against other usages.
One warrants mention, however, because it is receiving a surprisingly wide
usage. Amitai Etzioni distinguishes power "according to the *means* employed
to make the subjects comply" (1961, pp. 4–6). The types are "Coercive," "Re-
munerative," and "Normative." The classification is then claimed to be "ex-
haustive." Even a brief examination indicates that it is quite impossible to
classify many forms of power within this set of categories, because they are in
no sense mutually exclusive. Love, for example, may be all three at once. Rather
than being a classification of "means," it is in fact Etzioni's ethnocentric cognitive map of how he supposes subjects might perceive power being exercised over
them. As such, it may have ethnographic interest but seems analytically trivial.

[17] White (1943) was among the first anthropologists to insist on the importance of the energy basis of culture; however, he never followed up on his own
lead. A recent analysis of the subject is Howard Odum 1971. Readers not
familiar with the use of energy in the context of social science are urged to
refer to the first five chapters of this volume; the last six chapters should be
used with caution, as Odum does not employ the same rigor in cultural matters
as he does in the energetic.

tion. But, since societies will differently define what is important in the environment, it is not easy to draw up a formal list of elements that are of equal and common importance to all societies. What is possible, however, is to recognize that control over whatever elements the society does define to be of importance provides the student with a double-edged tool. He can compare this society's relative control over the environment with the control exercised by another society and thereby gain some notion of their relative position in the evolution of culture. He can also examine the actual organization of the controls exercised by members of the society and see how they thereby relate themselves to each other and to other societies with which they are in contact. This matter of control over the environment, then, gives us a tool that serves both for the internal analysis of any given society and for the comparison of one society with another.

The concept of energy must be used with caution. Concepts and definitions necessarily vary with the conceptual context in which they are employed. "In the world of science and engineering," writes Howard Odum, "power is defined precisely in terms of measurable units as *the rate of flow of useful energy*."[18] In speaking of *social power*, however, we are concerned not only with the flow of energy but also with how that flow is controlled and used by man.

Everything in the environment of man is composed of energy forms and processes and can be measured in terms of the amount of energy that is potentially available for conversion or is being converted. An *energy flow* is a process of conversion of energy from one form or state to another. In dealing with social power (as distinct from the engineering usage), we are concerned not so much with the rate of flow or conversion as with *the control that one actor, or party, or operating unit exercises over some set of energy forms or flows* and, most specifically, over some set of energy forms or flows *that constitute part of the meaningful environment of another actor.*[19] What is important here in distinguishing this

[18] Odum 1971, p. 26. Reprinted from *Environment, Power, and Society* by permission of John Wiley and Sons, Inc.

[19] The notion of power as influence stemming from a base of control is not new to political science, but it never seems to have been grasped as a central difference from other influences. Lasswell and Kaplan speak of the "power base"

concept from that set by Odum is that the energy forms and flows have to be relevant to some system of value and meaning, that is to say, be *culturally recognized*.

Now energy is important, indeed crucial, to man whether he culturally recognizes it or not; but it cannot be utilized as a basis for social power unless he does so. The term *environment* refers to the material, physical, or energy-form-and-flow aspect of man's social and physical habitat. Thus, not only do topography, climate, natural resources, etc., form part of the environment, but other human beings, sound waves (speech), behavior of others, etc., are also energy forms or flows and are also part of the environment. It is the actor's control of the environment that constitutes the base of social power; however, that base can only be operative if it is culturally recognized by other actors. The recognition may not affect the control; but it will affect the ability to use that control to influence others.

In speaking of "control over the environment," the word *control* refers to *making and carrying out decisions about the exercise of a technology*. The thing doing the controlling may be an individual or some social unit that has an internal power structure of its own. The notion of control necessarily includes both making and carrying out decisions, although the two phases are not necessarily exercised by the same social entity. The merit of the concept of *control* in this discussion is that it establishes the relative importance of the actors. In Figure 1*a*, $X$ is some facet of the environment of interest to both $A$ and $B$. The relative ability of $A$ and $B$ to control $X$ is a determinant in the relationship between $A$ and $B$. If (Fig. 1*c*) $A$ has relatively more control over $X$ than $B$, then $A$ is *superordinate* and $B$ is *subordinate*. If (Fig. 1*b*) their control is roughly equivalent, then $A$ and $B$ are said to be power *coordinates*. The

whereby $A$ exercises influence over $B$ because $A$ controls a value $B$ needs or desires (1950, pp. 83–84). Karl W. Deutsch notes that $A$'s power in this case depends on three things: "first, on $B$'s relative poverty and want in regard to some basic value of which $A$ controls a relevant supply; second, on $B$'s control of a relevant supply of some value which $A$ desires and which $A$ is trying to get by using its power over $B$; and finally, $A$'s skill and effectiveness in converting the potential of its power base into actual power over $B$'s behavior." (Karl W. Deutsch, *The Analysis of International Relations*, © 1968. By permission of Prentice-Hall, Inc., Englewood Cliffs, New Jersey. Quote is from p. 24.)

A ←——— Social Relation

Control

16

*The Nature of Power*

in terms of what people believe these energy potentials to be, rather
than what they may ultimately be shown to be, it is important that
we distinguish a *reality potential* (that which in fact turns out to
be the case) from a *cultural potential* (that which actors believe
to be true).[20]

Just as we can never really know reality, so we can never really
know the reality (energy) potential. We must always operate on
the basis of the ideas that we have about reality. In any relationship,
are constructed out of culture and experience. In any relationship,
each actor has distinctive ideas, a distinctive cultural potentia...
about the situation. After an activity or an interaction where t...
reality is in some manner tested, the cultural potentials of ei...
or both parties may change in accordance with their experi...
potentials of the actors.

But, through all this, the only bases of decisions are the c...
It should be noted that I am bringing in an aspect o...
that is, the meanings that people attach to the energy form...
implicitly involves energy forms. Therefore, my treatme...
up culture in analytical parts, that is, in terms of i...
pects, its meaning or value aspects, and its social rela...

The cultural potential ascribed to an individual in a...
is part of the culture; that is, it is the set of mea...
individual.
some set of energy forms or flows available f...

Another important distinction (made her...
convenience) is that between the *strategy* an...
It is derived from the military metaphor,...
to the over-all allocation of resources and...
refers to the immediate small scale of d...
deals in strategy when he considers t...
controls and location of energy form...
tactics when focusing on the proble...
these potentials into action. Paren...

20 These are discussed further in R...
21 "Tactical: involving actions or m...
of strategy by being of less impor...
magnitude or by taking place or b...
a base of operations"; "designed t...
*New International Dictionary,*...

(b)

ordinate distinct...
the elemental distin...
domains (where actors
tion (where they are coor...

A key concept in the de...
term is here intentionally use...
of knowledge, skills, and materia...
the order (i.e., space-time relations)
or achieve an energy conversion. To
change the arrangement of a set of parts

concept from that set by Odum is that the energy forms and flows have to be relevant to some system of value and meaning, that is to say, be *culturally recognized*.

Now energy is important, indeed crucial, to man whether he culturally recognizes it or not; but it cannot be utilized as a basis for social power unless he does so. The term *environment* refers to the material, physical, or energy-form-and-flow aspect of man's social and physical habitat. Thus, not only do topography, climate, natural resources, etc., form part of the environment, but other human beings, sound waves (speech), behavior of others, etc., are also energy forms or flows and are also part of the environment. It is the actor's control of the environment that constitutes the base of social power; however, that base can only be operative if it is culturally recognized by other actors. The recognition may not affect the control; but it will affect the ability to use that control to influence others.

In speaking of "control over the environment," the word *control* refers to *making and carrying out decisions about the exercise of a technology*. The thing doing the controlling may be an individual or some social unit that has an internal power structure of its own. The notion of control necessarily includes both making and carrying out decisions, although the two phases are not necessarily exercised by the same social entity. The merit of the concept of *control* in this discussion is that it establishes the relative importance of the actors. In Figure 1*a*, $X$ is some facet of the environment of interest to both $A$ and $B$. The relative ability of $A$ and $B$ to control $X$ is a determinant in the relationship between $A$ and $B$. If (Fig. 1*c*) $A$ has relatively more control over $X$ than $B$, then $A$ is *superordinate* and $B$ is *subordinate*. If (Fig. 1*b*) their control is roughly equivalent, then $A$ and $B$ are said to be power *coordinates*. The

whereby $A$ exercises influence over $B$ because $A$ controls a value $B$ needs or desires (1950, pp. 83–84). Karl W. Deutsch notes that $A$'s power in this case depends on three things: "first, on $B$'s relative poverty and want in regard to some basic value of which $A$ controls a relevant supply; second, on $B$'s control of a relevant supply of some value which $A$ desires and which $A$ is trying to get by using its power over $B$; and finally, $A$'s skill and effectiveness in converting the potential of its power base into actual power over $B$'s behavior." (Karl W. Deutsch, *The Analysis of International Relations*, © 1968. By permission of Prentice-Hall, Inc., Englewood Cliffs, New Jersey. Quote is from p. 24.)

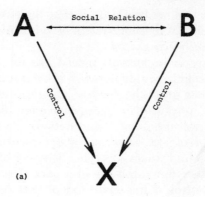

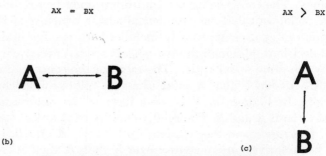

Fig. 1. Basic Components of Power Relations

ordinate distinction is fundamental to power analysis and provides the elemental distinctions that compose the structural elements of domains (where actors are noncoordinates) and levels of articulation (where they are coordinates).

A key concept in the definition of control is *technology*. The term is here intentionally used in a broad sense: it refers to a set of knowledge, skills, and materials (apparatus) necessary to alter the order (i.e., space-time relations) of some set of energy forms or achieve an energy conversion. To "alter the order" means to change the arrangement of a set of parts or the relative position

of the whole. Ethnographic descriptions of technology are sometimes used in a sense that excludes the ideational and evaluative
content of the activity. Here we specifically include the ideas associated with the materials, as well as the behavioral skills relevant
to the entire process. "Superiority" in control refers to a more effective or efficient complex of tools, skills, and ideas, taken as a whole.

For some purposes it is convenient to add a further element to
the definition of technology and, thereby, to our concept of control:
that of *organization of labor*. Traditional accounts usually handle
the organization of labor separately from technological activity;
however, whether one chooses to do this or not is really a methodological problem; it depends upon whether it is convenient. Certainly there are many operations where the roles of operators are
inherent parts of the technological process. For example, in comparing the potential power in two systems of production, the organization of labor may be so specialized within the total systems
that they cannot be compared without it. Certainly, the technology
of a nineteenth-century slave-labor plantation with its simple skills
would be difficult to compare with that of a twentieth-century agro-
enterprise that involves fairly highly skilled technicians, without
taking the organization of labor into account as part of the technological variable. However, for many purposes, the labor force
may be an independent actor within a power structure, and, as
such, its very organization may be a variable independent of the
other technological aspects. In many situations the role of labor
unions, for example, may vary independently of the specific technology that the workers employ.

A question that presents itself equally to the analyst and to the
actors within a system is that of the "real" control that may be exercised. That is, can an actor actually exercise the technology
ascribed to him, or is it merely believed that he can? The problem
is essentially one of determining the validity of a proposition, and
we have to recognize that one really never knows about the real
control of actors until after the fact, and even then it may remain
somewhat problematic.

Before actors actually exercise their controls, they can only
speculate about how much power can be brought to bear on a situation and, in many cases, about which of two actors may have
greater energy potentials at his command. Since decisions are made

in terms of what people believe these energy potentials to be, rather than what they may ultimately be shown to be, it is important that we distinguish a *reality potential* (that which in fact turns out to be the case) from a *cultural potential* (that which actors believe to be true).[20]

Just as we can never really know reality, so we can never really know the reality (energy) potential. We must always operate on the basis of the ideas that we have about reality, and these ideas are constructed out of culture and experience. In any relationship, each actor has distinctive ideas, a distinctive cultural potential, about the situation. After an activity or an interaction where the reality is in some manner tested, the cultural potentials of either or both parties may change in accordance with their experience. But, through all this, the only bases of decisions are the cultural potentials of the actors.

It should be noted that I am bringing in an aspect of culture, that is, the meanings that people attach to the energy forms. Culture implicitly involves energy forms. Therefore, my treatment will take up culture in analytical parts, that is, in terms of its formal aspects, its meaning or value aspects, and its social relational aspects. The cultural potential ascribed to an individual in a given situation is part of the culture; that is, it is the set of meanings ascribed to some set of energy forms or flows available for control by that individual.

Another important distinction (made here for methodological convenience) is that between the *strategy* and the *tactics* of power. It is derived from the military metaphor, wherein strategy refers to the over-all allocation of resources and plan of action, and tactics refers to the immediate small scale of disposition and plan.[21] One deals in strategy when he considers the over-all allocation of the controls and location of energy forms. He concerns himself with tactics when focusing on the problem of a specific mobilization of these potentials into action. Parents surely have strategic advan-

[20] These are discussed further in R. N. Adams 1970a, pp. 48–51.

[21] "Tactical: involving actions or means . . . that are distinguished from those of strategy by being of less importance to the outcome of a way or of less magnitude or by taking place or by going into effect at a shorter distance from a base of operations"; "designed to achieve a given purpose" (*Webster's Third New International Dictionary*, 1966).

tages over children. But children not infrequently are able to command their parents because of the immediate tactical circumstances. In a public situation, a mother may wish to scream and beat her child; but, since they are in public, the parent is inhibited from doing so. When we make casual remarks about "so-and-so having a great deal of power," we are almost always making strategic comments. When we say that "so-and-so knows how to use power," we will usually be commenting on tactics.

This concept of power has certain advantages. Since it is energy forms and flows in the environment that constitute the basis of power, there exists an objective element to allow for comparison of different cases, cross-culturally or over the course of evolution of a single society. The activities of the actors are based on rational decisions, which, in turn, are defined in terms of some set of interests and values that are a part of a continuing cultural process. They are not *sui generis* products of an individual's nervous system. Further, the manipulation or exercise of control by one actor over the environment of another is instantly translatable into an interpersonal relationship, which implicitly may be both coercive and cooperative, containing the potential operation of sanctions. Power is thus clearly a relational issue between parties, but it is also a relation that exists with reference to things that can be described as external to any particular actor: the energy forms and flows, and the equivalence of values.

The question of values and interests in any analysis immediately introduces problems. Here I am using the terms in the very broad sense of Anthony F. C. Wallace's "equivalence structures."[22] The crux of Wallace's exposition is that individual values and cognitive maps operating in a cultural situation need not be congruent or shared; indeed, they cannot in the nature of things be expected to be. Rather, the psychological framework with which each individual works must merely be such that the consequences provide the various actors with equivalent behavioral expectancies. They must have some organization of knowledge and emotion that permits them to make and act on common predictions concerning each other's behavior. There is a sharing of understanding and of expectancies, even though the specific unique form of any given individual's un-

[22] Wallace 1970, Ch. 1.

derstanding would surely, upon analysis, prove to be quite different in shape from that of other participants. Complementarity of behavioral expectancies is the crucial feature, not similarity of presumed meanings.

In the course of this essay, then, when we speak of "shared meanings," "shared values," or "common culture," we will be referring to a sharing of expectations about forms and behavior, systematized to permit interaction. Among other things, this distinction permits us to avoid a problem that disturbed Max Gluckman, which he referred to as the "error of 'psychologism.' "

In my essays I speak of whites and Zulu having common interests in peace and in low maternal and infant mortality rates and so forth, as one may speak of managers and workers having a common interest in a factory or mine continuing to work and produce. I have been told it is specious to say that workers have this common interest. Workers go to earn wages. I consider that this criticism is, in sociological or social anthropological analysis, to commit the error of "psychologism." The motives which induce the people to do certain things are not the same as the complex of social interests which their actions serve. . . . Nevertheless I believe that a common or shared social interest must be demonstrated in the action of persons.[23]

The distinction between "motivation" and the "social interest" being served is one way to draw the line between the variations in psychology that necessarily characterize participants in any society, and at the same time identify the shared expectations that are absolutely crucial for them to operate in any conjunctive way.

Gluckman's "social interests" are, however, also self-interests. Although shared with others, they are also specific to the individuals participating in the situation. When we use the concepts of shared values or interests in speaking of rational decisions, we will be concerned with decisions made on the basis of some recognized self-interest. It is important here to recognize that such an "interest" may be far removed from the classic image of material gain or the profit motive of economic man. Such interests are to be identified both through their complementary coincidence with interests of others in the society and through their place in a system of such

---

[23] Gluckman 1968, p. 87. Reprinted from *Local Level Politics*, ed. Marc J. Swartz, by permission of Aldine Publishing Co.

interests as manifested by an individual or congruently shared by members of a group. The empirical analysis of any given power situation requires that the analyst propose or assume some guiding interests on the basis of which a rational decision is made. Whether these interests as described by the analyst are really in some sense representative of the cognitive and evaluative map of the individual, or whether they are merely adequate constructions of the analyst, must in most instances remain a moot point.

It is apparent, however, that the issue of values, no matter how resolved, will at certain points be central to the analysis of power situations. A leading scholar of political science has expressed it as follows: "Power, though often spoken of as if it were a thing, is actually nothing of the kind. It is, as the Hobbsian definition suggests, oriented towards things, and anything can become the basis of power. A house, a love affair, an idea can all become instruments in the hand of one seeking power. But in order to convert them into power, the power-seeker must find human beings who value one of these things sufficiently to follow his leadership in acquiring them. Power, therefore, always presupposes several human beings who are joined together in pursuing a common objective."[24] Perhaps the central issue to keep in mind in discussing values in the context of power is that values are ascribed to things; they are qualities attributed to things by human beings. Thus, except in a metaphorical sense, it is incorrect to say that people seek values. Rather, they seek *things*, that is, energy flows and forms, upon which they have bestowed value.

In the exercise of power, it is control over valued things, that is, sets of separate, recurrent events that are placed in one category, that allows one actor power over another. The things (i.e., elements in the environment) can include even a given *state of mind* if the individual finds it sufficiently objectified to perceive its presence or absence. Some people value their tranquillity and peace of mind above eating hot dogs and candy bars; for them, it is rational to seek the former over the latter.

Power, in the social sense, is present in all social relationships. That it has many facets is one reason that the literature presents

[24] Carl J. Friedrich 1950, pp. 22–23. Reprinted by permission of the publisher from *Constitutional Government and Democracy* by Carl J. Friedrich, © 1950, Xerox Corporation, published by Xerox College Publishing.

such a range of approaches for description and analysis. That it has received much, indeed most, attention from those interested in politics is presumably due to the fact that it is most clearly manifest there. However, that it clearly extends far beyond the usual field of politics is also clear and may in part explain why many political scientists have felt the subject to be too diffuse or unfruitful for empirical analysis. The approach taken here is that an understanding of power is necessary not only to the study of politics but also to the study of culture itself, as well as the network of social relations of which it is the manifestation.

## 3. ADDITIONAL CONSIDERATIONS

*Power structure* refers to any systemic set of relationships through which actors or parties manifest their relative concerns about control over the environment and power over their fellow men. The following will deal with some of the more central characteristics of these relations: (A) Power and Control; (B) Reciprocity and Omnipresence; (C) Authority and Legitimacy; and (D) Types of Power Exercise.

### A. Power and Control

Perhaps one reason that power has been subject to so much disagreement is that it inherently involves two quite different kinds of relations. A simple illustration will clarify this. Let us say that a teacher has a certain amount of power over his students; at least the students usually feel that way. Were we to ask what the foundation of this power might be, the answer might include a number of things, such as his violence, his sternness, his intelligence, his ability to teach, etc.; but, no matter what else might be included, the salient feature would remain the fact that the teacher controls the grades and, thereby, whether the student can pass on to a higher class and pursue his career. If we are to see this as a power relation, then we must describe the scene as follows:

The teacher stands in a position that allows him specific controls over certain papers and marks on papers. These marks on papers are physical facets of the environment that are of particular interest to the student because he believes that his grades are of importance for his successful future, for his prestige among his fellows, for avoiding tongue-lashings at home, for staying in school, etc. The marks on the paper are part of the student's future environment, and the teacher controls them. By virtue of this, the teacher has power over the student.

Note carefully the difference: *control* over the environment is a physical matter. An actor either has it or does not. How he gets it is quite a different matter and need not concern us for the moment (see section D). But, once he has it, there immediately comes into being a particular quality in the relationship between the teacher and the student. The teacher now has power over the student. *Power* over an individual is a psychological facet of a social relationship in the sense that it may be said to have its physical locus within the nervous systems of the actors; it is social in that it exists by virtue of the complementarity of social concern of each actor with respect to the other.[25]

The difference between power and control is very important, even though in many analyses (particularly in macroanalyses) it is convenient to treat them indiscriminately. Control is a nonreciprocal relationship in the sense that it exists between an actor and some element of the environment that cannot react rationally to shared behavioral expectancies. This does not mean that the thing being controlled does not have its own peculiar behavior. A rock will act like a rock, a horse like a horse, a stream of water like a stream of water, etc., and a corpse like a corpse. Thus control is always contingent upon understanding the nature of the object

[25] Raymond Aron provides an interesting comment on the power/control difference: "French, English and German all distinguish between two notions, *power and force (strength), puissance et force, Mache und Kraft*. It does not seem to me contrary to the spirit of these languages to reserve the first terms for the human relationship, the action itself, and the second for the means, the individual's muscles or the state's weapons." (From *Peace and War* by Aron Raymond, copyright © 1966 by Doubleday and Company, Inc. Used by permission of Doubleday and Company, Inc.) My usage tends to parallel this, although Aron's use remains fairly limited to the military and political context and mine is specifically proposed for a broader context.

being controlled and thereby requires a set of techniques appropriate to those characteristics.

Power, however, is a social relationship that rests on the basis of some pattern of controls and is reciprocal. That is, both members of the relationship act in terms of their own self-interest and, specifically, do so in terms of the controls that each has over matters of interest to the other. The behavior that results from an awareness of power is such that the actor tries to calculate what the other individual might do that could affect the actor's interests.

Control, as a category, includes a great deal, perhaps more than one is initially inclined to allow. It not only includes such things as the physical act of holding a gun on a person, or holding title to a piece of property that another may need, or being in the position to sign or not sign the payroll, or pushing someone off a cliff; it also includes whether an individual has certain skills. Thus, sound waves are physical events, and, depending upon the individual's ability, the quality of a person's singing has the power to bring an audience to the concert hall or to keep it away. If the books published by an author bring people to buy them, then the author has some power. Even love must admit to operation in terms of control and power. A man who wants to keep the company of the object of his affection is quite in her power; by controlling her own availability and behavior, she controls a portion of the environment of intense interest to the man.

In speaking of the interest that one actor has in some portion of the environment controlled by another, it should be noted that I am specifying very little about the kind or quality of interest. The lover mentioned above, for example, may realize his interest in the girl by means of a platonic poetry-reading session, or in bed, or both. Power derives not so much from the kind of interest as simply from the fact that a sufficient interest exists to influence the individual's decision to attempt to realize it.

When it comes to describing a power structure or a system of power relations, it is important to recognize another facet of this matter. While control has to do with things, it is often the case that human beings are those things. The objections expressed by the women's-liberation movement in the last third of the twentieth century have as one concern that women not be treated as "sex objects" by men; that is, that they not serve as mere masturbation devices. The objection is that men tend to treat women, not as social entities, but merely as objects of the environment to be controlled. Whether or not the argument is valid, at least it illustrates that some women think they are the object of mere control.

Actually, direct control of human beings seldom can occur for an extensive period within primary or close relationships, simply because the controls of the other party provide part of the environment of the actor. But, in the chain of indirect relations found in complex societies or in the relations of great social distance among simpler societies, individuals may tend to be seen as mere elements of the environment rather than as reciprocal actors. Thus the actor in such situations becomes merely a member of a stereotypical category, and behavior toward him is not toward him as an individual with special interests, but as "stranger," "Communist," "nigger," "whitey," "slave," "sovereign," "piece of tail," "hippy," "the establishment," and so forth; and specific conduct is habitualized to deal with all members of a given category in some standard manner.

A classic situation in which a question of this kind required authoritative decision was that which faced the Spanish conquerors in the New World with respect to the American Indians. The question was whether the Indians were human beings or not. If they were, then they needed to be Christianized and, by the same token, could be organized and harnessed as human labor. Had they been subhuman, then, of course, they could have been treated merely as beasts of burden. Another case may be seen in the theory that "peasant masses" are incapable of revolt because they in fact hold no power. The counterargument (which seems unquestionably to be more realistic) is that they do have power, if by virtue of nothing else than their control over themselves. It has classically been the case within civilized history that entire segments of populations of "natives," peasants, unskilled laborers, etc., have been subordinated to a degree that clouded the question as to whether they should be treated as human beings or not. In most cases, the decision was made on the basis of whether they could manifest enough control over themselves that the superiors found that they had to negotiate with them rather than treat them as chattels. Failing in sheer control, reciprocity—and therefore power—was established.

The distinction between control and power also clarifies an aspect of power relations that has often proved a stumbling block: the interpretation of the use of force. Most students of power prefer to consider the direct application of force or physical coercion as being something distinct from power, and so it is considered here. Force is the exercise of control, not of power. The Israeli hostages held by Arab guerrillas in the Twentieth Olympiad in Munich in September of 1972 were essentially objects of control of their captors. Physically locked in an apartment, they were parts of the environment that were thought to be so prized by the Israeli government that the latter would release some two hundred Arab captives in Israel in order to guarantee the lives of the hostages. Force, as one kind of control, and power, as the set of psychosocial conditions for decision-making, are clearly distinct phenomena.

Thus far we have differentiated between power and control but, concerning the latter, have dealt with a diversity of manipulations. Some readers will be uncomfortable in throwing together the champion sword-fighter's ability to defeat his opponent, on the one hand, and, on the other, the judge's ability to pronounce sentence or the teacher's ability to flunk a student with a mere scratch on a piece of paper. All are cases of control in that all concern direct control of some meaningful aspect of the environment. It is important, however, to recognize that human beings' ability to symbolize leaves little untouched. In this case, it is clear that the judge's pronouncement or the teacher's giving a grade, while a physical act, also rests on the fact that there is cultural agreement as to the context and meaning of the words pronounced or the scratch on the piece of paper. What we have here is *control of a symbol*. The control of the scratch or voice is real: it is control of energy forms and flows. These energy forms or flows, however inconsequential or trivial in terms of energy, are collectively accepted as meaning a certain complex process. This meaning rests on the same question of legitimacy, agreement, as does the recognition of an authority (note: the *recognition* of the authority, not the existence of the authority; the latter exists merely by virtue of having control). Symbol control thus at some point rests on an allocation of power to a specific individual or unit to perform, under certain recognized conditions, a ritual act; and this ritual act is a symbol that carries an equivalent meaning to all sharing that particular culture.

Symbol control, then, is actually composed of a particular combination of control and power. Some set of people, or social units, that control some telling portion of the environment give their right of decision-making (i.e., their potential power) to some other person. To keep in bounds the activities of this individual, they agree upon some ritual control or symbol control that will signal when he is exercising this derived power under approved circumstances. The people granting the power want to restrict the use of this power to certain situations; the use of the symbol control, then, carries meaning only if used under the correct ritual circumstances. If used correctly, the power is recognized to be in force; if used incorrectly, the power will not be recognized.

A potent illustration of the use of symbol control is that of the officers and chief of state of complex societies (although it is also found in the most primitive societies). The president of the United States is practiced in signing his name to things. An act of signing (and the signature), however, carries very different meanings depending upon the ritual circumstances in which it occurs. Congressional bills are signed with one set of rituals; letters to little boys or girls are signed with another; placing the signature on some object to be abandoned on the surface of the moon occurs under yet another; etc. In all cases, the president has control of his signature, but power rests in his having acted under the appropriate ritual circumstances; the meaning of that signature and its control varies with a complex set of agreements established within the culture.

Complementary to the symbol control exercised by the president is that exercised by the ultimate sources of the control, the voters. Their control has to do with their vote. They cannot give or take away the right to exercise power in their behalf at will; they too can do it only under certain circumstances; thus, their power to control themselves is symbolically allocated every time they vote.

It is clear that, in complex societies, we most commonly deal with power and symbol controls. However, it is necessary to keep in mind the fact that, even within extraordinarily complex networks of power and symbol controls, there are embedded crucial relations in which real control remains the central issue. Some of these are "legitimate"; people have agreed that they will not collectively confront and challenge their exercise. Others are not so regarded.

The police, the military, boxers, football players, parents, children, and various other categories of persons are allowed and expected to exercise direct control over others under specific circumstances. Murderers, robbers, muggers, and so on exercise direct control, but without widespread collective consent; they are subject to challenge, although not necessarily successfully.

A final point to be made on the subject of control and power has to do with analysis. A description of a power structure would be incomplete if it did not contain information concerning *both* the control and the power aspects, particularly since some of the objects of control may well be human beings who, through other strands in the network, do participate within the power system as a whole. A problem faced by some new mothers is the degree to which it is necessary, advisable, or wrong to treat their newborn as a thing and the degree to which it is to be treated as a human being. As the child matures, of course, it increasingly acts like a specific human being, and the problem begins to resolve itself, as the mother learns (perhaps the hard way) what its particular interests are. In any complex system, identifying the relevant aspects of the environment is a necessary part of our understanding of how the power structure works, since the exercise of controls and power are often interchanged, or alternate, within the system. Hereafter, therefore, when the term *power structure* is used with respect to a specific case, it will include the relations of both power and control.

## B. Reciprocity and Omnipresence

Although in the analysis of a power structure it is advisable to deal with both power and control, the real dynamics of power are derived principally from the power relations. The reason for this is that the elements of the environment that may be brought under control are only of importance to the system as a whole insofar as specific interest is expressed in them and a technology is available or devised for handling them. When this occurs, then their control becomes a realistic matter of concern to other actors, and there is established automatically a power relation. The subsequent activities are carried out in terms of the actors' estimates of the situation, of their own changing interests, and of their predictions concerning what the other actors will do with respect to the controls.

To insist that power relations are reciprocal is not to say that they are equal, balanced, or equivalent. Quite the contrary: it is precisely in those cases where the power is unequal that the power aspect of the relation may most easily be seen to operate. It is important, however, to recognize that there are always at least two sides to a power relation and that, in the context of the relation, decisions will be made by all parties. Among political scientists who have concerned themselves with power, this is more recognized by some than by others. Carl J. Friedrich holds that "power . . . is a bond simultaneously embracing the leader and the led, the ruler and the ruled,"[26] whereas Robert Dahl formulates his entire argument and analysis of power around a paradigm that specifically obscures the distinction by differentiating "controlling units (C)" and "responsive units (R)."[27]

One reason that it is important to recognize the continuing reciprocity of power relations is that it makes it clear that power exists whether there is an unevenness in its distribution or not. Thus, power is usually not thought to be an issue between two friends. Yet it is specifically to keep power from being an issue that friends often take extraordinary precautions to avoid even giving the appearance of manipulating or using coercion. The person who requests that compliance be given with no breath of pressure or force will suggest that he is "asking as a friend." The individual who suddenly feels the pressure of power from one whom he had assumed would never so use it may say, "I thought you were a friend," or "I thought you loved me." The fact of the matter is that, between friends, both parties have considerable control (i.e., through making themselves accessible) and the issue is not to let it show.

One should not be misled by popular usage in this matter. When an individual states that he is "powerless," one should carefully note whether it is really the case, or whether he merely finds himself in a position where the power of another has so constrained him that none of the alternatives open to him are to his taste. The fact that an employee chooses not to offend or embarrass his employer does not mean that he does not have it within his control

26 Friedrich 1950, p. 23.
27 Dahl 1968, pp. 405–415.

to do so. If after many years of subordination he decides to exercise
the very little control that he has, that is, to offend, he may well
simply do it and lose his job.

This brings up another important characteristic of power systems: they are potentially present in all social relationships. Even
when they are intentionally being set aside or left unexploited, the
potential always exists. Also, the fact that the study of power has
usually been left to students of politics has obscured the fact that
it is to be found in all relational systems. "The truth is," observed
C. E. Merriam, "that only confusion will be created by trying to
draw too sharp and exclusive a line between political and other
forms of organization. The governmental, the legal, the political,
all have their analogues in other organizations, where similar phenomena of sub-, super- and co-ordination may be discovered, and
nothing is to be gained by attempting to trace impossible lines
between them."[28] Concerns of power play their role within families
and households, in recreation and sports, in religious and ritual
activities, and in artistic and esthetic performances, as well as in
the more commonly recognized areas of economic and political
action. But to say that power is omnipresent does not mean that it
is always, or even usually, manifest. So long as differences in control exist among actors, there will be the potential of power within
relationships.

This omnipresence need not be seen, in any sense, as a threatening or dangerous thing. Quite the contrary. Power is actually one
of the major dynamic forces in human society, or in any society.
It is a reflection of success in dominating and controlling the environment and is a measure of that success. The human species
as a whole—and societies of human beings separately—survive and
flourish by virtue of this control and remain integral by virtue of
the power exercised among their members. We may recall here
Balandier's argument that "power may be defined, for every society, as resulting from the need to struggle against the entropy that
threatens it with disorder."[29] While we can insist that the reasons
behind societal integrity are more complex than that and that

[28] Merriam 1934, p. 9. From *Political Power: Its Composition and Incidence*,
by Charles Edward Merriam. Copyright, 1934, by the McGraw-Hill Book Company, Inc.
[29] Balandier 1970, p. 36.

power does more than merely sustain order, Balandier does frame the relation between social power and the survival of the society in forceful terms. Aristotle placed emphasis on the converse of this: ". . . he who is unable to live in society, or who has no need because he is sufficient for himself, must be either a beast or a god: he is no part of a state."[30]

The omnipresence of power has one further consequence that must concern us before leaving the topic. Any study of power is, by its very nature, a study that can lead through a complex and involuted network of controls and influences throughout the entire society—indeed, throughout the entire history of mankind—if we allow it. While it would be methodological nonsense to allow any study to get so out of hand, there are two indicators of limits that any full-scale study of power should reach: it should be able to identify the actors or roles that operate at the two vertical extremes of the system, those at the very top and those at the very bottom. Without identifying the upper extreme, it is impossible to have a framework within which to trace the locus of the major controllers and power wielders in the system. And, without identifying the lower extreme, it is equally impossible to trace out the consequences of the activities that characterize the system.

If one is to concern oneself with the problems of pollution in contemporary western society, it is necessary to follow the lines of relation up to the national level, to the decision-makers who continue to provide economic and political protection for the major polluters, as well as to look down to the residents of the polluted areas, to the children and the infants who are subject to the toxic vapors and poisons that are being released within the region. Certainly the power structure of this event will not be comprehended until all the relevant actors are placed reasonably accurately with respect to their overlapping interests. The fact that power is omnipresent means that any study of its operation must attempt to trace out the full dimensions of its consequences.

---

[30] R. McKeon, ed. 1941, p. 1130. Reprinted from *The Basic Works of Aristotle*, Copyright, 1941, by Random House, Inc. By arrangement with the Oxford University Press. From "Politics," trans. Benjamin Jowett, from the *Oxford Translation of Aristotle*, ed. W. D. Ross, vol. 10, 1921, by permission of the Clarendon Press, Oxford. One must remember that, for Aristotle, the state was the society.

## C. *Authority and Legitimacy*

Our discussion thus far has made no reference to a pair of terms that are extremely common when matters of power are up for discussion: authority and legitimacy (and, by extension, legality). As with power, these terms have seen varied use in the literature. *Authority* has, in general, been used in one of two general ways. One has been to see it as a behavior, a quality ascribed to the exercise of control or power: "In short—it is not an original idea—a man's authority finally rests on his ability to reward and punish."[31] The other is to see authority as being more or less synonymous with *legitimacy*, for example: "A policy is authoritative [legitimate] when the people consider they must or ought to obey it."[32]

Given the concepts of control, power, and cultural potential, it is possible to order these residual notions without too much difficulty. Favoring George Homan's stance, I see authority as a term to be applied to someone who has power. Thus a political authority is a person with political power; and an authority in Chinese art is a person who controls information and knowledge about that subject. If we say that the Supreme Court has the ultimate authority, it is because it has the ultimate power. These uses may not all appear to be entirely parallel, but they reflect a consistency in using the term to identify a person or group that exercises power—or can exercise such power—over others by virtue of control over certain forms or flows of energy. The use of the term *authority* to refer to policy is merely a metaphorical extension from the individual who exercises the power or control to his mechanisms or means of

[31] George Homans 1961, pp. 291–292. Reprinted from *Social Behavior* by permission of Harcourt Brace Jovanovich, Inc.

[32] It is with no great pleasure that I record that this usage lies in some uneasy relationship to that of Easton: "Although the literature is replete with discussions about the nature of authority, the meaning of the term can be resolved quickly for our purposes. A policy is authoritative when the people to whom it is intended to apply or who are affected by it consider that they must or ought to obey it. It is obvious that this is a psychological rather than a moral explanation of the term" (1953, p. 132). Obviously I am allowing that, for some authority, people may consider not that they "must or ought" but rather that they *want* to follow it. The "must or ought" may derive from either power authority (fearing not to obey) or legitimacy (agreeing that it is correct to obey).

doing it. Power interests may be expressed through the enunciation of a policy, by laws, by orders, by innuendoes, by requests, by advertisements (propaganda), or, as mentioned earlier, by the simple exercise of force. To say that a given policy is authoritative is merely to say that it is backed up by power or control.

A recent case of this usage may be seen in the description of a change in parental authority in a Bahaman community. The community economy was based on a subsistence of agriculture and fishing. With economic development, wage labor became increasingly available to the younger generation. As it became clear that the youth were no longer dependent upon their parents for their subsistence and that they could get what they needed with money earned outside the family, the parental authority broke down. "Authority . . . exists because those who have authority also have power over those who obey them."[33]

Legitimacy, with which authority is sometimes associated or confused, has quite a different basis. In the terminology being employed here, *legitimacy* is a cultural potential about an authority, a law, an act, or what you will, to the effect that it conforms to "recognized principles or accepted rules or standards."[34] A thing is legitimate, then, when people agree that it is in some manner correct, proper, or the way it should be. The sources of the belief in legitimacy are varied, but in any event quite different from those of authority. Concerning authority, we ask: *What* is the basis of the authority? What is the real skill, or power, or control, that lies behind the assignation of authority? In dealing with legitimacy, however, the question hinges on *who*: Among whom is there agreement that the authority is legal or legitimate?

Although the basis for authority necessarily lies in an agreement among people recognizing it, that agreement, in turn, rests on performance or evidence of power, either past, future, or both. If the individual invested with authority fails to perform satisfactorily or to back up his decisions with power, then his authority is likely to be challenged. The basis for legitimacy, however, is in-

[33] Rodgers and Gardner 1969. Reprinted from *American Anthropologist*, vol. 71, no. 1, by permission of the American Anthropological Association.
[34] *Webster's Third International Dictionary*, 1966.

herently a matter of agreement and nothing more. There is no other test for it than the question of whether people continue to agree that it is so. Given the fact that this is the core of legitimacy, it is obviously the case that there can be considerable divergence about the matter. The real issue of importance, then, is how it is achieved. How does it come into being? And what are the conditions under which it is retained or dissolved? It will be clear that these are not easy questions to answer. They lie at the heart of culture, and to answer them successfully is, at the same time, to answer some crucial questions about cultural origins and processes.

While authority can readily be determined and can also readily be withdrawn or challenged, legitimacy presents a more difficult problem. Since it rests entirely on agreement, it is questionable whether it continues to be an entirely viable analytical concept in complex societies. Political scientists have long used the concept, but, given the degree of alienation and opposition built into advanced societies, it is to be doubted whether it is entirely applicable without severe conceptual reworking. The problem is not resolved merely by counting heads to determine whether "enough" people agree or not. The very disagreement is as important to the understanding of the system as is the fact of agreement.

The relation of authority to legitimacy is of particular importance in political matters, although in other aspects of culture it may be of little moment. We do not, for example, concern ourselves with whether an authority on Chinese art is legitimate or not, unless he is trying to use his knowledge as a power device. Since authority is often assigned (see next section) for specific abilities, it is not uncommon for legitimacy to closely follow on authority. In U.S. culture we recognize the father as the legitimate head of the household, but we do not extend his "headship" to any other institution, such as the baseball team or the practice of medicine. We do, however, tend to let other kinds of authority spread out, and grant them certain legitimacy. Great cinema personalities are sought for their recommendations concerning hair oil and candidates for president of the United States. Not all societies let legitimacy and authority slide so sloppily over the cultural landscape. Note in the following description of the Cuna Indians of Panama how they carefully differentiate between the proper areas of authority of their chiefs:

The Cuna have various spheres or sources of power—political and curing—based mainly on knowledge of traditions and ability to put them to use (here it is striking that chiefs wield what we would call political power but are chosen largely not for their shown political ability but for their verbal skills—knowledge of speaking traditions); medicinal—based on knowledge of native medicine; and various economic—leaders of such communal tasks as house building, buying and selling by boat in Panama, growing and selling plantains, etc., and also individuals who have acquired personal wealth thru farms or contraband dealings and have therefore gained power. So far, nothing unusual. What I do find interesting, however, is the remarkable Cuna fashion of keeping these various "power roles" absolutely and apparently discretely distinct. The chief, when building a house, is just another house builder—he has no say over what's going on and does not seem to even get the face-to-face deference one would expect for a chief and which he does get in his place of power—the evening congress. At the evening congress the chief is boss but outside of it he has no say. It is considered extremely improper and is even the source of chants and legends for a chief to exercise power outside the congress—if he participates in some event or sees some wrongdoing, he's got to wait till the evening and handle it in the congress. Similarly with each realm of power—they have their typical place and outside of this place the person in question is just another participant.

Related to this is perhaps what happens when a person in power is absent for some reason. Let's take chiefs where this is most striking. Each Cuna village has a string of chiefs who are ranked with regard to power. It is the highest ranking chief who is present in the congress who decides everything. Thus when a first chief is off visiting another village, he has no say in what is going on in his own. Even more striking, if the first chief is ill (even slightly) and stays home rather than go to the congress, the next chief takes over totally and may and often does make important decisions contrary to what the first chief would have done. Needless to say, this system leads to all kinds of maneuvering among rival factions, making use of the chief ranking system and the "absence rules."[35]

One of the most significant and obvious indicators of cultural and social change is the emergence of disaccord over the assignment of legitimacy. Since authority is assigned on the basis of performance, expected performance, or a cultural potential of power, there is at least some objective basis for agreement about where to as-

[35] Sherzer 1972. By permission of Joel Sherzer.

sign it. However, there are many reasons why disagreement manifests itself over legitimacy. In Latin America today there are often insurgents who claim that the incumbent government, while clearly having authority in fact, is not legitimate. In attempting to displace governments, a preliminary device is to try to destroy the agreement about legitimacy that may exist concerning them. Part of the strategy of change, then, is to deny this accord or agreement and to seek to have others do the same.

Given the distinctions that have been made, it is convenient to differentiate two kinds of authority. In one kind, power differences exist, based on differences in control. In the other, the skill of an individual is admired or desired by his fellows. We can therefore distinguish *power authority* from *skill authority*. An individual has skill authority because he knows best about something and is regarded as having special capabilities and controls. Just what he is regarded as best at doing may be quite divergent in different situations. In the case of the San Blas Cuna, it will be recalled, the various chiefs chosen have their authority highly restricted to specific things. In his classic article on the psychological aspects of leadership among the Nambikuara (a primitive people in Brazil), Lévi-Strauss observed, "Consent is at the origin of leadership, and consent, too, furnishes the only measure of its legitimacy." In the event of disorganized behavior, "the chief has no coercitive [*sic*] power at his disposal. The eviction of the bad people can take place only insofar as the chief is able to make public feeling coincide with his own opinion. Thus he must continuously display a skill belonging more to the politician trying to keep hold of his fluctuating majority than to an over-powering ruler . . . It is not enough to do well: the chief must try—and his people count on him for that—to do better than the others."[36] The headman of a collecting band has no power upon which to draw; he will be followed so long as he leads in a manner pleasing to his followers, that is, so long as he shows skill in his leadership. Similarly, the charismatic leader in a complex society may have no base of power aside from skill in projecting his personality.

The heads of modern states, however, rest their authority on a

[36] Claude Lévi-Strauss 1967, p. 53. Reprinted by permission of the New York Academy of Sciences and the author.

basis of power; some of them have proved positively inept in exercising skills of persuasion or in detecting what the desires of their subordinates may be. Power authority rests on the fact that the individual can exercise threat on the obstinate subordinate who is unwilling to conform. The school teacher who can flunk his students, the employer who can fire the employee, the government administrator who controls the budget, the military officer who can send a person up for court-martial, etc., are all examples of the kind of power that formal organizations make possible. Since formal units require sufficient power to permit a leader to be independent of the sheer allocative basis of the primitive band, we should find cases in those simpler societies that have achieved a more advanced technological control over the environment. Robert H. Lowie recognized such a distinction in North American Indian tribes. Most tribes had "titular chiefs," obedience to whom "continues no longer than the will of the chief corresponds entirely with the inclination of those he leads."[37] In contrast to these weak "peace chiefs" (who seemed more concerned with keeping the peace than with stirring up conflicts) there are among some peoples "strong chiefs," individuals who exercise real coercive force as a part of their authority. These Lowie cited as being found among the Incas, possibly the Aztecs, certainly the Mayas and the Chihchas, probably the Natchez of the southeastern United States, and, finally, where the police societies emerged among the Plains Indians.

To Lowie this emphasis on weak chiefs reflected a strong difference between Indian societies in America and societies found elsewhere in the world. He further felt that the power of the "strong chief" was derived in part through a "magnification" of his power that was possible by virtue of his allying himself with a religious specialist. From the standpoint of the present analysis, however, the differences between skill authority ("titular chiefs," weak chiefs, "peace chiefs") and power authority ("strong chiefs") are not to be explained through continental characteristics. The enhancement of power through religious activity may well be important, however, and this we explore more fully in Part Three.

[37] Lowie 1967, p. 71. Reprinted from the *Journal of the Royal Anthropological Institute*, vol. 78, nos. 1–2.

Principally, however, the issue lies in the fact that, in all cases cited by Lowie of what we would regard as "power authority," the societies in question were relatively highly developed; and, with the exception of the Plains Indians, which we will review shortly, all had fairly complex administrative organizations, with numerous persons living off the wealth or surplus produced by others. In all, we could expect the leaders to have encountered sources of independent power.

In summary, then, *authority* applies to an individual or operating unit that has power, control, or skill or, by metaphorical extension, to the means by which or the associated context within which this power or control is exercised. *Legitimacy* refers to an agreement about the correctness of anything—a form of behavior, a law, an act of power, an authority. It is, therefore, quite possible to have authority that is not legitimate, that is, where a power holder is believed to be holding or acting out his power in an incorrect manner or on an incorrect basis. It is important to keep the matter of legitimacy separate from that of power, since the latter is derived from control over the environment, irrespective of what one may think about it; and the other has to do with what people think about things, irrespective of how those things may really be. In matters specifically pertaining to power, I earlier employed the term *cultural potential* to refer to the manner in which people think about the controls and powers that may exist in a given situation. A specific cultural potential will often include some notions of legitimacy, particularly in political matters, but need not. It refers merely to opinions about how things are, whatever those opinions may be.

## D. Types of Power Exercise

The English language (like many others, evidently) has done a disservice to our understanding of power. There is no verb *power*. There is an English noun *power*, and absence of a verbal form seems to imply that there is some substantive quality to its referent. Consequently, our literature is loaded with notions of "empowering," "giving power," "taking power," "exercising power," "playing with power," "showing power," etc.; but, if we try to express the idea that power is exercised as a *verb*, there is no such word. The inconvenience is clear when we compare this to *control.* We can both "control (verb) something," and we can "give or take control." When we speak of someone "taking control," we are referring to an act whereby an individual participates in a *process*. But, if we try to speak of power in this way, we find that a person rarely "takes power" (usually only chiefs of state do); rather, he "takes the power." This substantive implication about power complicates our present discussion. Here, we are specifically regarding power as a process, a part of a relationship. While I can say, "The king controls the throne," I should not say, "The king powers his subordinates." Note, I am saying he *powers*, not *empowers*. *To power* would refer to the process whereby an actor exercises power, just as *to control* refers to the process whereby he exercises control. (Obviously, to "empower" means to give power to someone or something else, not to exercise it oneself.) I will not try the reader's patience by systematically using the word *power* as a verb, but I will resort to it on occasion for the sake of emphasis.[38]

Fundamentally, we are concerned with the following processes:

| | |
|---|---|
| "to control" | *A* controls *X*. |
| "to power" | *A* controls *X*, and thereby exercises power over *B*. |
| "to empower," or "to grant power"; "to be empowered," or "to derive power from" | (1) *A* controls *X* and "powers" *B* but grants control to *B*, thus relinquishing both control and power to *B*. |
| | or |
| | (2) *A* controls *X*, and retains control but permits *B* to act as if he controls; thus *B* can "power" in *A*'s place; *B* has derived power from *A*, but *A* retains control. |

[38] Robert Dahl observed that "unlike 'influence' and 'control' it has no conventional verb form" (1957, p. 202). There is, of course, an intransitive form used as *powered* and *powering*, but it carries the sense of *being empowered*, or *empowering*, still thus escaping the issue of having the usage refer to the process of exercising power. Spanish uses *poder* both as verb and noun, but the verb has the same usage as the English *to be able*, as the earlier Latin usage would indicate. Spanish speakers are equally unable to say simply that "El rey puede su inferior." Neither *power* nor *poder* can take a direct object.

To give control is the same as giving the thing being controlled. Thus an economic exchange would be a case where each of two parties grants the control of something to the other. When one gives up control, he also gives up whatever power may be contingent upon that control.

The situation in connection with giving power, however, is more complicated. One can either give up power through losing control over the relevant piece of the environment; or one may give over the ability to make decisions but retain the control. When we say that a person "grants power" or that another receives or "derives power," we may be referring to *either* of these two situations. There is nothing in English usage that would differentiate them. To keep these distinct, we will follow the general usage of saving the use of any form of transfer of power for the situation where the control is not transferred. Thus, if A relinquishes both control and power to B, then it will be referred to as a transfer of *control*, and it is assumed that all contingent power is lost by the earlier holder. When we refer to power that has been granted, delegated, derived, allocated, or what you will, however, we will be referring to situations where the original controller has retained at least some measure of his control and so has not relinquished the power that he would thereby exercise over the person to whom he may have granted power. What is transferred, under these circumstances, then, is the right to make decisions, with the assumption that the actor retaining control will backstop the new power holder by supporting his decisions.

This separation of decision-making from actual control is one factor that accounts for the incredibly complex elaborations to be found in human power systems. A moment's reflection will indicate that this ability to arbitrarily grant the right to make a decision is something that is probably uniquely human. It requires a number of degrees of abstraction to differentiate conceptually (1) the proposed act from (2) the decision as to whether to commit the act or not; and, then, (3) to further allocate the decision phase to someone else, while (4) at the same time retaining the actual control, and (5) therefore putting off till later the decision as to whether to agree to the decision made by the grantee.

If we leave aside matters of transferring or changing of control and focus only on processes of transferring power for the moment, we can distinguish the following:

| *If*: | *Then*: |
|---|---|
| $A$ controls $X$, and thereby $A$ "powers" $B$; | $A$ has *independent* power. |
| $A$ controls $X$, $A$ grants to $B$ decision-making power dependent on $A$'s continuing control; | $A$ has *granted* power to $B$; $B$ has *derived* power from $A$. |
| Each $A$ of a set of $A$'s retains control of its $X$; each $A$ grants to $B$ the right to make decisions; | $A_1, A_2, \ldots, A_n$ *allocate* power to $B$; $B$ has received *allocated power* from the set of $A$'s. |
| $B$ grants power to each $A$ of a set of $A$'s but retains control of his $X$; | $B$ *delegates* power to $A_1, A_2, \ldots, A_n$. The $A$'s, individually and collectively, have received *delegated* power. |

Let us now return to the varieties of power exercise. The simplest, where decision-making and control are retained by an actor, is *independent power*. The solitary hold-up man with a gun in his hand, the solitary lifeguard who must decide between saving two lives, the object of someone's infatuation—all of these individuals have the ultimate decision over what is to be done, what disposition is to be made of the environment of someone else. (In these three cases, it is unwise or virtually impossible for them to let someone else make the decision.) Independent power lies at the basis of the network of controls of all power systems. It has often been observed that processes associated with independent power usually revolve around issues of force, that is, who can physically manipulate the relevant aspects of the environment. The reason for this is simply that one most often observes independent power in action in those cases where the controlling actor has found it impossible to separate himself from decision-making. For most people, it is always easier to let someone else make the decision. The fact that we so rarely see independent power in action (especially in complex societies) should not obscure the fact that it is possible to identify independent bases of power and that, even where decision-making has been granted elsewhere, it may be withdrawn or later withheld by the controller.

An individual's possible independent power, under the simplest technological conditions, varies with age, sex, condition of health, intelligence, knowledge, skill, and many other specific and personal factors. Each individual's ability to control the environment will vary with these factors. As such, in simple societies independent power has its most important role. Among other things, it is crucial in determining why one person rather than another is chosen as a leader or headman. As technology advances, as the control over the environment becomes more complex, independent power changes in a rather strange way. Perhaps most important is that the exercise of control becomes more specialized; individuals become more specialized in abilities. Thus, while technology opens more of the environment to control and thereby increases the total independent power to be exercised, it narrows the specific range of controls available to most individuals.[39] Since ultimately the individual's control of independent power is limited by his own physical and mental abilities, there is an inevitable concentration of control. The technology, however, may permit a single individual to pack a tremendous wallop, for example, by placing in his hands the button to set off an atomic bomb, or by placing him near glaciers in that delicate state in which they will crack and tumble into the sea if he blows on his ship's horn. But his control of such massive events is completely dependent on a particular and usually uncommon concatenation of circumstances.

So, while advancing technology increases the amount of potential independent power, it also specializes the participation of and control by specific individuals. A corollary of this is that individuals become more interdependent; the increasing controls exercised by one increasingly impinge on the environment of others. Since the ability of any single individual to physically exercise control is restricted by the amount of physical and mental activity he is able to carry out in any given period of time, the whole nature of power takes on an increasingly different quality. Independ-

[39] This should not be construed as a contradiction of Malthus; technology opens *potential* environments; the social and engineering processes to realize this potential present different problems.

ent power, or direct control over the environment, becomes less
crucial except under critical circumstances, and other varieties of
power, those having to do with control over the environment of
the controllers, become increasingly important. In this linkage,
control gives power, and that power, in turn, provides further access to control of symbols and other energy forms. Thus, if *A* controls the environment of *B*, he may use that control to require that
*B* grant him yet further controls or symbol control over other environments that *B* controls.

It will now be obvious that the linkage of controls-with-power
and power-with-further-controls-and-symbol-control permits an indefinite strategic extension of the specific control and power of any
individual, provided that he can keep the multitude of controls and
powers adjusted and balanced in his favor. It also makes perfectly
clear, were it not already so, why a description of a power structure must include control, symbol control, and power.

There is a further point of importance about independent power. The quality of "independence" derives from the fact that within a given context or situation the power is uniquely exercised by
a particular unit, that is, a specific group or actor. This is easy to
identify where it is a simple matter of whether *A* or *B* holds the
knife. However, there are many situations where an actor, *A*,
grants his decision-making to another, *B*, so that the second can
effectively exercise the power of the first as if it were his own.
From the point of view of a third actor, *C*, it may appear that, for
practical purposes, *B* now has independent power. However, unless
the actual control has been shifted, the power is only shifted by instituting symbol control. In a contemporary capitalist state we say
that *B* "owns" something, but we actually know that "ownership"
rests on property laws, symbol controls, of the government; and
we know that the government not only can but may use these
symbol controls to exercise its own greater powers to set aside
these "property rights" when it finds it expedient to do so. The so-
called right of *eminent domain* permits the state to exercise this
independent power over its citizens. But of importance here is the
fact that, except for the symbol control of the state, citizens in such
states will treat property *as if* it were their own. It is, thus, independent power based on symbol control of the *environment*. In
fact, of course, they have the judicial and police powers of the

state on their side to exercise sanctions against those who would try to challenge their control. So, even though citizens do not have direct control over the physical property under these circumstances, for most purposes they act *as if* they did. Assuming that we understand the difference, it is terminologically convenient to refer to such power as "independent," whether it is based on control of substantial or of symbolic environments. So long as one citizen successfully acts independently against another, we may use the term; but if it gets to the point that he must call on the sanctioning powers of the state, or that he argues his rights against those of the state itself, then we must be careful to indicate the real basis of power.

Independent power is in the hands of the actor. Dependent power exercise leaves the control in the hands of one actor but turns over the decision-making to another. It is convenient to distinguish three kinds of such power transfers: *granting, allocating,* and *delegating.*[40]

Granting power consists of one actor or operating unit giving the decision-making power to another. It is involved in the simplest interactions and is usually conceived as granting someone a "right." Mutual dyadic granting between two actors or units would be equivalent to classical reciprocity and to Sahlins's "negative reciprocity" and "balanced reciprocity."[41] Simple dyadic granting of power is the most fundamental power operation to coordinate relations. It is done between units that anticipate a return approximately equivalent to that given. It thus includes cooperative, unsocial, friendly, hostile, conflicting, or, indeed, any quality of action. The point is that reciprocation is anticipated. What we will shortly describe as coordinated operating units are based entirely on this kind of power granting.

Allocated and delegated power are distinguished because they are the common forms of power granting that lead to various kinds

---

[40] In my 1970 volume I used the term *derivative* power to refer to the variety that I am here calling *delegated.* The reason for changing the terminology is merely one of stylistic convenience; *delegate* permits both a transitive verbal and a substantive usage, whereas *derivative* gives us an intransitive verb. The term *derive* can be used for any situation in which an actor receives decision-making rights from another source.

[41] Sahlins 1965.

of power structures. We differentiate the two on the basis of whether the power is transferred from many to one, or from one to many. If the receiver is unique and is granted some particular power that each of a set of grantors has to give, we will say that he has *allocated power*. However, if the receiver is one of various who receive power from the grantor, then we will say he has *delegated power*. Delegated and allocated power situations are structurally very different. In delegated power, where various grantees receive from a common source, each grantee's new power will necessarily be relative to that received by each of the others. Thus the president of a company is delegated more power by the board of directors than is a vice-president, or a manager of one of the sections, or the foreman of one of the work gangs; and government delegates more of its power to some individuals than to others. Since the delegator grants to various individuals, it means that he can manipulate his grants of power so as to exercise power over each of the receivers. So it is that the delegation of power necessarily makes the receiver dependent. So long as the individual with delegated power wants it, the superior has additional power over him.

In allocated power, the relation between the grantor and receiver is quite different. Since a grantor can allocate certain powers only to one party at a time, he cannot be as manipulative as the delegator can. Since power is allocated by many to one, in an election, many allocate their right to make decisions to only one of the various candidates.

Allocated power is the kind of power held by a headman of a primitive band, the power of the chairmen of many modern bureaucratic committees, the power invested in the United Nations, the power that binds an alliance or confederation of nations together. The participants are peers and can withdraw their allocated power at any time. When it occurs that the grantor cannot withdraw his allocation at will, then the power structure changes. The citizens of the United States have the opportunity once every four years to allocate their individually held power to select from a number of candidates for the presidency. Once they make their selection, their allocation has been made, and it is extremely difficult to withdraw it. Impeachment proceedings are complicated and require even greater political support. Because of differences in the mechanisms of possible withdrawal, the use of allocated power

*within* a modern democracy and that in a primitive band are very
different affairs. Where withdrawal is not difficult, however, as
among states belonging to a League of Nations or the United Nations, then we have a situation structurally similar to that of a
primitive band.

The distinction between allocated and delegated power is an
analytical one. In actual complex cases, both types of power will
be operative. Returning to our modern democracy, the people can
control symbolically and can allocate power for only one day every
few years; their rulers then effectively have independent power
and proceed to delegate power during the rest of the time. So, while
we may, for various reasons, reiterate that a democracy is a system based on the allocation of power from the many to the few, an
equally impressive fact is that, as in any complex system, the
major operations are carried on through the delegation of power
held *independently* by the superordinates.

The distinction between delegated and allocated power is made
in terms of whether power is granted from one to many, or from
many to one. This is a convenient technical distinction, but another equally important differentiation is involved. Both these processes entail one party holding relatively more power than the
other. In allocated power, the multiple granting of power by many
to one gives that one greater power than any of the other peers. In
delegated power, the grantor will not be able to delegate power to
many unless he already has more power than they do (thereby not
reducing himself to being a subordinate by virtue of the grant).
Thus, these processes of granting power inherently involve a concentration of power, either before or after the fact. So, while allocated and delegated power can be identified in terms of the relative
numbers of parties in the processes, they may also be identified by
the relative power positions of the parties. Delegated power is
granted by a superordinate to a subordinate; allocated power results in making a coordinate (i.e., a peer) into a superordinate.

There seems to be little question but that in allocating power the
allocators temporarily lose power and the recipient temporarily
gains it. In the delegation of power, however, the picture is by no
means as simple. Gluckman observed among the Lozi: "Delegation
of authority always creates power against him who delegates. The
Lozi say that when the king appointed his chief councillor to rule

for him, he made that councillor 'another kind of king' who could control him. For the chief councillor now represented the people against the king, as well as the king to the people."[42] This instance is one where the king's power is principally based on the allocated power of his people; thus the delegation to a subordinate actually placed that subordinate more in the position of a broker than in that of a bureaucratic dependent. In those situations where the delegator's power is either independent or derived from some yet higher source, then the delegation will not necessarily weaken him but usually will strengthen him, since it gives additional mechanisms for the exercise of his own power. The delegate, being totally dependent upon his good will, finds it unwise to misuse the power so delegated. Such a case is found in the political and economic support provided by the United States Department of State and Central Intelligence Agency to Col. Carlos Castillo Armas in Guatemala in 1954, or the military intervention of the Soviet Union in support of orthodox Communist party elements in Czechoslovakia in 1968. In both instances, the delegation of the power of the large nation to elements of the smaller nation extended the exercise of power of the former.

There is little question but that, when societies become more complex (which is to say when they have more power in them), the role of allocative power changes in important ways. It will become clearer after the discussion of operating units and the evolution of power that allocative power's relative importance declines, while that of delegated power increases. Autonomous or sovereign units based on allocative power are standard in primitive societies but occur only under rather special circumstances in complex societies. Today there are groups, such as the *guerrilleros* in Latin America, the militant blacks, Chicanos, and American Indians in the United States, the French-Canadians in Ottawa, and the Palestinian rebels and terrorists in the Middle East, all of whom have decided to withdraw some or all of their allocative power from the nations in which they live. As such, they are arguing that it is possible to seriously weaken powerful organizations, even nation-states, by withholding this power. The question is open. The with-

---

[42] Gluckman 1965a, p. 145. Reprinted from *Politics, Law and Ritual in Tribal Society* by permission of Aldine Publishing Co.

drawal to isolation from the larger society may weaken the superiors by the loss of some allocated power. But the subordinates also lose the benefits, the delegated powers, of the larger society.

Allocated power does, however, continue to play an important role in a number of situations. The leadership in complex societies, for example, may appear to be based on a range of independent controls. In one sense this is true, of course, but the controls are actually rather dispersed among a number of top operating units. The centralization in a president, premier, or some other chief of state depends on allocation by these power holders that surround him. The president of the United States needs to have the support of power interests in the country; but he also needs to be able to depend upon his immediate subordinates to carry out his own interests. Those immediately below him in both the national power structure and the governmental administrative structure must include many who allocate power to him, or else he will be unable to govern.

At many points, or in many niches, small or intermediate operating units based on allocated power are constantly coming into being in complex societies. So long as their interests do not infringe on those of the more powerful, they are likely to be left alone. But it is not uncommon that they will be seen as either threatening or useful, and attempts will be made to co-opt or subordinate them by granting or delegating power, or even by direct exercise of power over them.[43] So it is that social workers and community developers try to "organize" local groups that might aid in the development of the worker's activities.

Perhaps the most depressing effect of complexity on allocative power is to make it gradually indistinguishable from the direct exercise of power. Instances of this are to be seen where individuals can see no ready escape from the situation in which they find themselves and therefore often prefer to make the best of it. To take ex-

---

[43] "Among the most important structural characteristics of both the classless society and the mass society are the decline or disappearance of intermediate organizations—voluntary associations small enough for the individual to have an effective say in their activities—and the increasing distance between the leaders and the masses in all types of organization." (T. B. Bottomore 1966, p. 138. Reprinted from *Elites and Society*, originally published by Messrs. C. A. Watts in 1964, by permission of Pitman Publishing.)

treme cases, the "trusty" in the jail finds that life is better if he cooperates and works for the jailers. The lower-level bureaucrat will continue to suffer indignities rather than seek other employment simply because he knows his way around and is uncertain of a future outside. For a thousand and one reasons—security, survival, familiarity, or what you will—people usually prefer to contribute something to the context of their lives, prefer to have some active participation, prefer a favorable acknowledgment to a complete retreat, hostility, and marginalization. Given the opportunity, one is more satisfied in an organization to which he contributes decisions than in one where he is totally marginalized.

We have now described independent power and three kinds of dependent power. Before leaving this subject, it is useful to see how these work in some common kinds of complex power transfers. They are all composed of combinations of the four basic types.

*Patronage* or *clientage* relationship is a centralized reciprocity, a centralized mutual granting relation. Structurally it looks somewhat like a combination of allocated and delegated power, but it differs because it is the superimposition of a series of mutual granting relations between a single actor or unit and a series of other single actors or units. Between patron and client is a reciprocal granting relation. Because a single patron will tend to have various clients, the relation will superficially look like a mixture of allocation and delegation; but here there is no collective action on the part of the multiplicity, nor is there any necessary playing off of one client against another. Because it is created on a series of individual relations, clientage is important for building an individual's power and (as will be seen in Part Three) is very important in the evolution of power structures.

The patron-client relation may be initiated by either party. It is commonly assumed that it is the patron who is the initiator, because over the long run he stands to gain more, since he is the central figure in a series of relationships. It is important to keep in mind, however, that the client is as often, or more often, the initiator of the relation, for it is usually he who has the greater need. George Foster has illustrated this well for the Mexican community of Tzintzuntzan: "Tzintzuntzeños, recognizing their humble position and lack of power and influence, are continually alert to the possibility of obligating a person of superior wealth, position, or influence, thereby initiating a patron-client relationship which, if matters go well, will buttress the villagers' security in a variety of life crises that are only too certain: illness, the sudden need for cash, help in legal disputes, protection against various forms of possible exploitation, and advice on the wisdom of contemplated moves."[44] Perhaps the most telling evidence that it is the client and not the patron who is the crucial member of the relation is to be seen in the fact (as reported by Foster, but also true over most of the Catholic world) that saints may be patrons. Thus, individuals will seek the patronage of a saint to help them, as they would that of a living person. However it may be that one conceives of a saint's activities, he has seldom been found seeking out clients; it is the client who is the initiator. The patron's role consists in his need of some service that the client can provide; it also may be a step toward ultimate exploitation or, in some cases, even delegation.

Max Gluckman describes well the situation in the Barotse: "With the goods and the technologies available to the Barotse economy, the rich and powerful could not live in much finer houses, surrounded by relatively luxurious furnishings, or bedeck themselves with fine clothes; there was therefore no point in attempting to exercise their power to profit from sweating the labor or to expropriate the goods of underlings. Instead, they used their control over land, and goods to build up direct relationships with many followers." ". . . a man's prestige is determined by the number of dependents or subjects he has, much more than by mere possession and use of goods. Prestige and power are important in all

[44] Foster 1967. From George M. Foster, *Tzintzuntzan: Mexican Peasants in a Changing World*, pp. 229–230. Copyright © 1967 by Little, Brown and Company (Inc.). Reprinted by permission. In an earlier version of the essay from which this chapter was derived, Foster referred to the relation as the "patronazgo," a neologism which suggests that the patron rather than the client might have been seen to be the more crucial member of the relation; cf. *American Anthropologist* 63, no. 6 (1961): 1191. A more recent statement along the lines being argued here is to be found in Alexander Moore's discussion of patron-client relations in pseudonymous Atchalan, Guatemala: "But to describe the process in simple lineal terms, I say that a client first claims a sponsor, who in turn bestows some advantage upon him, which in turn must be validated by performance or achievement." With reference to the relations with two early Guatemalan presidents, Carrera and Barrios, he comments that "the highest patron, then, is the creation of his clients" (1973, pp. 116, 118). Reprinted from Alexander Moore, *Life Cycles in Atchalan*. (New York: Teachers College Press, 1973.)

these societies and enable a man to control the action of others; but he gains that control through establishing relationships of personal dependence with as many others as he can."[45]

Another central feature of the client relation is that the client may have little more than his own body and skill to give. He can give labor, loyalty, respectful behavior, clowning, etc. In contemporary western society, a dentist or doctor may speak of his clients; as such, they have the privilege of leaving the specialist and seeking another. Knights in European feudal society equally might change their allegiance; voters at election time are sought for their vote. Among Latin American creoles, "The client promises loyal support; the leader pledges supplies and help."[46]

*Extension of allocation or delegation* is a device whereby the recipient of either kind of power simply passes along the "right" that has been given him to another. Since the original recipient does not have the real controls, the act of extending decision-making rights to another can be tenuous and dangerous, but it nevertheless is much practiced, particularly in what we will call unitary domains. Under some circumstances, a further granting of power may provide structural solidarity. For example, in a religious situation, when power is allocated by virtue of a belief in the particular merit of the recipient, or to one who already has power and may be expected to reciprocate, the grantor stands to benefit. When the medieval pope crowned and consecrated a king, he was using power allocated to him and granting further power to the king. Since the king was also a recipient of allocated power, however, this really set up an interlocking series of power dependencies. In administrative organizations, there is often a practice of redelegation, such that lower-level administrators receive authorization for actions down a chain of delegated actors.

*Expropriated* power is the case where an actor who has power over another uses his superordinate position to deprive the subordinate of his own independent controls and powers. The state can expropriate properties of its citizens and residents because they are subordinate. Closely related is *exploitative* power, where the

[45] Gluckman 1965*b*, pp. 46, 4. Reprinted from *The Ideas in Barotse Jurisprudence* by permission of the author.

[46] Eric Wolf and Edward C. Hansen 1972, p. 74. Reprinted from *The Human Condition in Latin America* by permission of Oxford University Press.

superordinate does not actually remove the controls from the subordinate but uses his superior power to benefit disproportionately from the controls and powers of the subordinate. This, of course, would be the core of Marx's notion of the surplus value. More recently it has been traced by C. B. MacPherson in these terms: "Those who have the capital and land can therefore, by employing the labour of others, get a net transfer of some of the powers of others (or some of the product of those powers) to themselves." MacPherson recognizes this to occur in any society with a ruling class, but "What is unique about the transfer in the market society is that there it is maintained by continual competition between individuals at all levels."[47]

*Brokerage* includes a number of combinations of power transfers. Basically it consists of a central figure, the broker, who is granted, allocated, or delegated power by one or more parties. This power is used to negotiate with a third party (which may be one or multiple). The successful negotiation consists in obtaining that the third party also grants (or allocates or delegates) power to the broker so that he may then negotiate with the first party. The successful broker is he who (1) finishes the entire negotiation with advantages to himself and (2) has so satisfied the other parties that they are willing to seek him out as a broker again. A recent paper by William T. Stuart insists that the term *brokerage* must refer to "the instrumental significance of exchange in the patron-client relationship."[48] I see no virtue in these restrictions. To say that brokerage must refer to exchange and that it must refer to a patron-client relation simply reduces the utility of the concept. Marriage brokers do not necessarily work in a patron-client relation; and there are brokerage negotiations that do not involve an exchange (except in a metaphorical sense).

It is important, I believe, to distinguish between "cultural" and "power" brokerage. In the first case the broker is concerned with the changing of meanings and values or the use of certain cultural forms among members of some populations, when these innovations derive from the culture of another population. Thus the

47 C. B. MacPherson 1962, pp. 56–67. Reprinted from *The Political Theory of Possessive Individualism: Hobbes to Locke,* © 1962 Oxford University Press, by permission of The Clarendon Press, Oxford.
48 Stuart 1972, p. 34.

mestizo schoolteacher in a Latin American Indian community, the itinerant peddler offering urban products to rural dwellers, and the impresario negotiating the services of a singer with some local theater are all instances of negotiating the manifestation of cultural differences in the sense that Fredrik Barth has seen in the activity of entrepreneurs: "The entrepreneurial coup . . . is where one discovers a path by which something of little value can be transformed into something of great value . . . The information produced by such activity will render false the idea that people have held till then about the relative value of goods, and can reasonably be expected, to precipitate re-evaluations and modifications both of categorizations and of value orientations."[49] This kind of process may, but does not inherently, involve exchange. Teaching new meanings is not an exchange process between the mestizo schoolteacher and his rural Indian students. The students pay him nothing, and he "gives" them nothing.

The power broker, however, is involved in a process much more akin to exchange, although it can be argued that even here exchange is not inevitable. The power broker specifically wields power at each of two levels, or within each of two domains, and his power in one level or domain depends upon the success of his operations in the other. Thus the marriage broker is not successful unless he gets both families to agree; and the cacique acting between his "people" and the central government is not successful unless he gets something for both parties. A major role of power brokers is to mediate where confrontations do not occur.[50]

Although a broker exists to negotiate between the interests of two parties, or between the members of a lower level and those of a higher level, it nevertheless remains a tendency for the broker to favor one of the parties against the other. Initially, such a tendency may be due simply to any one of a series of possible preferences or obligations felt by the broker. As time goes on, however, and the broker has experience, the tendency will increase for him to favor the one who has the greater power over him; this, in turn, will often be the one who has strategically the greater amount of power in the system as a whole. As power increasingly concentrates in

49 Barth 1967, p. 664. Reprinted from *American Anthropologist*, vol. 69, no. 6, by permission of the American Anthropological Association.
50 R. N. Adams 1970*b*, pp. 321–322.

the upper reaches of a society, the brokers who operate between the local and higher levels pay increasing heed to the interests of those above them and concomitantly decreasing attention to the local interests. In multiple-level societies where brokers exist at each level, this produces an interesting phenomenon that can be called the brokerage or janus point in the system. The janus point is that point or area furthest down among the levels where the power concentrated at the top makes itself so felt that the brokers will favor the interests of the higher levels as opposed to the lower. In expanding systems, where power is increasing, it is often possible to trace the inexorable lowering of the janus point as more controls concentrate at the top.

This is illustrated by events at the University of Texas at Austin. When the university was founded in the latter part of the nineteenth century, there was a general accord from the top of the state government down through the faculty as to what the best interests of the university were. In the late teens there was a governmental crisis, and a split occurred between the board of regents and the governor, with the regents siding with the interests of the university. In the 1940's another crisis occurred, at which time the board of regents sided with the governor against the university interests as defended by the president of the university. Most recently, in the late 1960's, in another series of crises, the university administration sided essentially with the board of regents against what were considered by most faculty to be their own interests. Looking at these four points in time, the janus point in the system shifted steadily downward through the various levels of articulation of the system as the state became increasingly wealthy and powerful.

## 4. THE VARIETY OF OPERATING UNITS

In considering the structure of power in the world about us, we traditionally deal with varieties of social entities: individual human beings, family groups, voluntary associations, business corporations, nation-states, etc. Social scientists have from time to time concocted various analytical concepts for these units, but usually these have been restricted to some particular kind of unit. Thus the anthropologist has a complicated series of analytical concepts and typologies for kin-based and family organization, and the student of the organizations of complex societies has worked out types to help him both sort and analyze the actions of formal organizations. Here our interest is restricted not to a particular kind of unit but rather to the role that power plays in any and all human organizations. Since human beings have found it possible to organize themselves in an unnumbered variety of ways, both sequentially and simultaneously, we find it necessary to re-examine the range of human society in order to provide analytical tools that will enable us to make some significant statements about any specific human grouping and the relative power that it can bring to bear on a situation. We are going to apply the term *operating unit* to the varieties of organization that we are about to discuss.

Operating units are peculiar to the human species. They can form, dissolve, break into pieces, reform, and recombine, depending upon various factors. No other species can readapt its social organization as readily as can man, although ethological studies of various species show that such organizational readaptation among other species does take place when environments are changed (e.g., the differences in organization between animals "in the wild" and in a zoo, or the genetic readaptation of viruses). Man, however, not only can reformulate his organization; he can also belong to many such organizations at any point in time. Not only is he necessarily a member of some kind of kin organization and some larger "community" or "territorial" grouping, but in any complex society he will also be a member of various voluntary associations, recognized as pertaining to some ethnic category, some occupational sector, some educational stratum, and so forth. People with varying characteristics organize or are organized to obtain or protect various things: and, since organization provides one kind of power, these varying units are organizations of power, as well as benefiting from power based on whatever sector of the environment they may also control. In short, human operating units are of a wide variety and "subject to change without notice."

An operating unit is *a set of actors sharing a common adaptive pattern with respect to some portion of the environment. The pattern involves collective or coordinated action and some common ideology expressing goal or rationale.* An actor is a human being and/or an operating unit. This concept permits us to compare cases ranging from a fragmented set of Christmas shoppers concerned with making purchases from the environment, whose ideology consists of unconsciously shared interests, to highly controlled total institutions, such as maximum-security prisons.

Basic here is adaptation, a process inherently involving change premised on natural selection. An operating unit must adapt sufficiently well to the environment to survive. There is no need to confuse this with the exaggerated concepts of Social Darwinism, which applied the notion of the "survival of the fittest" to social groups and individual entrepreneurs.[51] Our concern, rather, is, in Theodosius Dobzhansky's terms, that "The statistical probability of survival or elimination, despite accidents, will depend on the degree of the adaptedness of individuals and groups to the environment in which they live." Of course, the concept of natural selection has most commonly been applied to populations and species; and, particularly in the hands of geneticists, it is seen to act through a selection of genes so that "carriers of some genotypes will survive, or will be eliminated more or less frequently than will the carriers of other genotypes, and the succeeding generations will not be descended equally from all the genotypes in the preceding generations, but relatively more from the better adapted ones. Therefore, the incidence of better adapted forms will tend to increase and the incidence of the less well adapted ones to decrease."[52]

In applying this notion to societies, we do not discard the question of genetics, but lay it to one side for the moment in order to examine another facet of the adaptation process. Rather than seeing the individual as a member of a reproductive population, we see him as a member of a series of organizations, each one of which exercises some particular adaptive activity; insofar as the individual pertains to a particular organization, the successful adapta-

[51] See Hofstadter 1955.
[52] Theodosius Dobzhansky 1967, p. 129. Reprinted from *Mankind Evolving: The Evolution of the Human Species* by permission of Yale University Press.

tion and survival of the organization will promote the adaptation and survival of at least some portion of its individual members. Such organizations, or units, may experience considerable change in membership, but obviously uncorrected loss would ultimately lead to extinction. Dangers to group survival are, therefore, of a different order than are those to individual survival. The operating unit is a concept that permits us to compare all kinds of groupings that survive.

Central features of the adaptation of an operating unit are (*a*) its controls over the environment, its technology (in the broadest sense) of handling or processing energy forms and flows, and (*b*) its power derived from other sources. Adaptation involves changing these controls, both as to their kind and as to the quantity of the environment being controlled. Units that strategically control more of the environment than others are said to be more powerful and also better adapted. In matters of power, of course, it is specifically control over an environment relative to others that is of interest. The focus of concern here is the way in which units are internally organized and how this internal organization empowers them. To explore this, a series of types of operating-unit structures have been proposed that vary in accordance with the presence or absence of a set of features (see Fig. 2). Five of these features have to do with the type of power being used internally and where it is focused; one has to do with the presence or absence of a basic shared identification of the members of the group. The empirical reality to which these models refer may be of any population size beyond the single individual.

The minimal degree of internal organization is the presence of parallel behavior (parallel adaptation) of a series of individuals or units, each of which has its own independent power, with no shared recognition that they are acting in parallel. The second feature is the presence of that recognition, an identification of commonality, with the consequent change in behavior of individual units to use this fact to their own advantage. The third feature is the appearance of coordinated action among those sharing common adaptation, such that a network of relations comes into being and members grant power to each other. This innovation represents the first appearance of the use of power within the unit, enabling it to act as a unit rather than as a set of coinci-

dentally related parts. The fourth feature is the allocation of power
by the members to one of their number to make decisions for
them; the fifth is the appearance of a source of power that this
now central member can use independently of any particular
allocation. The sixth and last is the delegation of power by the
central figure.

This set of features allows us to distinguish four major classes
of units. *Fragmented units* are characterized by no coordinated
activity, simply collective action. *Informal units* are characterized
by coordinated activity, but the coordination is entirely dependent
on the collective independent power of the individual members
(whether or not the power is centralized). *Centralized units* have
a central figure or authority, irrespective of what the basis of that
power may be. Its power may or may not be independent of that
independent power pertaining to the members. *Formal units* are
characterized by a central authority with sources of power that are
independent of the independent power of the members.

## A. Fragmented Units

The minimal amount of control and consequent power available
to any collectivity is that which separately pertains to each individual member in accord with his particular capabilities, strengths,
skills, and knowledge, together with whatever transferred power
he may have available to him. A simple aggregate of individuals
with such bases may be said to comprise an operating unit, providing the aggregate meets the criterion of common adaptation.
When a series of individuals manifest parallel or complementary
behaviors with respect to some aspect or facet of the environment,
they are carrying out a common adaptation and may thereby be
considered to be an operating unit, although in its minimal form.
Methodologically, it is useful to recognize this almost protounit
because it is often the first step that brings an otherwise totally
disparate and randomly assorted set of individuals (or units) into
some degree of common organization. When an entrepreneur seeks
to organize a group of people, he tries to find some common
adaptive interest, some activity or orientation already shared (perhaps unconsciously) around which he can try to build some
organization.

In a population characterized as a fragmented unit the partici-

Types of Operating Units

| Power Relation | Fragmented Units | | Informal Units | | Centralized Units | Formal Units | |
| --- | --- | --- | --- | --- | --- | --- | --- |
| Independent Variable | Individuals and Aggregate Units | Identity Units | Coordinated Units | Consensus Units | Majority Units | Corporate Units | Administered Units |
| Members have separate independent power | + | + | + | + | + | + | Variable |
| Members identify common membership | | + | + | + | + | + | Variable |
| Members grant power reciprocally | | | + | + | + | + | Variable |
| Members allocate power (centrally) | | | | + | + | + | Variable |
| Center (leader) exercises power independently of others | | | | | + | + | + |
| Center (leader) delegates power | | | | | | + | + |

Fig. 2. Types of Operating Units

pants may or may not identify with the collectivity. Thus, in the normal course of a downtown weekday, there is considerable activity of people using the city streets in order to get from one place to another. If a store is holding a sale, there may be a convergence of people on that store. Many fragmented units are like this, simply aggregates: people watching the movie; suburban husbands mowing the lawn on Saturday morning; college students going to class; and so forth. If it occurs, however, that for some reason the participants recognize the commonalities of shared behavior, and recognize that their orientation or interest is held in common, and therefore recognize their common participation, then *identity* is felt. The importance of distinguishing identity is that, when it is recognized, an individual participant may then be alienated from the collectivity and choose to give up the behavior in question. No fragmented unit, be it an aggregate or an identity unit, has any internal overt behavioral organization beyond the fact of the common or parallel conduct of the individuals involved.

Fragmented units may be of almost any size; and, insofar as we are concerned with simple *aggregate units*, there is no systematic, formal way of being sure of just how big one may be. *Identity units*, however, do permit delineation, since in the last analysis the possible participants may be asked with whom they identify themselves. Among the largest such identity units are what Edward Spicer has referred to as "peoples,"[53] large ethnically distinct sectors that recognize or claim some common origin and retain some common set of adaptive activities (such as language, rituals, sacred symbols, etc.). Jews, Gypsies, and Chicanos would be cases of "peoples." Other, nonethnic-based identity units would include aliens, refugees, and voters. The crucial characteristics insofar as power is concerned are that there is no unique and specific control exercised over the participants to coordinate them and that there is no organized allocation of decision-making that holds for all individuals who identify with the unit. Some Jews or Chicanos may organize, but there is no single organization to which all pertain. The organizations thus formed are not themselves mere fragmented units, but either informal or formal units that are using the ethnic identity as one criterion of membership.

[53] Spicer 1971, pp. 795–800.

A further important point about fragmented units, and one that continues to hold for other types of units as well, is that they are themselves composed of other operating units. In some cases, an individual human being is himself an operating unit. Fragmented units may also be composed of informal units and formal units, such as the cases just mentioned of Jewish or Chicano organizations. In Guatemala and Mexico there are Indian communities of diverse aboriginal languages and dialects. It has classically been the case that the members of these communities identify themselves as *naturales* (i.e., of a population that was native to the area), but individually until recently they have shown little particular interest in that identification for the entire population that went under that label. Instead, if asked, they would tend to identify themselves as members of a particular community of Indians, not of the larger Indian population as such. It is possible, therefore, to see the collectivity of individual Indians as an identity unit and the collectivity of Indian communities as an aggregate unit. In the former, there is identification, but no interest in coordination; and, in the latter, there is common adaptation to the environment in many respects, especially economic and political, but no particular identification between communities.

It may well have occurred to the reader that what distinguishes the identity unit from the aggregate is part of the problem of identification of social classes. "Workers of the world unite! You have nothing to lose but your chains!" obviously was an exhortation to members of an aggregate unit to identify with each other. The problem of class organization is precisely the question of shifting from an aggregate organization to one of identity, and thence to a consensus unit. The great problem with fragmented units is that they have no basis of power but the unorganized collectivity of individual independent power pertaining to the various members of component units. It is as if the cells of an organism could exist apart from their conjunction as interrelated parts of the organism and were able to recombine so that they formed a dog for part of the day and two cats during the rest of the time. Since human beings are organized by means of a number of operating units, any randomly selected set taken from a whole population may never have acted as an aggregate, not to speak of having identified with each other. Certainly the growing body of industrial laborers of the countries of the west in the early nineteenth century was an aggregate but was hardly an identity unit.

## B. *Informal Units*

If the "workers of the world" were able to unite; if the Mexican-Americans of the United States or the Bolivian migrants in Argentina were able to coordinate their efforts so as to elect their fellows to political office; if the Indian communities of Guatemala could agree to initiate cooperative political activity toward their common defense and interests; if these fragmented units could directly interact and coordinate—then we would be witnessing a process whereby individuals and units were using their common identification as a basis for granting to each other rights to make decisions for them, or decisions in common. They would be coordinating their activities around some series of interrelations, interactions, and activities.

The *coordinated unit* marks the minimal degree of such coordination. The manner in which extended families interact and the way that Australian hunting and gathering family bands separate out over a wide territory, interrelated through classificatory kinship and recognized rights of access to common portions of their environment, illustrate this degree of coordination. So long as there is no leader of the whole to whom is allocated the authority to make decisions for the whole, then the unit operates in a regulated but somewhat random manner. Individuals and groups grant certain rights to others, primarily on a reciprocal basis; that is, each retains certain rights for himself but grants to the other certain rights in return for which he receives some. Thus power is reciprocally granted within many dyadic sets and collectivities, but there is no concentration beyond that manifested by mutual coordination.

Coordinated units are of many kinds—indeed, as many as there are bases for reciprocal action. Their principal importance in evolutionary terms is that they form the major basis for the emergence of more highly centralized units, which find new forms of adaptation. All centralized units themselves form coordinated-unit networks with other centralized units. Therefore, the mere presence of a centralized unit is a signal to the observer that there will also be present one or more coordinated units. Within any extensive identity unit it is almost inevitable that there will be many co-ordinated units, often interrelated among themselves.

A feature of coordinated units that has pestered some investi-gators is their apparent lack of a clear-cut boundary. The kindred, as defined by George Peter Murdock,[54] is this kind of organization, as are the relationships between the various family units that comprise a bilateral network of extended families. Bands are co-ordinated into tribes; nations may be coordinated in organizations of common markets. A feature of coordinated units is that its members are equivalents in the sense that they are members of an identity unit; but this does not mean that they are equal. It is usually the case that they are not regarded as equals but rather that they are ranked (a subject that will be explored in greater detail in Part Two).

The apparent lack of a boundary for a coordinate unit is due to two circumstances. One is that the basis of the coordinate or recip-rocal bonds between any two members may not be precisely the same as that between another pair. Thus the coordinated kinship network has many different kinds of relationships linking the various members. Unless some arbitrary definition is given that excludes certain kinds of relations from consideration, then there is no boundary. Consequently, boundaries may be defined some-what differently, depending on who it is that makes the definition. The other feature that tends to make boundaries nebulous is that it is very easy to add or drop members, since the decision can be made by any individual. From the point of view of the investigator who is trying to "fix" a unit, the easy appearance and disappear-ance of relations can be trying; but, after all, that is the investi-gator's problem, hardly a problem for the members of the unit.

Not only primitive, but also complex societies are full of identity and coordinated units of one kind or another. The Democratic and Republican party memberships of the United States are cases in point. In contrast to the centralized party organization that charac-terizes the Communist party, or the PRI of Mexico, the major United States political parties are composed of millions of members who remain somewhat consistent in giving their vote to party members and, in some cases, in periodically working for a political

[54] Murdock 1949, pp. 46, 56–57.

campaign. Individuals may abandon the party without any previous notice; and the party, in turn, has no power to ostracize its
members.

Within each of these parties, however, there are further and
more highly organized sets of actors who choose to allocate their
decision-making to a select series of individuals—to leaders, chairmen, and candidates. When they do this, the internal nature of the
unit shifts in an important way. By allocating power, by centralizing the decision-making ability, it is now possible for these more
highly organized units to divide the labor in the face of new
tasks, to avoid overlapping efforts, etc. These are *consensus units*;
the individual members may withdraw their allocated power at
their own discretion; that is, they will obey the leader only so long
as they find it convenient in their judgment of their own needs.
But, insofar as they do grant power, they centralize it, and this
permits them to act in concert for some interest that is common to
the collectivity. In all coordinated and consensus units the individuals who are granted or allocated the right to make decisions
are characteristically sought out for their ability, wisdom, or skill
to accomplish what the members want. They have no special power
beyond that allocated to them; so they have absolutely no way at
the outset to exercise force over the members. As we will see, this
remains basic to political organization in all human societies.
Primitive family bands are so composed, and it may be presumed
that this basic dependence on allocative power remained the major
source of power in the group until well into the Neolithic period.

However, social organization based on allocative power is by no
means limited to primitive society, and it continues to play an important role in more advanced societies. Most of what are regarded
as "voluntary associations" are organizations in which the members have agreed to subordinate their rights of decision-making in
order that they may have certain other advantages. Leaders are
chosen because they are felt to be the best prepared for the particular task at hand, but they cannot use force or control-based
coercion to obtain cooperation.

It is possible to differentiate among informal units on the basis
of the degree to which loyalty is expected of the members. Where
the expectation of loyalty is high, there is an additional element
that enhances the power of the leader. Not only can he expect

support in his decisions from the members, but, to encourage recalcitrant members to conform, he can expect the availability of one special source of control, that is, he may be able to expect a coalition of the members to use control against the stubborn member. Where such loyalty by the members is manifest, the leader finds he has, through this dependable allocation, a source of power that is in effect independent of that allocated by any one adherent. For this reason, we differentiate two classes of centralized informal units. One is based entirely on consensus, and individuals are completely at liberty to diverge and withdraw their allocated power at their own convenience. The other has, in addition, a loyal majority that can provide the leader with additional independent power to support the exercise of the power allocated to him. This we call a *majority unit*.

The variety of circumstances that lead a consensus unit to convert to a majority unit are not entirely clear, but it is certain that they involve the recognition on the part of the leadership and members that the welfare, if not the survival, of the unit depends upon keeping the members' behavior in line. In order that it may occur regularly, it is apparently the case that the society must achieve superior controls in general, that is, have grown in the amount of power available within the system. A classic case in the literature that illustrates the appearance of the use of force because of the increase of control over the environment is that of the Plains Indians "soldier" or "police" societies.[55]

Symmes C. Oliver's ecological study of the Plains Indians classifies the various tribes and bands into: (1) "True Plains Indians," (2) the hunting and gathering peoples that never achieved the level of tribal organization that the True Plains people manifested, and (3) peripheral farming tribes which, because of their less mobile subsistence and more abundant resources, formed permanent villages.[56] The True Plains Indians, according to Oliver, were

[55] This case is much described, perhaps most significantly in Lowie 1967, pp. 63–68. (This source contains a further bibliography.)

[56] Oliver 1962, pp. 1–90. The True Plains Indians included the Comanche, Kiowa Apache, Kiowa, Arapaho, Cheyenne, Teten Dakota, Crow, Assiniboine, Gros Ventres, Blackfoot, Sarsi, and Plains Cree. The hunters and gatherers included Basin Plateau groups, northern Shoshone, and Algonkians and Athapaskans of Canada; the farmers included the Omaha, Mandan, Iowa, and Oto.

characterized by primary dependence upon bison hunting, such that for most of the year the basic social organizational unit was "a local group small enough to subsist by hunting and gathering, but large enough to furnish protection against hostile war parties and raids."[57] During this period,

. . . there was no need for strong social controls, since the band was not hunting as a unit, and individualistic enterprise was what was required. In the summer months, however, when the whole tribe came together, the entire situation was different. Many people were together in one place, and these were people who owed allegiance to different bands. There were important ceremonies to be organized. And, above all, there was the communal buffalo hunt to be undertaken, upon which so much depended. Order was necessary in the tribal encampment, to prevent disputes. Strict discipline was necessary on the hunt, because individual hunting was inefficient . . . It was at this time that the police societies always functioned. Over and over again, the point is made that the most important job the police societies had was in policing the communal hunts. For most True Plains tribes, this was the only time when formal social controls were instituted . . . It may be noted that the role of the police societies was integrative in another way. They not only were responsible for *punishing* offenders but also tried to *rehabilitate* the guilty persons by bringing them back within the tribal structure. As Provinse put it, "Conformity, not revenge, was sought, and immediately after a promise to conform was secured from the delinquent, steps were taken to reincorporate him into the society."[58]

The poorer hunters and gatherers, whose ecology did not permit the formulation of larger annual tribal encampments, had no police societies at all, since they were clearly unnecessary for the maintenance of social control. In contrast, the peripheral farming groups not only had police societies but also operated the full year around, not merely during the summer bison hunts.

All the Plains Indians were fundamentally organized as con-

[57] F. Eggan, cited by Oliver 1962, p. 54.

[58] Oliver 1962, pp. 61–62. Reprinted from *Ecology and Cultural Continuity as Contribution Factors in the Social Organization of the Plains Indians*, originally published by the University of California Press; reprinted by permission of The Regents of the University of California.

sensus-based informal units. The differential distribution of the police societies illustrates how increasingly abundant environmental resources permitted increasing controls over the environment, which led to periodically or permanently larger groups and greater intragroup power. The hunting and gathering marginals had no such coercive device, whereas, when in larger groups, the True Plains Indians evolved a mechanism for the use of certain members as a physical controlling force against other members. And, in the more evolved group with developed agriculture, the environment and technology added even more power to the system, such that these coercive mechanisms became permanent parts of the Indian social organization.

The police societies can also be seen as operating units tentatively marking off a new level of integration within the Indian society. The True Plains societies were, then, transitional between the hunting and gathering marginals, where such units did not occur, and the farmers, where they had become an established part of the social order. It should not go without mention here that Lowie saw these conservators of order as a step toward complexity.[59]

## C. Formal Units

The degree of power achieved in the Plains Indians' farming societies tends to extend beyond that of the informal unit. The police societies became permanent organizations due to the greater environmental control allowed by permanent agriculture. In some cases, this gave the leaders a degree of continuing power that was somewhat independent of the single member's individual allocated power. This kind of arrangement is what lays the basis for one in which the leader may not only have power independently of the single members but also have enough power to delegate it. The presence of such controls indicates a dependability of available pow-

---

[59] Lowie 1927; see especially p. 101. Max Gluckman also finds seeds of complexity in the police societies, but emphasizes that they show "that social cohesion develops as men who are allied in terms of one customary rule of association (band-membership) are grouped under a different rule (soldier-society membership) with others who have a different allegiance under the first rule" (1965a, p. 90).

er unknown to most hunting and gathering societies. In an overview of human society, perhaps the most common basis for such
independent power is the availability of armed men—Janizaries,
troops, police, a gang of thugs—a group that depends upon its leader to have sufficient controls and power to support it. However, in
complex societies, where so much of the operation of power is delegated to others, there are many other sources of independent power. Among the most important are the controls over land and other
basic survival and production resources. In considering the importance of an independent basis for the support of the judiciary, the
*Federalist* observed: "In the general course of human nature, a
power over a man's subsistence amounts to a power over his will."
It seems unavoidable in the broad picture that, of the various independent powers that leaders exercise in formal units, that which
ultimately derives from controls over a people's subsistence basis
will be the most important.

The shift from the informal to the formal unit is a particularly
important one. The delegation of power by an authority may not
appear in itself to be such a markedly drastic change in a system,
but it reflects the fact that there is so much power invested and concentrated in the leadership that the leader not only can afford to
grant some of it to others but must do so if he is to keep the situation in hand. It thus also marks the point at which an individual
member's allocated power ceases to be the dominant source for the
activities of the unit as a whole, being replaced by a totality of
power that the leadership has been able to collect. It marks the end
of the freedom of the individuals or the operating units to go their
own way, to leave the scene if it is not to their liking; it marks the
beginning of the bureaucratization of society. There is presumably
some maximum size of a human organization that can be based on
allocated power alone. We know of no limitation on the size of an
organization that controls resources beyond those controlled by its
members. Scholars have variously seen "civilization," the city,
writing, and various other indicators as being indices of the major
change in human social evolution. All these, of course, are external
manifestations of such change. Certainly one analytic aspect of
that change is the shift from a society based solely on allocated
power to one where additional independent power becomes available; and that, of course, occurs with the additional control over

the environment provided by the domestication of plants and animals.

Such formal units, however, are also thereby extremely varied. We need only contrast the power exercised by a Barotse king, the pope, the manager of a bank, a Polynesian chief, and an American president to see the varieties of relations involved. In order to bring within the scope of our treatment such excessive diversity, I have differentiated two kinds of formal units, the *corporate* and the *administered unit*. The corporate unit has all six features of power and identity in operation. Not only do the rulers have independent power and delegate it, but the members have independent power and allocate it, as well as sharing varieties of power-granting networks and holding common identity with other members.

The term *administered unit* is chosen to indicate that this residual category comprises units that exist within larger corporate structures (such as the nation-state) and have either independent power or delegated power as their source but are characterized by an administrative organization, or bureaucracy. All corporate units have some such administration, but in complex societies there are many units that draw upon existing concentrations of power, and these may lack one or more of the six features that characterize the corporate unit. Most common are those organizations, recruitment to which is by force: the conscription to the military, the imprisoning of criminals, the locking up of people whose deviant behavior is attributed to mental deficiency, etc. In organizations such as these there is, obviously, little chance of allocated power, and the independent powers of individuals may be so constricted that they cease to even contribute them to any reciprocal granting. In extreme cases, such as solitary confinement, it can be argued that even the individual's independent power ceases to be at his own disposition.

There will be no attempt here to analyze the varieties of such administered organizations, since they are a rather specialized class and should be examined separately. Most organizations, however, that we find in operation in complex societies, as well as all those in primitive societies, can be fairly adequately analyzed in terms of the six basic types of power structure; the organizations that dangle, as it were, from the concentration of power at the top of the system will comprise the variety of administered units.

## 5. POWER DOMAINS AND LEVELS

The devices that can be used for mapping a power domain are the operating units that include the actors, and the domains and levels of articulation that these operating units form among themselves. In describing a structure of power, we are as much concerned with the internal organization of the units as we are with their interrelations. The internal structure is intimately related to the external structure; and, indeed, for some purposes one may ignore the "boundaries" entirely and deal simply with the power relations that extend as a network through the entire universe. Within such networks, there are two major concepts which, taken together, provide the principal framework for analysis of a power system. These are *domains* and *levels of articulation*.

### A. Power Domains

A domain is any relational set in which there are two or more actors or operating units of unequal relative power with respect to each other. If *A* has greater power over *B* than *B* does over *A*, then *B* is said to be within the domain of *A*. However, the term *domain* becomes useful in cases of multiple-party relations, where *A* has domain over a number of subordinates.

Domains may be differentiated on the basis of a number of variant properties. Among the most important is whether the relations permit multiple access from the subordinate to the superordinate. Where this is not the case, the domain is unitary (Fig. 3*a*); where it is the case, the domain is multiple (Fig. 3*b*). In a unitary domain there is only one immediate superordinate for any subordinate. Thus, in contemporary North America, the modern family has only one mother; the United States has only one president; most corporations have only one president; a school system has only one superintendent; etc. Insofar as subordinates to any of these have no other access to power aside from the channels established by the relation with the single superordinate, then the subordinates are in a unitary domain.

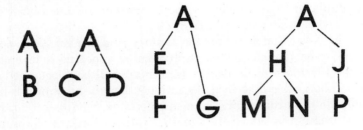

(a) Unitary Domains

(b) Multiple Domains

(c) Mixed Unitary and Multiple Domains

Unitary:   A – E – H/K

Multiple:  A – E/F/G – L/M

Fig. 3. Unitary and Multiple Domains

In *multiple domains,* the subordinate has access through two or more channels. Thus the clever child who finds that he is refused a favor from one parent may turn to the other in the hope that he (or she) will provide it; the small nation refused a concession or aid from the United States may turn to Russia (and vice versa); the peasant or rural laborer who finds he has no success in getting his employer to provide better conditions may turn to a labor union or a revolutionary organization; etc.

The distinction between the unitary and the multiple domain seems to be of such obvious utility that it appeared independently in the literature of the 1960's (and may well have occurred earlier). Julio Cotler described the unitary domain as "interconnected multiple radii converging on a single vertex."[60] This he contrasted to a situation in which the "multiplication of means of communication brings together the interconnections of the radii that have, until now, been unconnected."[61] F. LaMond Tullis elaborates somewhat further in posing the two forms as "Ideal Types I and II" and presents them as a "preview of a formal model of political change" in which "political modernization among the peasantry is therefore to be understood as the successful resolution of structural binds in favor of a move toward Ideal Type II."[62] This is

---

[60] Cotler 1969, p. 65 (translation mine). This idea became fairly popular among Peruvianists as "the triangle with no base," emphasizing that the relations tended to center on the superordinate and that there was no effective coordination of efforts among the individuals in the lower level. I believe that this has been an unfortunate image, because it has drawn attention away from the fact that a successful concentration of the independent powers held by those at the bottom would probably constitute an effort on their part to move up to the next level and confront the erstwhile superordinate. Thus, the "triangle with no base" continues to be just that, with the change being that there are now probably two triangles, each composed of the same "empty" base, but with two different apices. Although I first encountered the "triangle with no base" in Cotler's work, it has been attributed to William F. Whyte (see his 1974 reprint, pp. 537–538).

[61] Cotler 1969, p. 72.

[62] Tullis 1970, pp. 42–50, quotations from pp. 45, 49. Reprinted from *Lord and Peasant in Peru: A Paradigm of Political and Social Change*, Copyright © 1970 by the President and Fellows of Harvard College, by permission of Harvard University Press. In a footnote (p. 45) Tullis notes that "Frederick W. Frey, *The Turkish Political Elite* (Cambridge, Mass., 1965) has created a typology of power structures (p. 442) during the process of political development in which he posits essentially the same thing, i.e., that in 'traditional' polities the masses are isolated and atomized from each other in a power linkage sense, but that in modern democratic 'mass' polities they are totally incorporated and linked up in a pluralistic and multidirectional way."

A more recent variant on the unitary/multiple distinction is that of Nancie

essentially the same argument that I published in terms of power domains in 1966.[63]

Any complex domain of more than two levels usually includes both unitary and multiple subdomains (see Fig. 3c). Thus a system may have a single ultimate decision-maker (the king, president, etc.), but the channels of access may vary. Presidents of the United States, with such broad areas of potential power, have tended to try to preserve unitary domains between themselves and the larger constituency. Thus various presidents have established a set of White House advisers and aides who serve as a filter or strainer for people wishing to have access to the president. The system is so successful that some members of the cabinet have been unable to gain access to the president. It is possible to inhibit access completely. However, for individuals within such a system, there is usually the possibility of multiple access: Secretary of the Interior Walter J. Hickel, when he wanted to reach President Nixon on urgent business, tried through various informal as well as official channels. In fact, all were closed to him.[64]

A shift from a unitary to a multiple domain is one of the most important kinds of structural change that has occurred in the course of economic and political development in recent years. The classic hacienda of Latin America is one in which the laborers are bound to the hacienda through one or another means. Debt peonage, physical isolation, cultural isolation through inability to speak the national language, and the use of violent repression toward individuals who attempt to escape the system have been among the more characteristic features of this system. The haciendas essentially tried to retain a unitary power domain at a regional level such that the laborers could not have access to any source of power beyond the hacienda. In terms of the structure of power, one of the major facets of developmental and revolutionary activity in de-

---

L. González, using the two models to describe variant forms of the patron-client relation (1972).

[63] The 1966 paper was originally read in 1963; the political modernization and evolutionary aspects were introduced at that time and expanded in R. N. Adams 1967, Ch. 15, and 1970a, p. 65.

[64] Hickel 1971, pp. 243–244.

veloping countries has been directed at destroying these older unitary domains by instituting new channels of access and thereby establishing multiple domains in their place.[65] This has fundamentally constituted part of a process of concentrating power at the top, that is, in the national government.

Multiple domains, where lower-level subordinates have more than one access to power being exercised over them, profoundly affect the behavior of both the superordinates and subordinates. In a unitary domain (Fig. 3*a*) the superordinate $A$ can differentially delegate power among the subordinates, thereby keeping them fragmented so they cannot or do not combine their power against the superordinate. In a multiple domain (Fig. 3*b*), however, the subordinates, $T, U, V$, and $W$, for their part, may try to play the $A$'s off against each other. The importance of multiple domains is that subordinates have alternative routes of access to delegated power.

A question that necessarily interests any domain member who either desires or fears a change in domain structure is whether the combined power of the subordinates within a domain is equal to or greater than that of the superordinate. The answer to the question depends on two facts: (1) the state of organization of the subordinates and (2) the availability of other-than-allocated power, that is, independent or delegated power, to any of the members, but particularly to the superordinate. Figure 4 illustrates the problem. In 4*a*, $A$ controls members of an unorganized set, $E, N$, and $D$, each of which independently is too weak to confront $A$. In 4*b* they have organized, and in 4*c* they confront $A$. $A$, in order to beat the $E$-$N$-$D$ combination, seeks delegated power from $H$, whose position until now has been ambiguous. In 4*d*, $H$ grants the delegated power, thereby allowing $A$ to counteract the $E$-$N$-$D$ organization. In 4*e*, $A$ has successfully used the delegated power to subordinate the $E$-$N$-$D$ combination but in so doing has itself become subordinate to $H$. $A$ then proceeds to divide and conquer $E$-$N$-$D$ (see 4*f*).

A variant on this is the position of some African tribal chiefs under an indirect colonial-rule system. Prior to the colonial situation, the chief depended mainly on allocated power and possibly some independent power. The colonial superordinate could dele-

[65] This process is treated at length in R. N. Adams 1970*a*, and 1967, pp. 225–272.

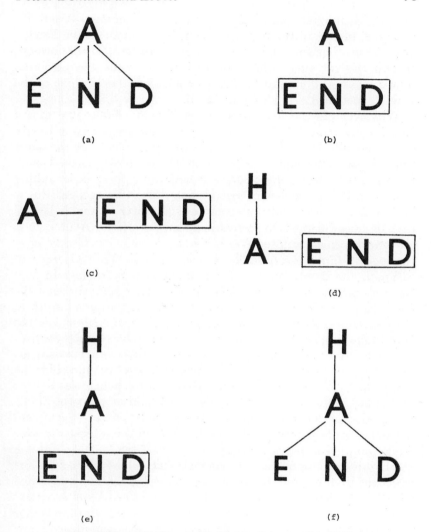

Fig. 4. Change in Domain by Confrontation and Delegation

gate more power to him, thus making him somewhat independent of the allocated power and dependent on the colonial authority. He thereby became less responsive to the interests of the subordinates and more responsive to the colonial officials.

A common error in dealing with domains derives from a carry-

over of a common English usage. There is a common usage, for
example, of the "domain of God," or the "domain of the Devil,"
or of some other spiritual entity or notion. In terms of the present
system, this can only result in confusion. Let us analyze the actual
power relations that may exist in such a case as the "domain of the
Devil," specifically a Christian Devil.

Whatever else he may be, the Devil exists differently in the
imagination of each believer and can act simultaneously in totally
different and contradictory ways in different places at the same
time. As such, the expression "George is in the power of the Devil"
means that George (or someone) believes that there is something
called the Devil that has power or control over George. All this is
clearly a matter of cultural potential. However, when it is said
that, because George is so possessed, he has power over Arthur, then
the issue becomes confused. What kind of controls does George have
that permit him to exercise power over Arthur? While George can
call upon the Devil, can he delegate this power to Arthur? In fact,
George's power over Arthur depends on Arthur *believing* that the
Devil can do things through George—and so Arthur *allocates* to
George these symbolic controls and powers. For, if Arthur does not
believe that the Devil exists or that George has any special controls
or powers, he will simply pay no heed. George can exercise his
Devil's power over Arthur only if Arthur chooses to grant him the
ability to do so. He may do it through a genuine belief that George
in fact has the power; or he may do it just to humor George along.
So the kind of domain of power that George has here is dependent
not upon the real controls that he has but on the allocated power
others may wish to grant him.

All this will sound terribly materialistic, and so it is. It tries
to locate in time and space the phenomenon we are concerned
with, and to determine precisely what energy forms and flows are
involved in it. Thus, while the analyst can never know whether
George is really possessed by the Devil (i.e., we cannot ever know
the reality potential), it is important to know whether Arthur is
going to seriously attribute that possession to him, and what
George believes (cultural potential).

## B. Levels and Confrontations

In our traditional conceptualization of human relations, domains serve to classify what have usually been conceived of as "vertical" relationships. In fact, however, it is obvious that within and among domains there are coordinate relations, and that over the long run they are as important as superordinate and subordinate relations. The concept of "level" comes to mind when we try to find an organizing notion for these coordinate sets. In trying to apply the notion, it becomes apparent that it has never received systematic attention for use in this capacity. As intellectual devices, levels have long been used to indicate some kind of emergent phenomenon, implying that whatever is assigned to a "lower" level is somehow antecedent, historically or structurally, to that appearing at a "higher" level.[66]

As with many ideas in the social sciences, the term *level* came into common usage long before any systematic concepts were formulated. My intent here is to adhere to a specific set of definitions for the term in the hope that we can move toward a more systematic and rigorous usage of it. In order to do this, I am going to differentiate *levels of articulation* and *levels of integration*.

A level of articulation is to be found wherever there is a continuing confrontation; and two adjacent levels are marked out wherever there is a continuing superordinate-subordinate relationship. Thus, within some domestic units, parents and children comprise two levels. In a business, levels are found clearly differentiated between the president, vice-president, manager, senior employees, and junior employees. In capitalist complex societies with wealth or affluence differentials, socioeconomic strata marked by cultural differences serve to differentiate such levels. Much of the confusion that led Rodolfo Stavenhagen to insist upon the distinction between social stratification and social class[67] could have been avoided if the stratification issue had been seen in terms of a differentiation within any society that is complex or expanding. As societies expand their control over the environment, either through technology or through power derived from outside sources, they will differentiate into levels. If these are dependent upon the particular skills or attributes of specific individuals, and their occupants change over

[66] Edel gives a helpful discussion of the general use of the term *levels* in the social sciences (1959). See also Bunge 1963, Ch. 3.
[67] See Stavenhagen 1967, pp. 126–151.

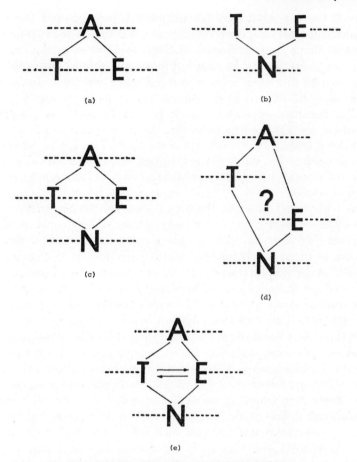

Fig. 5. Determining Levels of Articulation

time, then they tend to be thought of sociologically as "ranks," and they reflect an operation of the human mind in ordering the universe around it. In more complex societies, entire segments of the society will be separated out as operating units and ranked among themselves. These are "social strata." The relevance of rank, stratum, and social class to the power analysis will be further discussed in Part Two.

In practice, a level exists when two actors determine that their relative power is approximately coordinate. There are various ways of determining this. One way is for two actors, $T$ and $E$, to recognize that they are inferior to the same superior, $A$ (Fig. 5$a$); or that they are superior to the same inferior, $N$ (Fig. 5$b$); or that they are intermediary between the same superiors and inferiors (Fig. 5$c$). Of course, none of these is definitive, because this merely establishes where the two parties stand relative to a third. The precise question of whether $T$ and $E$ are on the same level (Fig. 5$d$) will ultimately depend on a confrontation between the two (Fig. 5$e$).

The real test, the confrontation, takes place when two actors are so related that their activities test the relative power of each. "A confrontation," says F. G. Bailey, "is a message which the receiver has no option but to receive and to act upon."[68] It may be hostile or friendly but is not necessarily either. It may simply be an incident when the relative powers of two parties are simultaneously brought to bear on a situation. The outcome of a confrontation determines the status of levels by clarifying what the relative power of the two actors may be. It may be just about equivalent, and they would therefore be on the same level; or it may be that the power of one is greater than that of the other, and that one is therefore superordinate and the other subordinate. Apart from this, the determination of levels usually must rest on estimations, usually based on the relative status of the actors with reference to some third parties or with respect to the amounts and kinds of the environment they control.

Having now indicated what I think is a useful concept for the term *level of articulation* in the context of power theory, let me point out that it varies significantly from the more common notion of *level of integration*. Julian Steward, who is the most responsible for establishing this concept firmly in anthropology, early recognized that it was similar to that of organizational levels in biology. "In the growth continuum of any culture, there is a succession of organizational types, which are not only increasingly complex but which represent new emergent forms."[69] "This concept of levels

[68] Bailey 1970, p. 104. Reprinted by permission of Schocken Books Inc. from *Stratagems and Spoils* by F. G. Bailey. Copyright © 1969 by Basil Blackwell Publisher.

[69] Steward 1955, p. 51. Reprinted from *Theory of Culture Change* by permission of the University of Illinois Press.

of sociocultural integration is useful in analyzing the internal structure of complex contemporary systems as well as characterizing the successive emergence of qualitatively new levels in historical development."[70]

Steward first published concerning this topic in 1951; subsequently there increasingly appeared in the literature descriptions that had recourse to "levels" as a way of handling diverse, contingent, and related cultures that occupied different segments of what was clearly a single, although complex, society. In 1954 Betty Starr identified for the Tuxtla region of southern Mexico six levels within which some sense of communality was felt: (*a*) household group, (*b*) dooryard group, (*c*) neighborhood, (*d*) village, (*e*) municipio, and (*f*) region.[71] The next year John Gulick published an analysis of change within a Lebanese village in terms of what he called "spheres," derived from E. E. Evans-Pritchard's analysis of the "balanced oppositions" and "group segmentation" of the Nuer organization.[72] Gulick's analysis includes both coordinated and centralized operating units as the spheres but was theoretically rather more imaginative than most of the other work that has appeared to date. In 1959, G. W. Skinner, working from definitions set by Lasswell and Kaplan, proposed a series of "loyalty levels" for a rural Indonesian area, but his use was more descriptive and less analytical than those of Starr and Gulick.[73] Similarly, that by Dwight Heath seems to have no theoretical function, but serves as a conceptual and classificatory device of the materials of the specific ethnographic case.[74] In a more generalizing vein,

[70] Ibid., p. 5. In 1942 Robert Redfield wrote an introduction to a volume called *Levels of Integration in Biological and Social Systems*; about 1958 Redfield was to refer to Steward's work as "the single impressive achievement in the presentation of a national entity as a societal system, by an anthropologist . . . The essential conception earlier put forward was of a structure of parts making up the larger whole. These parts are . . . 'levels of integration' (or of 'organization') . . ." (Margaret Park Redfield, ed. 1962, p. 387. Reprinted from *Human Nature and the Study of Society: The Papers of Robert Redfield*, © 1962 by the University of Chicago, by permission of the University of Chicago Press.)

[71] Starr 1954.

[72] Gulick 1955, pp. 159–171.

[73] Skinner 1959.

[74] Heath 1972.

Marshall Sahlins refers to "levels of organization . . . a sector of social relations" in his general work on tribesmen,[75] and Eric Wolf had recourse to the "levels of communal relations" as a framework for his summary article on Middle American Indians.[76]

Until recently, however, proposals that levels might have some theoretical utility have been rare. In a structural analysis of Quechua mythology, John Earls suggested that four levels of power relations were discernible in Incaic and post-Incaic thought, and that a particular affinity between the second and fourth levels present in Incaic times had tended to disappear today. Earls speculated that the repeated appearance of a messianic myth in historical Quechua society reflects that this affinity is not dead in the mentality of the Indians.[77] Another theoretical usage of levels is Henry T. Wright's application of the concept of "levels of administration" to archaeological sites in the Middle East. He argues that "a state can be recognized as a society with specialized decision-making organizations . . . receiving messages from many different sources" and that "the number of levels of administrative hierarchy in an organization was a function of the rate at which that organization would have to process information regarding the activities it conducted."[78] Given this, and the evidence provided by size of sites, settlement patterns, and artifactual remains, it is possible to infer the degree of administrative development of a region.

What, then, is the relation between levels of articulation and levels of integration? Essentially, it is the same as that between the description of the events in one place at one time, or in a restricted place over a restricted time period, and the conceptualization of those events made by people who have to discuss them and have to keep a cognitive map of the society within which they are operating. It is the difference between the "ethnographic" and the "ethnologic,"[79] that is, the difference between the description of a particular case and a general conceptual system that must encompass this and other cases. Sahlins pointed out that levels of integration

---

[75] Sahlins 1968, p. 15.
[76] Wolf 1967.
[77] Earls 1973, p. 411.
[78] Wright, forthcoming. Used by permission of the author.
[79] Goodenough 1956, p. 37. Cf. Rappaport 1968, pp. 237–241.

are classifications of sociocultural units with distinctive cultures;[80] and classifications are, obviously, mental constructs made by an observer or analyst.

Levels of articulation, like the operating units among and within which they are found, are classificatory devices to identify specific replicative events, repetitive interactions manifesting a certain pattern. A given level of articulation may be very short-lived, or it may survive for extended periods. The levels depend on the continuing interaction of operating units with roughly equivalent power. In a given society, therefore, the identification of levels of articulation poses the standard ethnographic task of nailing down the time-space coordinates of a set of replicated behaviors and finding their relations to other behaviors. This, under normal circumstances, can provide a picture that is cumbersome and too complex for meaningful comparison with other cultural situations (either of other cultures or of the same culture at an earlier point in its history). Both the people living in societies and the observers of societies find it necessary to classify sets of levels of articulation into larger classes, and the resulting system of conceptualized levels is what we are calling levels of integration. Levels of articulation are constructed out of the observation or recording of interactions and transactions among human beings; levels of integration are constructed out of data on levels of articulation, with some conceptual and cognitive dimensions that are brought to that data from our existing generalized cognitive map of the world. The latter factor means that in the formulation of levels of integration we will be subjecting the data to the processes and constrictions set by our cognitive abilities and limitations. This is not to say that the formulation of levels of articulation is not equally subject to such constrictions, but in their formulation there is no necessary attempt to classify or group the data; it is necessary rather to recognize it, identify it, and differentiate it.

Later we will return to this subject, because levels of integration are specifically pertinent in any approach to the evolution of cultural systems. For the moment, we can deal with both kinds of levels without bothering to differentiate them. At this point in the study of levels, we are still dealing with a variety of reported phe-

[80] Sahlins 1960, p. 33.

nomena, and we are far from finding standard usages. It is my impression, however, that for the study of complex society, levels of articulation and levels of integration will prove to be indispensable conceptual tools.

Levels necessarily reflect not only differentiation of power but also the relative concentration of power. When new power enters a system, the amount of power at the top will increase disproportionately, and the possibility of forming yet further levels will also increase. The mechanisms by which this occurs are most commonly allocated and exploitative power (i.e., the few can take or receive some from the many; delegated power, on the other hand, necessarily leads to deconcentration, dispersal of decision-making to lower levels).[81] To speak of levels, then, is to speak of a phenomenon that is necessarily present in any society wherein there is any allocation or granting of power at all; and this means all human societies. Levels, however, are particularly analytically useful as power in a system increases. It is here, where the various sources and bases of power may be obscure, that it is therefore both useful and necessary for the analyst to seek out the order of actors with respect to each other.

If one keeps in mind that the addition of new levels requires increasing the concentration of power, then a number of complex-society phenomena will be clarified. In the first place, the very emergence of government depended upon a sufficient concentration of power so that higher levels could come clearly into being. A rather problematic case in the literature in this connection points up this problem.

Edmund Leach in his classic study, *Political Systems of Highland Burma*, details the difference between three types of com-

---

[81] Kent Flannery has suggested, following Slobodkin, that, "when variables exceed their goal ranges, they subject systems to stress that can lead either to breakdown, or to evolutionary change. Perhaps as a result of the system's attempt to return a runaway variable to its range, new institutions or new levels appear in the control hierarchy (segregation), or higher order controls become strengthened (centralization)." (Reprinted, with permission, from "The Cultural Evolution of Civilizations," *Annual Review of Ecology and Systematics*, Volume 3, page 412. Copyright © 1972 by Annual Reviews Inc. All rights reserved.) This describes a stimulus that would mobilize the power of "higher order controls" but would not explain either where they got the power or why they might decide to mobilize it.

munity political organization, two pertaining to the Kachin and one to the Shan. The Shan were wet-rice cultivators, Buddhists, and an autocratic caste society with a highly prestigious king, or *saohpa*. The Kachin practiced hillside agriculture. The Kachin *gumlao* community was politically egalitarian and based on specific kin-lineage relations. Leach believes that the second type of Kachin political community, the *gumsa*, came into being from time to time in imitation of the Shan stratified organization. In *gumsa* communities, the kin basis was superseded by an overlord and a ranked organization. Leach argues that there is no ecological explanation for the shift from *gumlao* to *gumsa*, or the reverse (both of which occurred). But in two places he does specify the "influence of favorable economic circumstances"; "with economic luck and plenty of relatives a Kachin chief has a chance of becoming something very close to a Shan *saohpa*." The shift from the Kachin to the Shan type implied important changes in power structure: "The transition from Kachin-type organization to Shan-type organization involves the substitution of a straight landlord-tenant relationship based either on common lineage or affinal dependence."[82] It seems clear that the Shan organization involved a number of levels of articulation, whereas the *gumlao* clearly did not. The *gumsa* organization seems to have been the formal, overt attempt to establish Shan-type levels, but without achieving the necessary economic (i.e., power) base to stabilize them.

One explanation of the general state of political instability that Leach reported for this entire area might profitably be explored in terms of the actual power that the *gumlao* and *gumsa* rulers had available to them, in contrast with that necessary to maintain a full-scale Shan-type stratified organization. Leach apparently despairs of identifying ecological factors that would explain the shifts from *gumlao* to *gumsa* or the reverse, but he is quite clear that a shift from Kachin (*gumsa*) toward Shan was due to economic success. In one instance, he infers "that it was the trade in iron more than anything else which gave the early Jinghpaw power and which enabled the *gumsa* to become feudal satellites of the Shan princes rather than their serfs."[83] Leach takes pains to avoid con-

[82] Leach 1965, pp. 9, 266, 288.
[83] Ibid., p. 251.

cluding that *gumsa* tendencies among *gumlao* organizations may have resulted from the same kind of change, but one wonders what else might have led to such a case. Certainly the *gumlao* rebellions he describes as occurring periodically against the *gumsa* organizations, especially during times of weakening Shan power, suggest that *gumsa* leaders easily involved themselves in exploitation; the response was rebellion, and there was not enough power to sustain the *gumsa* organization.

The introduction of power, however, can come by two means, and one may lead to a *gumlao-gumsa*-Shan type shift, whereas another can lead to quite different results. Here again, a case from Leach serves as an illustration.

Once the British had established peace in the Kachin Hills their policy was one of maintaining the *status quo*. Wherever possible village boundaries were recorded and treated as fixed. This meant that in the more congested areas it ceased to be practical for a village to grow in size, for if it did so land would run short. In this way the relative status of the chiefs of different communities tended to be stabilized. *Gumlao* principles of government were disapproved but countenanced in some cases. Chiefs were turned into agents of government; succession was supposed to follow traditional law and custom, but appointment was always subject to approval by the British administrator. By these means Kachin chiefs were reduced to a dead level of petty mediocrity. Except in the relatively unadministrated areas of the north, there ceased to be great chiefs and little chiefs; they were just chiefs, who in most cases were no better than minor village headmen.[84]

Thus does Leach describe the effect of British colonial delegated power in a situation where only a few levels existed. Colonial structure replaced whatever power might have been concentrated at the top local level and left that level a weak, intermediate affair. The significance of this process is evident in areas of development attempted through the direct delegation of power by stronger nations. The stronger nations not only are in a better position to take care of themselves but also tend to drain power off from the developing nations rather than allowing it to concentrate there. The angry protests of third-world nationalists that the "imperialist" powers continue a postcolonial exploitation under the guise of "foreign

[84] Ibid., p. 245.

aid" has necessary truth in it. A "foreign aid" that would only serve to drain the United States of its own power certainly is not what United States planners had in mind.

A few further comments should be made on the nature of confrontations. It was earlier pointed out that confrontations need not be hostile. Indeed, the term covers a wide range of approximately coordinate relations (no matter who may be judging them to be coordinate). If a confrontation takes on any character at all, it is likely to become either conflictive or cooperative. While the recent sociological literature has placed much emphasis on the difference between conflictive and integrative theories of society, it must necessarily be the case that all relationships implicitly involve both. A positive relation at one place in a system requires that there be a negative elsewhere. A major issue in power analysis is to clarify just what the significance of each may be. Also, irrespective of whether a particular confrontation seems to be one or the other, the alternative social consequences are the same. Two actors may remain in some kind of dynamic equilibrium; one may eliminate, assimilate, subordinate, or encapsulate the other; or either or both actors may merely retreat from the confrontation and terminate the relation temporarily or permanently. Which of these alternatives may occur does not depend on whether the actual process is one of "conflict" or "cooperation." Any of the results may occur from either kind of relationship.

Indeed, the conflict-cooperation dichotomy, as with most dichotomies, obscures more than it reveals. While it tells us that there are relationships characterized by tension and violence and others characterized by a mutual dependence, the emphasis on these polar features hides two important aspects of the matter. One is that cooperation and conflict are both ways of getting the same goals. William Graham Sumner in 1906 labeled as "antagonistic cooperation" the behavior whereby actors provided mutual aid in order that each individual could better compete for life; and P'etr Kropotkin, ten years earlier in his classic *Mutual Aid*, pointed out that "sociability is as much a law of nature as natural struggle" and provides "under any circumstances the greatest advantage in the struggle for life." The other is a point made by Marx and more recently by Max Gluckman with reference to the interdependence between otherwise hostile Blacks and Whites in South Africa and

Rhodesia, namely, that classes within a capitalist system (and, we would argue, within any complex system) are necessarily interdependent.[85]

Indeed, as is often the case in the history of ideas, the current emphasis on "conflict" in social science derives in part from an earlier overemphasis on its contrary. The move away from the focus on functional integration is as much due to the intellectual, political, and emotional climate of the times as it is to serious scholarly overview.[86]

An important aspect of the analysis of the network of relations that is implicit in this formulation is that it is possible to trace out any particular empirical set of relations in terms of a conceptual framework that encompasses the entire network of relations known to and imagined by man. Moreover, it is possible to speak of a minimum level of relations and a maximum level, in both general and specific terms. The probable minimal level of relations, if we stick strictly to human social relationships, is that between an infant and his immediately next-older sibling, during that period of their lives when there is no clear-cut power differential. In a more general way, the domestic household unit is probably the nearest form that we have of a minimal level of adult operating unit for most societies.

The maximum level presents a different picture, since we must distinguish specific cases of independent domains where there are no superiors. Since the advent of the spread of capitalism based on western colonialism, however, there are very few such really autonomous domains. We are instead dealing with a few world powers, the collectivity of which must be regarded as forming the maximum level. These are in one dimension represented by the permanent membership within the United Nations Security Council. An examination of the maximum level, both actually and theoretically, leads us to the conclusion that it is not structurally possible for a single domain to exist at the maximum level for any length of time. Theoretically the reason is fairly obvious in that the very notion of a level is defined in terms of the presence of

[85] Sumner 1906, pp. 16–18; Kropotkin 1904, p. 57; Gluckman 1971, pp. 127–166.

[86] See, for example, Dahrendorf 1959; Horowitz 1969, p. 304; Lenski 1966, Ch. 2.

members of roughly equivalent power. As is the case at any level, the membership at the top level must be multiple. The empirical world here may be deceptive, since one might argue that Trujillo's thirty-odd years of power in the Dominican Republic and the long rule of Stalin are cases of such concentration. But the issue is precisely the fact that they were heads of state within a community of states, all of which had heads. Thus to say that power concentrates at higher levels is not to say that it concentrates in one domain at these higher levels. On the contrary, the fact that the concentration is multiple, in a number of domains, provides the major dynamics for the process.

The argument is that at the *maximal level* there will be a much greater per capita concentration of power than at lower levels but that there cannot for long be a single, monolithic concentration at this top level. The actual mechanism that supports this notion is probably that any single actor who succeeded in achieving top dominance would be subject to continuing threats by others seeking to replace him. There is no question that, among those competing at the top, there is a singular desire on the part of most to be superior to all others. But a plurality at the top generally prevails, since no one can long obtain sufficient power to *both* control his internal domains *and* dominate over his competitors. It is probably structurally impossible for a single world government to exist, although confederationlike entities have existed from time to time (e.g., the League of Nations, the United Nations, etc.). The same problems that inhibit the appearance of a world government inhibited the appearance of government among primitive bands: the top leaders are basically *totally* dependent upon the allocated power of their peers and thus have no independent basis for permanently dominating them.

This analysis requires a conception of human society that includes the entire history of the human species. Power relations have interarticulated with each other through time as well as over the face of the globe. One of the reasons that we find today we must deal with "underdeveloped" societies as being different from "primitive" societies is that the former are products, not merely of technological primitiveness, but also of the exploitative power of colonial and expansive power domains that have been extended over them by the more powerful nations. The middle class of the

United States is linked to the peasant cultivators of China, to the primitive agriculturalists and hunters of New Guinea, and to the copper miners of Africa not merely because they are genetically related to common ancestral populations but also because they are members of domains in confrontation with each other, and because of that fact the behavior of one may well have serious consequences for the behavior of the other.

The structure of power of any particular microcosm can be related to the structure of power of a macrocosm that envelops it; and the macrocosmic structures increasingly determine what can take place in the microcosms.

## C. *The Expansion of Domains and Levels*

All operating units exist among populations of similar units. Whether we deal with domestic units, family bands, towns, nation-states, feudal domains, or what you will, there is always a community of such units, each differing in one way or another from the next. When new sources of control become available to such populations, we can say that new power enters the system, and not only is it the case that the specific units will tend to grow in the amount of power they exercise, but the system of units will also expand into greater domains and increasing levels of articulation.

While in a general way we can hold that the fundamental cause of such expansion is the increase of energy flow in the system, it is important that we clarify some of the specific devices and variations in this process. Expansion can take place, theoretically, through an increase in the human population, an increase in the amount of energy flow generated by improvements in technology, or both. Figure 6 shows what theoretically would happen if either of these separate kinds of expansion took place alone. Figure 6b shows the expansion over 6a if the population increases with no per capita increase in control over the environment. This presumably is the basic kind of growth that took place over most of the Paleolithic period, when technological growth was so slow that it rarely afforded one generation a particularly noticeable advantage over its predecessor. The same kind of pattern has surely recurred at various times in human history, but with the size and complexity of the operating unit varying with the degree of advance of technology and condition of the environment. In this

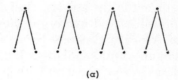

(a)

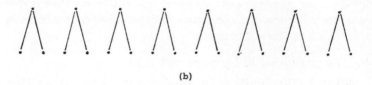

(b)

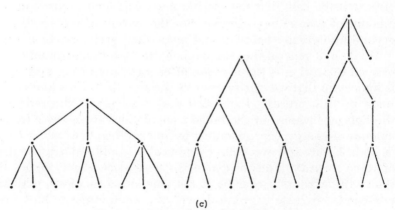

(c)

Fig. 6. Ideal Types of Domain Expansion

kind of expansion, the successful survival of new groups depends on the adaptive solution reached in the new environment. When human populations grow with no improvement in technology, groups of essentially like structures bud off and separate to another habitat. Thus the environment, already the scene of opportunities and restraints in the form of topography, climate, flora, fauna, etc., becomes more complicated through the addition of new human groups. If we assume that population density is a function of ecology and technology and that these do not change, we could not expect that a concentration of people would have to occur to necessitate the appearance of new levels of social organization. However, in areas where regular or seasonal abundance permitted an assemblage of larger aggregates, the contact between groups would require some tentative form of organization for social control, as was the case with the True Plains police societies discussed earlier.

Contemporary highland New Guinea provides cases where such demographic expansion with little technological change has apparently been somewhat contained for generations with extensive warfare. Ethnographic observation over the past few decades, however, has made it clear that the recent introduction of strategic technological improvements, such as the sweet potato and steel tools, has led to a continuing expansion that illustrates the budding-off process. E. Richard Sorenson describes the expansion of the Fore and attributes it to the introduction of the sweet potato about one hundred years ago.[87] H. C. Brookfield and Paula Brown hold that the expansion has been in progress for years.[88] In the case of the Fore, the major expansion until recently was into open neighboring land so that there was no direct conflict with other groups or their own expansive core until recently.

Figure 6c poses the other ideal condition, where there is an increase in power per capita, but there is no increase in the number of people in the system. As the figure suggests, this may take a variety of forms, since the number of levels to emerge will depend upon the amount of increased power added. Whereas there probably have been many empirical cases that have approximated the condition of population increase with no per capita power increase, cases of the contrary are probably all but nonexistent. The reason is that, when the amount of power in a system does increase per capita, one of the first things to happen is the incorporation of people to handle it. This is basically what C. Northcote Parkinson proposed in his now famous law: "Work expands so as to fill the

[87] E. R. Sorenson 1972.
[88] Brookfield and Brown 1963.

time available for its completion."[89] While Parkinson created his
law on the basis of British Admiralty statistics between 1914 and
1928, he later traced the increase from 1938 through 1967, only to
find that not only was there an increase, but even the rate of
increase had grown. "Whereas 1914 represented the culmination
of an arms race, when 4,366 officials could administer what was
then the largest navy in the world [125,000 officers and men, 542
vessels], 1967 represents the point at which we [i.e., the British
Empire] have become practically powerless, by which period over
33,000 civil servants are barely sufficient to administer the navy
we no longer possess [83,900 officers and men, 114 vessels]."[90]

Parkinson's observations have been the subject of a more extensive and less amusing treatment under the rubric *bureaucratization*. Reinhard Bendix has traced the growing ratio of administrative personnel to production personnel in a number of industrial
nations from the turn of the century:[91]

| | | | |
|---|---|---|---|
| United States | 1899: ratio= 7.7%; | 1947: ratio=21.6% |
| France | 1901: ratio=11.8%; | 1936: ratio=14.6% |
| Great Britain | 1907: ratio= 8.6%; | 1948: ratio=20.0% |
| Germany | 1895: ratio= 4.8%; | 1933: ratio=14.0% |
| Sweden | 1915: ratio= 6.6%; | 1950: ratio=21.0% |

In comparing Bendix's numbers of productive workers or Parkinson's number of active seamen to the administrative staffs that
support and command them, it should be noted that the latter include both "service" (in the sense of tertiary sector) and upper-
echelon personnel. The increased power in the system is reflected
in the increased levels of articulation in both classes of persons.
Unlike the situation of sheer population increase with minimum
extra power, where expansion replicated like units, growth of
power per capita leads necessarily to power concentration, and
this leads necessarily to increasing the number of levels. (I should
point out here that this analysis is intentionally not treating the
factor of social circumscription, to use Robert L. Carneiro's term;

[89] C. Northcote Parkinson 1957, p. 2. Reprinted from *Parkinson's Law and
Other Studies in Administration* by permission of Houghton Mifflin Co.
[90] C. Northcote Parkinson 1971, pp. 4–5. Reprinted from *The Law of Delay*
by permission of Houghton Mifflin Co.
[91] Bendix 1956, p. 214, Table 6.

this will be taken up later in discussion of the evolution of power structures.)

While an increase in levels marks a concentration in power, an increase in domains necessarily marks a differentiation or division of powers. The nature of this division, however, will depend upon a number of factors, important among which are whether the domains are unitary or multiple and how much relative power is delegated to them. It might be worth mentioning in this connection that one should not be misled by "tables of organization." These charts of boxes, lines, arrows, etc., are favored pastimes of bureaucrats, who use them to show lines of communication, authority, and responsibility within their organization. Such tables are, in anthropological jargon, "folk culture" traits of bureaucrats, their "ethno-administration"; they portray the world (in this case the bureaucracy) as some of the actors want to see it, or think it should operate. In fact, of course, a map of the real power structure will usually look very different from a table of organization. Indeed, tables of organization usually tend to obscure the precise bases and lines of power and exaggerate or minimize the number of real power levels or domains and even omit crucial power units. It is often the case, for example, that, when higher-level officials do not wish to be bothered with things going on in lower levels, they will insist that all transactions follow the tortuous table of organization; when they want to get a message through, however, they will quite easily bypass any number of intervening levels. These two modes of action are often referred to as "formal" and "informal." The difference, however, is more important than the terminology suggests, for the table of organization often becomes an officially propagated myth that obscures the real operation of the power structure.

The specific mechanisms that lead to the emergence of new levels are probably complex, but Gregory Alan Johnson has suggested with respect to primary state development that "overloading of decision making organization" may be crucial.

A state is defined as having a *hierarchically structured* decision making organization. Hierarchy or vertical specialization allows coordination in horizontally specialized systems. . . . horizontal specialization allows increases in the amount and diversity of work done by an organization. If the tasks performed by individual specialists are completely unrelated, hierarchical structure is not necessary. If, however, these tasks are related, as in the case of the decision making organization of a state, coordination between and among specialists is necessary. This coordination is provided by a specialist at a second structural level of the organization, and a two level hierarchy is formed.

The amount of information processed is probably also the major determinate of the complexity of information storage and retrieval facilities used by a given society . . . Conversely the type of facilities used by the decision making organization of a society should provide a relative measure of the amount of information processed by that organization. Further, development over time of such facilities having increasingly large information storage capabilities should provide a measure of the increasing amount of information processed.[92]

While in theory it does not require very much mass-energy to carry information or even to make decisions, it does when the decision-makers are human beings. Given the fact that the information has to be processed within the limitations of the human mental and physical capabilities, it is quite clear that increasing amounts of information-carrying energy forms require an increasing number of people and an increasing amount of coordination. Since the expansion of coordinated activity does not inherently work in a coherent way, centralization, or the emergence of a new level, is the only way to solve the overload problem.

Information theorists have tended to discuss this kind of problem in terms of "information overload." For reasons that will be discussed in Part Two, this is a misunderstanding for the fundamental elements of the process as they act in most phases of human society. The issue is not the amount of "information," a thing which is, in itself, without quantitative dimensions. Rather, the quantification hinges on the amount and kinds of energy forms that carry the information and what those forms entail. Thus, at the base, the handling of the energy forms is the problem that forces societies to establish higher levels of articulation or, in failing, to suffer disadvantageous consequences in the face of natural selection.

A final point needs to be made here. Just as an increase in power

[92] Johnson 1973, pp. 3–4. Reprinted from *Local Exchange and Early State Development in Southwestern Iran*, Anthropological Papers, No. 51, by permission of the Museum of Anthropology, University of Michigan.

or population will lead to increased levels or domains or both, so a decrease in power will have the contrary effect. The reduction of power in a system will necessarily lead to a reduction in levels of articulation, just as depopulation will reduce the number of domains. This reduction can be seen in former provincial-rural centers in the American Midwest and West and in the Argentina pampa. In their most exaggerated form they have been totally deserted, have become "ghost towns." More commonly, however, they are physically marked by abandoned buildings and by social organizations simplified and totally subordinated to outside power centers. Many operating units in complex societies, however, leave no such obvious residues, and the archaeologist will be hard put to find evidence of the former importance of women's afternoon teas or backroom meetings of politicians, both units that operated due to a temporary concentration of a certain amount of power and evaporated when this power was withdrawn. On a grander scale, it can be asked what happened to the offices and organizations of the Carolingian Empire of the ninth century, or the Byzantine Empire, or, even today, the British Empire. Domains and levels are, in a very real sense, constructs of power; lacking that power, they will simply disappear, except in the minds of those who remember, or in the architecture and documentary residues that provide future archaeologists and historians with employment.

# PART TWO

# Energetic and Mentalistic Structures

# 6. A NOTE ON STRUCTURE, MIND AND MATTER, AND CULTURE

The first part of this essay was devoted principally to conceptual matters, in an attempt to provide basic concepts that are necessary in order to exploit the concept of control over energy for social analysis. It was not possible to entirely avoid theory in that discussion, nor was there any particular value in trying to do so. The process of concentration of power as more energy passes through the system is a process that was mentioned a number of times and is fundamental to our understanding of human social evolution.

Part Two could as well have been Part One. It too deals with concepts, but concepts of a more general nature; it goes further into theory, theory that I regard as fundamental to our understanding of the operation of human society. I chose to discuss the nature of power first, because I believe it is always necessary to have something around which theory is being discussed so that we do not permit ourselves to be totally involved in theory with no reference. There is, however, no attempt at an axiomatic or formalistic treatment, as desirable as such formulations may be. Formalism is a double-edged instrument; what it gains in specificity of information, it loses in meaning; what it gains in clarity for some readers, it loses for others. In any event, formalism can only work with theories that are carefully hewn, and, while I hope that such might evolve here, it is not yet the case.

Part Two places the concern for power in the larger context; and, as a first step in that direction, a note of clarification is in order about the use of the term *structure*, a word subject to a variety of usages in modern literature. I have tried consistently to use a delimited concept, one permitting a rather wide application, but still distinct from those usually associated with "system," "organization," "institution," "*Gestalt*," etc. Let us start with Pierre Maranda's simple Lévi-Straussian definition: structure refers to "those properties of a system that remain invariant under a given group of transformations." The crucial matter here is that structure "presupposes the existence of an order which is to be discovered or read into phenomena. Order means a system whose properties can be mapped in terms of a constant set of related propositions," and the propositions are, themselves, defined by a statement of the rules by which they are generated.[1]

When dealing with cultures, what is order for one operating unit may be disorder for another. Moreover, within a single society, what may appear orderly to one observer may be chaos for another. The quality that is structural, that is, that orders, must, therefore, be seen to be relative to the given observer. As David Maybury-Lewis remarked, "A myth is therefore bound to have a number of 'structures' that are *both in the material and in the eye of the beholder*."[2] This relativity of structure is crucial to its more general usage. The structural order in any set of events will be that which seems to a specific observer to be unchanging when comparing separate events in space or in a continuing chain of events through time. Returning to Maranda, "Structuralism seeks to understand how societies preserve their identity over time." This "identity over time" must be identified in someone's mind.[3]

There is only one order, and that is nature's; there are as many structures as man is capable of discerning or inventing. Moreover, those that he chooses will be those that are, for whatever reason, of interest to him. If we keep in mind that, in discerning structure, the observer is looking at what is regarded as both orderly and continuing, then we can say that what is structural is that order that is relatively unchanging—specifically, unchanging when compared with those things that are changing. And to move one step

---

[1] Maranda 1972, p. 330. Reprinted, with permission, from "Structuralism in Cultural Anthropology," *Annual Review of Anthropology*, Volume 1, page 330. Copyright © 1972 by Annual Reviews Inc. All Rights Reserved.

[2] Maybury-Lewis 1969, p. 119 (italics added). Reprinted from *American Anthropologist*, vol. 71, no. 1, by permission of the American Anthropological Association.

[3] Maranda 1972, p. 331.

further: those things that are unchanging also are not *changeable* by certain actors or elements in the situation; that is, they are beyond the control of some actors or operating units. This does not mean they are beyond the control of all actors, however; and thus we have structures that are beyond the control of some people, but subject to control by others.

While it is probable that few students of the subject have thought of structure as being reducible to something as simple as "that which is out of control," I believe the notion has much to recommend it. In the first place, it makes it impossible to fall into the superficial contradiction of holding that structures are "a stable arrangement of parts" and then insisting that they can be readily changed by the deliberate action of man. The importance of stability or continuity can only be appreciated when that stability or continuity is clearly set against some contrasting degree of instability; there is no such thing as absolute stability, clearly, so we must be able to state what context we are using to differentiate that which is the same or different.

Since we are concerned with man, it seems not unreasonable to explicitly use man as the measure for what is stable or unstable. That is to say, from man's point of view, the cosmos is effectively a stable system; we have no reason to think that the sun will burn out before man does, or that the gravitational collapse that is postulated as the ultimate source of energy will complete itself or coquettishly stop before man evaporates. These things, we would hold, are structural to all mankind. However, in the view of the astrophysicist, the cosmic system may not appear at all stable; rather, it may appear to be in constant flux.

Similarly, while the surface of the earth undergoes constant modifications, both independent and due to the efforts of man, there are some major dimensions over which man has little control: the general composition of the earth, the composition of the atmosphere, the amount of solar energy intercepted by the earth during a given period of time, and so forth. Like the cosmos, these things have generally been taken as being structural for man. However, here we approach uncertainty. Man may exhaust some of the earth's resources; he may change the composition of the atmosphere. If he does these things, can we say that the terrestrial system is structural to mankind? The question is tricky: in one sense the terrestrial system is structural to man because, even though his occupancy of it is causing it to change, he has no evident control at the moment over that occupancy or many of its ramifications. This is no paradox. Consider the fact that individual men are steady-state systems: they must have a regular input and output but maintain a more or less constant weight for most of their lives. That is to say, if a man wishes to remain a steady-state system, he must then assure the requisite processes that will permit him to do so; that is, he must eat and breathe, and he must eliminate waste products and degraded energy. Man can choose not to be alive, that is, to give up these inputs; but he cannot do so and remain a steady-state system. So being *that kind of a system* is structural to each and every individual. *Being*, however, is not necessarily structural to each individual, since some can terminate this readily and sometimes do.

From man's viewpoint, we can conveniently distinguish structures which somehow involve the nature of man himself (such as that just discussed) from those which we believe exist independently of man's earthly tenure (such as the nature of the cosmos). This distinction is made entirely for our convenience, using man's own controls as a marker in the continuum of possible things to be controlled. Also, we can distinguish structures that are independent of man until he succeeds in exercising controls (such as the geological structure of a landscape prior to man's habitation thereon). The Lévi-Straussian concept of structure clearly applies to those structures that in some manner concern the nature of man, since it is the physical, chemical, and neurological composition that determines what he can control.

In a more profound way, however, all structures involve the nature of man. Just as it has been generally agreed that Maxwell's demon could not have operated without some expenditure of energy, so the question of what is structural depends upon the fact that man stands in the cosmos. Structures are comparisons; comparisons do not exist independently in nature but are made by man. If there were no man, there would be no structures. The reader should not turn away in disgust here. I am not saying that the things we classify as structural or not structural do not exist independently of man; only that structures require man's differentiation of their consistencies to constitute them. But it is in a less profound sense that the notion of structure is of immediate use. For not only is mankind as a whole surrounded by structures, but we also need to carry the relativity further and recognize that every human collectivity or operating unit—indeed, every human individual—can divide the world up into that which can be controlled as opposed to that which cannot. If one's knowledge permits, he can then get some probabilities on what the uncontrollable will do and try to take advantage of them or, at the least, to get out of the way. The important point is that structures are *entirely relative* to the operating unit for which they are structural. What may be structural for a peasant may well be under control by landlords; and a part of the structure that an army confronts is specifically controlled by its opponent. Each individual enjoys (or suffers) a unique set of structures. Thus for me, the author of this essay, there exists a potential readership that is, in the main, structural. I do not even know who most of them (that is to say, *you*) are. And, now that you have read this, what has taken place in your nervous system has become structural for you and for me, but obviously in different ways.

To say that something is out of control is not to say that it cannot change or even that it may not, at some time, be controlled. But, to see the issue clearly, we must return to our basic definitions. Control rests on a technology. We control that which our technology permits us to manipulate in some appropriate manner. So one way of destructuring something is to invent a technology that will permit us to control it. The same argument holds when comparing one actor or operating unit with another. If one has the technology and the other does not, then what is structural for the second is not structural for the first. Also, what appears structural from one position or standpoint may not be from another. For the adolescent child or young adult there is much that is structural in the parental home; but there is much of that structure that ceases to be relevant when he or she leaves home. Lévi-Straussian structures are held to be unchangeable by the entire human species; however, extending the term as implied above, the social structure described for an African society by a British social anthropologist may be relatively unchangeable by living Africans, although it may well be changing due to factors that are extrinsic to the society or that are intrinsic to the mentalistic structures of the African members. The structure of myth is supposedly beyond the control of myth makers.

Dealing with structure in this manner has the advantage of permitting us to use the term as a verb. Thus, when one acts, and converts energy, he has permanently structured part of his environment, that is, permanently placed some elements of it beyond control. When man devises and invents new elements of culture, he is thereby further structuring his culture, that is, he is adding things to it that will have to find their place among the other elements and will permanently change the particular pre-existing arrangement. This usage also permits one to investigate the amount of structuring in terms of the amount of energy conversion that was involved in the activity and the amount of complexity (i.e., the number of interrelations in the system) that has resulted from it. In the evolutionary sense, we can perfectly well speak of the increasing structuring of the environment within which the actors operate; the structure of power is to be found in the set of relations that are beyond the control of the species as a whole, of some particular society, or of a specific operating unit.

I will, then, be using the term *structure* to refer to the order in any set of relations that is beyond the control of some particular actor or element. I will be especially concerned with two particular kinds of structures. One is clearly Lévi-Straussian and refers to an order which we find among external events but which we suspect is imposed on those events by the human mentality. We suspect that they are transformations of mental activities of man. We cannot be sure of this, however; so we find it methodologically sounder simply to refer to the order among the set of external events themselves and be satisfied to indicate our suspicion that this constant external order is in some manner made possible because of a constant internal, mental order in the minds of men. These structures will be referred to as mentalistic structures, even though their mentalistic quality lies somewhere between an inference from external evidence and a figment in the imagination of the observer, and their locus could also be argued to be in a social dimension.[4]

[4] Abner Cohen sees political anthropology as being specifically concerned with two variables, power and symbolism: "Analysis in social anthropology has consisted in the study of interdependence, or of dialectical interaction between

To the other kind of structure we not only attribute *no* mental design but also insist that there cannot be any such implicit design except in our representation of it. These structures specifically have to do with the operation of energy as an aspect of phenomena. In this we are concerned with what might be called "the order in physical nature," an order having to do with the behavior of energy forms and processes to which the universe, including man's intervention, is subject. Most specifically, this order is derived from the First and Second Laws of Thermodynamics, as applied to social and cultural phenomena.

It should now be evident that I have entered into one of the most ancient of dualisms, mind and matter, the spiritual and the mundane.[5] Do not, however, be misled by the history of the distinction or by metaphor. I am not saying the world is somehow inherently composed of such a dualism; I am, instead, using these two sets of concepts and rules of order as a methodological device to examine the operation of the world, specifically the human world. I will be explicit (but it will also be implicit from time to time) that I regard the "mentalistic" to be quite as physical as the other and its behavior to be quite as hobbled by its own particular energetic composition as is the behavior of a falling rock. But, in dealing with man the actor, much of that which is regarded as "cultural" or "sociocultural" can be seen to have constantly been conditioned by two sets of conditions: man's mental structure, on the one hand,

---

the two variables." (A. Cohen 1969, p. 223. Reprinted from *Man*, n.s. 4, published by the Royal Anthropological Institute.) Cohen's brief review omits a definition of power, but he does hold the study of the two to have been important in social anthropology. It will be clear that I regard the distinction he makes to be of perhaps even greater moment than he allows.

[5] Bateson points out that the Judaeo-Christian tradition makes a dichotomy of *matter* and *order*, and in the First Book of Genesis: "(1) The problem of origin and nature of matter is summarily dismissed. (2) The passage deals at length with the problem of the origin of *order*. (3) A separation is thus generated between the two sorts of problems. It is possible that this separation of problems was an error, but—error or not—the separation is maintained in the fundamentals of modern science. The conservative laws for matter and energy are still separate from the laws of order, negative entropy, and information." (Gregory Bateson 1972, pp. xxiii–xxiv. Reprinted, with permission, from *Steps to an Ecology of Mind*, copyright © 1972 by Chandler Publishing Co.)

and the energetic structure, on the other. Moreover, I will argue that there are energetic structures that are, themselves, structural to the mentalistic structures; that is, that mentalistic structures operate within conditions set by energetic components, and that, in a different manner, the reverse is also true. I will also propose that some short-termed mentalistic structures change specifically in accord with the energetic changes. Finally, I would hold that all mentalistic structure is ultimately reducible to energetic structures, or that the structures here differentiated as "mentalistic" and "energetic" are merely facets of some other structural dimension. To enter that, however, is beyond my competence and the scope of the present essay.

To insist that structure is relative to specific actors or operating units is to insist that no specific structure is universal, except in regard to some specific class of phenomena. Thus, if Lévi-Strauss's analysis of myth is in some sense correct, it is only correct so long as men's minds are so constructed that they spin myths with that kind of structure. Once we place time and space limitations on our subject of study, then it becomes a relative matter as to what length of time is sufficient to warrant labeling something as "structure." What is structural in the life span of a butterfly may be a matter of incidental control to us. The habits of adults appear structural to small children but quite changing and varied to the adults themselves.

If we allow that structure is thus relative and putatively terminal, then we must ask how it is that structure comes into being and how it terminates. We cannot answer these questions for structure in general, but we can propose some answers with respect to mentalistic structures and their effect on energetic structures.

In the contemporary social-science literature the term *structure* appears principally as a noun or an adjective. Consider it, however, as a verb.[6] Working with our earlier definition, to say that *something is structured* is to say that it has been taken out of some-

---

[6] Piaget is the principal scholar to use *structure* in a verbal sense, and his usage is somewhat more generalized than that which I employ here, connecting structure with the general adaptation of a "subject" with an environment and seeing in all genesis the emergence of structure and in all structure the necessity of a genesis (Piaget 1969; 1972).

one's control.[7] Structuring is a dynamic process present in all human activity. A product of a given human activity that has the effect of placing something out of control may be said to be the structuring effect of that activity. At the very minimum, human life involves a constant energy transfer through the changing chemical composition of the environment; for example, respiration structures the atmosphere with more carbon dioxide and less oxygen.

This approach to structure places the question of the importance of the unconscious in structuralism in a somewhat different light. Unconscious events are structural because they are beyond control; but bringing them to the level of consciousness may not serve to bring them under control; that is, becoming conscious of them will not necessarily make them less structural. The same may be said for cosmic events. The stars will remain in their respective places whether or not we come to understand how they got there. The only reason that the unconsciousness need loom large in Lévi-Straussian structures is that it is one way to guarantee that the events in question are subject to no overt human control.[8] For us, however, to be unconscious is merely one manner of being beyond control; there are, in addition, many others, and the concerns of structural analysis should be much broader than a unique concern with unconscious patterns. Just as the structure of the mind determines what we do with nature, so do the structures of nature determine what the mind has to work with and, indeed, what the mind is capable of.

Before taking up the nature of energetic and mentalistic structures in more detail, and at the risk of boring my anthropological

---

[7] I adopted this usage in an earlier paper that, at the time of writing, had not yet appeared in print (R. N. Adams 1974a).

[8] Ino Rossi apparently comes to a similar conclusion through a much more sophisticated jungle. Of Lévi-Strauss he says, "The preoccupation with the unconscious is a preoccupation with discovering the basic structures, which are common to the mental mold of the sender and the receiver of the message, and which enable a genuine intersection of two intentionalities. In this sense, the unconscious is the only guarantee of objectivity of phenomenological analysis itself and the intrinsic link which would make of phenomenology an essential complement of structural analysis rather than its mere external verification." (Rossi 1973, p. 43. Reprinted from *American Anthropologist*, vol. 75, no. 1, by permission of the American Anthropological Association.)

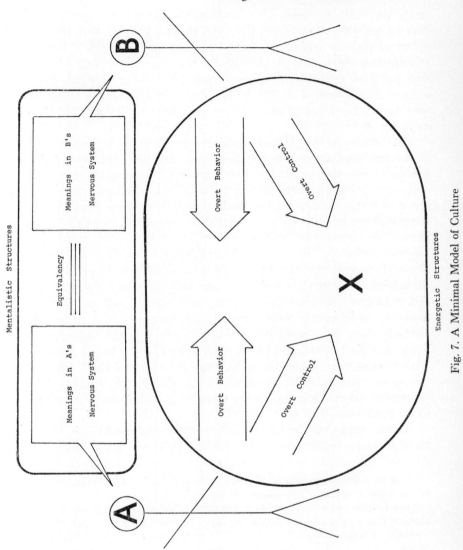

Fig. 7. A Minimal Model of Culture

readers, I want to make quite clear how I use the term *culture*. Anthropologists have taken an unwarranted delight in keeping this term fuzzy; to be incorporated in the present theory (and it is quite central in that regard) it must be specific. Figure 7 is a model of culture in its minimal form. It states that two actors, $A$ and $B$, have an interest in something energetic, $X$, and that as a consequence they have some kind of social relation, which is itself composed of some kind of patterned energetic activity. $A$ and $B$ each have some relative degree of control over $X$ (ranging from equal to very unequal), and power therefore exists as a part of the relation with respect to $X$. $X$ may be any kind of mass-energy form or process that is in some manner, directly or indirectly, perceptible to the actors. This includes the more obvious things, such as houses, land, guns, telephones, stone tools, etc. It also includes sound waves emitted as speech, neurochemical processes within one's nervous system, light reflected from some object that permits one to "see" it, etc. The only conditions to be met in order to qualify as an $X$ are that the thing in question be energetic in nature and that awareness may be had of it. In matters of social power, it must also be accessible to control through some known technology available to man. Mere control is not enough, however, for the actors must have some comprehension of each other's interests. It is here that we must resort to the methodological dualism and postulate that there exists within the nervous system of each a condition we will call a "meaning." Two aspects of this meaning are crucial. One is that it specifically concerns $X$, that is, that it involves some kind of mentalistic image, model, portion of a cognitive map, or evaluative quality that has been associated by the actor with $X$ and for which $X$ is in some sense an objectification. Both $A$ and $B$ have such meanings. Also included within the meanings is postulated an understanding of the nature of the meanings held by the others. Meanings present some problems, both to the actors and to the observers. There is no way that either actor can know with great detail just what the meanings are like. They are lost in the black box of the nervous system; and, until such time as neurological research provides us with better tools, we have no way to surely identify many aspects of meaning with biochemical processes. Another is that, as ideas, they may be extremely inaccurate with respect to the real nature of $X$. Similarly we, as observers, can have only approximate knowledge about the two sets of meanings and about the real nature of $X$.

When the two meanings are such that they elicit responses of the actors that conform in some manner to their expectations, then we say that the meanings are *equivalent*. We are not pretending that we know how equivalent or how congruent but simply that responses are elicited from the actors that permit them some degree of prediction of the behavior of the other with respect to $X$. When this is the case, then we say that a social relation exists between $A$ and $B$.

A social relation is not merely the presence of some degree of mutual predictability but also involves overt and covert behaviors that relate to the interest in $X$ and knowledge of the meanings of the other actor. In this way, all *social relations are premised on the equivalency of meanings and exist with respect to some energetic form*, X. *Culture may be said to exist when this equivalency of meanings with respect to X exists.*

The well-recognized characteristic of culture that differentiates human behavior from that of other species lies in the fact that new meanings and recombinations of meanings can quite rapidly be assigned to existing forms, and existing meanings can be extended to new forms. An object that meant little yesterday may be of great value today. In a general way, a central problem to all social sciences is the discovery of regularities in these apparently capricious and arbitrary shifts in meaning. By way of example, some hypotheses that relate them directly to certain energetic aspects of the $X$'s in the system include scarcity theory in economics, deprivation theory in social psychology, Engel's Law in economics, and the occurrence of symbolic inversions in cultural anthropology. Each of these proposes systematic relations between energetic qualities of things of interest to actors and the meanings those actors have.

In emphasizing these aspects of culture, I would hope that it is obvious that I am considering culture in the tradition of symbolism. The reason I do not place heavy emphasis on its uniqueness to the human species is that I regard that position as deriving from a particular focus on what distinguishes man from other animals. My interests are with how man operates in his environment; in that, much that he does is very animal-like indeed. The relevant aspects of culture, then, stem from the fact that it reflects a human ability to manipulate, juggle, and play complicated games with symbols at various levels, to arbitrarily endow anything, literally anything, with meaning and then proceed to act on the basis of the meaning rather than the thing. Culture, in a very real sense, is an extension of genetic processes of variation from the inside of the body to an outside-inside correspondence. Culture comprises those regularities that occur as human behavior simultaneously follows the laws of energy, on the one hand, and the rules of mental structuring, on the other. What we call "social relations" comprise the meanings we have about the energetic behaviors that relate to various energetic $X$'s that are of (mentalistic) common interest to us as actors.

## 7. THE ENERGETIC

### A. Energy and Flow

The anthropological study of energy processes, or energetics, is based on the First and Second Laws of Thermodynamics.[9] The First Law states that energy can neither be created nor destroyed but that it can change its form. The Second Law is more difficult to state, particularly in a form relevant to the present context, but essentially holds that in making its changes in form (which we shall here be calling "conversions") energy is necessarily reduced from a higher organization, negative entropy or lower entropy, to a lower organization, or higher entropy. *Entropy* refers to a state (within a closed system) of ultimate and irreversible dispersion of molecules that can be thought of as waste heat. Those versed in the physical sciences may argue that the Second Law in particular was devised to describe processes going on within specific kinds of closed systems and that it cannot necessarily be applied to the world or the solar system, not to speak of human society. My position is that the Second Law, whether borrowed or not, must be used for its heuristic value; without it there is little basis for sig-

[9] This section of the present essay is a considerably revised portion of my 1973 paper (R. N. Adams 1973*b*). Although it should be obvious from the text, I want to be explicit that I am *not* using power as a metaphor for energy, as does Lord Russell (1938) and as Bierstedt (1950) implies.

nificant theory. But, unless good reasons can be adduced to the contrary, we can treat the sun-earth-society system *as if* it were a system to which the Second Law (as well as the First) is applicable. If in the long run the Second Law proves to be misapplied, it is at the moment instructive and suggestive.

Since energy is being used as a variable in this essay, and since energy forms and flows are the empirical phenomena to which we are directing our attention, it is worth a moment's time to clarify what is meant by the terms in the present context. For energy, there are two usages that seem common in the work to date: energy-qua-energy and a broader concept of energy-in-all-its-forms. It should probably go without saying that I am not considering here such usages as "psychic energy" or "the energy of a poem" or other metaphorical usages that have caused the term to be carelessly used from time to time.

Taken in the first sense (i.e., energy = the ability to do work), the usage is close to that implied by "action," a concept that lies at the core of some approaches used in the social sciences. Certainly the better measurement of the behavioral activities of man will benefit a number of research areas and, most specifically, provide the social scientist with an independent scale against which to compare activities and processes that otherwise are difficult to handle. However, taken in this sense, the "flow" concept is hardly new to the social sciences. The use of energy as a more rigorous basis for measurement may be seen as a potentially superior way to handle action. Certainly the investigations of Eliot Chapple, Roger Barker and his associates, and the work-flow students of a few decades ago,[10] as well as various other approaches, make it clear that the conceptualization, as well as some kind of measurement, of the continuity of human activity has long received serious attention.

It is energy taken in the wider framework, however, that permits its use to cut to the core of a number of social-science areas and contribute to a broader interdisciplinary approach. When I say "wider framework," I have in mind the fact that the general relation between mass and energy, on the one hand, and that between information and mass-energy, on the other, are fairly well established. Research in energy flow must, I think, conceive its task

[10] Chapple 1940; Barker and Wright 1955; Roethlisberger and Dickson 1939.

to be the articulation within the man-ecology field of matters usually separated into these three areas, to deal with "energy" no matter what form it may take. Taking the mass-energy-information complex, or just "energy-complex," as a whole is in no sense a sneaky way of getting the kitchen stove into the act, but rather provides a legitimate basis for relating a kitchen stove that has long been in the act, but ignored, to other events through common concepts and not analogy.

It is common in human behavior that individuals and societies reconceptualize, re-evaluate events that form part of their environment, and that they can and do mix mass phenomena with energy phenomena, as well as confuse and interchange both with information phenomena. Understanding human behavior requires that we deal with this apparent muddle. The object is not to analyze human behavior into categories of mass, energetic, and informational components, but rather to be able to handle transformations from one of these areas to another with at least the same facility as, but hopefully more systematically than human beings do in their daily life. To focus on the mass-energy-information complex is to focus on a material world, to insist that, whatever it is that the social scientist may study, that thing must be of that world, or it cannot be studied. It is here that we need to employ a methodological dualism: we must for certain purposes resort to a mentalistic-energetic differentiation which, in fact, I would not subscribe to in theory. The reason for handling the mass-energy-information complex dualistically is that we not only want to be able to find the regularities between energy as mass and action, and in its manifestation as information as well, but we also want to explore how these energetic processes relate to those which have generally been subsumed under terms such as *value, cognition,* and other mentalistic labels.

This question of making a clear distinction between the mentalistic and the energetic for methodological purposes is not trivial. The failure to keep these things straight has produced some peculiar analogies and dubious theorizing. Of perhaps greater importance, the lack of effective relational concepts and propositions has forced scholars to switch arbitrarily from one energy form and value set to another. Thus, Wassily Leontief's Nobel-Prize-winning input-output analysis makes clear sense when dealing with the full energy-complex phenomenon, but that sense presents extraordinary methodological problems. He therefore resorts to a common measure of quantity: monetary units, which, at best, vary in both price and value from time to time.[11] Obviously the use of such an analysis may still be great, but it can hardly be denied that there are serious problems when converting from one society to another, from one culture or another, or, fundamentally, from one mind to another. Such input-output analyses are hard to use in historical and evolutionary comparisons, as the continuing discussions over the nature of primitive economies so amply illustrate. Nathaniel B. Guyol has argued convincingly that the use of monetary terms for quantification of national production

suffers from the same weaknesses as the usual measures of production, namely, variations in the value of money from one time to another, differences in the prices of commodities from one place to another, and varying rates of change in the prices of particular commodities from one time to another. Energy data, and specifically data on the quantities of energy effectively used, could be substituted for either volume or value data in the productivity equation and might yield better results, because *the physical volume of work performed in doing any given task at a given rate of speed tends to remain constant until there is a significant change in the technology of production.*[12] (Guyol's italics)

The core of concern is then with the continuum of mass-energy-information, practically all of which lies in the world external to any of us. Since epistemologically it cannot be directly known, we conceive of two kinds of structures that we seek to describe with respect to it: the mentalistic and the energetic.

Within the energetic, it is convenient to differentiate two phases of activity. We will be concerned with the change from one energy *form* to another, the conversion of mass to energy or one form of mass or energy to another; and with the fact that both mass and energy occur within discernible patterns that can be explored for certain purposes in the language of information theory. We are also concerned with the direct role of man in the activities of

[11] Leontief 1968, pp. 345–346.

[12] Guyol 1971, p. 136. Reprinted from Nathaniel B. Guyol, *Energy in the Perspective of Geography*, © 1971. By permission of Prentice-Hall, Inc., Englewood Cliffs, New Jersey.

energy form, with his *control* over mass and energy processes. This control is an energetic process in itself, that is, a "physical," or "material" event, the actual (technological) manipulation of energetic phenomena by human activity.

What has occasionally been overlooked is that, in the human cultural system, energy flows *always* carry information. Thus, as social scientists we must be more systematic in seeing flow as always having dual results: (1) the effect of new energy-mass conversion in a system, with a concomitant loss to entropy; and (2) the effect of information on a meaning system. Given these two aspects, when we speak of control of energy forms, we may equally well be speaking of control over the energy process itself, or over the information it carries, or both. What is controlled in the case of information is the marker,[13] the energetic form that is the vehicle with the pattern elements that comprise the information. Since information itself is a pattern, control of information is only realistic if it is control over the energetic information markers.

Gregory Bateson has argued that information really has zero dimension and that "no variable of zero dimension can be truly located. 'Information' and 'form' resemble contrast, frequency, symmetry, correspondence, congruence, conformity, and the like in being of zero dimension and, therefore, are not to be located."[14] I believe that exceptions can be taken in one sense to Bateson's view,

[13] "Von Newmann used the term marker to refer to those observable bundles, units, or changes of matter-energy whose patterning bears or conveys the informational symbols from the ensemble or repertoire." (J. G. Miller 1965, p. 194. Reprinted by permission of *Behavioral Science*.) Miller, in his own argument, correctly makes explicit that "matter-energy and information always flow together . . . Which aspect of the transmission is most important depends upon how it is handled by the receiver" (p. 199). But elsewhere, in dealing with inputs and transmissions, he seems to slide back into the more traditional, and confusing, concrete separation of mass, energy, and information: "Each of these sorts of transmissions may consist of *either* (a) some particular form of matter; (b) energy, in the form of light, radiant energy, heat or chemical energy; *or* (c) some particular pattern of information" (pp. 223–224; italics added). It is necessary to re-emphasize that mass-energy *always* carries information; the only questions are whether it reaches anyone's nervous system and, if it does, whether anyone cares what significance or meaning that information may have for him.

[14] Gregory Bateson 1972, p. 408. Reprinted, with permission, from *Steps to an Ecology of Mind*, copyright © 1972 by Chandler Publishing Co.

since the locus of these informational patterns, when transformed into human nervous processes, also thereby becomes part of culture.[15] Apart from this, however, control of them rests entirely on control over their energetic components or manifestations.[16]

Information in the nervous system, then, is a transformation of that exterior to it, and it is called meaning. The gap between meaning and information, the different interior and exterior coding of which Bateson speaks, is a broad one. The statistical notions of "uncertainty" and "order" (which we will discuss shortly) have been central in information theory and may well serve within the strictly closed system of a telephone wire, but they cannot be expected to work so well in the two nervous systems that are using the wire for communication. Technically, information flow (i.e., communication) refers only to the first of these; it refers to the movement of energetic markers in space or time. It is no different from any other energetic flow. However, it occurs that this *information transfer* has been confused with *meaning transfer*. Thus, in anthropology, when one speaks of message flow, the speaker seldom confines himself to a strictly information-theory usage; he is often intentionally implying that there is some innate cognitive consistency between what started out in one nervous system and what arrived and became embedded in another. Quite clearly the codes or meaning systems within any two human beings must of necessity be rather different; and, even when a code may be agreed upon, the question of interpretation of meaning still leaves much to be desired.

Just as important as being clear on the usage of *energy* is to be clear on the usage of *flow*, or process. The literature on flow has used the term for various processes that are quite different, and which have at times gone undifferentiated in the thinking of some writers. As in the use of *energy* for *mass-energy*, there is nothing wrong with this broader usage if we are clear that there are differentiations within and if we are prepared to recognize the differ-

---

[15] See White 1949, pp. 282–302, in an essay entitled "The Locus of Mathematical Reality."

[16] The notion that we can usefully deal with information as mass is purely metaphorical. Calhoun poses the notion of "ideomass" but can only promote confusion unless he means it in terms of dealing with the energetic component of the information marker, not the information aspect. (See Calhoun 1973, p. 269.)

ences when they become significant in particular problems. Five
ways of using flow have become evident to me:

1. flow as *transport* and *storage* of matter;
2. flow as *transduction* and radiation of energy;
3. flow as *transformation* of information;
4. flow as *conversion* from one state to another;
5. flow as energy cost of *triggering* energy release.

Perhaps the element common to all is that the expenditure of
energy at one point has a systematic consequence for the change in
the state of energy at another point. This permits the two to be
seen as parts of a system. Of particular interest to us in this context
is the fact that, within social organizations, the differential distribution of energy controls will permit actors at one point in the system
to exercise social power over others elsewhere in the system merely
because of the differential control. It is therefore not surprising that
power has also been seen to operate as a flow. Our usage confirms
this in that it is not uncommon to hear such an expression as
"power flowing to the top."

The first usage, flow as transport or storage, is the simplest to
perceive and acts as the archetype for the use of the term in the
rest of the cases. It can refer to water moving through an ecosystem, biochemical compounds moving through trophic levels,
dollar bills moving through hands, etc. The differentiation between
transportation and storage is merely a time-space separation of
aspects of the event, with storage allowing for zero change in space.

The second use of the term refers to the movement of energy in
space, such as in solar and thermal radiation, evaporation, convec-
tion, conduction, and other transductive processes. This obviously
includes a rather broad range, but it is probably in this sense that
the term *energy flow* is most correctly used.[17]

Serious difficulties begin to appear in the third usage, where
there is an apparent movement of energy through a system but

---

[17] David M. Gates 1962, p. 4: "The term 'flux' when applied to radiant
energy refers to the total amount of radiant energy of all wavelengths crossing
a unit area of surface per unit time, in units of cal per $cm^2$ per min. When
applied to the movement of water or mass, the term 'flux' refers to the amount
crossing a unit area per unit time in units of grams per $cm^2$ per min." Reprinted
from *Energy Exchange in the Biosphere* by permission of Harper and Row.

where the significant issue is not a movement of energy or matter but rather the transference or the transformation (in the sense of changing from one form to another) of a pattern or arrangement of mass-energetic parts. In a way, when one speaks of the flow of information, he is speaking neither of flow nor of energy in any of its known forms. Bateson has pointed this out quite clearly: "When a billiard ball strikes another, there is an energy transfer such that the motion of the second ball is energized by the impact of the first. In communicational systems, on the other hand, the energy of the response is usually provided by the respondent."[18] Anatol Rapoport noted that "so far no theory exists, to our knowledge, which attributes any sort of unambiguous measure to this 'flow.' "[19] "To be defined as a quantity of information a signal must be selected from a set or matched with an element of a set. It is misleading in a crucial sense to view 'information' as something that can be poured into an empty vessel, like a fluid or even like energy."[20] We are dealing here with separate energetic systems. The information marker does not energize the nervous system; it triggers it (more on this below). What appears to be flow is a replication of pattern at different points in time-space. The pattern exists only by virtue of being embodied in some mass-energy form, but whether it takes one arrangement or another may be of little consequence to mass-energy in itself. This usage is clearly metaphorical, and this should serve to warn us that some of our own cultural meanings have slipped into the picture. Most specifically the idea of "order" or "organization" is the way we describe information. It is, as Bateson has pointed out, a thing of zero dimensions; as such, it can hardly be accumulated, added, or built up. This will concern us later.

The fourth usage refers to the change that occurs in time when there is energy conversion, or change in the state of energy. This can refer to chemical conversion, such as the burning of fuel; thermal conversion, such as water becoming steam; photosynthesis; subnuclear conversion, as in the atomic bomb; etc. The major issue here is that mass-energy is seeking an equilibrium state with its environment. When the environment changes in critical or stra-

18 Bateson 1972, p. 403.
19 Rapoport 1968, p. 139. Reprinted from *Modern Systems Research for the Behavioral Scientist*, ed. W. Buckley, by permission of Aldine Publishing Co.
20 Ibid., p. 140.

tegic ways, the mass-energy system must convert into a new state. Such conversions are unidirectional in that the energy lost to entropy in a conversion is nonrecoverable. However, in some instances, such as the shift from ice to water, other energy may be added to restore the earlier state. This does not avoid the entropy loss; it merely means there is more energy around where that came from.

The fourth usage is particularly important in the mundane world of daily life. It is the energy that is expended in every activity, whether human or extrahuman, somatic or extrasomatic: the forging of steel, the dry cleaning of a suit, or the dusting of a bookcase; the eating of nuts, the cultivation of rice, or the mining of ores; the playing of chess, the building of a skyscraper, or the arranging of books on the shelf. All require energy expenditure. Some appear "reversible," such as rearranging books; but they really are not so, insofar as energy loss is concerned; those involving chemical or subnuclear changes are totally irreversible. Using the term *flow* in these activities may refer merely to movement of mass-energy between two points in the system.

The fifth usage of flow refers to processes that appear to be a type of transduction but in fact must be seen as a trigger mechanism.[21] It occurs when energy of one system is applied to the en-

---

[21] Fifty years ago Lotka made clear the importance of trigger mechanisms: "We have been accustomed, in thermodynamics, to disregard mechanism. In dealing with energy conversions by trigger action we must make a complete change of attitude. Here everything depends on mechanism. If we find any degree of regularity in the conversion factor, this must be due to regularities in the mechanism, i.e., in the human organism, and its social aggregation" (1921, p. 194). At that time the economists' concern with energy was by no means new, and Lotka cites work by G. Helm (1887), W. Ostwald (1909), and Winarski (1900). It is not clear to me whether Margalef is distinguishing the trigger from the release in his use of the term *energy gates*: "Natural selection is not as wasteful as it is assumed to be in popular books because it uses energy that would be lost anyway in keeping an ecosystem running. The energy gates at the places where species interact—or where they interact with environment —are the organs by which selection is achieved and evolution occurs, the rate of evolution depending on the efficiency of the gate." (R. Margalef 1968, p. 81. Reprinted from *Perspectives in Ecological Theory*, © 1968 by The University of Chicago, by permission of the University of Chicago Press.) The term *work gate* as used by Odum clearly does refer to one kind of trigger mechanism. However, Odum generalizes the term *work gate* to "refer to any multiplicative interaction

vironment of the second so that the second must seek a new equilibrium, thereby changing the state of the second system. In a more
elaborate form, it includes the energy cost or input into the productive process. There has been some confusion of the energy that
actuates the trigger and the energy released from the separate
system by virtue of the trigger action.

This usage is particularly important in our understanding of the
real mass-energy processes, both in contemporary life and in the
evolution of human society. Quite clearly the crux of our current
energy crisis is that we do not have adequate trigger devices in
sufficient quantities to effectively channel and strategically release
the great amounts of energy that are, in fact, all around us. Triggers require energy expenditure themselves (i.e., energy costs, or
energy cost of production), and the ratio between the amount of
energy expended in actuating the trigger and that released by the
system is an extremely important one. Ecosystems, for example,
have been differentiated in accord with their degree of maturity. A
feature that distinguishes the immature from the mature ecosystem
is that, in the former, the energy cost (respiration) is relatively
less than the amount of energy that is released *within* the system
(the gross production). In the ideally mature system, the energy
cost is equal to the energy released so that there is a steady state
of the whole and no further growth. The marvelous Rube Goldberg
inventions of a generation ago were supermature systems that required an inordinate amount of expenditure of energy for a minis-
cule product.

Trigger mechanisms are of many types, but one of particular
interest to human cultural systems is that which conveys to another
system information that changes the energy state of the second.
Since information is carried by energetic markers, that is, actual
energy forms or processes, information input really does involve
energetic input; however, it is the precise patterning manifested by
the trigger energy that permits it to have the effect it does. So we

---

of two flows and the forces they exert" (1971, p. 44, Figs. 2-4, 2-6). While the
notion of *gate* in this sense may be useful for chemical reactions, it is misleading when carried over to cultural trigger actions, since in the latter we do not
know what, if any, regular relations may hold between the amount of energy
released and the amount utilized to actuate the "gate" or trigger; that is, we do
not know what the multiplier in "multiplicative" may be.

may speak of the action as if information from one system triggered off a change of state in another. Most commonly, a trigger action will bring about a change in state that will continue until the second system reaches another state of equilibrium.

Trigger mechanisms are of many kinds, and of particular interest in the context of the present study are two that are contained in man's ability to reconstruct his social organization. It has elsewhere been noted that the organization of all species seems principally determined by the interworkings of a basic genetic composition with ecological circumstances. This interworking, especially among "higher" animals, often involves remarkable degrees of adaptation. And, indeed, this adaptation of a species through various subspecific populations in distinctive habitats is precisely a way of hastening the energy flux within the species as a whole.

In human organizations, however, culture permits, indeed almost forces, man to reformulate the meanings of organization, to seek new things for them to do, and to invent new ones. These new and reformulated organizations, or operating units, are constituted so as to adapt to some particular perceived problem, and many of these perceived problems involve serious issues of energy release. Thus, while the human individual has genetic limitations, his organizations are not so limited. By setting up different "purposes" and "goals," such units become newly adaptive. Thus the energies of man, unlike those of almost all other species, are not expended merely on one or a minimal set of social organizations but rather can be allocated among a whole series of different, changing, and often expanding organizations, each of which through its adaptation serves to trigger the exploitation of a certain niche in the external world.

Obviously the mere fact of allocating the daily caloric expenditure of man among different operating units cannot increase the somatic calorie output. Man can no more subvert the First Law of Thermodynamics than he can the Second. What such allocation does do, however, is to permit him to increase the number of organizational trigger mechanisms, to spread out his somatic energy in small chunks as cost of production in a number of niches and trigger devices. The importance of this may be seen in the nature of time utilization in hunting and gathering bands. Consider Richard B. Lee's report on the !Kung Bushmen: "!Kung Bushmen of Dobe, despite their harsh environment, devote from twelve to nineteen hours a week to getting food. Even the hardest working individual in the camp, a man named ≠oma [sic] who went out hunting on sixteen of the 28 days, spent a maximum of 32 hours a week in the food quest."[22] During the remaining time, women carry on various domestic tasks, and both men and women spend an inordinate amount of time in visiting, entertaining, and dancing. While the actual amount of time spent in nonproductive work obviously varies with different societies and different ecologies, many other studies reported in the same volume support Lee's observation and have led Sahlins to characterize the hunters (with his usual felicity of language) as the "original affluent society."[23]

This means that if man has increased his "surplus time," over the evolution of culture, he has done it because he already had surplus time. The crucial process, then, was not the time so much as the technology, the invention of trigger mechanisms and energy-extractive mechanisms. In this way man has succeeded in gradually dedicating more and more of this primal surplus time to the process of hastening the performance of the Second Law of Thermodynamics, of hurrying energy through his cultural system. By devoting more and more time to the cost of production, and thereby increasing production, he actually has increased the amount of human life that can be sustained and, thereby, the amount of human time to be spent in nonproductive activities. The proportion spent on leisure, however, has ceased over time to be proportionally shared among all the producers and has become a specialized occupation of a limited class; and as a result the producers increasingly have had to spend more time in production; to borrow again from Sahlins: man sentenced himself to hard labor for life.

Another way that operating units act as trigger mechanisms is by concentrating decision-making power. This can be seen structurally as the formation of ever more-inclusive operating units and as the appearance of higher levels of integration, levels from which decisions are made that affect increasing numbers of people lower in the organization. As more energetic processes and

---

[22] Lee 1968, p. 37. Reprinted from *Man the Hunter*, ed. Richard B. Lee and Irven De Vore, by permission of Aldine Publishing Co.

[23] Sahlins 1972, Ch. 1.

forms enter a society, control over them becomes disproportionately concentrated in the hands of a few, so that fewer *independent* decisions are responsible for greater releases of energy. Thus, in a large, complex, but coordinated organization a single decision will trigger a chain of subsequent dependent decisions, leading to the release of much more energy than would have been possible were the various subsequent decisions (1) not coordinated and (2) therefore not ordered to trigger off the planned releases. The establishment of concentration of power at higher levels of organization is a direct way to harness and release ever greater amounts of energy.

Social power, the ability to get somebody else to do what you want him to do through your control over energetic processes of interest to him, is the central issue in all these organizational processes. The exercise of social power from distinctive operating units and from different levels of integration is certainly one of the most important types of trigger device available to man. Without it, any technological device requiring the activity of more than one man would receive only sporadic or random attention. The evolution of culture has seen a steady increase in the energy cost of production, such that the pattern characteristic of mature ecosystems is a possible alternative in the future. Manual arts comprised the major trigger actions in the most primitive societies; that is, the energy actuating triggers was human energy. As culture advanced, man increasingly has had recourse to extrahuman triggers: first hand tools, then domestication of plants and animals, then harnessing of wind and water, later machinery and fossil fuels, and most recently subnuclear actions. The total per capita energy cost of trigger action has increased steadily. Man, in his immense anthropocentricism, has tended to congratulate himself and see this only as a per capita decrease in the human energy input; until recently, he tended to overlook the cosmic significance of the massive amounts of nonhuman energy required for this advance.

Flow, in the area of information and meaning, must be treated with considerable care. Since I have opted for an approach to the interior-exterior connections that will use a combination of energetic and structural analyses, the entire area of communication, information, meaning, and energetic structure is one that must be dealt with, and energy flow analysis is an important tool in this process.

## B. The Second Law—and Order

If we can assume that we agree to use energy in the energy-complex sense and to explore the problem of the relation of meaning and information, we are nonetheless left with some problems of interpretation of just how energy works.

One part of White's original statement on energy has perhaps contributed to a continuing misunderstanding about the application of the Second Law. "The second law of thermodynamics tells us that the cosmos as a whole is breaking down structurally and running down dynamically; matter is becoming less organized and energy more uniformly diffused." So far so good; but White continues in a more dubious vein: "But in a tiny sector of the cosmos, namely in material living systems, the direction of the cosmic process is reversed; matter becomes more highly organized and energy more concentrated . . . Biological evolution is simply an expression of the thermodynamic process that moves in a direction opposite to that specified for the cosmos as a whole by the Second Law."[24] Is White correct that living systems have in some manner "reversed the cosmic process"? If so, the Second Law isn't much of a law.

A different view is given by Erwin Schrödinger: "Everything that is going on in Nature means an increase in entropy of the part of the world where it is going on. Thus a living organism continually increases its entropy—or, as you may say, produces positive entropy—and thus tends to approach the dangerous state of maximum entropy, which is death. It can only keep aloof from it, i.e., alive, by continually drawing from its environment negative entropy—which is something very positive . . . What an organism feeds upon is negative entropy."[25] Schrödinger points out that living organisms do not in any sense reverse the cosmic process; rather, if anything, they hasten it. Their very life depends on a continuing conversion of energy from higher forms to entropy

[24] Leslie A. White 1949, p. 367. Reprinted from *The Science of Culture*, copyright 1949, by permission of Farrar, Straus and Giroux.

[25] Erwin Schrödinger 1967, p. 76. Reprinted from *What Is Life?* by permission of Cambridge University Press.

—or feeding on negative entropy, as he puts it. The fact that man is not a mechanism that is building up energy concentration, but rather one that is expending energy faster by virtue of the life process, is of extreme importance; a misunderstanding about it has perhaps led some anthropologists astray.

But Schrödinger's own argument proceeds to perpetuate another dubious notion that has been subscribed to by many social scientists:

An isolated system or a system in a uniform environment . . . increases its entropy and more or less rapidly approaches the inert state of maximum entropy. We now recognize this fundamental law of physics to be just the natural tendency of things to approach the chaotic state (the same tendency that the books of a library or the piles of paper and manuscripts on a writing desk display) unless we obviate it. (The analogue of irregular heat motion, in this case, is our handling those objects now and again without troubling to put them back in their proper places.) . . . Thus the devices by which an organism maintains itself stationary at a fairly high level of orderliness (= fairly low level of entropy) really consist in continually sucking orderliness from its environment . . . Indeed, in the case of higher animals we know the kind of orderliness they feed upon well enough, viz. the extremely well-ordered state of matter in more or less complicated organic compounds, which serve them as food stuffs. After utilizing it they return it in a very much degraded form—not entirely degraded, however, for plants can still make use of it. (These, of course, have their most powerful supply of "negative entropy" in the sunlight.)[26]

[26] Ibid., pp. 78, 79. The argument that there is a buildup of order that in some manner corresponds to the entropic process is popular. Ubbelohde holds that it is not a totally closed question as to whether life may "evade" the Second Law (1955, Ch. 13), and Boulding is more impressed that the "castles of order do get more and more complex" than he is that "the building of more and more complex little castles of order [is] at the cost of increasing chaos elsewhere" (1968, p. 162). Even Bateson, who so deftly and creatively picks his way among the latticework of energy theory, trips briefly on this matter: "We may compare the seeking of information with the seeking of values. In the seeking of values it is clear that what happens is that man sets out to 'trick' the Second Law of Thermodynamics. He endeavors to interfere with the natural or random course of events so that some otherwise improbable outcome will be achieved." (Bateson 1966, pp. 419–420. Reprinted from *Communication, The Social Matrix of Psychiatry*, by Jurgen Ruesch, M.D., and Gregory Bateson. Copyright © 1968, 1951, by W. W. Norton & Company, Inc., New York, N.Y.) In an article marked by enthusiasm, Maruyama argues that deviation-amplifying cybernetic processes,

What does Schrödinger mean by "orderliness" in the environment? When he refers to misplaced books, he refers to a possible analogue; but later he refers to nutritional consumption of "higher organizations" of energy and their conversion into degraded forms. The suggested confusion here is whether the "orderliness" is an actual difference of the degree of integration of the physical form, so that its "breakdown" by conversion would lead to a series of lesser ordered forms (such as conversion of meat to feces, or an atomic-bomb explosion); or whether it is merely orderliness in the eye of the beholder, that is, books that appear disorderly to the owner may appear quite orderly to the maid who places them upside-down on the shelves after dusting.

This is no minor point; a good deal of discussion of entropy in communication and information theory hinges on the process of order and disorder; is it a real process, or is it a metaphor?

A recent illustration may clarify that, at least in one aspect, it is indeed metaphorical and not energetic disorder. "Free energy implies some ordered structure, comparable with that of a store in which all meat is on one counter, vegetables on another, and so on. Bound energy is energy dissipated in disorder, like the same store after being struck by a tornado. This is why entropy is also defined as a measure of disorder. It fits the fact that a copper sheet represents a lower entropy than the copper ore from which it was produced."[27] Is refined copper sheeting a *higher order* of *organization* than the ore from which it is extracted? Presumably the copper in the ore is bound with various impurities, other minerals and elements, that have to be separated out. Not only does this process require an input of energy cost of production to make the separation (which energy is lost to entropy), but the very energy holding the ore together presumably is also converted

---

like Maxwell's demon, somehow elude the Second Law of Thermodynamics; he is led to this by noting that information can increase rapidly in these processes, but by paying no attention to the fact that there must be an energy expenditure for the processes to take place (1968, p. 306; originally published in 1963). Flannery, in his generally perceptive paper, repeats this confusion (1972, p. 423). The reader may also be interested in material cited by J. G. Miller (1965, p. 194) from De Beauregard and Zeman concerning the relation between information and negentropy.

[27] Georgescu-Roegen 1973, p. 40.

to entropy. The higher "organization" that the resulting copper sheet manifests *is orderly in terms of the culture in which it was processed*, but it is clearly of a less highly complex matter than is represented by the original ore. The converting of ore to sheet copper is exactly parallel to Mary Douglas's description of man's concern with other parts of his environment: "In chasing dirt, in papering, decorating, tidying, we are not governed by anxiety to escape disease, but are positively re-ordering our environment, making it conform to an idea."[28] In removing the copper from the ore, we are "making it conform to an idea"; we are not, however, instituting a new and higher degree of order in the total system. We are instituting or maintaining a degree of order in the cultural system but at the expense of order in the natural system. That cultural order lies wholly in our mind's eye. Splitting atoms, diverting rivers, eliminating trees, killing Jews, infidels, or Communists have all at one time or another been part of man's way of introducing more order into his cultural world; but let us not think of these as some kind of reversal of the cosmic process. Quite the contrary; they hasten the cosmic process, the conversion of energy, and the building of entropy.

It is difficult to be sure whether scholars so distinguished in the fields of energy study could have been swayed by the carrying over of a metaphor of "order" from organization-in-meaning via organization-in-information to organization-in-energetic-forms. The important issue is that we not do it. Lotka observed correctly, I believe, that the Second Law of Thermodynamics cannot be contravened by mere human action, nor even by the life that natural selection acted to promote: "In every instance considered, natural selection will so operate as to increase the total mass of the organic system, to increase the rate of circulation of matter through the system, and to increase the total energy flux through the system, so long as there is presented an unutilized residue of matter and available energy."[29] The crux of Lotka's argument is that evolution, as a mechanism following the Second Law of Thermodynamics, succeeded in accelerating "the circulation of matter through the life cycle, both by 'enlarging the wheel,' and by causing it to 'spin

[28] Douglas 1970*a*, p. 12. Reprinted from *Purity and Danger* by permission of John Farquharson Ltd.

[29] Lotka 1922*a*, p. 148.

faster.' "[30] Lotka's principle states that, in evolution, natural selection favors those populations that convert the greater amount of energy, that is, that bring the greater amount of energy form and process under their control. In cultural evolution, the extension of biological evolution in this as in other matters, trigger mechanisms have enabled even greater quantities of energy to be released. Societies that have accomplished this have achieved immediate adaptive advantage thereby, although in the long run the specialization implied may diminish their adaptability for the future. It has already been suggested that trigger devices enhance energy flow, not only by the release of energy they permit, but also by the release of energy involved in their own operation, that is, in the energy cost of production.

The notion that there are "islands," or "castles," or local order, may be considered a metaphor for the much more important discovery by ecologists of the nature of the achievement of steady states in ecosystems (to be discussed shortly). One can look upon these steady states as "islands" of organization in an informational sense; but they are by no means counterentropic preserves of energetic forms. Rather, they are devices whereby energy is hastened to entropy rather than radiated back into space, or converted into equilibrium forms, which, for the time, have neither input nor output. Indeed, if the terms *island* and *castles* of negative entropy have any application, it is to portions of the inanimate world, not the animate.

The problem of "order" in these contexts is not one that has been overlooked, although it remains one for which the solution is still far from clear. Lotka observed years ago that the notion that evolution proceeds "from less probable states to more probable states" is probably meaningless unless one can state some rather important conditions. "It is meaningless unless the characteristic with regard to which probability is reckoned is explicitly or implicitly indicated. Probability is essentially a matter of classification. An improbable event is one that is a member of a small class, and whether it is so or not depends, clearly, on our system of classification. For this reason, the broad statement which has sometimes been made, that the direction of evolution is from less probable to more probable

[30] Ibid., p. 149.

states, is not only inadequate, but is really meaningless. It is indefinite in failing to specify with regard to what characteristic probability is to be reckoned; and it is incomplete in failing to call attention to the fundamentally important connection between the particular probabilities in question, and available energy."[31] Mathematicians have long warned that "All particular configurations are a priori equally improbable."[32]

The confusion, which is so profound in the literature that it should be a subject of special research, is easily resolved. The greater the energy in a system, the more complex will be that system. But complexity is not the same thing as order. As Maranda stated, "Order means a system whose properties can be mapped in terms of a constant set of related propositions."[33] We may add that propositions are *mentalistic* phenomena. Thus a given complexity may be very well ordered, or may be very disordered; and a set with a given order may be either quite complex or quite simple. Unfortunately, the mischief of information-theory disciples is to have confounded these two notions. A very high energy system may appear either very ordered or very disordered.

## C. Man in the Ecosystem

A decision that has to be made in all studies of energy in human society is what framework one ought to use in order to best bring out the kinds of answers one is seeking. At the outset we can identify certain energetic characteristics of man and his particular universe in systematic terms: (1) Man, the individual, is a dissipative system, that is, a system that requires a regular input and gives a regular output. It is called dissipative because, if the input were to be stopped, the system would continue and eventually dissipate itself through the output. (2) Man is a member of a species which, because its component members are human beings, must also be a dissipative system. (3) Individuals do not operate

[31] Lotka 1925, pp. 34–35. Reprinted, with permission, from *Elements of Physical Biology*, © 1925 The Williams and Wilkins Co., Baltimore.

[32] Rapoport 1968, p. 141. See also Burgers 1963, cited by J. G. Miller 1965, p. 201; according to Miller, Burgers "holds that the distinction between order and disorder is made by the living observer and is not inherent in the physical world as viewed by physicists." See also Tribus 1961.

[33] Maranda 1972, p. 330.

in terms of the species, but in terms of societies or communities, and these also are dissipative systems, for the same reason that the species is. (4) Communities or sets of communities pertain to larger collectivities of communities extending from regional groupings to empires. (5) Communities or sets of communities and the larger units are parts of ecosystems, that is, systems of energetic interchange.

All dissipative systems share a number of characteristics by which they may be contrasted to equilibrium systems.[34] They all require energy flow to continue in existence; they all exhibit a state of homeostasis during some phase of their existence; they manifest a regular succession of states until the homeostatic condition is achieved; and their growth and ultimate size are determined by the amount of energy that flows through them.

Dissipative systems can, however, manifest different states, depending on the relative input-output ratio: (1) in expanding systems input is greater than output; (2) in declining systems output is greater than input; and (3) in steady states, input is equal to output. According to the Second Law of Thermodynamics, all dissipative systems must ultimately be terminal. The three states just mentioned, therefore, describe phases of the life cycle, trajectory, or succession of such a system.

Figure 8 indicates the approximate curves of some known systems involving human beings. Of those indicated, the human life is the only one with an internal, homeostatically limited life span; all the rest are determined by elements external to themselves. The ecosystem and the human empire manifest the first two phases, expansion and some portion of a steady state. The first two, the human population and human culture, manifest thus far only the first phase, that of expansion. Macrohistorians, such as Spengler and later Toynbee, have speculated on the mechanisms that produce those curves peculiar to the human societal curves. The development of the study of ecosystems, however, has permitted a more cogent understanding of the nature of such systems and the role that energy plays in them.

In ecosystem studies[35] the expanding phase of the dissipative

[34] Blackburn has spelled out these features (1973, pp. 1142–1143). Ashby refers to equilibrium systems as "energy-tight" systems (1958, p. 3).

[35] Odum 1971; Margalef 1968.

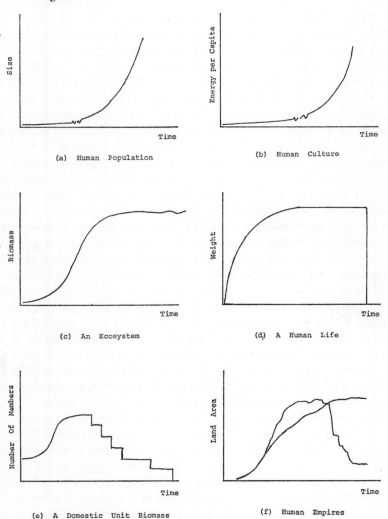

Fig. 8. Some Schematically Portrayed Dissipative Systems. Developed after Blackburn 1973, Taagepera 1968, and others.

system is seen as its immature phase; the steady state, as maturity. Each phase has many characteristics that are only now being exploited for their implications in human development.[36] Among

[36] Rappaport 1971a; Margalef 1968.

the issues that are quite clear, however, is that the structure of an expanding system is quite different from that of a steady state; and, in its macrocareer, the human species has known only the first of these. Also, a steady state implies achieving some kind of an equilibrium with the environment. This equilibrium is dissipative, however; that is, it is not an equilibrium system at rest but one that depends on a regular input and output. As such, the environment must provide the regular input. A steady state, then, not only reflects something about the internal structure of the organism (i.e., the size of the candle wick, the genetic template determining life span and body size) but also reflects the environmental structure of the system. Finally, when we look at such curves as that of the human life, the species and culture, an empire, or an ecosystem, we are clearly looking at complex sets of subsystems; and, in the case of the last four, these subsystems are capable of continuing survival even if the macrosystem should fragment, so long as the requisite input for the parts continues available.

These systems and subsystems provide us with a framework within which to see the career of man and the evolution of social power. The "empire" is, of course, only one kind of human society, and the model given for it in Figure 8 can apply equally well to any human society at any level where the input to the system is composed of live individuals. What this curve gives us, then, is the trajectory or succession of combinations of operating units.

An argument was earlier entered that there is no "natural boundary" between the individual and the species. It can obviously be argued that, for a viable system, one individual is not enough, and that the species has never (so far as we know) acted like a unit (or at least an effective one). Where to draw a line around any particular subset within the macrohuman whole is arbitrarily decided by the investigator. The fact that many investigators have been interested in reproductive or economic units has led to concern with families; concern with minimal survival groups has led to attention to communities; interest in power systems has led to attention to nations; etc. But, in every case, the boundaries were chosen because (correctly or not) it was believed that the unit so enclosed would provide a fruitful field of study.

Attention to the broader ecological area led Roy A. Rappaport to propose that the study of human society (and here he was concerned specifically with an agricultural New Guinea society) could usefully consider three units: "the local or ecological population; the ecosystem; and the regional population."[37] Rappaport suggested these units in the context of dealing with a primitive agricultural society and also within the context of an anthropology that had recently discovered ways of handling ecological and economic processes. Starting from a somewhat different standpoint, but in an attempt to move toward the same goal at which, I believe, Rappaport was aiming, I want to suggest a more general model, one that will serve research on any society, not just the primitive or preindustrial; and I believe that there is a better tool for anthropology than the ecological-economic complex that I believe dominated Rappaport's thinking at the time he proposed these units.

Let us distinguish four systems:

1. *The research focus operating unit* is an arbitrarily chosen complex that includes a human population whose members share a common adaptive stance to an environment within which it is presumed to operate. In the case of Rappaport's study it was the Tsembaga local group of the Maring people; but it could be the highlanders of New Guinea, or it could be a domestic group, a community, a nation, a group of people temporarily joined in a common task, etc. Rappaport's "local, ecological population" would be a specific case in point. This would also include the classical anthropologist's "society" and its "culture."

2. *The power system* is a system that comprises all the human populations with which the focal operating unit experiences exchange (i.e., input and output) of energetic forms and processes, including material items, energies expended on directed activities, energetic markers carrying information, etc. The term comprehends Rappaport's "regional population" but is considerably broader. The "regional population" was proposed because Rappaport was particularly interested in "aggregates distinguished by the criteria of regional continuity and exchanges of personnel, genetic material, and goods."[38] The concept of the power system encompasses not only the regional population, one that is defined in terms of social, economic, and genetic exchange, but also the

[37] Rappaport 1969, p. 184.
[38] Rappaport 1968.

power relations (which are always potentially reciprocal) that directly affect the focal operating unit. This expansion of Rappaport's usage is necessary because in the contemporary world it is evident that few human populations live in sufficient isolation to avoid being severely influenced by the action of power systems, many of whose operators stand beyond the limits of the "regional population" as defined by Rappaport. In cases, such as Rappaport's study, which have a specific concern with economic exchange, it may well be useful to distinguish the "regional population" as a subunit within the power system; this, of course, is a matter of research strategy, for the general model I am suggesting must be left open to allow for focusing interest on other operating units as research aims demand.

Members of a power system need not reside contiguously with the unit being focused upon in research. Thus, to understand a Guatemalan village it is necessary to recognize power relations that relate it to various governmental offices, market places, stores, kinsmen, etc., who operate at varying distances, and some of whom never have occasion to come directly to the village. The general problem is no different with an urban population that may serve as a focus for research: a ghetto, a street-corner group, an executive office, a governmental bureau, etc., are all subject to varieties of external relations that provide part of the human relational system within which they operate. It should be explicit here that I am using "power system" in a broad sense to include not only the "political" and social relations, but also the economic and genetic relations, after the fashion of Rappaport.

3. *The ecosystem* as defined by Rappaport for anthropological usage is a "system of material exchanges among the populations of the several species and non-living substances occurring within a demarcated area."[39] In this matter I must not only expand or extend Rappaport's concept of the ecosystem, but must also so stretch it that it may offend the more traditional field of ecology.

It is very convenient to deal with a given pond, ocean shore, or rain forest as a somewhat closed "ecosystem" and to handle the things beyond this as merely input sources. Of course, there are limits on the utility of the model when the inputs badly damage

[39] Rappaport 1969, p. 184.

what might otherwise be an orderly steady state. This concept of the ecosystem can stand, *providing there is no feedback* to the sources of the input, such that subsequent inputs are changed as a result. A crucial aspect of the ecosystem is that it includes within it all those zones between which there is *exchange*, but none which experience only a one-way movement (i.e., either input or output, but not both). Thus we usually do not think of the sun as being part of the forest ecosystem, but rather as the source of an input to it.

There are at least two ways that this varies from the emphasis taken by the ecologists who have been responsible for the development of the ecosystem concept. First, they have tended to be much looser with respect to just what the boundaries of a system may be, that is, to be arbitrary as to the boundaries. In this they surely have the right of precedence and practice on their side. In doing empirical work, to insist on complete differentiation on the input-output basis could be both difficult and in many cases not of great significance. However, I propose this as an ideal type and obviously do not pretend that empirical work will necessarily find such a strict usage always necessary. Second, and perhaps more important theoretically, the ecologists tend to use as a cardinal criterion for an ecosystem its stability, its achievement of a steady state, the presence of homeostasis.[40] The presence of a steady state, or of a relatively low frequency of fluctuation, has an appeal that evidently has served the ecologists well. Obviously there is no virtue in taking issue with the utility of the ecologists' model. But, if we look again at Figure 8, it will be obvious that in dealing with the human species we are dealing with systems that may be in expanding states for extended periods; during this time, there is a regular input and output, and it seems to me that it is wiser to emphasize the existence of exchange rather than the question of relative equivalency of exchange. One of the characteristics of human occupation has been the fact that most societies have been ignorant of whether they were exploiting a mature or an immature ecosystem, that is, whether they were interrupting an expanding ecosystem or draining the energy resources from a mature, steady-state system. I believe the difference is important in dealing with

[40] Margalef 1968, pp. 11–12.

human society because the human species itself has been a con-
tinuingly expanding system; it has never achieved a steady state
as a whole, although there have probably been periods during
which human subsystems have maintained a homeostasis.

I suspect that one reason that the notion of equivalency of exchange has proved attractive may have less to do with its research
utility than with a continuing preoccupation in western studies
with the question of equilibrium. A system in a steady state is
not, technically, an equilibrium system, since the latter is one that
exchanges neither matter nor energy with its environment. Myron
Tribus and Edward C. McIrvine have indicated, however, that
such equilibrium systems really are in a sense out of equilibrium
with their own environment.[41] That is, the course of the environment is to follow the Second Law; equilibrium systems seem to
be temporary hangups[42] in the course of this process. The fact that
steady states give the illusion of being equilibrium states, that they
allow a subtle continuation of the habit of seeing the human species
and human societies in an organismic analogy, I suspect may have
something to do with the apparent value placed on such systems.
Of course, there is a much more important reason, which will be
discussed later: if the human species and its cultures do not achieve
some kind of steady state, there are a good many reasons to suspect
that we will not have to worry at all.

Whereas Rappaport chooses to find the ecosystem within a
"demarcated area" but leaves this area undefined, I would define
it as the area within which energy-complex feedback affects subsequent activity. It can be seen that the "natural" ecosystem seen
in this light will exclude, besides the sun, the upstream of the river
that pours water into it and any other input that continues un-
affected by the output events within the system. This proposes that
an ecosystem is a system composed of subsystems related by exchange of elements of the energy complex, when exchange is
defined as comprising *both* input and output.

It will be obvious that the power system as defined earlier is one
within which there is feedback. Moreover, it may well include
feedback from beyond the borders of what is traditionally re-

[41] Tribus and McIrvine 1971, p. 125.
[42] Dyson 1971, p. 20.

garded as the ecosystem. Consider the pond. So long as events are no cause for extraecosystem interest, then it remains comfortably isolated. But what happens if a conservationist happens on the pond and finds drainage from some nearby oil wells, and this input is changing the ecology of the ecosystem? If he does nothing about it, then we could argue merely that the input has changed, and with it the ecosystem. But, if our conservationist stops the oil input and, indeed, removes the oil from the pond, then I would argue that he has become part of the ecosystem of that pond; and, if the pond is then placed as a conservation sanctuary, such that no new inputs will occur without feedback to the conservation head-quarters, there triggering action to do something about them, then, by any logic, the headquarters are part of the ecosystem.[43]

However, there is an important exchange difference between eco-systems and power systems. While power systems receive inputs from larger ecosystems, they are themselves ultimately finite within those larger systems. While man may manipulate lesser eco-systems, the fact cannot be avoided that he, along with his par-ticular power system, ultimately must be seen to lie well within a maximal ecosystem, the biosphere. For this reason, the power system and the ecosystem are not, in the ultimate case, two separate intersecting systems, such as are Rappaport's ecosystem and regional system, but are hierarchically arranged. I hasten to add, however, that, in the case of a particular research focus operating unit, it may well be the case that the particular interest will turn on a lesser ecosystem that has been particularly caught within a larger power system. However, the researcher should never forget that every power system resides in a larger ecosystem, whereas the reverse is not the case, and that human energetic inputs into an ecosystem are but a part of the total inputs.

4. *The universe* is the source of external energy input, princi-pally solar radiation, the major input to our system; and therein is found entropy, the major output. The structure of the universe is not of immediate methodological importance to the understand-ing of the lesser ecosystems and power systems of this world, but we have to pose two phases of it to make the system work: the ultimate energy source is gravitational collapse, whereas the output

[43] Odum 1971, pp. 58–60.

of our system is sheer entropy.[44] Here, one might wish to insert
an intervening system, the biosphere, and I would argue that that
is perfectly acceptable.

Figure 9 suggests the major energy-complex flow relations between the various kinds of systems here discussed. In it is suggested
another characteristic that is relevant to the understanding of these
systems. All of our systems (universe, ecosystem, power system,
and focal operating unit) are scenes of energy conversion, that is, the
conversion of energy to entropy. Flow between systems, however,
tends to be either through mass or energetic transduction (radiation, etc.). The process also involves a predominant movement of
energy from the larger to the smaller system until it finally becomes lost to entropy, reflecting the Second Law of Thermodynamics.

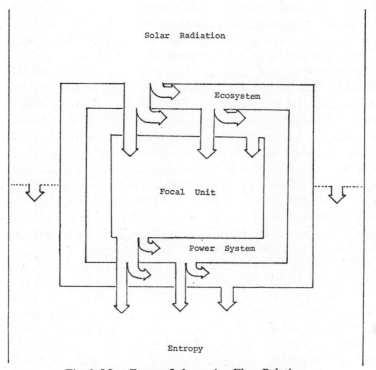

Fig. 9. Mass-Energy-Information Flow Relations

[44] Dyson 1971.

A crucial question now arises concerning the output from the focal unit. In sheer energetic terms, the focal unit receives more from other systems than it returns in usable form to them. In fact, most output of the focal unit is not to these other systems, but to entropy. The many things thought to flow in a social system, such as messages, energy devoted to labor, etc., are in energetic terms lost to entropy and are not actually transduced into another segment of the ecosystem or power system. This energy, however, is not merely lost to entropy. For what it often does is to take advantage of energy stored in the terrestrial system and trigger its release, thus liberating considerably more than itself.

## D. Human Society: An Expanding System

Let us return to the main theme, the energetics of human society. It should be noted that to use energy as our principal variable in no sense denies that the various forms that energy takes (i.e., various kinds of minerals, nutrients, organic substances, gases, etc.) have differential significance for man. We are claiming not that man somehow "lives by energy alone" but that all environmental elements that man uses or produces are, themselves, forms of energy and that this makes it possible to use energy as a variable for helping to understand the human condition.

Consider, for purposes of the present discussion, the human species, not in any of its several parts, but as a particular set of energy forms. Man as a form of energy, his behaviors, his control of stock, and the energy conversions in which he is involved constitute an independent variable. The dependent variables are certain facets of social organization, most specifically the pattern of evolution of the power structure.

Man himself is an energy form in several capacities. First, he is an energy converter. He incorporates (or "captures," as Leslie White says) energy forms in his biological system (oxygen, nutrients, etc.) and converts them into degraded forms and waste heat. He further incorporates wide varieties of elements, compounds, and organisms into his cultural system and similarly degrades them. In the process, man and his cultural system convert these energy inputs into what we shall be distinguishing as *products* (i.e., an output of energy conversion defined as being useful in man's cultural order), *waste* (i.e., an output of an energy conversion defined as useless to the cultural order), and *entropy*, the low-grade, waste heat that is the finality of the system.

Upon being conceived, man begins a life cycle wherein he is first an expanding energy-conversion system (i.e., has a greater input of energy than output). Over most of his adult life he acts as a steady-state system (i.e., a varying equilibrium system wherein the input and output are equivalent over a period of time). In his declining years, he becomes a declining system (i.e., one wherein input is less than output). Schrödinger is possibly poetic, but certainly not referring to man, when he refers to death as "the dangerous state of maximum entropy." What happens at death is, obviously, not that man is converted to entropy, for the corpse remains in a continuing degraded state. Rather, man has ceased to be an energy converter. He may still be of some use (depending upon the order projected by the particular culture) for an eye bank, for ornaments on a medical student's bookshelves, or for making lampshades.

As an energy converter, man elaborates extrasomatic devices to aid his adaptation to a degree unknown in other existing species. These elaborations form part of what is usually termed his "culture," and the specific complexes of tools, skills, knowledge, and behaviors that are used in the adaptation to and manipulation of energy are his "technology." The culture-building process is costly in energy; and the cost is an index of the level of advancement the culture has reached.

Besides being an energy converter, man is also collectively treated as a large existent stock of a particular kind. Social distance and masses of people make man appear more like stock. However, it needs to be emphasized that the notion of stock is somewhat metaphorical, since it is man the energy converter that composes it, not necessarily man in storage. But when we are considering the species as a whole, demographically, it is possible to conceive of man in this light, since the mere mass and its differential distribution are of considerable importance.

The distinction between man-as-converter and man-as-stock often appears in the context of man-the-actor being contrasted with man as a collectivity acted upon. In dealing with operating units, we differentiate a particular aspect of relations (i.e., power) dependent upon the different controls that individuals exercise over the energy forms around them; in this we are dealing with man the converter.

Figure 10 schematically analyzes the processes by which man converts energy into culture (as separate from converting energy into human biomass). All elements of the environment that come within the human technological system pass through phases of this process, moving from pristine environmental form to one form of stock or another and mostly ending in entropy and waste. The diagram is not intended to show the entire ecology of the process, and it omits the auxiliary energy inputs to production. It also does not try to indicate the complexity of the interdependent phases in the process of manufacture (Georgescu-Roegen's copper sheet is only a way station in this long process). By virtue of extraction the elements are placed under control and undergo a sequence of alterations between conversion (when they undergo extraction, manufacture, or consumption, i.e., are processed through usable forms by man) and stock (when they are stored and transported). In each stage of manufacture we are dealing with a different product. Finally, however, the product is offered up for the most important conversion process, consumption. Here man takes

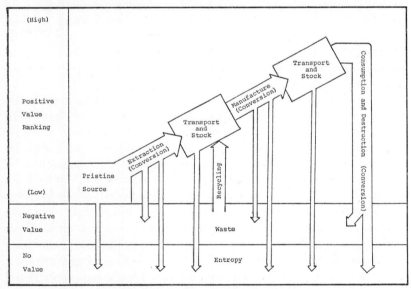

Fig. 10. Energy Flow and Value Ranking

and destroys or casts it away by eating it, shooting it off, wearing it out, or occasionally, with durable objects of stone and the like, just calling it a monument and leaving it there. Monuments are pretty high-class stock. At every turn in the system there is loss of part of the original energy input to waste and entropy. Some of this waste, of course, re-enters the system for recycling (indicated by the arrow going from "waste" to "stock"). Also, there is an "energy cost" in support of the technologies at work (refrigeration, light, heating), many of them extremely costly in energy usage. The manufacturing processes themselves, of course, use great amounts, but so do many consumption events, such as great fiestas, potlatches, crusades, wars, etc. Every cultural event has an energy cost component.

We are concerned here with the energy input in production, in the processes of manufacturing and extraction, and with how these processes relate to the structure of power. From the point of view of energy conversion and the energy cost of production, everything that happens to a product prior to the instant when it is consumed can be regarded as part of the production process. The multiple activities of what economists and demographers call the "third sector," or the "service sector," are that range of institutional and individual efforts that surround the modern production process. The goods and paper work involved before the automobile is dumped in the heap or the coffee is drunk are expenditures of energy, losses of energy to waste and entropy, which are dedicated to the preparing of something for consumption.

The central function of consumption and destruction was well expressed by the ecologist Alfred Emerson, who noted that death is an adaptive phenomenon. For a species or population as a whole to continue to adapt, there must be output as well as input. In making this observation, Emerson was seeing a population as a stock of converters, requiring constant recruitment and elimination of members. Similarly, consumption is the necessary destruction and devaluation of the nonhuman energy forms that man has brought within his system to promote his own survival. Both capitalistic and Marxist economists have emphasized production, the input phase of the process. The underplaying of consumption has left half the picture unexamined and surely has contributed to the rapid onset of the population and energy crises.

If we recognize that consumption, destruction of stock, is as important as production to human life, then it follows that the basis of power lies not merely in control over the means of production, but in the *total set of conversion processes,* including consumption and destruction. Jack Goody, in his examination of military technology in Africa, observed that the "various political systems are correlated not so much with differences in the ownership of the means of production (nor yet in the objects of production themselves) but rather in the ownership of the means of destruction and in the nature of those means."[45] He was, of course, specifically referring to the technology of war and destruction of human stock as well as cultural stock. Today this has become painfully evident, not merely through the inability to adequately distribute products, but through the accumulation of nonbiodegenerable waste in the human-environmental system. Since production in advanced societies has never been gauged to its inevitable output in waste and entropy, we now increasingly face the problem of how to cope when the crisis may well be past a point of convenient return.

The relative attention paid to different energetic activities at various points in this continuum varies from one society to another, but all societies obviously have to handle these energy processes. The classic Hindus seem to have used this chain as the basis for ranking their social strata, through giving specific rank to occupations related to different points of the process, but principally in accord with the degree of involvement with energy forms and processes (see Fig. 11). At the bottom of the system were those who were not even ranked, the outcastes, who had to do with waste materials, human and animal, and dirt in general. Next higher

[45] Goody 1971, pp. 42–43. Reprinted from *Technology, Tradition and the State in Africa* (New York and London: Oxford University Press) by permission of the International African Institute. It has been Marxists probably more than Marx who have not allowed sufficient importance to the control over the means of destruction and of consumption. Marx clearly recognized that consumption was part of the production process in a number of ways. Production is simultaneously consumption, just as consumption requires production. Also, production creates the need for consumption; and, finally, consumption completes the act of production. Followers of Marx have, however, tended to focus on production modes and means rather than the broader conversion process. See Marx 1971, pp. 22–28.

Energetic System

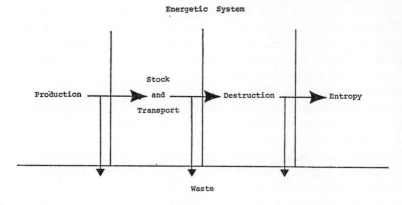

Caste System

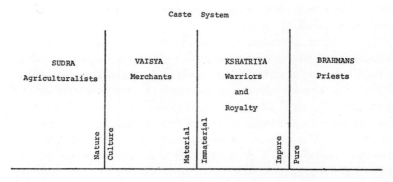

Fig. 11. Modified Classic Hindu Caste Rankings according to Position in the Energetic Process. Louis Dumont (1970, pp. 67–68) deals with the successive dichotomization; Harold A. Gould (1971) gives bases for caste characterization. Bases for binary distinctions are my guesses, based on various literature and the role of energy processes. Dumont (1970, p. 68) identifies the Vaisya as "farmer" and the Sudra as "unfree servant."

were those who actually accomplished conversion through production, the Sudras; production was agricultural labor and obviously involved constant expenditure of energy and contact with natural resources and material things. Next higher were the members of the merchant caste, Vaisyas, who handled the products, the stock. Next were those who did not traffic in materials but held power authority through control of force: the Kshatriyas were the royal and warrior caste. At the top were the Brahmans, who had achieved a state of purity, of freedom from life processes, and lived on allocated power alone; they, too, had nothing to do with the material processes.[46] If one observes the ranking here, it can be seen to reveal a set of binary differentiations concerning the processes of energy: (*a*) the ranked are separated from the unranked in terms of the castes being opposed to the outcastes; (*b*) the Brahmans, the highest caste, are opposed to all other castes on the basis of purity/impurity; (*c*) the lower two castes are opposed to the upper two castes on the basis of dealing with the material versus dealing with the immaterial; (*d*) the top three castes are opposed to the Sudra on the basis of dealing with cultural things versus natural resources. This kind of structural analysis can be pursued, but my purpose here is merely to illustrate how energy processes seem to give a pattern to the criteria for the social ranking system in one society.

The core of the energetic problem confronting humanity today is expansion, both cultural and biological. It is the already apparent consequences of an unchecked growth that have brought the whole subject of energy to public notice; the implications for social science have yet to be widely realized. A good case may be made that every major problem facing mankind today is either directly or indirectly a consequence of this expansion. And, to confuse matters, many social-science theories have been formulated around consequences of expansion, but are naïve with regard to this fundamental dynamic.[47]

It has already been noted that the human species has two semi-independent aspects of expansion, that of the biological stock, the

[46] I should hasten to note that Indian caste rankings vary greatly, and I use here a simplistic system described for 650 A.D. by a visiting Chinese Buddhist. The structural analysis given here is entirely tentative and would have to be pursued and checked out against other variants of the system before any serious claims to structure could be made. These materials are from Gould 1971, esp. p. 3.

[47] See Daly, ed. 1973 for one of a wide set of papers and books that have appeared recently on the question of energy in contemporary life. The major contribution of the social sciences is posited, hopefully, for the future; to date,

human biomass, and that of the cultural stock of materials and symbols. The population expansion obviously varies with cultural factors, but it must be assumed that it is only by maintaining a rate of reproduction slightly beyond the probable death rate that even a steady state can be assured. In general we must assume that the human stock will increase at some exponential rate unless cultural or environmental limitations are imposed.

Growth of the cultural stock, however, obviously is a different problem. Culture consists of a continuing conjunction of two facets, energy and meaning, or "matter and mind." The energy component clearly expands; whether they are durable forms such as carved granite, or constituents extracted from the environment, processed and consumed, or transitory sound waves or bodily movements, we are dealing with things that can be quantified, measured, and compared. What distinguishes them as cultural, however, is not their energetic quality or quantification, but the meanings and values that have been arbitrarily assigned to them. It is this conjunction of value and meaning with a particular type of energy form that constitutes culture. The problem in applying the concept of "growth" or "expansion" to cultural stock is that, while it is appropriate to the energetic aspect, it is by no means relevant to the psychological behavioral aspect. This is illustrated by a problem that came up in anthropology with respect to the notion of "complex cultures" a few years ago. Certain scholars insisted that Australian aboriginal society had a "complex culture" because the meanings attached to and the structure of the kin relations were rather intricate. At the same period the term *complex societies* was coming into vogue as a way of referring to societies with a very high energy content, societies with an industrial base.

---

they have been thrown into turmoil by the fact that much of the theorizing of the previous forty years was within an equilibrium-seeking model. The "functionalism" of British social anthropology and North American sociology began to lose its luster in the 1950's, when a contrast was found with the so-called "conflict theories," such as those of Marx. This view of events, however, misses the more central issues. It is a question neither of functionalism nor of conflict, but rather of the expanding nature of the systems about which these theories have been built and the fact that neither set of theories was entirely gauged to the more basic questions of the nature of the energy processes of the systems they described.

We cannot treat quantitative culture growth and expansion in mentalistic structural terms but must treat it in whatever measurable or quantifiable aspects of culture we can deal with, that is, energy forms or processes. However, even here we cannot fully escape the structural side, for the differentiation of form, the very distinction between one form and another, is patterned by mentalistic aspects of culture. But, while the discrimination of "things" is based on cultural criteria, their quantification must be based on the energy forms that are thereby segregated.

With our focus on the amount of environment under control, it may be useful to specify some major kinds of energy forms that are of particular importance in the use of power. Toward this end, I would propose the following set of dependencies:

1. The nature of any particular kind of *natural resource* will permit only certain kinds of *technological applications*. (One cannot have a fuel technology in the absence of fuel. This is not to deny the ingenuity of man, but simply to remind us that there are physical limits beyond which a given technology will not work.)

2. In any given environment (with some given set of natural resources) the amount of *economic production* possible will be limited by the *technology* at hand. This is not to deny that other technology may be devised, or that other resources may be imported, but to argue that there is a limit beyond which a given technology cannot get more out of a given environment.

3. The amount of *production* within any social system sets limits on the *total population* that may survive within that system. This is not to deny that there are often ways to increase production and that other circumstances, such as wars or revolutions, may also reduce populations, but merely to insist that production sets limits on population.

4. The size of a *population* sets limits on the number of *operating units* that can be expected to operate within a given environment. This is not to deny the limitless ingenuity of man's capacity to invent new kinds of interests, but it reflects the facts that operating units have to do with adaptation and that a population of a given size will be capable only of some finite set of adaptive behaviors.

All of these factors (natural resources, technology, production, population, operating units) refer to energy forms and flows, identifiable by attendant ideas, behaviors, and contingent arti-

factual materials. In any society, the elements to be found in each
are themselves potentially subject to control and thereby serve as
bases of power. Power, in a social system, increases with the expansion of control over any of these phenomena.[48]

Some of the dependencies proposed are, I believe, generally accepted. Certainly those between natural resources, technology, and
production seem hardly contestable. That between production and
population growth is supported by a number of kinds of studies. In
general Malthusian terms, the major checks on population growth
have classically been hunger and disease, and the second is frequently produced by the first.[49] Another kind of data comes from
contemporary demographic studies that generally show correlation
between increases in income and decreases in mortality and increases in fertility.[50] In the absence of either immigration or emi-
gration, mortality and fertility are the two principal factors that
collectively produce an increase in population.

There seems to be little question that the first two major revolutions in man's control over his environment, the agricultural and
the industrial, brought in their wake significant increases in the
rate of population increase. Prior to the agricultural revolution, the
average rate of world population increase was 5 people per year;
from then until 1650, a date that can be used for the beginnings
of the Industrial Revolution, the average was 625 people per year.
From 1650 until 1960, the average annual growth of populations
was 7 million, and, for the period from 1960 to 2000, it is estimated
that an average of 90 million people a year will be added to the
world's population. "In the long run," concludes Marvin Harris,
"production has determined reproduction."[51]

The final set of elements in our chain of dependencies is that

[48] Bierstedt suggested that "Power would seem to stem from three sources:
(1) numbers of people, (2) social organization, and (3) resources" (1950, pp.
730–738). Interpreting Bierstedt narrowly, his three items would correspond
to population, operating units, and natural resources. The remaining elements,
technology and production, clearly are suggested by Marx's notion of "means
of production."

[49] Thompson 1956, p. 976.

[50] Spengler 1959, p. 812.

[51] Data cited by Harris (1971, p. 223) from Deevey 1960. See also Polgar
1972, pp. 204–205. The distinction between the two "revolutions" was originally,
of course, introduced by Childe, in 1936.

which holds that social organization, here specified in terms of operating units, expands and becomes more complicated by virtue of a growth in population. It will be recalled that earlier in the essay I made an ideal type distinction of what would occur should either population or nonhuman sources of control increase without the other (see Fig. 6). As I emphasized then, neither of these cases is really possible within the range of macroscopic growth. What in fact happens is that, as populations grow, they both expand their social organizational forms *and* increase the quantity of nonhuman energy forms that they bring under control.

The best demonstration of the first of these points is to be found in a cross-cultural study by Michael J. Harner. Harner worked with a sample of 1,170 societies and found impressive evidence that the development of chiefdoms and states clearly follows upon, that is, comes after, the expansion of population. Harner specifically proposed that the mechanism that accounts for this is the relation between population and resources. As population expands the pressure on resources becomes greater, and it is specifically the result of the scarcity of resources that leads to changes in the social organization. Harner proposes this in order that it contrast "with existing theories based upon concepts of surplus or simple energy growth, which have consistently failed to explain, in terms of a single process, evolution in" descent, political organization, and class stratification.[52]

Harner notes in comparison that his position "differs from Marxism in emphasizing the importance of scarcity in the means of production. Scarcity (demand exceeding supply) is essential if the means of production is to provide a base for social power through its ownership or control. Thus, the major material means of production in a society actually will not be the base of social power if there exists a plentiful supply of it beyond demand." "Essentially . . . the control or ownership of scarce and, therefore, valued means of production is the source of social power."[53]

From the standpoint of the present paper, however, it is necessary to return to dependencies that Harner does not take into

[52] Harner 1970; quote is from pp. 84–85. Reprinted by permission of the author and *Journal of Anthropological Research* (formerly *Southwestern Journal of Anthropology*).

[53] Ibid., pp. 70–71.

explicit account, namely, the relation between production and technology. In a volume that has had considerable impact on anthropological thinking in these problems, Esther Boserup proposed that not only does population pressure account for development, but specifically it accounts for the improvement or advance in technology in agricultural societies.[54] Boserup's argument is that population pressure on agriculturalists results in improvements in technology, specifically, the gradual reduction of the length of time land lies fallow, and that results in greater production. The increased production, in turn, allows further population expansion, thus keeping the process going.

It must be interjected here that both the Boserup and Harner positions depend (as does the present paper) on the assumption that natural selection may well have eliminated populations that failed to increase production or change their social organization. What is being said, in effect, is that, no matter what the motivations may have been, those who failed to see the threat to their survival and to take the necessary steps to readapt their systems simply are either not now around to be counted, or opted for one of a number of alternatives that were less developmental but that permitted them to survive.

It is also useful to introduce a further line of thought that complements Harner's concern with social organizational expansion. Robert Carneiro argues that the increased complexity of social organization (in his case he is concerned specifically with the emergence of the "state") does not have the same results in all environments.[55] If, for the sake of exposition, we contrast environments that are open for further population expansion with those that for some reason circumscribe the population, then the alternatives are different. When populations can expand over open lands without opposition, they will tend to do so. However, they may be circumscribed by the fact that the natural environment is inhospitable to their technological and other abilities, in which case they will be "environmentally circumscribed"; or they may be located along with other societies in an area of particularly rich "resource

---

54 Boserup 1965; Spooner, ed. 1972.
55 Carneiro 1970, pp. 733–738.

concentration" for their given technology, and thereby see moving as being profoundly disadvantageous. In the second instance, as their population and/or the population of neighboring groups grow, they will become "socially circumscribed."[56]

Carneiro's argument then suggests that, where resources are especially attractive over those of alternative areas, the response of populations is to come into competition, then probably conflict, with other groups experiencing parallel problems, and that this leads to allocating (to use our terminology) more power to a headman, and to offensive and defensive alliances. This means that such groups would concentrate or centralize power, and that they would seek coordinate action with other groups where this would be to their advantage.

It is not possible here to pursue this set of arguments further. There remain some important questions, however, to which we should at least allude before moving to other aspects of the evolutionary problem. The set of arguments outlined above has been concerned with agrarian societies and, most specifically in anthropology, with such societies of the preindustrial period. I believe it is possible to apply the same kind of argument, that is, that population pressure accounts both for the adoption of improved technology and for societal growth, to societies of the industrial and of the so-called postindustrial period.

Given the specific form of the elements of the argument, such an answer would not be inevitable. However, if we look to the structure of the argument, I believe it is possible to see that it does, in fact, have relevance to the later eras. Couched in its starkest form, the argument says that *when, for whatever reason, those who make decisions for a society are deprived of necessary resources, they will attempt to improve their control by increasing the energy in the system, by strengthening their social organization, or both.* The things that make industrial societies different from preindustrial societies lie in a change, not in this basic pattern, but in the nature of the elements that operate in it. Most specifically, "who makes the decisions for a society" changes, as does what comprises "necessary resources," the inherent nature of

[56] Carneiro credits Napoleon Chagnon with suggesting this term.

the controls, and the manner in which the social organization may be strengthened.

In complex societies with multiple levels of articulation, then, the decision-makers are those who rule, and what they perceive as being necessary resources will not necessarily be the same as that perceived by others lower down in the society. What appeared necessary to Hitler did not appear so to all Germans; nor did what appeared to be necessary to President Nixon seem equally important to all North Americans. Also, what is needed to keep a contemporary nation going is so extensive and varied that no one can be aware of its entirety. Similarly, a "scarcity" has to be perceived years in advance if it is to be avoided, and population pressure becomes highly relative to the specific means of transport and market conditions that influence the distribution of goods. Also, technological advance is considerably more complicated than merely shortening the period that the land is left fallow. When a technology depends upon a long chain of sequential processes, however, and when innovation may take years of experimentation and theorizing, it is not necessarily possible to come up with solutions that can be directly applied. While the concentration of people makes it more likely that innovations will be conceived, their applications may be much more time-consuming.

Finally, in industrial societies the notion of strengthening the society involves such things as military build-ups and "thought control" as well as mere centralization and unification. But the fundamental issues are the same, even though the manifestations become highly intricate. The logistics of the application of controls and the manipulation of power become ever more entangled. In short, human society today still survives on the basis of control over the environment, but the elements involved in the process are more complex.

There is more to the process of survival through natural selection, for it is clear that some societies are continually more successful, whereas others seem less so. This is particularly evident in more advanced societies, where technological differences are more evident, or where a constant aggressivity is evident. Two or more societies in confrontation over limited resources may resolve their conflict in one of two ways: one may become superior to the other, in which case the second is absorbed, destroyed, or in some manner subordinated; or they may find themselves to be approximately equal and remain at a stand-off. If technology is still simple, this stand-off will be manifested by periodic intensifications, encounters, oscillations between conflict and cooperation. But through the evolution of human society the ability to systematically develop technology and to intentionally incorporate other societies as a means to strengthen the position of one's own society has steadily increased. Where societies at a stand-off engage in this we have what I have called "structural escalation," the process whereby survival with respect to other societies is seen to depend upon one's ability to expand one's control over the environment. Survival, a maximal value in most surviving societies, is linked to expansion of energy control.[57]

In the mid-twentieth century, structural escalation was evident in the precept or dogma of development. Early in the Industrial Revolution it was possible to distinguish developmental societies from nondevelopmental societies—that is, societies that were becoming hooked on expanding their control over the environment, from those that had not taken up the habit. In the middle of the twentieth century one's political philosophy made little difference, since development had become the opiate of the world's governments. Concepts about development vary from place to place; in the high-energy societies, population expansion is increasingly being seen as a threat rather than as an asset to survival, but cultural expansion is still in fairly high repute. The claim that the purpose of development has been to "better peoples' ways of life" should not obscure the fact that this is only one view of its purpose; that is not all that it does. Since many of the problems in the "ways of life" that need "bettering" are due to an earlier developmental philosophy, mercantile and industrial structural escalation, it rings

[57] While I earlier proposed this term (1970a, p. 89), Benjamin J. Cohen has more recently arrived at the same conclusion. He argues that imperialism is due to the fact that the relation between states or national sovereignties is anarchic and competitive; and, consequently, internal domination is a logical concomitant of that situation. Cohen refers to this anarchic state of affairs as a "defect," but it is clear both that it is quite orderly and necessary and that it cannot be otherwise. See Cohen 1973, p. 245.

untrue to claim that development is being done as a favor to the energy-poor peoples of the earth. In fact, it is the high-energy nations that promote the developmental dogma, because it is they who are converting most of the energy and think that it is necessary for survival at their level of cultural expenditure. Lower-energy nations favor it for the same reason, but with less fervor.

In short, early in humanity's career man adapted, through a variety of different cultures, to almost all the environments the world has offered. Over this vast geographical area and through slow climatological changes, different technologies evolved. The increasing control afforded by these developments had a number of effects. For one, the species as a whole became more secure, since a local catastrophe or technological failure did not mean that other adaptations would suffer a like fate. By the same token, what was significant for one population became insignificant for others; the species' security thrived on cultural differentiation. Another consequence of differential technology was increased control. Both stock and conversion devices variegated and expanded. Each increment of growth in this sphere of energy forms and processes meant a new basis of power; and each increment in the exercise of power meant that the social organization had, in a sense, to expand to contain the new influences. However, this expansion has been occurring at a continuing and increasing energy cost. For the low-energy-level societies, the cost continues low. As the number of people increases, the effects on the environment become more marked. As technology advanced, the environment began to suffer permanent and irreversible changes. Agriculture led to the clearing of forests and grasslands, to erosion and climatological change; industry has led to the spoilation of subsurface minerals and the pollution of the total environment with indisposable and toxic wastes. Every increase in extraction of energy increased the cost, both in the energy spent on the conversion and in the energy lost as the raw materials found their way to final consumption and waste.

The cosmos has been not reversed but rather continues moving irreversibly converting low entropy to high; and, on earth, the process is the same, with man as a part of this process, not a separate agent to it. Increasing population and improved technology are entropy-hastening processes. It is, as Georgescu-Roegen remarked, "as if the human species were determined to have a short but exciting life."[58]

It may be argued that over the course of much of man's existence he could not have been aware of the effects, particularly the long-term effects, of his habitational process. But most cultures at all levels have shown considerable knowledge, or a sense of disaster, about the environment about them, and many have instituted and often ritualized dogmas that promote conservation measures. It is possible that industrial man knows more, but very likely our increased knowledge is a function of the amount of damage we are doing. Indeed, if there has been lack of sensibility to man's effect on the environment, it is in the latter days of advanced and rapidly progressing civilizations. Advanced production technology has proceeded with little attention to the problem of destruction; the input process from the environment has far overshadowed concern with the output or the limits of resources. It may well be, as C. S. Lewis observed, that "Man's conquest of nature turns out in the moment of its consummation, to be Nature's conquest of Man."[59]

## 8. THE MENTALISTIC

### A. Binary Distinctions and Levels

Of the many issues that distinguish "natural" and "social" sciences, certainly one of the most central has been the use of mentalistic variables. There is no doubt that their gradual elimina-

[58] Georgescu-Roegen 1973, p. 47. A more extensive discussion of the increasing energy cost of production will be found in section 8D.

[59] Lewis 1973, p. 327. Rapoport, in discussing speculation about Maxwell's demon, remarks that the demon had to create entropy in order to do his job, and thereby eventually disposed of himself. "This, in turn, leads to speculations concerning similar processes in all 'organizing' activities, the perfection of technology, accumulation of scientific knowledge, etc. Are we becoming 'de-

tion from physics and biology was the mark of the paradoxical success of mind over matter. In the social sciences, however, they not only remain but in many areas continue central to an entire apparatus. Power, especially in the analysis of empirical cases, requires that we treat the subject of "values," for it is precisely in this area that the human species has differentiated itself into different societies that treat with the world in profoundly different ways.

Of all the areas to which social science has dedicated itself, values must be the most foggy and imprecise. Whereas many other areas of psychology and sociology have advanced impressively in recent decades, our understanding of values remains fundamentally little better than it was years ago. In the present section, I will look at values from a standpoint that I believe is at least coherent and useful to the present theory of power and control. I do not propose it as "the approach" to the subject. Rather, I think it is a better crutch for the present exercise than some others and one that may help until such time as values can be consigned to the museums of the intellect that house other and earlier trappings of vitalism. The basis of the argument rests on structuralism. It begins with the central notion of binary differentiations; it argues that this provides the basis for ranking and that ranking, for practical purposes, can handle most of what we mean by *value*.

In the discussion of operating units, the shift from a gross or mass aggregate to a unit of some coherence was first signaled by a process that was simply called identification, the recognition that there was some collectivity that was a "we" and that it was somehow differentiated from something else called a "they." Identification consists of the decision by some actors that they are in some manner more similar among themselves than they are with respect to some set of others and that, by contrast, the others are in some manner dissimilar.

To speak of dissimilarities or differences places us squarely within the mentalistic structural realm. We must assume that the world about us is made up of things that vary in similitude and, further, that our powers of observation are not entirely misleading

---

natured' to the extent that we 'order' the world to suit our needs?" (Rapoport 1968, p. 138).

in telling us that two horses are more alike than are a horse and a ladder. But we also have good indications that where we draw the line between similarity and dissimilarity depends greatly on our own experience and that it is always a *relative* boundary. So, irrespective of what the real world may be like, the distinctions we draw must accord with our own mentalistic structures. Bateson has pointed out that this dualism to which we have recourse is probably "based on the contrast in coding and transmission inside and outside the body." In dealing with this internal world, that of "communication, organization, etc., you leave behind that whole world in which effects are brought about by forces and impacts and energy exchange. You enter a world in which 'effects'—and I am not sure one should still use the same word—are brought about by *differences.* . . . I suggest to you, now, that the word 'idea' in its most elementary sense, is synonymous with 'difference.' "[60]

Also, in its simplest form, "difference" is merely that; it says nothing about the basis, the form, or the related meanings. The identification of similarity as against dissimilarity (the basis of Durkheim's mechanical solidarity) reveals a binary differentiation, the mechanism that is fundamental to Lévi-Strauss's structural analyses (and, indeed, the entire resurgence of structural studies in recent years) and can be seen in the operation of all cultures, whether simple or complex. It is probably not extreme to suggest that the basis of binary differentiation in human culture rests first on this inside-outside distinction, the segregation of the *me* and something else; and, as Lévi-Strauss has indicated, we then proceed to make further distinctions, indefinitely.

In understanding binary differentiation, it is important that it not be confused with its manifestation when combined with another evaluation. To differentiate is one thing; the criterion on which differentiation is based is another. I do not know whether the mere fact of identification, that is, of making a binary differentiation, may be said to imply the immediate bestowal of something we may want to call value; and I am not sure that it really makes any difference. Once the differentiation we make is submitted for codification in culture, it must find its place in the existing mentalistic structures. However, it may be the case that a differentiation

[60] Bateson 1972, pp. 454, 452–453.

is made on the basis of some criterion that already has evaluative or ranking priorities implicit in it. To single out persons because of their sex is one thing; to do so because they are particularly repulsive or attractive representatives of the sex is something else. But differentiation may occur without such a clear-cut evaluation, such as that made by a busy cashier among the individuals who line up to pay through her window. But the same cashier will begin to recognize some loyal customers in terms of how they act toward her and find preferences for some over others.

Binary differentiations may become fixed for various reasons, but one way to perpetuate them is by labeling. Out of the cognitive framework of the actor, the object being differentiated receives attention because of some of its features; and, usually, the application of a label will have some associative relation to that feature. However, labels can be flagrantly misleading, and differentiation may occur without the individual being able readily to clarify and formulate a label appropriate to the criterion lying behind the differentiation.

Culture is thus constructed through successive binary differentiations. Lévi-Strauss's own vision of this process projects it as being the core of culture building, and he describes the cultural reconstruction of a group of Australian aborigines who were herded together in a camp:

So, although the social organization is reduced to chaos by the new conditions of life imposed on the natives and the lay and religious pressures to which they have been subjected, the theoretical attitude continues to flourish. When it is no longer possible to retain the traditional interpretations, others are worked out which, like the first, are inspired by motivations (in Saussure's sense) and by schemes. Social structures previously simply juxtaposed in space are made to correspond at the same time as the animal and plant classifications of each tribe. According to their tribal origin, the informants conceived the dual scheme on the model of opposition or resemblance, and they formalized it in terms of kinship (father and son) or directions (east and west) or elements (land and sea, water and fire, air and land), or again in terms of the differences or resemblances between natural species. They took these various procedures into account also and sought to formulate rules of equivalence. If the process of deterioration were halted, there is no doubt that this syncretism could serve as the starting point of a new society, for working out an entire system with all its aspects adjusted.[61]

While there can be discussion as to whether the I/other, inside/outside dichotomy is fundamental to all further binary distinctions in some generic sense, it cannot be doubted that it is of continuing fundamental importance. It applies not merely to an individual but to every identity operating unit that comes into existence by virtue of its application and to every new energetic form or process that comes within the realm of a social relation. So the fact that many categories and labels may be used does not reduce the daily binary decision-making activity required of each individual, no matter what the energy level of his society or the amount of power he may have.

Binary differentiations are, of course, combined, recombined, replicated, further subdivided, cross-correlated, and generally subjected to continuing further binary processes. One such case was suggested by the caste-system classification given in Figure 11. Louis Dumont, in arguing his fundamental analysis of the caste system, found he had to begin with this binary differentiation and simply pose the further elaboration of the same process.[62] Students of this aspect of mental activity have for some time reported that there seems to be a limitation on the number of taxonomic dimensions that the human mind can comfortably handle within a social-communication context. The number has been proposed as lying around six[63] or seven.[64] Among the most recent illustrations of this is a study of folk taxonomies by Brent Berlin, Dennis E. Breedlove, and Peter H. Raven that presents a convincing case that "There are at least five, perhaps six, taxonomic ethnobiological categories which appear to be highly general if not universal in folk biological

[61] Claude Lévi-Strauss 1966, pp. 158–159. Reprinted from *The Savage Mind*, © 1962 by Librarie Plon, 8, rue Garancière, Paris–6ᵉ; English translation © 1966 by George Weidenfeld and Nicolson Ltd., by permission of the University of Chicago Press and George Weidenfeld and Nicolson Ltd.

[62] Dumont 1970, pp. 56 ff.

[63] Wallace 1970, p. 82.

[64] G. Miller 1956.

science . . . The five ethnobiological categories are arranged hierarchically and taxa assigned to each rank are mutually exclusive."[65]

The most significant alternative suggestion to the six- or seven-
level phenomenon is one based on an observation by Lévi-Strauss
that the "figure of two thousand appears to correspond well, in
order of magnitude, to a sort of threshold corresponding roughly
to the capacity of memory and power of definition of ethnozoologies
or ethnobotanies reliant on oral tradition."[66] Ira R. Buchler and
Henry A. Selby have shown that the approximate figure of 2,047
would be the number of items, classes, or terminal taxa that would
be found in a taxonomy composed of eleven levels with systematic
binary partitioning.[67] It is not possible to pursue the question of
specific numbers here, but it does lead us to an important set of
issues with respect to our understanding of levels of social organization.

In the first part of this work I argued for a distinction between
levels of articulation and levels of integration, using the first term
to refer to the levels that may empirically be found in the course
of interactions in a society and the second to refer to the classification of levels that a society was likely to utilize in describing its
own organization. The number of levels that we may expect to

[65] Berlin, Breedlove, and Raven 1973, p. 240. Reprinted from *American Anthropologist*, vol. 75, no. 1. There are ample cases cited by Wallace (1970) and
G. Miller (1956) of the ubiquitousness of these numbers. In the present context, it is perhaps of interest to observe that J. G. Miller's general work on living
systems suggests "seven levels of living systems . . . but I do not argue that
there are exactly these seven, no more and no less" (1965, p. 213).

[66] Lévi-Strauss 1966, p. 154.

[67] Buchler and Selby 1968, pp. 305–309. A further suggestive outcome of
their analysis shows that, if one systematically pursues binary partitioning of
classes from the first through the eleventh level (where there remains only 1
of the 2,047 original taxa), the number of deleted taxa at level seven is 32, at
level eight it is 16, and at level nine it is 8. These figures of 8, 16, and 32
correspond closely with the breaking points observed by Piaget and his colleagues in the learning and developing behavior of children. "P. Greco has
shown that the construction of natural numbers only occurs according to what
we might call a progressive arithmetization, the stages of which would be approximately characterized by the numbers 1–7; 8–15; 16–30; etc. Beyond these
limits, progress beyond which is rather slow, numbers still involve only inclusive aspects (classes) or serial ones so long as the synthesis of these two
characteristics remains outstanding" (Piaget 1972, p. 42).

find in folk or oral tradition systems has been argued to be on the order of five or six. I believe that this figure serves effectively for human societies, no matter what their level of complexity or their degree of literacy. In the next section, dealing with the evolution of power systems, I find it convenient to use approximately seven levels of integration. James G. Miller has observed that "six banners in one of the halls of the United Nations Palais des Nations in Geneva depict six levels of social organization. They say: Family, Village, Clan, Medieval State, Nation, and Federation."[68] While this approximate coincidence means that I am not very original, it also means that I am probably also quite human in my mental structural potential. Perhaps the telling argument that levels of integration are determined by the nature of our minds, rather than the number of events in the external world, may be seen in examining what happens in the lower-energy societies. If six or seven levels is the number reached by our civilization, we should expect that, if the numbers were going to be determined by the amount of energy, simpler societies would have fewer. This, how-

TABLE 1

Levels of Operating Units in Kapauku Papuan Society

| Reported Operating Units | Kinship Levels | Political/Legal Levels |
|---|---|---|
| Phratry | Phratry | |
| Sib | Sib | |
| Subsib | Subsib (moiety) | |
| Confederation | | Confederation |
| Lineage | Lineage | Lineage |
| Sublineage | Sublineage | Sublineage |
| Village | | Village |
| Household | | Household |
| Polygynous family | Polygynous family | Polygynous family |
| Nuclear family | Nuclear family | |

SOURCE. Based on Pospisil 1958*a.* The differentiation follows indications in Pospisil 1963*a* and *b.*

[68] J. G. Miller 1965, p. 213, n. 16.

ever, does not seem to happen, as can be illustrated with some
examples, which will, incidentally, serve to bring up some other
issues of importance as well.

Leopold Pospisil's description of Kapauku Papuan political and
kinship organization reveals the presence of two overlapping but
separate hierarchies or levels. Table 1 shows ten types of operating
units reported by Pospisil. There are, additionally, political factions
that form around the Big Man and include a range of client-
supporters who congregate irrespective of their kin relationship to
the Big Man. These may occur within any of the political segments:
confederacy, lineage, sublineage, or village.[69] While Pospisil clearly
differentiates the relative importance of the various units and their
differential functions, the separation into two sets is mine, and, to
the degree that it misreads his report, the fault is mine. While there
is only one political head-of-family, in the kinship area he is responsible for two possible levels of families.

In the Koṅku region of Madras State, India, Brenda E. F. Beck
describes a case in which the two systems have become much more
differentiated but still retain an important residual identification
(Table 2). In the Indian example the nationally defined and imposed levels of the nation and the state stand above the local levels
as seen locally. It seems likely that the same must now be true
if one were to attach the imposed districts of the national administ-
istration on top of the Kapauku system.

Finally, to compare these two cases with a technologically complex, high-energy society, let us look at the system of levels in the
United States (Table 3). In the United States there are many
variations, depending on whether the neighborhood is a viable
political unit and whether one thinks more in the town-county-
state system, or more as an urban resident. But, again, the issue
is less that there are precisely six such levels than that the system
includes around six. Also, of course, the number of kinship levels
in the United States has atrophied, and there is no correspondence
whatsoever between the two hierarchies beyond the family level.

There are a number of points to be made with respect to these

[69] See Pospisil 1958b, p. 82; 1963a, p. 41. Since the factions may occur anywhere, I have omitted them from Figure 13. They do permit an increase in
political levels from time to time. Also, Pospisil devotes almost no attention to
them in the sources consulted (see also 1958a, 1963b).

TABLE 2

Political and Kinship Levels in Koṅku

| Political Levels | Kinship Levels |
|---|---|
| (India) | |
| (Madras State) | |
| Koṅku (*NāTu,* political region) | Caste |
| *nāTu* (administrative and ceremonial region) . . . . . . . . . | Subcaste (*jāti*) |
| *kirāmam* (revenue village) . . . . . . | Clan (inherited common name; exogamous) |
| *Ūr* (hamlets—about 400 people) | Lineage |
| *ur* (particular settlement) | |
| *kuTumpam* (household unit) . . . . | Family |

SOURCE. Based on Beck 1972, pp. 2–4. The levels connected by dots are said by Beck to correspond to each other: "Subcastes are often associated with subregional or nāTu territories, and clans are often linked to a kirāmam area" (p. 4).

TABLE 3

Political and Kinship Levels in the United States

| Political Levels | Kinship Levels |
|---|---|
| United States (nation) | |
| State | |
| County/city | |
| Town/section of city | Distant relatives |
| Neighborhood | Near relatives |
| Family unit . . . . . . . . . . . . . . . . . . . . . . . . . . . . . . | Family unit |

examples. The first concerns what happens to the systems of levels as the societies become more complex; or, to put it more correctly, what the nature of the complexity process is when seen through what happens to levels. In the Kapauku Papuan system the political levels are marked by the fact that each has a headman, who is responsible for solving disputes that occur among the units that exist within his scope of authority. Thus, these are clearly levels of articulation composed of *consensus* units. However, they differ from levels of articulation where headmen have been able to get additional independent power, such as some Big Men may achieve, as is the case in any chiefdom or more advanced system. Here, the levels are entirely based on allocated power. As a consequence, there can be little real delegation of authority from the higher levels to the lower levels, because headmen at the higher levels do not have any more power than is allocated to them. Given this, they really have little to delegate back beyond that which they have been given—by the very people to whom they would delegate.

The kinship levels are levels of articulation composed of co-ordinated units, in that they have no authority or points of confrontation. Rather, they act more as circles of social distance, in the sense that Sahlins attempted to define exchange relations.[70]

In comparing the Kapauku Papuan with the Koṅku region and United States systems, it is possible to see why kinship separates out as the systems become more complex. Kinship units are fundamentally coordinated units. If it becomes necessary to exercise external power functions, they do so first through internally allocated power and, presumably, later through other kinds of power exercise. But, as power continues to enter the system, there is a problem as to whether the units should centralize in order to be able to exercise power themselves, or give up the power roles, remain as coordinate units, and serve other functions. Pospisil makes explicit that the phratry, sib, and subsib are not politically organized and essentially are without political function. They are especially important in marriage and religious matters and also are relevant to matters of inheritance, although secondarily, since most men will have sons or brothers as possible heirs.[71] In the Koṅku case the two systems are differentiated such that three of the five political levels have retained a kind of identification, but the subcaste/*nāTu* and the clan/*kirāmam* correspondences are not functional in the way that the lineages and sublineages are among the Kapauku Papuans. In the United States system there is no correspondence whatsoever

---

[70] Sahlins 1965. Pospisil (1963*b*, p. 33) sets forth three broad categories of serial distances used by one Kapauku; the *imee bagee* consist of twenty-three categories of relatives; the *ojaa bagee* may include anyone of interest, friend or stranger; the *jape bagee* include all those of traditionally hostile confederacies.

[71] Pospisil 1958*a*, p. 16.

between the two systems above the family level, and even the family has little legal importance except in the few states where communal property laws still hold.

In very general terms, the differentiation of the system, such that kinship increasingly plays a lesser role in affairs of the society as societies become more complex, seems unquestionably related to the nature of reciprocity systems. When power begins concentrating in the system, kinship units must either centralize or be replaced by other units that can centralize. Thus, confederations and political factions are already displacing the sibs among the Kapauku Papuans. In general it appears that some of both things happen, but the ultimate displacement of kinship is due to its inability to keep the qualities of both types of systems.[72]

Incidentally, this fits with what we know of the use of kinship organization as a power device in more complex societies. Whether it is a question of the rationalized incest of the Pharaohs and the Incas, or the royal intermarriage of European royalty, or the family interlinking holdings of the Du Ponts and the Rockefellers, in each case we have devices for coordinate organizations to retain power in systems where it is expected that there will exist pretenders for their controls.

This displacement of the kin system has, of course, been observed by everyone. Behind the immediate reasons just suggested, however, there is a more profound structural process at work. We will have occasion to observe in the evolution of power systems that the centralizing process must use different basic social relations than are used in coordinating processes or were used in prior centralizing. This gives the impression that emerging new relations displace or marginalize those that were of principal importance earlier. Since kin relations provided the earliest societies with their principal relational idiom, it seems inevitable that they will be unable to serve that purpose when new levels of integration emerge.

The problem of whether levels of integration are products of the human mind or are indicative of differentiation in a power system really is no problem at all. They are, in fact, both. In

---

[72] Godelier expresses what I believe are fairly parallel notions but has them too well wrapped in productive forces and productive relations for me to be sure. (See Godelier 1972, pp. 95–96.)

analyzing a sector of United States society from top to bottom, we find many separate sectors with encapsulated sets of articulation levels, either formed by administrative fiat or having emerged within some semiprotected niche in the system. Obviously the United States is not limited to six levels of power relations. But the collective historical authorities of the United States have found it convenient not to multiply the number of administrative political levels; rather, new interior domains are established, within which the necessary additional levels may be constructed. Thus, within the state or the federal government, there are many bureaus and agencies, each with its own system of levels. To integrate the entire system, however, we find that we stick with about six levels; and, for this reason, I find it convenient to retain the original usage proposed by Julian Steward—"levels of integration"—for the over-all system, and apply "levels of articulation" to the empirically discovered levels of power differential within any part of the system under study.

Among the things that become clear when dealing with levels, whether taxonomic of operating units and people or of other classes of events, is the very strong tendency to rank those that occur more or less within the same level. This notion is a help in the matter of values. While few satisfactory conventions have emerged with respect to quantification of meaning, it has long been customary to speak of quantity of value: e.g., "to have great value," "to increase value," "surplus value," etc. I would argue that such a usage is fundamentally metaphorical and that it has helped obscure a more naturalistic approach to the whole question of meaning and value. The general idea of value is premised on the notion of ranking; and, as a consequence, it has been possible to speak of values that are ranked higher as being "greater" or having "more value." Further consideration of this, however, will suggest that value, like meaning, cannot be quantified. Ranking is not a device that necessarily orders objects in terms of their quantity. Rather, it is an ordering that may be based on any criterion whatsoever. When we rank the beauty of women or the quality of food and use the expression "more," we are speaking metaphorically; there is no quantification, in an energetic sense, involved. This is hardly a new observation and has long been implicit in the insistence on cultural relativism; but it becomes especially important when we conjoin energy forms with meaning and seek to clarify their relationships.

The problem of quantification in meaning in some sense is a false problem. Unless one is referring to quantification of energy forms to which the meanings are attached, there can be no quantification: it is clear that, to introduce value, meaning, or mentalistic structure into the discussion, they must be phrased as unique features or characteristics of specific societies or operating units. No cross-cultural comparison, not to speak of measurement, of mentalistic structures is possible without taking some existing structure as a point of departure. One can either argue (after Lévi-Strauss) that the structure of myth is the same for *all* primitive humanity or argue that there are structures in myth that are necessarily unique to a given operating unit or individual. But, whichever way it goes, one has to start somewhere, with some body of cultural material, some distinctions already made with meanings already assigned. However it may be done, any quantitative statement that does not refer to energy forms can be immediately and incontestably contradicted by anyone with different definitions and arbitrary meanings. Lévi-Strauss may prove to be immortal, but not because anyone could ever prove him to be right or wrong.

## B. *The Nature of Ranking*

Returning now to the question of creating value, we can propose that: *given a universe of multiple elements that are in some manner regarded as equivalents*, it then follows, as inevitably as the recurrence of binary differentiation itself, that *the pieces will be ranked with respect to each other*. The anthropological literature (particularly since the rise of modern structuralism) is loaded with illustrations of this.

Irrespective of how we might choose to formulate the ranking process in mentalistic terms, it is important to see it as a sociological process with mentalistic structural concomitants. Ranking is carried on with respect to a universe of energy objects or processes that have been defined as being equivalent by some typology or taxonomy. Such a universe may be all automobiles, or all General Motors automobiles, or all Cadillacs, or all Cadillacs of 1972 model, etc. In considering this universe, the observer may be content to leave it as an undifferentiated whole; but usually

not, if he has time or curiosity. He will instead begin to differentiate, and with the differentiation he will find some reasons to
prefer some over others, and he will end up with a ranking. The
formulation of a taxonomy or a classification does not have value
implicit in it, but *the very establishment of the ranking implicitly
sets up an order of priorities*. Once we have established a priority
for things, then we have also implicitly introduced the process of
maximization, the process whereby the individual, when given
alternatives, seeks that which lies higher in his hierarchy of ranked
preferences or avoids that which is very low.

This process of (*a*) binary differentiation, (*b*) taxonomy making
and classification, and (*c*) ranking with the implicit bestowal of
priority is not some random, unorganized activity, unrelated to
the question of power and control. It is, rather, a mentalistic structural concomitant of overt control. What the individual does, both
on his own and collectively in coordination with others, is to create
in his mind a picture of the world, a picture that appears to him to
"make sense." Once having this "sense" in his head, he then tries
to assume that the world is, in fact, constructed as his mental
model says it is. Once again let me quote Mary Douglas's observation: "In chasing dirt, in papering, decorating, tidying, we are not
governed by anxiety to escape disease, but are positively reorder-
ing our environment, making it conform to an idea."[73] Ranking,
then, is an attempt to arrange events in the external world so that
they will behave as our mental limitations dictate and will reflect our ability to handle them. It becomes a way to put order in
the environment, to imbue things with a positive or negative value
that permits them to be maximized, minimized, or optimized.

Given the importance of ranking as an activity common to all
human beings (and presumably to all nonhumans that have to
make decisions about adaptation to the environment), it is unfortunate that one of the most influential recent works (in English)
dealing with the evolution of power structures presents ranking as
something that is of no real consequence for the most primitive of
people and only becomes of importance when man has already
achieved control of agriculture.

A major thesis of Morton Fried's work on political evolution is

[73] Douglas 1970*a*, p. 12.

that early human societies were egalitarian and that ranking appeared with what we might think of as tribal societies or chiefdoms. "Ranking," says Fried, "exists when there are fewer positions of valued status than persons capable of filling them . . . Rank has no necessary connection with economic status in any of its forms, though it frequently does acquire economic significance."[74] The emphasis on the independence of ranking from the economic order is important for Fried because he identifies the next major change in society, the appearance of social stratification, wholly on economic grounds: "Stratification . . . is a system by which the adult members of a society enjoy differential right of access to basic resources."[75]

This delineation and the related definitions are unfortunate. There is a major problem connected with Fried's use of "ranking," and it spills over somewhat into his treatment of "stratification." While it is useful to identify what Fried has called a "ranked society" as one in which ranking occurs somewhat after the manner in which he has described it, it is misleading to define social *ranking as such* in this manner. Ranking is a process whereby the elements of some universe are ordered such that they vary consistently along some arbitrary dimension. In the sense of ordering things, ranking obviously did not await the appearance of the neolithic; it was already present in subhuman societies.[76] The thrust

[74] Fried 1967, p. 52.

[75] Ibid.

[76] Irwin Bernstein reported in a specific study of this issue that, for 22,000 scored interactions among seven groups of monkeys, "Inspection of data for agonistic episodes reveals that 'dominance orders' existed and were stable in all groups except the green monkeys." (Bernstein 1970, p. 89. Reprinted from "Primate Status Hierarchies," *Primate Behavior*, vol. 1, by permission of Academic Press and Dr. Bernstein.) M. R. A. Chance, in a review article on primate rank order, argues that dominance does not rest solely on behavioral attributes in aggression or competition but also involves a question of *focus of attention* on certain animals: ". . . the attention-binding effect of an animal in a group is essentially the quality that puts it in a behaviorally focal position, and which also tends to place it near the group's spacial center." (Chance 1967, p. 509. Reprinted from *Man*, vol. 2, no. 4, published by the Royal Anthropological Institute.) Chance reports that common to all the literature he reviewed was "persistent centripetal attention by subordinate members of a rank order toward more dominant members or toward a supremely dominant individual" (ibid.). The emphasis on "focus of attention" gives the impression that there is good

of Fried's argument is not that all kinds of ranking were absent but that societies were not employing ranking as a significant device in the early stages. In claiming this, however, Fried places the student of comparative societies in the difficult position of trying to explain what man was doing sociologically all those years before he developed agriculture. The fact of the matter is that he was, among other things, ranking people.

Ranking is obviously not applied only to binary differentiations, such as to distinguish the king from all the rest. When applied to human society it is much more widely used as a coordinating device. Through daily and yearly experience there are times that someone must be first, someone else second, etc., simply because the nature of the situation precludes everyone acting simultaneously. Ranking is the device used to determine who shall act in what order. When a group of people agree on ranking, they are not necessarily permanently stigmatizing an individual with some inferior or superior status (although they may be). More commonly they are saying, "given this situation, the following ranking will be used." R. Lauriston Sharp, for example, describes the social organization of the aboriginal Australian Yir Yoront as comprising twenty-eight roles for each individual, half of which he or she employs with people of the same sex, and half with those of the other sex. "The nature of the fourteen masculine roles which are played by every Yir Yoront man means that every individual relationship between males involves a definite and accepted inferiority or superiority. A man has no dealing with another man (or with women, either) on exactly equal terms. And where each is at the same time in relative weak positions and in an equal number of relatively strong positions, no one can be either absolutely strong or absolutely weak."[77] What Sharp describes is a coordinate set of relationships, and Yir Yoront society would, on the basis of it, have to be described as a purely coordinate unit. But, even in this minimal sense, rank is an important part of the picture. It is also con-

---

reason to think that the rest of the primates are employing a basic structuralism in their behavior just as we do—that we come by it honestly.

[77] Sharp 1958, pp. 4–5. Reprinted from *Systems of Political Control and Bureaucracy in Human Societies*, Proceedings of the 1958 Annual Spring Meeting, by permission of the American Ethnological Society.

sequential that we recognize that it is there, not merely because it shows that rank does operate in extremely primitive societies but also because *the ranking of objects involves inherently making a judgment and inherently bestowing value.* The value may be nothing more than saying that whoever goes at the head of the line ought to be one who knows where the line is going. Those who are reluctant to recognize ranking in these "egalitarian" societies are faced with a difficult question: where do values come from, if they are not inherent in ranking?

Fried's definition of ranked society has a more serious difficulty, however. I think it is impossible to classify any society as non-ranked, given his definition. Again to the Yir Yoront: "Yir Yoront cannot even tolerate mild chiefs or headmen, while a leader with absolute authority over the whole group would be unthinkable."[78] Well and good; this sounds like Fried's nonranked, egalitarian society. Sharp then poses the question as to how technological operations get carried out and answers it by posing an illustration wherein a young man who has no immediate consanguineal relatives to whom he may turn can suggest to those who are subordinates in the ranking system that they invite others to help him in the task at hand. This clearly is a differentiation, and there is some ranking.[79] While it appears that there may be only one, or at best a few, of these per family, is it correct to say that this man, who has met the qualifications, is the *only person capable of making that suggestion?* He is probably the only one, or one of the few, that people will listen to, but surely there are others who would also be capable of doing it. If this is so, then the Yir Yoront would have to be regarded as a ranked society by Fried's definition. As we look further into Sharp's description, however, it becomes clear that there are a number of such ranked positions which are in fact occupied by only one person each, but for which it is hard to argue that the actual position holders are the only ones capable of achieving the position. Not only are there shamans, but also Sharp makes it quite explicit that "heads of families" do have clear-cut authority over others through their roles as fathers, husbands, or senior males over the lineage mates who are younger than they. He notes

[78] Ibid.
[79] Ibid., p. 6.

that the heads of the families "acknowledge no higher political authority."[80] So, besides the ranking inherent in kinship, a head of the family is ranked over all other members; in some extended families there surely must be a number of men who would be capable of handling the job.

In a more general sense, this has not gone unrecognized by other scholars: "Power is strengthened by the accentuation of inequalities, which are its precondition, just as it is the precondition of their maintenance. Thus the example of 'primitive' societies that might be called egalitarian shows both the generality of the fact and its most attenuated form. Positions of superiority and inferiority are established according to sex, age, genealogical situation, specialization and personal qualities."[81]

The literature on ranking quite naturally pays specific attention to the hierarchical aspect of the systems involved. I believe it is of considerable importance that ranking be appreciated within the perspective of the system within which it operates; in this capacity, it acts as a coordinating device, establishing reciprocal relations within the larger set. One reason that this aspect has been somewhat underplayed is that some ranking systems achieve extreme differences between grades or ranks, and it is a little hard to stretch the notion of equivalence or reciprocity under these circumstances. The problem here is in the confusion of an ideal, ideological, or symbol system with an energetic system. There is no question but that the pay of a senior captain in the army will be vastly greater than that of a new recruit and that the captain has an extraordinary amount of power over the recruit. This we would readily recognize as a clear case of a power-domain relationship. However, between the captain and a lieutenant the difference is by no means as great, and in many things they will work essentially as equivalents—that is, they are both members of a single generally recognized set. The ideological aspect of this is the grouping of these ranks together as a part of a set of lower-echelon officers. The rank difference helps to coordinate their activities and under restricted circumstances gives one power over another. But the nearness of their ranks leads this to be a mark of *relative equivalence*

---

[80] Ibid., p. 7.
[81] Georges Balandier 1970, pp. 37–38.

when they are compared with noncommissioned officers or with generals.

Ranking then serves to give stability to relationships and to set up rules for clear-cut distinctions between the elements within some specific set. In this respect, then, we would expect to find the phenomenon of ranking to be akin in structure to that of levels of integration, also a mentalistic product. What rank does is to take a limited set of categories, which constitute some universe, and establish priorities among them. This has caused some confusion in understanding social stratification in somewhat advanced societies. The arguments of Louis Dumont in this regard are most instructive, particularly when reinterpreted within the framework of the present theory. For purposes of the discussion to follow, the reader may wish again to refer to Figure 11.

Dumont takes issue with many Indianist scholars who identify the caste ranking as originating in power inequalities, a position he illustrates with a quotation from F. G. Bailey: ". . . the ranking system of caste-groups was validated by differential control over the productive resources of the village."[82] Dumont holds that the ranking of the castes is a matter of ritual status, of ideology, not power. He points out that to insist on the power basis in examining empirical cases of caste in India "leaves a residuum which is not reducible to the clear and supposedly basic notions of power and wealth. This unresolved duality . . . hangs like a millstone round the neck of contemporary literature."[83] Power, in the sense of "legitimate force," does not characterize Brahmans and so can hardly be called upon to account for their position at the top of the system.

I believe that, by re-examining the argument in the light of the concept of power being used here, Dumont and the "materialists" whom he takes to task may both be shown to have certain reason on their side. Dumont thinks of power solely in the sense of the use of force. If we recognize, however, that allocated power continues to be of major importance in all systems and that what has been

[82] F. G. Bailey, *Caste and the Economic Frontier* (Manchester: Manchester University Press, 1957), pp. 266–267, cited in Dumont 1970, p. 76.

[83] Louis Dumont 1970, p. 75. Reprinted from *Homo Hierarchicus: An Essay on the Caste System,* © 1966 by Editions Gallimard; English translation © 1970 by George Weidenfeld and Nicolson, Ltd., and by the University of Chicago, by permission of the University of Chicago Press.

called "religious" specifically refers to situations where the collective allocated power of a population is expressed in a sacred ideological idiom, then it can be seen that the situation is not that the Kshatriyas (the warriors and royalty) have power and the Brahmans (priests) have no power, but rather that the Kshatriyas have independent power of arms, whereas the Brahmans have the allocated power of the religion. Thus the higher ranking of Brahman over Kshatriya in the Indian caste system does not pose a question of whether "power" (in the sense of force) or "ritual" (in the sense of status ranking) is more important in explaining the system, but rather indicates that both operate conjunctively, but independently, within the framework of the total power structure. Because Dumont's concern is with the system of ranking, he sees power (qua force) as being subordinated to a ritual system based ultimately on the purity-impurity contrast. It appears to me that the ritual subordination merely reflects the fact that until recently the need for allocated power was clearly as important for social integration within the society as a whole as the kind of energy controls available to the political rulers. In other words, allocated power was necessary because direct energy controls were not enough. One test of this may, perhaps, be seen in observing what is happening to the ritual ranking under the emerging controls available in an industrializing India, where the allocated power is being directed away from the religious idiom to the political, and the kind of force available to political rulers is considerably greater than in the precolonial period. The result is a severe series of changes in the caste system. Even in the colonial period, with the first elements of industrialism emerging, the caste system provided a basis for politico-social stability that was quite advantageous for imperialists.

The importance of this argument may be seen in the fact that the ritual status emphasized by Dumont is a ranking system, or what he prefers to call hierarchy: *"the principle by which the elements of a whole are ranked in relation to the whole."*[84] I prefer the term *ranking* to *hierarchy* because I believe that the latter has other better uses (and it is hard to use as a verb), and I find it hard to think of any ranking that does not implicitly involve "elements of a whole being ranked in relation to the whole." In terms

[84] Ibid., p. 66.

of the present theory, ranking (Dumont's "hierarchy") is in the first instance a characteristic of coordinate sets. But when societies grow large, and when the power of the complex agricultural but preindustrial systems becomes increasingly concentrated in controls over the means of production, then the ranking pattern (i.e., successive binary differentiations) will be applied to larger chunks of society, and it becomes convenient to differentiate the process as social stratification *of some kind*. What seems to confuse thinking in the Indian case, what set Dumont against the "materialists," is that the dichotomy drawn gives the allocated power of Brahmanism a higher ranking than that allowed to independent material power, in much the same way that Allah in Islam might be said to have higher status than a secular ruler in the eyes of believers. If one reflects on any sovereign social entity, however, whether at the band level or the national, it is the ideology that provides the identity to the unit, and it has to be through allocated power that unity continues during peace as well as war. No society of man has ever relied on sheer "powering" for solidarity; rather, "powering" comes into being (*a*) after there is some basis for differentiation of controls and (*b*) when the solidarity of allocated power fragments because of conflicting interests.

One need merely look to the contemporary United States, where much allocated power is given to the government, and examine the confusion present in her people over whether a president should be impeached. When the president claims a mantle of sacredness for his office, as has been the case during the writing of these pages, the people are divided both socially and, within themselves, individually, as to how they should react. Many still have a "religion" for the sacred and have not been willing to accord this to the president. But the church has long been fragmented and subordinated in the United States, and so the question of who gets the allocated power is an unsolved one.

If the reader shrinks at thinking of the difference between the Brahman and the Untouchable as being one of rank rather than power, he should remember that the caste system is a mentalistic set of relatively few elements; and, as Dumont and others have made perfectly clear, it operates only very imperfectly in the real world. Dumont is surely correct in seeing the five categories as ranked; on the other hand, his "materialist" opponents surely are not wrong in observing that those who control more strategic portions of the environment tend to fall into the upper brackets, and those with less, into the lower.

## C. Value Classes

I have been arguing that values do not mystically appear, but arise out of larger ranking processes. An earlier tendency in American anthropology[85] to siphon off values and study them as if they were in some manner independent of the energy forms and processes, and possibly even of the mental structures, which produced them has not been as fruitful as was once its promise. Within the present approach there are two ways of dealing with values that are somewhat in line with the more traditional manner but yet permit us to keep a clear relationship of the value system with operating units and energy forms, acts, and objects. Choices are usually made between specific things and much more rarely from among abstract categories. Yet, when we speak of values, we find that people often include easily within a single range of discourse value both as things and as categories. Thus there is a difference in discussing maximization depending on whether we say (1) that George is trying to get his pay raised or (2) that George is trying to get "wealth." The first is a specific, perhaps month-by-month pay check; the second is an abstract category that may mean rather different things to different people and in the language of different operating units.

It is useful, then, to distinguish *value classes* or categories from *valued objects* and *acts*, or energy forms and processes. "Wealth," "honor," "prestige," and "love" are all categories, into which different people or operating units might classify very different acts or objects. Classes of values are usually ranked too, such that, in some discourse, honor might be held to be a higher value than wealth, or the reverse. Similarly, among acts and objects, a young man might place the manifest affection of a young lady above the privilege of a trip around the world. He has made a ranking, placed the value of one object over that of one act.

Values, like *all* culture traits, exist *only* in a context of sets of social relations, within or among specific operating units. It is to

[85] Kluckhohn 1951; Albert 1956.

be assumed that every informal and formal operating unit, from identity units on, has some system of values, some ranking of priorities, shared by its members or carried as policy by its leaders, that permits it to deal with those aspects of the environment with which it is particularly concerned. An individual actor will have as many value systems as there are operating units within which he participates. It is not the place here to take up the problems of individual conflict that arise from this fact, and they are well recognized in the literature under other rubrics, such as "role conflict." But it is important in our concern with the genesis of values to recognize that the emergence of a new operating unit implicitly demands that some new set of values, of priorities, come into play. It is probably the case that all reasonably well-established operating units are engaged in a kind of value dualism. They try to maximize certain objects, acts, or events and minimize others. And along with this, they offer for these choices rationalizations couched in the idiom of value classes that they rank most highly within the context of the event.

An individual faces a problem that is not common to more complex operating units. Not only must he choose among ranked objects and acts when they may occur in quite different ranking sets; he will also be acting roles in a number of different operating units, and the relative ranking of the units must be allowed for. In making a particular empirical choice, he may find that the choice is between an object valued highly in unit $A$ but rejected in unit $B$, and that he values unit $B$ over unit $A$; and he is in a dilemma.

There may be some kind of master ranking that permits one more readily to make certain choices. Edward Banfield, as a result of work in a southern Italian town, proposed the following "predictive hypothesis" that he felt underlay the conduct of the people he was studying: "Maximize the material, short-run advantage of the nuclear family; assume that all others will do likewise."[86] I have found this to be useful as a model for setting up similar propositions for other operating units. Its structure requires that you identify the principal operating unit in your hierarchy of

[86] Edward Banfield 1958, p. 85. Reprinted from *The Moral Basis of a Backward Society*, Copyright 1958 by The Free Press, a corporation, by permission of Macmillan Publishing Co.

units and that you identify the principal value class in the hierarchy of that unit. And it finally provides you with a guide as to the value maximization of other units in your environment.

Maurice Godelier suggests a formulation similar in certain respects to what I am recommending here. He argues that there are "structures," such as "kinship," "political relations," "religious relations," which collectively comprise the structure of the society and simultaneously set the value hierarchies.

. . . the dominant role played by a given structure means that there is a hierarchy of structures in a society, and this hierarchy, it seems to me, is the basis of the hierarchy of *"values"* i.e., *the norms of prescribed behavior*, and, through this hierarchy of values, the basis of the hierarchy of needs of individuals and groups. In order to explain the rationality of the economic behavior of individuals, it is not sufficient to know the hierarchy of their needs and explain the social structures in accordance with this.

On the contrary, one has to start from structures, the relationship between them and their precise roles, if one is to understand the rationality of individuals' behavior . . . Ultimately, by way of the hierarchy of "socially necessary" wants, the hierarchy of structure determines, on the basis of the productive forces of the society, the distribution of social labor among the different kinds of production . . . The intentional rationality of the economic behavior of a society's members is thus always governed by the fundamental, unintentional rationality of the hierarchical structure of social relations that characterizes this society.[87]

Godelier is, essentially, trying to establish that the hierarchy or ranking system of "values" will be founded in a structure and that this structure, in turn, finds its place in a ranking with other structures in accordance with its importance among the "productive forces of the society." If I were allowed to substitute "system of power" for "productive forces of the society" and "operating units" for "structures," then the two formulations would, at least superficially, be fairly similar.

When we speak of values, then, we are referring to a set of mentalistic structural formulations, based in the first instances on suc-

[87] Godelier 1972, pp. 98–99. Reprinted from *Rationality and Irrationality in Economics*, trans. Brian Pearce. Copyright © 1966 by François Masper. Reprinted by permission of Monthly Review Press.

cessive and overlapping binary distinctions, each particular set of which pertains to some particular operating unit (i.e., is shared by its members). That similar or even apparently identical sets may be held by more than one operating unit is of interest to cultural analysis but not to epistemology. With a multiplicity of binary differentiations, we rank sets, categories, or classes of objects and acts (energetic forms and processes) in the external world. Since these ranked sets are numerous, they can be described in terms of taxonomic levels, and a single value ranking may include both value classes of some generality and specific energetic forms. Thus the human being ignores the classic scholarly distinction between the class and the thing. In all cases, however, the particular ranking systems themselves will form part of the equivalencies of meanings pertaining to some operating unit. Moreover, the specific rankings will serve those operating units as part of their adaptive equipment to deal with the external world, to make choices and decisions.

These value rankings are subject to change, specifically of two kinds: (1) those that occur because of the operation of natural selection on those operating units or individuals whose rankings are antithetical to their own survival and (2) adaptive changes that occur when experience provides feedback through information and meaning such that the categories are reranked, reformulated or redefined, discarded, or combined into a new pattern. The processes in the second case are extraordinarily complex and are the subject of much of psychology and social psychology, as well as portions of anthropology, economics, political sciences, and, directly or indirectly, the entire range of biomedical sciences concerned with the operation of the nervous system.

Just as the choice to use mentalistic structures as a subject of analysis is a methodological decision, so the greatest danger in their use stems from methodological carelessness and poor judgment. Generative and transformational linguistics, as well as structural anthropology, have been both exciting and suggestive, once again establishing within these fields the importance of rationalist principles alongside the earlier, more dominant empiricism. But the reassertion of rationalism does not assure that it will be used correctly; just as the use of empiricist methods gives no guarantee that their findings can be asserted to be correct. The greatest benefits in structural analyses (of mentalistic structures) come from the first levels of analysis, those regarded by structuralists to be the most superficial. As the models created trace further transformations into more profound or deeper structures, they become more generalized. This, in itself, is not without purpose; but the models that result are increasingly the product of the analyst's own prior mentalistic framework and less the product of the history of a community in the external world.

A myth extracted from a single Bororo informant and then from a number of his fellow tribesmen permits us to establish elements of structure that derive directly (always recognizing the empirical pitfalls in gathering such data) from individual performance. As these models are compared with those of other Amazonian tribes, we find there are more variations; and we seek regularities; and, in so doing, we are driven to deeper levels of generality, such as classifying contrasting sets as being representative of a "culture-nature" contrast, or a "purity-impurity" contrast, or a "we-they" contrast. When we do this, we move away from the particular demographic-social universe; and, by the same token, we have achieved a level of profundity that becomes methodologically uncertain. For, while it has been possible *to analyze* in this fashion, it does not prepare solid ground for synthesis, that is, a return to specifics. Thus we can reduce an American patriotic fable and a Bororo myth to a common model; but, once done, we have no assurance that the model will help us construct a new myth that will be acceptable to a significant community. A major reason for this synthetic weakness is that mentalistic structures pertain, not only to individual nervous systems, but also to social operating units of one kind or another. The selection and evolution of parts and their particular recombinations and transformations within the social context are directed by factors operating as social variables whose vehicles are human nervous systems. Mentalistic structures held by operating units are social constructs.[88] These constructs are carried out in the context of real societies, confronting real problems of survival and readaptation within a welter of ecological and social factors and forces. The specific conjunction of these forces at any point is, for the participant, seldom predictable, even where he is

[88] Cf. Berger and Luckmann 1967.

familiar with much that has previously occurred in that society and in similar contexts; without some theory of that conjunction, only the most generalized kinds of syntheses can be attempted concerning the outcome.

To pursue the question of synthesis, then, we must be willing to use mentalistic structures wherever they may appear to be useful, and not necessarily in the manner that has been more popular among the structuralists with an inclination toward the genetic, the seeking of more profound models. While we may be able to formulate interesting hypotheses about the ultimate genesis of mentalistic models, man makes decisions on the basis of more immediate and "superficial" structural models; and, indeed, it is probably the case that new models are less the product of hypothetical deeper structural levels than of the immediately preceding similarities and binary contrasts. For, whatever may be the case about the deeper levels of structuralism, it is also the case that man can and does constantly form binary differentiations on the basis of the immediate, including both immediate percepts and concepts. On this basis, he further binarily segments, recombines, and elaborates, achieving products which may at one and the same time be of extraordinarily simple appearance but mask a tortuous history of social and mental construction, both conscious and unconscious.[89] The basic argument here is that for purposes of analysis we must distinguish the mentalistic from the extraindividual energetic (that is, exterior to any particular individual, not exterior to all individuals) and that we must further distinguish the particular social context, that is, the operating unit and its adaptive problems, within which specific mentalistic structures are occurring. This allows us to identify both the ecological and the societal factors that are conjunctive with certain mentalistic phenomena.

Remembering that our mentalistic-energetic distinction was a purely methodological one, we must then recall also that all mentalistic phenomena are also fundamentally energetic in character; they are, after all, part of the individuals who entertain them. They are composed of energetic elements, and the "meaning" they have is merely an individual's way of making conscious and potentially exteriorizing information that is organized with the compo-

[89] Cf. Lévi-Strauss 1966, pp. 66–74; 1972, esp. p. 11.

nents of his nervous system and in accord with the structural composition of that system. Given this fact, then mentalistic structures and their component informational elements are subject to processes of natural selection just as are any other energetic processes, and we can only assume that such selection processes are continually at work internally within the individual, and intrasocially not only within each operating unit but also among operating units in the society. Since all our thoughts are formed by such contrasts and serve to form others, we find ourselves fluctuating between one extreme (or apparent extreme) and another. When things get too noisy, we want quiet; when we work hard, we want to relax; when we eat too much, we stop; and so it goes with everything we do. There is too much, then too little, and we fluctuate. Every operating unit carries out its activities with specific rhythms. The domestic unit is dominated by the twenty-four-hour cycle, the community by the annual round, the North American national political system by the four-year presidential cycle, and so forth. Each of these contains points of extremes on a continuum.

The nature of the relationship between what I am here calling the "mentalistic" and the "energetic" has also received the attention of Lévi-Strauss. In a 1972 paper, he argues that the process of coding of which the mind is capable is essentially coherent with the structure of the rest of the world. "For nature appears more and more made up of structural properties undoubtedly richer although not different in kind from the structural codes into which the nervous system translates them, and from the structural properties elaborated by the understanding in order to go back, as much as it can do so, to the original structures of reality." The value in recognizing this correspondence and interaction for Lévi-Strauss is that it permits him to dispose of the "threat of falling back toward some kind of philosophical dualism."[90]

While sympathizing wholeheartedly with Lévi-Strauss's desire to avoid metaphysics, I confess that I am not convinced that his willingness to identify correspondences between structural processes of the mind (in which he is here including both sensory and cerebral processes) and structural features of the external world may not be premature. Even allowing that he is correct with re-

[90] Lévi-Strauss 1972, p. 22.

spect to the nature of these elemental processes (a matter on which
I am not prepared to opine), the more important aspect of structural analysis lies not so much in these pristine, original phases as
in the application of elementary mentalistic (structural) patterns
to much more complicated external phenomena. The correspondences suggested by Brent Berlin and Paul Kay[91] between the
primitive appearance of white and black as basic color terms and
the sounds /a/ and /p/ are suggestive at this elemental level; but
questions about the dichotomy between nature and culture or communism and anticommunism will be little clarified if one seeks
the kind of ecological structures Lévi-Strauss indicates.

The problem lies not with the immediate argument proposed by
Lévi-Strauss, but rather with its ramifications if once adopted. Essentially he holds that mentalistic structures can construct models
of energetic events because the inherent structure of the mental
process is part of that of the rest of the energetic world. While the
latter part of this is quite acceptable, the proposed cause is problematic. It would lead us to assume that all the constructs of culture
are in some sense a reconstruction of the structure of the real world.
If this were the case, we would hardly need a special science of
culture or an area of study called "structuralism." It is hard to
find an exact analogy for the proposition, but it is a little like arguing that the construction of culture follows the principles of biological inheritance. If that is true, then it is important indeed, and it
would eliminate much of the work of cultural anthropology. But it
is at the very least questionable that the structural properties of
the mind have the capacity of reproducing the model of the atom,
without requiring of the investigator that he embark on a reconstruction of the history of science.

In contrast to Lévi-Strauss's proposal, I would argue that we will
gain more from structural study by looking to the relationship between any structural transformation or model and the immediately
anterior environmental and life situation; if older conditions are to
be found reflected in usages current today, it is because they still
hold a similar or structurally parallel meaning to that present at
their genesis. The purpose, as I earlier suggested, is to seek not the
conditions of pristine genesis but rather the principles of constant

[91] Berlin and Kay 1969, pp. 104–110.

regenesis. Given the fact that binary distinctions are operating constantly and that they are part of the daily grind as well as of evening pleasures, it would be useful to find sets of metavalues to which all or a significant set of our value classes could be referred, a larger categorization to which they pertain or of which they are special cases. It is certainly the case that Lévi-Strauss's nature/culture dichotomy and Mary Douglas's purity/danger contrast provide us with metaclasses in which it is possible to see a great many ethnographic events performing in a systematic and orderly way. Of course, the particular objects and acts so classified may vary greatly, even within a fairly small society. The I/other distinction that is obviously so central to both social psychology and cultural study, as well as to any social organizational analysis, is common to all societies.

Within the present context there is such a distinction, that of control/out-of-control, which seems to act as a metaclass for a great many classes that have been suggested in the ethnographic literature, as well as having been explored in the comparative analyses. I had the occasion in the course of the final days of preparation of this book to review a series of thirty-odd papers concerning the ethnography of power in Oceanic and New World areas.[92] After the question was posed as to whether they conformed to a control/out-of-control classification, it became increasingly evident that the major binary classes that were reported within the context of interest in power did indeed rest on the question of relative control. Value classes, as well as specific things or types of things, were ordered in terms of their relative controllability, their relative accessibility to human manipulation. Among those mentioned were the following (the relatively greater control being indicated by the first mentioned):

| | |
|---|---|
| order | disorder |
| pure | impure |
| natural | supernatural |
| safety | danger |
| human | superhuman |

[92] These papers were presented at the 1974 San Francisco meeting of the American Association for the Advancement of Science and are currently being prepared for publication by Raymond Fogelson and myself.

| predictable | unpredictable |
| familiar | unfamiliar |
| known | unknown |
| clear | ambiguous |
| observance of etiquette | failure to observe etiquette |
| culture | nature |
| central place | periphery |
| responsibility | irresponsibility |
| understandable | incomprehensible |
| social relations | aloneness |
| belief | disbelief |
| rational | irrational |

and so on. The list, while not endless, is certainly limited only by the human imagination and ability to compare. These, it must be remembered, are value classes, and into them are placed various objects and people, as well as specific behaviors. The suppression of women in highland New Guinea societies piles a number of these classes together in order to indicate how completely unpredictable and undependable women are (from the man's standpoint).

It does not require excessive imagination to see the central quality of control in the mental world of man. The notions of threat, scare, and shock are all things that reflect a relative lack of control on the part of the actor. It seems not unlikely that, if we are to reach basic metavalue classes that stand for all mankind, they will necessarily reflect this very focal issue, the issue that is, incidentally, the central concern of social power.

In our current state of ignorance there is no end to the subjects to be explored; I want, however, to bring the discussion of values and mentalistic structures to an end by exploring a few propositions and illustrative attempts that seek regularities between the energetic and the mentalistic.

## D. Some Mentalistic-Energetic Regularities

It should be recognized at the outset that the values of an individual may change in response to energetic factors from within the organism as well as from the environment. I am not going to concern myself in what follows with the first of these. In the context of society as a whole, the operation of the individual human organism in this respect is clearly of secondary significance and, even where critical, is probably quite unpredictable.[93] It is in any case beyond the scope of the present work, which is concerned with the relation between the exterior energetic field and the social units that cope within it.

Consider, then, the proposition that the readiness to change a mentalistic model and its related projections in the external world varies with the previous consistency experienced by the actor with respect to his capacity to exercise control and power. This position essentially holds that the individual's control and power, his adaptive stance at a given point in time, will either reflect some degree of consistency in those matters or will reflect some change. It is the variation in consistency, not necessarily the absolute amount of control, that plays the major role in determining the changes in the mentalistic structures. Consistency is not to be construed as some kind of dead-level constancy; it may be a regular rate of growth, or a regular decline, or a regular oscillation; it may be any kind of consistency that permits prediction of what will come and the adjustment of adaptive behavior to it. If such a regularity should change, then the mentalistic models will change so as to manifest binary differentiations, and in some cases (e.g., the "inversions" discussed below) to create actual contrasts.

What can be said if the power and control situation is subject to irregular but continuing fluctuations? Presumably, the mentalistic elements will reflect this, but the actors may well find a regularity in the very fluctuations that permits a new adaptation with attendant predictive possibilities.

Another factor is the degree of rapidity of the control or power change that may occur or confront an individual or unit. When it is abrupt, this will be reflected in a sharp and overt change in the

[93] I am persuaded by the arguments of G. Lowell Field and John Higley, who hold that "The behavior of influential persons is not merely at present poorly understood and unpredictable; their behavior always contains enough elements of arbitrariness, capriciousness, or mere lack of obvious explanation to render it permanently outside precisely predictive theory." (Field and Higley 1973, p. 3. Reprinted from *Elites and Non-Elites: The Possibilities and Their Side Effects* by permission of MSS Module Publications.) Their position certainly holds for a theory of the kind being presented in the present effort; I would be inclined, however, to think that a theory of this capriciousness might be possible but would be a separate task.

projection of values. In effect, values can change as fast as does the system of power and control. Here again, however, the more general classes of values will show less change, and the more specific classes will change more precipitously.

Changes of this kind have recently become known as "symbolic inversions" and can be illustrated by consequences of the 1954 United States Supreme Court decision concerning racial integration of schools.[94] In the years that immediately followed, the expression "Black is beautiful" was increasingly heard, in contrast to the dominant value associations of the white-dominated and white-oriented United States society; it reflected both the fact that the black population had been delegated power from the federal government and the fact that they could use it on the local level to achieve better schooling; and it also reflected the possibility that this slight increase might lead to a further increase if they were to make a serious effort to get it. One of the major ways that intentional changes are thrust onto a society (whether ultimately successful or not) is by insisting on a self-fulfilling prophecy. This is not too distantly related to the "big lie" as practiced by the Nazi dictatorship under its propaganda minister, Goebbels, or to the notion that the role of science in the study of society is to "make history," not merely to study it. In any case, such a change is an inversion of the earlier symbol ranking. In Figure 12 it will be seen as having changed the power sign of the government toward the blacks; with this change in power, which provided them with some delegated power, they then reversed the signs of their relative appreciation of things black and things white.

Upon reflection, it will be seen that what I have just described is little different from the contrasting ranking given to certain critical symbols, or "diacritics" (to follow Fredrik Barth's usage), that mark the boundaries between two societies or operating units that are concerned to retain their own individualistic identification. Some college students in the United States use something, often an animal, as a symbol for their university, and it contrasts with those used by other competing universities. A student will rank his particular symbol above those of all other universities. Since this

[94] *Brown* v. *Topeka Board of Education*. This aspect of symbolic inversions is explored at greater length in my forthcoming article, "Power Correlates of Changes in Symbols."

Time 1:   Before   Supreme   Court   Ruling

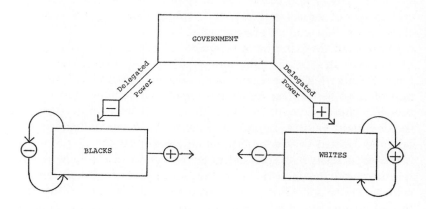

Time 2:   After   Supreme   Court   Ruling

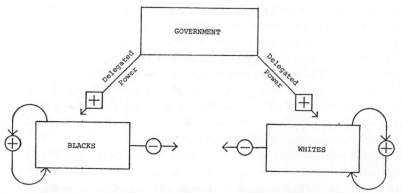

Fig. 12. Association of Power and the Symbol Change from "White Is Beautiful" to "Black Is Beautiful." From R. N. Adams (forthcoming).

holds true at each university, any specific case is an inversion of ranking of any other particular case. National flags can be considered in somewhat the same manner, as can the representative symbols of any corporate unit or any other unit that stands in some position of competition with another.

Contrasting symbolic inversions may be seen to mark severe boundaries in social relations, whether in space or in time. I would argue that they will always mark changes in power structure, either accomplished, underway, or projected. From the standpoint of a given operating unit, they will be seen as important to its survival, in the sense of retaining its identification and avoiding confusion or assimilation with other units.

In passing it may be noted that inversion shows, probably better than any other case, the essentially binary character of basic ranking. Most value changes, however, involve more than simple inversion of ranked elements and consist of changing the ranking, in which elements may appear or disappear, be moved up or down, promoted or demoted.

The adaptation that a society, or any operating unit, has with its environment will continue so long as inputs and outputs remain constant. This is safely true, because it is both tautological and trivial. But as a tautology it draws our attention to the fact that the "consistency of experience" referred to earlier has to do with adaptation and that the relation of mentalistic changes to the experiential is part of the operating unit's response to a change in the environment. Mental images are an important component in decision-making, since so much of the adaptation of a unit takes place in terms of those images. The crucial point here is that, with the change in images, certain decision-making consequences change; this may well alter the ability to respond in the future. If adaptation is the "capacity to respond,"[95] then the mental structures of man clearly set limits on his adaptation, and the fact that they change by binary steps means that they frequently cannot be altered so as to take into account the real change in the environment. The particular binary changes may approximate something appropriate to the change in control, but they may well also switch the image to something quite different and maladaptive. In the culture of the United States, to "lose one's temper" is contrasted with "keeping one's temper." When driven by the frustration of inabil-

[95] Slobodkin 1968, p. 197. Actually Slobodkin says, "Functionally, adaptation can be thought of as altering the capacity to respond, rather than constituting a response." (Reprinted from *Population Biology and Evolution*, ed. Richard O. Lewontin, by permission of Syracuse University Press.) I suspect Slobodkin would agree that the "altering of the capacity to respond" is merely the verbal usage; a given state of adaptation may hold merely on the basis of its capacity, and not on an alteration of it.

ity to affect the environment in the way he wants, a man may switch from "keeping" to "losing" his temper when this is inappropriate to the situation, resulting in a further loss of real control; this in turn may further constrict his ability to act.

The tautology is also trivial, but its triviality too is useful, because it calls our attention to the fact that few societies known to modern man have enjoyed this kind of steady-state existence, and no society composed of modern men can claim to have experienced it. As a consequence, the general principle just enunciated may be true, but its utility may be of more theoretical interest than practical or empirical note. Its virtue, however, lies in the fact that it calls our attention to certain specific areas of focus if we are interested in the relation between the mental world and the physical experience.

Adaptation, as "capacity to respond," can be thought of as occurring at a number of levels. Bateson, followed and expanded upon by Slobodkin, has proposed that adaptation to perturbations or changes in the environment will follow a series of responses, where time permits, such that the members of a population will first attempt to cope behaviorally; failing in that, they will begin to make physiological changes; and, failing further in that, the population will experience genetic changes.[96] Each of these "levels" is seen as being progressively more "profound," taking more time, being more difficult to accomplish and more irreversible if successfully achieved.

Bateson has also observed that, in contrast to information, values are images that direct us in our attempts to deal with our environment.[97] If the environment does not seem to conform to them, then we will try to reform it to meet the form of the image. Information, by contrast, is composed of environmental elements that serve to change our images. It is not surprising to argue, then, that, if the environment is already in conformance with our images, we shall not try to change it. When we find it to be out of kilter, however, then our images direct us to do the kind of ordering that we discussed at some length earlier. The value ranking of operating units evolves gradually through experience with what seems,

[96] Bateson 1972, pp. 346–363; Slobodkin 1968, pp. 194 ff.
[97] Bateson 1966, p. 42.

within the relevant context, to work best with respect to some particular elements of the environment, that is, in particular situations. So long as behavior is coherent with that ranking, and so long as the environment seems to respond properly to the effort, there will be no change in the values.

Change in such ideal steady-state systems is signaled by the fact that efforts to control energetic forms become less effective or suddenly cease to work at all. Failure to be successful, this incoherence between mentalistic idea and energetic performance, can then lead to a variety of individual responses, but adaptation consists in selecting those that permit one to continue to respond to the environment in some effective way in spite of the change.

Let us think of a mirror image of the Bateson-Slobodkin model of levels of response to perturbations in the environment and conceive of a variety of value classes that differ in their scope of generality, that is, differ in the number of subclasses, objects, and acts that may be included in them. Those very general classes that have broad scope, such as "the good," or "virtue," could be considered to be relatively profound, whereas those with much more limited scope, such as "a cold drink," would be less so. One such range from most specific to most general would be the following: this glass of beer I am drinking—glasses of beer—beer—alcoholic drinks—drinks—consumables—processed organic products—manufactured products—goods—utility— . . . and, depending on the system of value, perhaps the last would be good or evil. (One should not introduce the notion of "level" here without having reference to some specific empirical case, because most certainly this would involve us in some kind of taxonomy.)

Now change in values will proceed somewhat after the fashion of the Bateson-Slobodkin levels. First, responses to alterations in the environment will bring about shifts in the more superficial values. If these do not serve, then the class of greater scope will be weakened. So, when we find that the Adams brand beer, which we formerly loved, is getting bad, we shift to another; but perhaps all beers begin to affect us adversely, and so we try wine; when it seems wrong, perhaps we turn to a nonalcoholic drink, and so on. Quite obviously we cannot proceed indefinitely into the more general classes, or we would die.

So the more general classes change more slowly than do the

more superficial. This is not merely because rapid changes would be contra-adaptive, as in the case just cited, but because general classes not only are broader but also overlap. Specific things like consumables may fall within both a larger class of utilities and a larger class of pretty things. The hierarchy of values is not a series of separate pyramids, but rather a series of overlapping pyramids wherein particular objects and acts are classified into different, more general classes. Changes in more general classes come about more slowly, but do regularly occur. Probably the most common process at work is the gradual elimination of specific subclasses or specific objects and acts from the more general class. Thus "virtue" used to be a well-recognized and broad value class in western culture, but, over the years (principally I suppose since the onset of the Industrial Revolution), the specific elements of what was classified as virtue have been gradually eroded. Such subclasses as thrift, chastity, good works, and honesty have each given way to the changing world of experience and tended to fade and fragment, so that elements of the class continue to be honored by specific operating units, but in no way is the class as a whole widely subscribed to today. Few would know what one was talking about if one were to call for a nation to act virtuously.

Thus the profundity of the value class that is affected by changes in the energetic world will reflect to some manner the degree of general disruption of the familiar environment. In this sense, then, the more general or profound the class, the more structural it will be to our societies and operating units; that is, the more difficult is it for us to change. Whether I will have a drink of beer now I can probably decide with little hesitation; whether I will give up drinking beer altogether is more difficult; to give up alcohol entirely, yet more difficult; and so on.

There is no reason, incidentally, to think that the particular *ranking* of a set of values will reflect the degree of profundity. That is, we may rank possession of a new car very high on our list of preferences at some point; but this is very specific, and it is subject to change much more readily than might be a lesser-ranked value, say for tranquillity (or excitement), which is much more general. In ranking values, we must respond to the known elements available in the environment, and these may at any one time be a mix of classes of greater and lesser specificity.

A further possible reason to see general value classes as changing more slowly than the specific harks back to the earlier discussion of the limitations of taxonomic elements. If value classes do exist in a taxonomic scheme, then we should expect to find that there would be a crude taxonomy of classes, such that there might be some basic set which, for the philosopher so inclined, would be enunciated at any level within the range of six or seven.[98] Since any such class will be held to include a great number of acts, it is clearly easier to change the content of the class than the general class labels. Thus the canons of beauty change, but beauty remains a valued class.

Another generality that may be ventured about values is that, *as operating units have more experience, that is, as they have had to readapt more often, their general scheme will be such as to rank value classes of greater generality higher and those of greater specificity lower.* This reflects the fact that experience will usually show that the high ranking of specific objects and events is more often frustrated than the high ranking of a general category or class. The general value class can remain high because it can be satisfied with a variety of specific elements, whereas it would otherwise be continually battered by unhappy experience. Thus the degree to which general classes are ranked over the specific reflects the greater experience of the individual.

The relation of value change to power is particularly interesting. Power, as has been repeatedly argued, is an omnipresent aspect of social relations; both the decision as to whether to exercise it and the specific nature of that exercise must be made always in conformance with some value ranking of potential outcomes.

Unlike many aspects of formal culture, changes in power relations and experience can be extremely sudden. While we are accustomed to think of values as being things that tend to be particularly tenacious, we have already observed that this tenacity is

[98] This sent me back to Plato, who identified five types of virtues: wisdom, temperance, courage, justice, and holiness (Jowett, trans. 1937, I, 118, *Protagoras*; p. 349 of Jowett's 3rd ed.). In the *Republic*, he omits holiness (Jowett, trans. 1937, I, 696, *Republic, Book IV*; p. 453 of Jowett's 3rd ed.). Aristotle is much more inclined in this, as in many other things, to simple binary distinctions; virtue is divided into the moral and the intellectual (McKeon, ed. 1941, *Nichomachean Ethics*).

probably related to their degree of specificity. There are, however, a good many things that can be dealt with specifically, and there are clearly differences among a number of specific objects and acts that may be valued very highly and are not readily subject to change. So we must seek some other factors in this matter. One of these, perhaps obvious but nonetheless important, is that the classes that are perceived to be particularly strategic to the current adaptative capacity of the unit will be ranked highly and, by the same token, will be resistant to change. An aspect of this, however, is the question of how accurate the appreciation of the strategic role of some items may be; and a factor in that is the question of length of experience that was mentioned earlier. An individual must learn, if he does not in some sense invent, what is of crucial importance for the survival of an operating unit.

This general attack on the mentalistic area and on values in particular cannot pretend to solve all the problems of synthesis alluded to earlier; indeed, I would argue that, as a whole, they are impossible of solution. It does suggest some ways that reasoning from the energetic universe to the mentalistic will clarify our understanding. In symbolic inversions, I invoked social power as an intervening device, because it specifically linked the two. There are also other ways to seek this linkage, through changes in the environment that may not involve an intervening power linkage. Two such cases are Bennett's rule on the shift from starchy staples, and Engel's Law.

M. K. Bennett has proposed that an increase in a society's income will be accompanied by a decreased dietary use of starchy staples and an increase in a broader mix in the diet. Bennett surmised that the constant shift he observed in food practices "presumably . . . has a basis in human psychology, in a general rule that populations will enhance the variety of their diet when they can afford it."[99] There is no immediate reason to take issue with this mentalistic ascription, but it is worthwhile pointing out that there is also an explanation that may be derived directly from the Second Law of Thermodynamics and Lotka's principle.

[99] Bennett 1954, p. 218; see also his pp. 25–33.

Bennett's argument can be stated in the following terms: when an increase in income signals an increased energetic input to an operating unit, the output will change such that starchy staples, foods that are specifically of a high caloric content but are produced with low caloric cost of production, will be displaced by foods that themselves have a much broader range of caloric value but will have a higher energy cost of production. In the course of cultural evolution, natural selection early favored those human populations with sufficiently varied diet to sustain the population over lean as well as good times. With the appearance of statelike organizations, rural agriculturists became subsistence peasants. A dietary concomitant of this change was the reduction of the variety of foods consumed, with a concomitant increased dependence on one or a few high calorie producers with low energy cost of production. Since the so-called starchy staples fit this description, dependency increasingly focused on them. The increase in energy costs associated with economic development or social mobility led to the appearance of a wider variety of foods that did not rest in the fact of any increase in per capita caloric intake (which might also occur) but merely in the increased energy input into the food-production process. Since there is an upper limit on the calorie consumption possible in the human diet, an increase of input cannot effectively raise the amount of caloric output indefinitely. The consequence is, then, an increase in the energy cost of production of food. This necessarily brings about a shift to the production of foodstuffs that require a higher energy input for an equivalent per capita caloric output; and this takes the form of a shift away from energy-cheap, high caloric producers to foods with less relative caloric output per unit of input.

This general process has been recently confirmed for the United States in a study by John S. Steinhart and Carol E. Steinhart. Between 1940 and 1970, improving technology of agriculture provided for an increasing output of food for consumption. However, the increase in consumable food cost ever more energy in the production process, so that over that period the number of kilocalories necessary to increase the consumable food by one kilocalorie increased from below five to almost nine. The authors also observed that the curve relating these two variables was leveling off, so that it was approaching the point where no technological improvement would make it possible to obtain any more consumable kilocalories, no matter what the increased cost of production might be.[100]

The more general principle that this is following may be stated as follows: As a society develops, that is, as energy input per capita increases, the energy cost of production will increase relative to the total increased energy output.[101] This can be derived directly from the Second Law and Lotka's principle[102] and can be seen to apply not merely in the energy cost of production of foodstuffs but also in all industrial and agricultural production.[103] The fundamental reason for this is that, for most kinds of production, human labor provides the cheapest input in terms of energy; as other energy sources are tapped, the energy cost of production must necessarily increase. It should be noted here that this applies to the developmental situation, that is, where there is an increased input of energy per capita, not necessarily to situations of growth where biomass increases with no concomitant per capita increase.

A related economic theory that states input-output relations is Engel's "Law" to the effect that "the proportion of a consumer's budget spent on food tends to decline as the consumer's income goes up."[104] As with Bennett's formulations, this also states an input-output relation that follows basic energetic principles. The phenomenon described by Engel is a direct consequence of the fact that the adult human organism enjoys a trophic steady state, with a maximum consumption limit per unit time. An increase in income can elaborate costs for food, but there is a limit to the normal human being's ability to consume food. A continuing increase in energy input into the domestic budget must necessarily lead to a relative decrease in the proportion that is food. Put in energetic terms, the individual is limited in his capacity for somatic conver-

---

[100] Steinhart and Steinhart 1974, pp. 310–311.

[101] Adams 1962, pp. 88–89.

[102] Lotka 1922*a*, pp. 148–149.

[103] Cottrell makes the agricultural case clear in his pioneering volume (1955, Ch. 7).

[104] H. S. Houthakker 1968, p. 63. Reprinted from *International Encyclopedia of the Social Sciences*, Copyright © 1968 by Crowell Collier and Macmillan, Inc., by permission of Macmillan Publishing Co.

sion of energy. If he is to increase the amount of energy converted in his environment, it must be through recourse to trigger mechanisms that release extrasomatic, that is, nonfood energy.

In both the Bennett and Engel cases, we are dealing with changes that originate, as we would expect, in the environment, that is, in a change in the availability of food products. In both, the human capacity for consumption was involved: a somatic upper limit that constitutes a natural selection over how much, and therefore what, can be consumed. Values changed as the capacity to produce changed; but the capacity for digestive consumption remained fairly constant. In both cases, in contrast to the symbolic inversions discussed previously, the changes were slow and probably quite unconscious to many people involved. But both these cases and symbolic inversion reflect changes in value systems, and they also reflect the fact that the rapidity of the change may be closely related not to the ranking of the value but rather to its profundity, on the one hand, and its specificity, the direct linkages it may have with energetic elements of the external world that are themselves being subject to changes in power and control, on the other.

A final case of external changes that are much studied but about which we know remarkably little theoretically may be seen in the sequence of rank promotions that takes place during the process of manufacturing or production (see Figure 10). With the original bestowal of ranking on a natural resource, there is, at every stage in the extraction and production sequence, a promotion of the value ascribed to the object in question. Economists have regarded this as the "value added" that occurs during the manufacture and subsequent handling of the material. In the energy system, "value" is "added" when energy is expended on the further processing or handling of the object. There are both the energy cost of production and the energy of the material lost in any conversion process. This addition of value, equated with loss of energy, continues until the object in question reaches the act of consumption, at which time it is demoted in rank, perhaps merely to a lower level, but more likely to being excluded entirely from the ranking system. Most societies have a category of total waste, which essentially excludes the degraded material from further consideration.

Nicolas Georgescu-Roegen sees this as the heart of the economic process: "The true economic output of the economic process is not a material flow of waste, but an immaterial flux: the enjoyment of life." He then argues that "this flux—which, as an entropic feeling, must characterize life at all levels—exists only as long as it can continuously feed itself on environmental low entropy. And if we go one step further, we discover that every object of economic value—be it a fruit just picked from a tree, or a piece of clothing, or furniture, etc.,—has a highly ordered structure, hence a low entropy." "It is . . . because of the particular scarcity of environmental low entropy that ever since the dawn of history man has continuously sought to invest means for sifting low entropy better. In most (though not in all) of man's inventions one can definitely see a progressively better economy of low entropy."[105]

It is not yet clear what kind of consistent relationships we may eventually find through the history of human culture between ranking, energy cost of production, high entropy build-up, and other facets of this entire process of man's ecology of energy.[106] Until we have some studies directed specifically at this matter, much of what is said (excluding neither Georgescu-Roegen's remarks nor the present paper) must remain somewhat speculative. The now age-old western conundrum of whether mind or matter is the dominant actor is, like much of our metaphorical thinking, more a device that keeps us in ignorance than one that helps us understand better the Nature that is Man. Our mentalistic structures did not come into being independently of their own energetic nature; but neither is the behavior that is a consequence of that nature's composition in any sense a pre-existing model for it. Our putative understanding of the world is our own invention, but one which in some manner has been determined by our own nature.

[105] Georgescu-Roegen 1973, pp. 42–43.

[106] Odum (1971) touches on this area in a number of places, and, I must confess, to me quite unsatisfactorily. While avoiding the energy-flow-is-like-money-flow metaphor (cf. Parsons 1963), Odum contents himself with an analysis based on the converse, that is, money-flow-is-like-energy-flow (Ch. 6). He also suggests value correlations of a more obvious kind (i.e., in terms of stored potential energy or in terms of energy replacement costs or time loss in complex systems; see pp. 155–156) but does not approach the problem of how cultural systems actually *do* evaluate energy forms.

# PART THREE

# A Model of the Evolution of Power

## 9. THE FRAMEWORK

Much of the recent theoretical and conceptual modeling of the evolution of society has been carried out by a coordinate unit of professional anthropologists, most of whom have, in one capacity or another, been connected with the University of Michigan or Columbia University. Many were first- or second-generation students of Leslie White or Julian Steward. The first generation depended more on ethnographic materials, while the second and, indeed, a third, now emergent, have worked more with prehistorical materials and, naturally, recognize the influence of a much broader group of scholars.

The present effort depends more on an ethnographic base, but, as will be seen, relies on archaeological materials for confirmation of some otherwise speculative ventures made on the basis of power analysis. It should be explicit at the outset, however, that the entire model is theory building based mainly on deductive suppositions from the principles of power operation and suggestive clues from prehistoric and historic evidence. The building of theory, whether done by historians or by social scientists, must trace a pattern something like this; differences will tend to lie in the nature of the stimuli that trigger propositions and hypotheses. No one, including myself, can find the model proposed here entirely satisfactory; it is an attempted synthesis which, I hope, will serve to introduce some correctives into the general current thinking. For the reader whose interest lies totally in contemporary problems, the dedication of the final portion of the book to this subject may appear esoteric; seen from an anthropological perspective, however, it is not. Rather, it is trying to view the operation of power from the widest perspective, so that we can better understand which of past processes are currently replicating.

## A. Evolution: General and Specific

The differentiation that Sahlins made between general and specific evolution[1] continues to be fundamental to our understanding. If we see every human operating unit as attempting adaptation, we are simply proposing that, from the individual on up, human beings are constantly experimenting with specific ways of controlling their environment. All evolution is, then, specific. The term *general* refers to a conceptual model that traces the line of maximal evolutionary development through the course of human history. It is not a line followed by any single society, any more than the history of a society is to be traced by following the life trajectory of any single member. General evolution is the outline of the evolution of the species; specific evolution is that of any particular subunit of the species during any period that it exists as a distinctive unit.

Care has to be taken with the concept of general evolution, however, for it is easy to slip into a Victorian anthropocentrism. We must be clear on the criteria being used to define this maximal trajectory. Sahlins is explicit in seeing general evolution as the "passage from less to greater energy transformation, lower to higher levels of integration, and less to greater all-round adaptability."[2] The first two of these readily apply to the evolution of the human species as we know it thus far; adaptability, however, is another matter.[3] If we use L. B. Slobodkin's notion of adaptation as the capacity to change, then there has long been evidence that the human species' ability to adapt can probably not be argued to be superior to that of many viruses and insects; the very complexity that is imposed by virtue of controlling so much energy forces human society and culture into rigid and conservative behavioral patterns that inhibit its future capacity to change. Thus, in speaking of the general evolution of life, we clearly can differentiate species that achieve survival and continuing adaptation

[1] Sahlins 1960.

[2] Ibid., p. 38. Reprinted from *Evolution and Culture*, ed. Marshall Sahlins and Elman R. Service, by permission of University of Michigan Press.

[3] A forthcoming paper by Roy A. Rappaport, "Energy and the Structure of Adaptation," argues this point and effectively discusses some mechanisms involved from the point of view of ecological and systems theory; it was presaged by Slobodkin 1968.

through genetic change as opposed to physiological or behavioral change. Whether the total amount of energy being processed will serve as a criterion must first be asked in terms of life as a whole. Within this framework, the adaptation of species evolves through symbiotic processes, wherein the presence of a particular set of species and resources provides elements of a niche for a given specific form. It can be argued that, taken as a *whole*, life has shown a tendency to increase the amount of energy being processed through vital processes over its history. Whether this continues as a steady curve (apart from man's role in it) is not clear. It does not follow, in any case, that the ultimate superior harnessing of energy by a single species (what would amount to a centralization of control of life by a single species) will prove adaptive in the long run. Indeed, there is every reason to think that such a centralization can never be achieved, and, even if it could, it conceivably could eventuate in disaster for the centralizing species.

When we speak of the general evolution of the human species, in contradistinction to the general evolution of life, we must also doubt whether the tendency to harness more energy, and thereby inherently to move toward a concentration of energy within the hands of increasingly fewer subunits of the species, is adaptive. What we observe here is equivalent to the immature and mature phases of the ecosystem model (see Figs. 8 and 18). Man's evolutionary specific trajectory thus far traces the rising portion of the sigmoid curve; it is quite reasonable to see in this phase of the curve the general evolution of man, in contrast to the curve traced by any specific subunit of man. This does not mean, however, that the increase in the processing of energy, which provides us with the best index of this portion of the curve, will continue to be a satisfactory index when the curve begins to level off toward a steady state. Indeed, one of the problems that faces us currently is the modeling of this second section of the curve, a leveling-off process that is inevitable, given the fact that the biosphere ecosystem on which we depend is finite. We must then modify Sahlins's earlier differentiation to recognize that general evolution thus far follows the increasing-energy-cost pattern he described; but the fact that it is becoming nonadaptive indicates that we must begin experimenting with alternatives.

Returning, then, to the evolution of power as the particular dimension of the evolution of culture that interests us here, we want to differentiate among varieties of specific evolution. The term *pristine* has been used to refer to the first emergence of some particular evolutionary manifestation. Morton Fried, in particular, distinguishes between "pristine and secondary situations, applying this distinction . . . to the development of stratification and the state. A pristine situation is one in which development occurs exclusively on the basis of indigenous factors. In such a situation there is no external model of more complex design to help shape the new society. Neither is there the presence of a more complexly organized society to stimulate the process of development." Fried emphasizes that societies obviously evolve in contact with other societies, but that the term *pristine* applies when "none of the external cultures are any more complex than the one being considered."[4] Secondary situations of development are all those that are not pristine.

A possible minor point needs to be observed with respect to Fried's usage. When we identify something as pristine, we are not necessarily identifying it as being in the line of general evolution. Thus two societies in confrontation may each invent and develop some new kind of technological or social organizational form to deal with the problem. Both could be pristine. One, however, might prove to be more successful and eliminate the other. Thus the world has probably witnessed the emergence of many pristine forms that proved inadequate to the adaptive demands of the situations they confronted. General evolution traces the emergence of those pristine forms that were naturally selected for survival.

All but one final portion of the model constructed here concerns the rising fortunes of man, a period of ecological immaturity for the species. What we observe in the process is the appearance of increasingly complex forms of societal organization, coupled with an increasing variety of cultural forms. Discussions of cultural evolution have, until recently, tended to pay most attention to the characteristics of the maximal level of integration achieved. Thus, in contrasting a hunting band with a chiefdom, the band organization is usually compared with the profile of the chiefdom; less attention is paid to the interior of the chiefdom organization,

[4] Fried 1967, p. 111.

the subunits that compose it. Herbert Simon has observed that "The time required for the evolution of a complex form from simple elements depends critically on the number and distribution of potential intermediate stable forms."[5] He argues that any larger or more inclusive organization depends on the appearance of "subassemblies" that must have a prior appearance in some form or another. Thus, in the grossest of outlines, evolution traces the appearance of new building blocks, some few appearing at successively higher levels, but many more occupying intermediate loci within the larger structure.

A criticism that has inevitably been leveled at attempts to draw the profile of evolution has been that the intermediate forms, the "subassemblies," are very different from the organizations of a similar scope that still stand in some maximal position. Thus, while we can compare the hunting band to a neighborhood of suburban United States in terms of their internal organization, clearly the exterior relations of the two result in violently different characteristics. The difference, by no means a superficial matter of cultural forms, rests fundamentally in the nature of the total power structure of the band, on the one hand, and the suburb as a part of a larger, world-encompassing society, on the other. The difference is easy to see in the case of the incorporation of tribal Indians of the South American lowlands into the civic societies of nations, such as Brazil,[6] or the increasing dependence and dislocation of the arctic Eskimo. The particular processes of adaptation and subordination that have been operating in this regard since the domestication of agriculture have varied, and they comprise the ongoing subject of study of many anthropologists.

Figure 13 attempts a schematic picture of some of the principal evolutionary variations that are involved in societies at different levels and tries, simultaneously, to suggest structural parallels that may be sought through a comparison of them. Contrasted are societies of distinctive levels of integration, indicated by the vertical columns; within each box are terms commonly applied to subdivisions or "subassemblies," operating units peculiar to these levels. Since each column represents a maximal domain with a different number of levels, the diagram permits us to differentiate

[5] Simon 1965, p. 66.
[6] Ribeiro 1970.

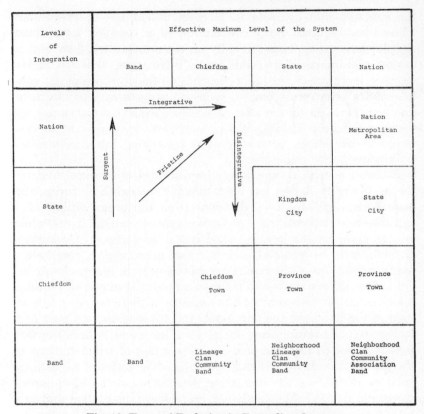

Fig. 13. Types of Evolution in Expanding Systems

schematically four kinds of evolutionary processes: the *pristine*, *surgent*, *integrative*, and *disintegrative*. In terms of the present analysis, the feature that distinguishes surgent from pristine evolution is that in the former case the operating unit in question is expanding within an existing domain with an inevitable confrontation with the maximum power holder of the domain, should its surgency continue to that point. In the pristine case there is no other superordinate power holder in the domain of the emerging unit, and the ultimate confrontation must be with other maximal domains.

Fried has applied the term *pristine* to the appearance of the state when no other more advanced state was present. I would apply the term more broadly to any surgent social unit that expands to a more complex status, but does so from the top, that is, not from within or from a lower level, but from the maximal level. To be concerned with whether certain of the formal traits used in surgency or pristine evolution are borrowed from existing states is to classify variant structures in terms of formal features. If we concentrate sheerly on structure, however, we can apply the term not merely to the appearance of the archaic Near Eastern states, or to the appearance of chiefdoms or the Incaic kingdom in Peru, but also to the emergence of the Japanese nation from its involuted isolation to a major industrial power. The formal features of Japanese development have borrowed from abroad, especially in technology. The evolving power structure, however, can perfectly well be argued to be an indigenous process. It is probably the case that most instances of pristine emergence at the various levels have been ultimately unsuccessful. Since the absolute number of such units is reduced as communities of societies shift from a coordinate to a centralized condition (these forms will be discussed shortly), it is inevitably the case that a majority of the maximal units at one level of integration will become subordinated at the next. Hawaii, prior to its political subordination to the domain of the United States, was a pristine evolving society. Thereafter, it was integrated within the expanding U.S. domain, and its indigenous organization rapidly disintegrated and was replaced by new operating units based more on Western religious, political, and economic relations.

The horizontal arrow in Figure 13 indicates the evolutionary integration of subordinate entities by those of greater scale. In this process we are concerned with the effective level of regency of the maximal unit in question. For example, during the period when the western part of the United States was still in territorial status, the effective governing power came directly from the local military post, even though the ultimate source of delegated power was the national capital. Thus, the effective power exercised by the nation over the Indians of that time and place was rather on the order of that exercised by a technologically advantaged competitive chief, but one with inexhaustible further resources. With the creation of reservations for Indians and the conversion of territories into member states of the federal union, the Indian population became less militant and more dominated by a government bureaucracy. Within the national setting today, the Indian communities vary from those on reservations to enclave communities, urban and rural, that try to compete with other sectors of the resident United States population.

A parallel integration occurs at the regional and state levels within nations, such as those achieving independence in Latin America in the early nineteenth century, which were essentially not integrated at the national level until the appearance of new resources and markets in the latter part of the century. Thus the states of Brazil continued with a high degree of autonomy until the 1930's, as did some of the southern states of Mexico. This incorporative process is essentially unidirectional, however; and, as such, it implies both the destruction or clear transformation of the links or bonds that formerly provided the lesser units with their integrity and the subordination of such units to new kinds of linkages that tie them into the larger organization. Indeed, it is a cardinal feature of both surgent and integrative evolution that the idiom expressing the new relationships between the lesser unit and the greater will be different from those that have served as the internal bonds holding the lesser unit together. This will be clearer as we discuss the emergence of higher levels shortly.

Disintegrative evolution refers to that aspect or phase of the evolutionary process whereby the social operating unit in question breaks up. It is quite familiar in the break-up of domestic units, businesses, empires, and kingdoms, and it is fundamentally due to the termination of the power bases that held the societies together. Disintegration through conquest usually involves simultaneous integration of the residual components into the conquering domain. As a form of social process, the varying elements of disintegration could probably stand considerably more research in view of the increasing emphasis that is being placed on the importance of achieving steady-state conditions in the anthropocentric ecosystem.

## B. The Growth Sequence

The model of evolution presented here diverges in some important respects from the general models which have preceded it and from which it may be said to have evolved. Two major differences are that it poses the evolution of power systems (*a*) to have followed a multiple track whereby (*b*) a set of processes to be called the "growth sequence" is replicated successively as new levels of integration emerge. To make clear the nature of this variation, let us look to some earlier schemes.

In his germinal essay Sahlins casually reintroduces the old primitive society–civilization dichotomy, *societas* and *civitas*; within the first, he further proposes three progressively higher forms, the *band*, the *tribe*, and the *chiefdom*; and, within the second, he proposes the "archaic form."[7] The two specific discussions of recent years with the greatest influence have been Elman R. Service's *Primitive Social Organization*, in which he followed the band-tribe-chiefdom sequence, and Fried's *The Evolution of Political Society*, in which he rejected that sequence and substituted the notions of egalitarian societies–rank societies–stratified societies–state. Fried argued that "there is no theoretical need for the tribal stage in the evolution of political organization" and that the phenomena cited to illustrate such a condition "may well be the product of processes stimulated by the appearance of relatively highly organized societies amidst other societies which are organized much more simply."[8] In proposing the stratified societies, Fried found himself with an ethnographically residual and void category. He argued that this particular evolutionary phase was necessary theoretically but that it could not have survived in a pristine condition because it became almost immediately converted into the state. I will return later to these proposals by Fried: the nonimportance of existing "tribal" groups and the importance of nonexisting "stratified" societies.

Fried's influence has been great, and one hardly finds a contemporary ethnographic or archaeological synthesis that does not resort to his formulation. Differences between his own and his colleague's views seemed solved when Service offered a compromise model of three general classes: egalitarian society (which would include tribes and bands), hierarchical society (possibly including Big Men domains and certainly chiefdoms), and "Archaic Civilizations or classical empires."[9]

With this closing of the ranks by my predecessors, I hope that

[7] Sahlins 1960, pp. 36–37.

[8] Fried 1967, pp. 173, 170; see also 1968a.

[9] Service 1971, p. 157. This first appeared in Fried, Harris, and Murphy, eds. 1967, p. 167.

the present work will not be taken as regressive and Pollyannaish for intentionally reinstituting the band, the tribe, and the chiefdom, and using the state only as a very generalized concept.[10] My reason, as will be evident, is that the terms are appropriate to describe elements in a sequence that is more analytic than those presented by Service and Fried. I venture back to abandoned territory not because these later formulations are unsatisfactory (in fact, I think they are better in broad outline than the earlier), but because the earlier can be bettered by more attention to variables that I am going to use here: types of exercise of power;[11] the simultaneously dual character of the growth process; and a recognition that the evolution of society has followed some unchanging basic principles throughout its course. With respect to the last, I have learned as much about the "primitives" by looking at society in its highly differentiated industrialized form as I have about the latter by reading of the "primitives." I can presume to this, not because I am any more convinced than Fried that we are anywhere dealing with pristine examples of human society in its earlier state, but because I believe that simplicity and primitiveness have common structures that are related to the amount of energy they process. Low-energy operating units confront certain basic common problems, whether they exist now or ten thousand years ago; and where their responses must be made under similar constrictions they will manifest similar structures. They will vary, obviously, insofar as environmental constrictions (Kent Flannery's "socio-environmental stresses")[12] differ, and also as they may have been influenced by societies with different adaptive modes, formal elements of which may have little adaptative or selective effect.

There is a fundamental growth sequence that repeats itself through the course of human social evolution. It consists of three phases which, taken collectively, may be seen as a complete and terminal sequence. These are identity, coordination, and centralization. *Identity* is the process earlier described for the formation

---

[10] The state must be regarded as part of one of the intellectual dichotomies among which we can include status/contract, mechanical/organic, *Gesellschaft/Gemeinschaft*, folk/urban, traditional/modern; all, including prestate/state, continue to have some utility.

[11] See sections 3D and 4.

[12] Flannery 1972, p. 409.

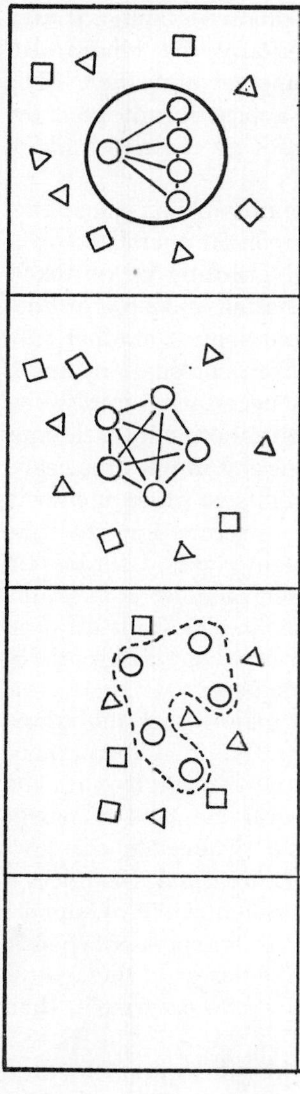

| | Identity | Coordination | Centralization |
|---|---|---|---|
| Growth Sequence | Identity | Coordination | Centralization |
| Operating Unit Type | Fragmented Identity Unit | Coordinated Unit | Consensus, Majority, or Corporate Unit |
| Types of Power in Operation | 1. Independent power of each constituent unit | 1. Independent power of each constituent unit<br>2. Power granted reciprocally between individual constituents | 1. Independent power of each constituent unit<br>2. Power granted reciprocally between individual constituents<br>3. Power concentrated in central unit (whether by allocation, delegation, new independent source, or some combination) |

Fig. 14. Operating Unit Types in the Fundamental Growth Sequence

of an identity operating unit, through which a number of separate units (individuals or more complex operating units), which are neither articulated nor related in any way, identify each other as being similar in some respect. The degree of mutual awareness need go no further than a common identification (although it may for other reasons). Identity is fundamentally the binary differentiation of some set of "we" from some set of "other." The other may go relatively undefined, that is, appear infinite; but the "we" will have specific markers or diacritics by means of which they are separated from the rest.

*Coordination* is the direct or indirect condition that comes into being through the interaction of the component members on a coordinate basis, that is, when reciprocal granting of power is established. There is no categorical subordination and superordination of any subset of the totality as over and against another subset. Ranking is an important mechanism for coordination, but it may be done on any basis and does not necessarily imply significant control or differential power. Coordination of relations creates a coordinated operating unit and thereby implies that each member grants certain decision-making rights to other members (not necessarily the same for each dyad), in return for which he is similarly granted approximately equivalent rights. Coordinated units are, then, founded on the fact that each member both grants and is a recipient of a certain amount of power. The trade-off need not be equal, but neither can it be centralized or differentially focused on any one member or subset of members.

*Centralization* is the condition when a majority of the whole focus relationships on a minority or on one. The precise relationship between the individual members of the collectivity and the centralized individual or unit will vary with the kind of power exercised and the amount of power in the system. In the low-energy units, it is based solely on allocated power, and the unit is a consensus unit; if there is available a real concentration of support from the majority or from some external independent power source, the unit is a majority unit; and, if the power of the central figure is so augmented that he must delegate it to exercise it, then the unit constitutes a corporate unit.

I have described the three phases of the growth sequence as they would occur to a single set of operating units or individuals. The crucial feature of these processes is that *the centralization of one unit usually occurs as a part of the coordination of that unit with other units*. To put it in another way, the centralization of a unit at one level is a dialectic link with the coordination of that unit with others at the next level. This is why each level except the top one necessarily undergoes the entire growth sequence. At any point in evolution, the top level will consist of a coordinated set of relations, although it may show oscillatory tendencies toward and away from centralization. This is the case because centralization at one level is simultaneous with coordination at the next. A unit centralizes as a response to external pressure, and in human societies the only continuing pressure is that exerted by other societies. This pressure from other societies demands external coordination, at the same time that it attempts internal centralization.

Most discussions of cultural evolutionary models have used a notion of stages, steps, or levels of integration that depicts stages or levels as a ladderlike succession of phases, each following the preceding one. The present model still uses the level of integration as a framework but emphasizes the growth sequence of coordination and centralization (see Fig. 15). When one set of component operating units undergoes the identity-coordination-centralization sequence, what happens next, in a sense, is that it stops. While centralization may be tightened up, there is no new kind of basic structure to which the units can move. Furthermore, they cannot centralize any more than the amount of power available will permit; if there is a great deal of power, then it will be used in centralization at the next level. So the dialectic linkage of centralization at one level initiates coordination at the next and starts a new growth sequence at a higher level. This repetition of the growth cycle in a time span as brief as human history is made possible by the human mentalistic binary differentiation process: the ready "creation" of new units out of combinations of old ones is a peculiar characteristic of our species; it is achieved through the process of coordination. So it is that the combination of mentalistic structure and energy expansion leads social organization through a repetitive set of growth sequences, each successive one requiring much more energy than the previous one and, by the same token, inevitably appearing if more energy is pumped into the system.

Figures 15 and 16 employ only the sequence of coordination-centralization. There is no need to include identity in the diagram, because it is an implicit prerequisite to coordination, and at this level of macrodescription it would unnecessarily complicate the presentation. Although the points have been made before, I want

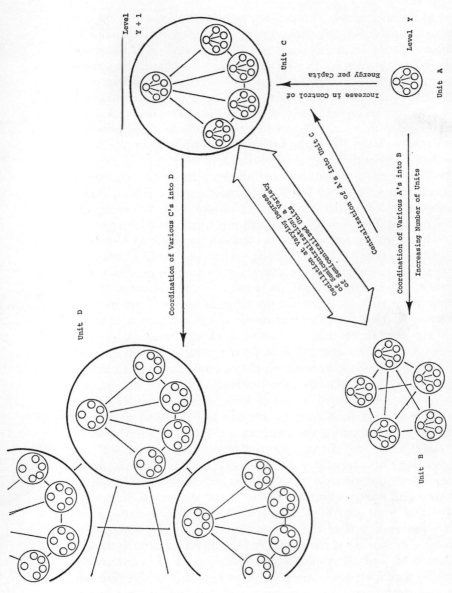

Fig. 15. The Growth Sequence. Beginning at any level ($Y$) below the maximal level of the system, Unit A undergoes coordination with similar units, thereby forming Unit B. As increasing energy per capita is controlled, Unit B oscillates through various phases until it centralizes as Unit C. The centralization of Unit C simultaneously occurs as Unit C is being coordinated with like units into Unit D. The emergence of Unit C constitutes the full appearance of a new level of integration ($Y + 1$).

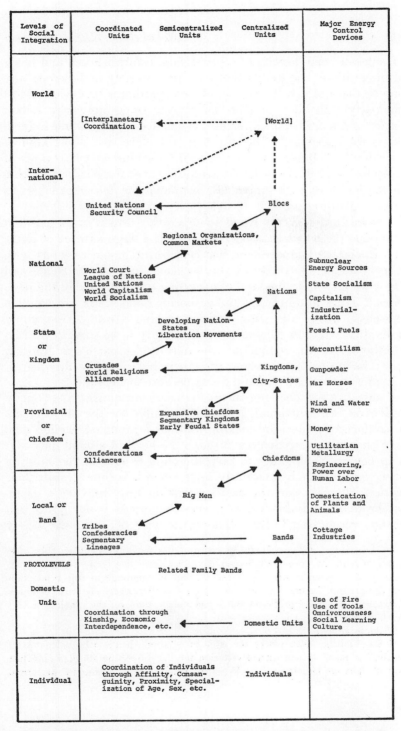

Fig. 16. Schematic Model of Evolution of Power, with Suggested Coordinated and Semicentralized Forms. Note that the correlation with technology is for pristine societies and is only intended to be suggestive.

to reiterate some aspects of coordination, centralization, and levels of integration. The first is that coordination may be based on any one or more of a wide variety of linkage idioms or devices. Most obviously, kinship, common languages, trade networks (silent barter and more complex forms), avoidance behavior, and so forth serve this purpose.[13] The question, therefore, is: What kind of coordination? Based on what criteria? Leading to what kinds of relations? Coordination fundamentally leaves the decision-making in the hands of each individual, or among the decision-makers in larger operating units.

Centralization occurs when one operating unit is in the position of having the power to make decisions for a large number of units. It is important to understand that centralization can vary (*a*) with respect to the specificity of the decisions that can be made and (*b*) with respect to the kind of operating unit that makes the decisions.[14] Thus, in a hunting and gathering band, there can be some consensus about allocating decision-making about curing to an individual who has demonstrated his ability to be superior to that of others. And the individual who may lead a particular hunting party has to be one to whom the others have, for the time being, allocated power of decision-making because of his skill.

Centralization does not mean that decision-making necessarily resides in one individual. It is quite possible for the set of elders to comprise the decision-making unit; or a group of women who take charge helping another through the birth of a child may also help her decide whether to keep the child or not; or the hunting party may decide by consensus as to when it is time to shift their tactics. The fact that the decision-making body may be a group rather than an individual is a very important issue that is not always recognized.[15] The ethnocentric bias of our own society

[13] The nature and complexity of coordinating bonds is a subject that takes us far beyond the present discussion. Hymes (1968) has pointed out how difficult it is to readily categorize even the use of language in this connection. For the present, I simply have to deal with this in categorical terms, however, realizing that a more profound and broad-scaled attack on the problem is very much in order.

[14] Paula Brown 1951.

[15] See Vansina 1962, where the issue of a "single leader who delegates authority" is taken as a principal criterion for the differentiation of a classification of African kingdoms. The Western social scientist comes by his ethno-

tends to see the role of the individual decision-maker as being so important that a dominant binary contrast has been to pose it as the opposite of some kind of "group" or "democratic" process. The issue has been blurred, because the question is not whether a single individual makes the decision, but rather what are the constraints under which a decision is reached. Thus the leader of a consensus unit makes decisions under the constraint that a poor decision will simply not elicit appropriate action. In contrast, a decision reached through consensus of a group of elders may in fact reflect the fact that one of them is specifically respected for his opinion on the matter at hand, and tentative solutions will be discussed until one appears that seems to meet the constraint of receiving his approval. How often have we heard that a leader did or did not himself actually make the decision, that he was or was not influenced by advisers?

Centralization is a relative thing; it is quite as important to know whom it excludes as whom it includes. The fact that in more complex societies, such as chiefdoms, individuals may seem to exercise extraordinary power must not obscure the fact that such an apparent concentration of power can only be had and maintained by cultivating continuing allocated power, irrespective of whether it is done in a context of fear or of charisma.

Perhaps the best example of the centralization of power in the hands of a set of multimembered operating units is that found in some West African societies, an outstanding case of which is the Yakö society of southern Nigeria. The Yakö were governed by a complicated set of voluntary associations. Underlying this collection of associations, however, the Yakö population consisted of some forty thousand people residing in five villages. There was absolutely no coordinating government between these villages: they would probably have to be regarded collectively as an identity unit. Each village was composed of a set of wards with between three hundred and five hundred adult males divided into between five

---

centricity in this matter honestly. Since Henry VIII, English-speaking citizens have been familiar with the single sovereign's supremacy, and Europeans have generally adopted it since the Treaty of Westphalia in 1648, "which expressly confirmed the right of secular sovereigns to determine the religious duties of their subjects" (Watkins 1968).

and eleven localized patriclans. The patriclans in turn subdivided into a number of patrilineages.

At first glance, this system would appear to have (above the household) some four levels: patrilineage, patriclan, ward, and village, with a nascent fifth level in the form of the panvillage identity unit. But, if we examine the actual organization of power, we discover that the series of voluntary associations to which power is allocated all exist at either the ward or the village level. Thus the patrilineages and patriclans are not part of the power levels of articulation. The situation is a little like that cited earlier for Kapauku Papuans, where the coordinate kin relations have been described ethnographically as if they were structurally on a par with the elements that constitute the levels of power articulation. The Yakö do, indeed, provide a particularly interesting case, since theirs is an organization that has succeeded in instituting a series of consensus units, the voluntary associations, as the focal figures in the centralizing process. Some of these units are able to exercise coercive force, as one of the ward-level associations can exercise power independent of that allocated to it, and two of the five village-level organizations specifically can do this.

Were we to classify the Yakö society in terms of the model about to be described, it would be identified as a chiefdom, but one where the concentration of decision-making is, in C. Daryll Forde's words, "widely distributed among a number of independent and over-lapping agencies. Wider political relations then largely resolve themselves into modes of cooperation with and competition between such associations."[16] Here, then, instead of a single chief receiving allocated power and holding some independent power, that power is distributed among the associations, which are themselves a ranked, coordinated set of operating units.

There is nothing that says that such coordination can last forever, particularly when subjected to the influx of new objects of control, and therefore of new sources of power. In the model that follows, the fact that centralization may take a variety of forms and be invested in a number of different operating units must be recognized to be the more common pattern, not a deviation therefrom. Investiture of total power in a single individual is by far the

16 Forde 1967, pp. 122–123.

exception in human history and has usually triggered such ultimate events as the French Revolution or the murder of the tyrant. It is more common that tyrants survive because they are allocated power from a supporting body of immediate constituents who find them convenient, irrespective of the larger terror they may invoke.

## 10. LEVELS OF INTEGRATION

The model of the evolution of power (see Fig. 16) is constructed with five levels of integration, preceded by two protolevels and capped by an imaginary, futuristic cosmic system for intra- or interplanetary space fans. The number of levels of integration, as has been observed, are products of convenience for handling the material; if one were to examine any particular case he might find that the number of levels of articulation involved vary from the number used here. By far the greater amount of ethnographic material that I have reviewed fits well into this system. Where there is question, it stems from one of two difficulties. One is that there is simply not enough data (without extensive case-by-case research) to have a clear picture of the relative nature of power sources within the society; the other is that I have not worked out index ranges of amounts of energy controlled appropriate to the various levels. The second of these is clearly a program for future research; when and if it is accomplished, it should give a basis for being less dependent on the classic levels of integration, replacing them with an index of power development. In view of this, the present model must be seen as merely one of a continuing series of way stations toward the better formulation of the processes of evolution.

Each level of integration includes two facets of reality: on the right in Figure 16 (under Centralized Units) are the designations for classes of operating units with a centralized internal organization. As has already been indicated, the particular power structure of the centralization will vary. In the higher levels, however, the amount of power centralized increases, and therefore the power exercised from the center (which is necessarily coherent with its particular structure) is disproportionately greater. On the left (under Coordinated Units) are coordinated sets or communities of centralized units of the type indicated on the right. A terminology for the centralized units is readily available, as was suggested in the earlier discussion of the growth sequence. However, the centralistic bias that characterizes our thinking about these things has left us with few terms appropriate to the kinds of coordinate units of which chiefdoms, kingdoms, and nations are a part. A practical reason for this lack of consistent terminology, however, is that coordinate units may be formed on the basis of a wide variety of criteria; given our formalistic mode of perceiving things, it is more likely that we will characterize these in terms of the particular criteria and form that they take than that we will see them as members of a larger class of such units. So the terms designating the coordinate sets should be taken as merely illustrative, and in no sense do they pretend to characterize the variety of such sets that may have occurred.

## A. Protolevels

Protolevels are included here to make clear that the major processes replicated at each level are present in lower orders of development. Individuals are centralized organisms, a coordinated set of which is the collectivity that makes up the *domestic unit*. Similarly, the domestic unit is a centralized entity that, collectively with others, comprises the *band*. Neither the individual nor the domestic unit standing alone is a viable organization. They may survive for limited periods alone, but ultimately they cannot survive apart from a higher coordination. Individuals, such as the Japanese hiding out on the Pacific islands after World War II, may survive many years alone, but they obviously cannot reproduce themselves, and their very success in isolation simultaneously marks them as a failure for the species. Coordination takes place through a variety of basic cultural mechanisms—fundamentally, common language, consanguinity (principally filiation), affinal alliances, and other cultural traits usually conducive to mutual survival within the environment. Individuals cannot survive on the basis of coordination alone; there must at least be minimal periods when they act with some degree of centralization (such as care of the sick, childbirth, child care, and other activities requiring centralized decision-making); or else, like the separate individuals, they will not survive.

The basic sociological unit in the system is the domestic unit. Note that I am not labeling this the "family," although it obviously is fundamentally composed of familistic relations. The domestic unit is the centralized unit that provides the necessary basis for the reproduction of individuals. Given genetic drift, it is unlikely that a sequence of endogamous domestic units could survive indefinitely. One such immaculately conceived unit can hardly account for the rest of the species; it requires the coordination of a set of such units. So the local level is proposed as the minimal human social organization that can survive over various generations. Even here the species could not have survived had only one coordinated unit existed at this level. There were many such units that, taken together, constituted a continuous territorial coordination perhaps after the classic pattern of the French dialects. But any classification or taxonomy is arbitrary; and, so long as we understand that survival of a single such coordinated unit would be uncertain, we may begin our evolutionary sequence here.

Before proceeding to the phases in the levels of integration, an examination of the domestic unit may prove instructive. The cycle of the domestic unit replicates the growth sequence, somewhat after the style of ontogeny recapitulating phylogeny. Figure 17 shows how the domestic unit evolves through the sequence of operating units established earlier, including an initial step as an aggregate unit. In the first generation, there is an assortment of nubile men and women; their common marriageability permits them to be classified as an aggregate unit; that is, they are independently pursuing a common type of goal, that is, someone of the opposite sex. At some point, the members of two pairs find they are drawn to each other and, in so doing, form two identity units. In courtship they establish reciprocal relations which, plus the subsequent alliance, convert each pair into a coordinate unit. These coordinate units then produce offspring, a development that converts each of them into a centralized unit (without worrying for the moment about whether the father, the mother, or both together constitute the centralizing element). The offspring, constituting the second generation, proceed through childhood as subordi-

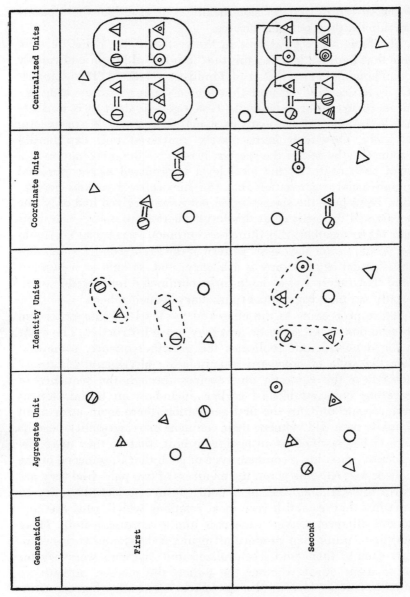

Fig. 17. Growth Sequence of the Domestic Units

nate members of these centralized operating units until they reach nubility and initiate a repetition of the sequence by behaving like members of an aggregate unit. By the simple device of domestic-unit incest rules, with a requirement to marry a person of the opposite sex of the same generation, a cross-cousin marriage system is established within two generations.

The point of this little exercise is not to explore the coordinate game of kinship rules but to show that the domestic unit, as illustrated in the generationally repetitive pattern, follows a growth sequence that is, in fact, a cycle of increasing internal power concentration. The expansion and concentration of power, then, is implicit in the protolevels of social evolution, as it is in the individual life cycle. It is not something somehow emergent or epiphenomenal in later stages of evolution but is structural at the very lowest level. This extraordinarily important fact has been somewhat obscured by anthropologists' excessive concern with the analysis of the coordinate aspect of kinship relations. That there is power in families and domestic units has not gone unrecognized, but the presence of expansionistic power dynamics as a process central to the lowest socially operative levels makes it clear that expansion is not something reserved for later stages of cultural development.

Domestic units are coordinated through territorial exclusivity, consanguineal and affinal relations, linguistic similarities and differences, and other cultural forms that mark them as relatively more or less related. In Figure 16 the coordinate phase of the domestic unit refers both to the fact of coordination and to the empirical situation holding among bands during certain seasons when they are separated in order to take the best advantage of a scattered resource base or of seasonal ecological variations. Their coordination is periodically intensified in seasonal or otherwise periodic rituals with which they are all familiar. This seasonal separation, then, alternates with periods of greater communality.

In the growth sequence between the domestic and local levels there is a transitional position between a loosely coordinated set of domestic units and a centralized set that would constitute a band. So far as I know, there is no particular name for this; it is indicated in Figure 16 by the term "related family bands." Since intermediate phases reoccur at higher levels, it becomes convenient to institute a category of a "semicentralized" phase. It will become evident that most societies empirically fall and, indeed, oscillate within this range, between the polar extremes of centralization and coordination.

## B. *The Local Level: Band and Tribe*

The band is the most primitive viable form of centralized human social organization. Its centralization is based entirely on allocated power, and the nature of the decision-making has often been described in the literature.[17] I have already commented on the importance of balanced ranking among these peoples; but ranking, even at this very low energetic level, can readily manifest a much more flamboyant quality and can be determined on some basis other than sex, age, and individual capacity. Contrary to some popular thinking, there is evident among some bands a differentiation in rank through accumulation of better control over the environment. Edwin A. Winckler has summarized:

Hart and Pilling (1960) have described the trading in claims to women that makes up a political career among the Tiwi [an aboriginal Australian population]. The reward of a successful career is not accession to political office, but the organization of wives of various ages into an efficient team for collecting food, providing a higher standard of living for the political entrepreneur and attracting younger or less successful men to his camp. The maturation of such a political career over the life cycle of individuals is an important determinant of the distribution of people and resources at particular points in time, and conveys a sense of organized political process that focus on episodes of "conflict resolution" would not.[18]

When we explore further, we find that the Eskimo and Xavante (Brazil) headmen,[19] as well as the Tiwi (Australia) headmen,[20] do have notably more wives than other members of their bands and, possibly in some part as a derivative of this, that headmanship

---

[17] See, for example, Lévi-Strauss 1967; for discussion, see Service 1966, Ch. 4.
[18] Edwin A. Winckler 1970, p. 310. Reprinted from "Political Anthropology," *Biennial Review of Anthropology, 1969*, ed. B. Siegel, by permission of Stanford University Press.
[19] Laughlin 1968, p. 317.
[20] Pilling 1968, p. 141.

not infrequently tends to follow in a particular hereditary line. So, in situations of very little power differential, the success of individuals in competition with each other can result in the introduction of a new basis of ranking.[21] This is ranking of relative adaptational success, and its presence in one Australian aboriginal population means not that it would be found in all band organizations of this level, but that it, too, can exist.

The role of the headman is to lead where his followers choose to follow. The position may or may not be particularly sought, but to keep it the individual must be skillful at making decisions that will appear appropriate to the members of the band. Many writers have emphasized the lack of authority manifested by the headmen of bands, but, as I suggested earlier in this essay, "skill authority" is as important in the continuing evolution of power as is "power authority." The emphasis in the literature on "lack" of authority rather than on a particular *kind* of authority has drawn attention away from the very important fact that the band is frequently and necessarily centralized if the population is to survive and utilize the best skills available.

The band also stands at a terminal phase in a growth sequence. Further demographic growth can only result in the simple mechanical expansion of the band. This would require either the budding off of new coordinated units, or the building up of new units on top of existing ones, thereby creating new levels of articulation. J. B. Birdsell recently reviewed the literature on hunting-band size and concluded that the Australian "dialectical tribe" (a set of bands coordinated by common dialect) "statistically approximates 500 persons." He sees this figure to be a function of communication possibilities.[22] The size of each band, however, seems to average twenty-five, based on census data from three

---

[21] Adaptational success sometimes appears masked behind other processes. Forde reports that, among the Yakö of West Africa, the Ikpungkara cult had higher prestige than the structurally similar and older Okindom cult because the former was newer. However, probably of greater importance, it addressed itself to problems that arose with the increase in population—land scarcity, cattle theft, rights to housing, etc. Thus the newer society, because of the timing of its appearance, was more critical to survival and gained higher ranking. See Forde 1967.

[22] Birdsell 1968, p. 232.

separate populations of hunters (India, Africa, and Australia).[23] Special circumstances may lead to larger groupings, but Birdsell's review indicates that there are probably fewer exceptions than was once thought.

The potential size of bands, then, must be seen both in terms of their acting alone and in terms of their acting in more intensive coordination with other bands, that is, as tribal or portions of tribal organizations. For reasons that probably combine ecological and power factors on the one hand and formal historical factors on the other, the particular internal organization of bands will vary. Peter Rivière makes an interesting comparison between two South American village Indian groups, the Trio and the Akwe-Shavante. Both depend on slash-and-burn agriculture, hunting, fishing, and gathering. The Trio, living in villages of some 30 people, have no dual factionalism within their communities, but see each village as the minimal unit of integrity and integration. The Akwe-Shavante live in villages of 80 to 350 people that are split into factions in support of one or another chief, usually along lineage lines.[24] In this way, it is possible even on the lowest level of viable human organization to see the emergence of decisional conflicts, which, were expansion to continue, would eventuate in the differentiation of new levels of integration.

Expansion and adaptation of band organizations have occupied most of human history. The Big Men of Melanesia and New Guinea, to which the Akwe-Shavante chiefs may be likened, provide the classic illustration of pristine evolution from the band toward the chiefdom. Big Men, relying on a variety of social linkages, try to concentrate social power so as to move to a higher level. For reasons not entirely agreed upon by specialists, their failure is apparently inevitable, and they are ultimately replaced by competitors. Competition and conflict between bands do not lead to enclavement and incorporation, because no band has sufficient power to retain social power over another. Therefore, if a band successfully confronts another because of social or ecological

[23] Ibid., p. 235; see also Martin, who arrives at a similar figure for the Havasupai of North America (1973).
[24] Rivière 1970.

circumscription, the result must be to scatter or displace the neighboring population. Captives may be killed, possibly eaten, or enslaved; and, if needed, they will be married or adopted.

It is when the larger social order has achieved higher levels of integration that the problem of the nature of band incorporation and lower-level organization becomes important. Chiefdoms, relying on the allocated power of people, are willing to incorporate neighbors if they are not immediately in need of the resources and if the lesser units are willing to give loyalty to (which means they may be frightened into accepting dominion under) the foreign chief. At the band or local level, however, the real basis for expansion is the larger coordination of the tribe, which permits the aggregation of sufficient number of people to form the foundation of a chiefdom. Since the very existence of the tribe has been doubted, we turn to that subject for a moment.

I earlier alluded to Morton Fried's conclusion that no such thing as the "tribe" ever existed among pristine primitives. "Most tribes seem to be secondary phenomena in a very specific sense: they may well be the product of processes stimulated by the appearance of relatively highly organized societies amidst other societies which are organized much more simply. If this can be demonstrated, tribalism can be viewed as a reaction to the formation of complex political structure rather than a necessary preliminary stage in its evolution."[25] I have already indicated that I find the notion of the "tribe" to be a useful one; and it is useful precisely as a label for the coordinate relations that exist among various bands or villages. Fried could not do with the "tribe"; I cannot do without it. Indeed, if there were no word *tribe*, I would have to invent one or leave the category with no specific designation. As it stands, the local level of integration is the only one for which there does exist an apt term to designate the coordinate unit.

The kind of coordination that takes place at this level may introduce new energetic elements that are not usually found within a single band, since a collectivity of bands may occupy a much more extensive territory than can generally be the case with scattered domestic units. Where the ecology permits, trading may

[25] Fried 1967, p. 170.

evolve, based on the variations in resources among tribal components, thus establishing another coordinate linkage which, later, may extend to other tribes.

Some tribes, such as the Plains Indians cited earlier, fluctuate essentially in a pattern that replicates the coordination of the domestic-unit-within-a-band organization, but at a higher level. Others, like the Plateau Tonga of Africa, essentially continue as a series of villages, semishifting, but linked through a wide variety of kin, ritual, and other kinds of countervailing obligations.[26] For the tribe, "The formation of regional polities, however, is frequently difficult. . . . Higher unity has to contend with the segmentary divisions of the infrastructure, with economically self-centered local groups prepared to define and defend their own interests against all comers."[27]

It becomes clear at this level that coordination need not always be friendly. Warfare or, better said, raiding, for women or loot or occasionally "slaves," is an important part of the relational system that must be seen as a coordinating device. Slaves, in this context, are usually people who are appended to the band or tribal unit, who may have special work tasks, but who usually occupy the role of resident outsiders. They have nothing to do with the chattel slavery that appears when societies evolve to higher levels of evolution. Of course, kinship and language continue to be important in the linking of these components. But the systems may become much more extensive. Arthur R. Sorensen, Jr., has reported, for example, from the Brazilian-Colombian border region, that there are more than twenty-five different linguistic groups, but that every individual is fluent in three or four languages or more, and there are four *linguae francae*. This rather extreme situation is due to the presence of patrilineal exogamous grouping where languages are kept strictly accountable. Thus every child must speak his father's and his mother's languages, as well as those of some of his neighbors.[28]

Sahlins has also analyzed a particular form of predatory expansion that occurs with a particular type of tribal organization,

[26] Gluckman 1965*a*, pp. 91–97, from material of Elizabeth Colson.
[27] Sahlins 1968, p. 17. Reprinted from Marshall D. Sahlins, *Tribesmen*, © 1968. By permission of Prentice-Hall, Inc., Englewood Cliffs, New Jersey.
[28] A. R. Sorensen 1967.

the so-called "segmentary lineages."[29] Drawing specifically on the
*tar* of the Tiv of West Africa and on the villages of the Nuer, he
makes a convincing case not only that these fit the general coordinated situation that is logically necessary but also that, further,
they could only occur in an *intertribal* situation, that is, they could
not occur in response to chiefdoms or more highly evolved forms
of organization. This, of course, specifically argues against Fried's
contention that the tribe came into being as a reaction to such more
advanced organizations. The predatory cases are, as Sahlins points
out, rather special cases, however; and there is no need to take
issue with a more general form of Fried's argument. Indeed, if
the tribe is a coordinate organization, it would follow that the
centralization of a tribe toward the general status of chiefdom
would come about specifically as a result of the pressures of social
circumscription. Thus, while not necessarily being a reaction to
more advanced societies, as Fried suggests, the centralization would
be a reaction to other groups.[30]

One of the things that disturbed Fried about attempts to define
the tribe was that the boundaries that served to identify tribes were
exactly the same as those used to identify and differentiate bands.
To him, "most so-called tribes" seemed "at close range to be curious
melanges rather than homogeneous units."[31] And, in this, I can
only agree; that is exactly the way they are, and that is precisely
why they so aptly fill the structural necessity of a coordinated
entity that relates bands, lineages, clans, and/or villages. Without
them, there could have been no further evolution to chiefdoms.
When we find a category that is structurally necessary and for
which the literature is full of cases, then perhaps we ought to go
along with the implication and allow that the tribe is a useful
concept.

When confronted with the question of why domestic units would
find it convenient to form more centralized bands, certainly as
good a reason as any is for better survival, so long as the environ-
ment/technology complex permitted. There is safety in numbers
when it comes to defense against other expanding units. When we

---

[29] Sahlins 1968.
[30] Sahlins 1961, p. 342; Fried 1967; 1968*a*.
[31] Fried 1968*a*, p. 13.

address the same question to the amalgamation of tribal components (bands, villages, lineages, clans, etc.), the answer is the same. While there are advantages to extending the area of peace, there are also advantages in being able to go to war. When one finds constraints on expanding production through peaceful means, control over the means of destruction can be equally useful.

Whatever the impulse, Lucy Mair has suggested on the basis of East African materials that there are two important conditions that must be fulfilled before one can expect a chiefdom (her term for this position is "kingship"—we will interpret it as a chiefdom) to develop.[32] One is inherited ritual power, and the other is an ability to attract and keep a following. She gives two examples (the Gusii and the Mandari) where a transition to chiefdom may have been underway through the attachment of clients, supporters who, in these cases, usually came from neighboring societies or other, less successful components of the same tribe. These people were, for one reason or another, refugees who attached themselves to the local headmen to get protection and support for the wherewithal necessary for marriage, etc. The Alur of western Uganda had chiefly lineages that were thought to have *ker*, a certain chiefly quality that was needed for ritual and political activity and was obtainable only through inheritance. Since this power could be had neither through imitation nor through economic success, chiefless people would request the Alur to send a chief's son to be their chief. The new chief would, at a later point in time, declare his independence of his father and proceed to rule alone. Mair is especially concerned to show that kings could come into being without conquest, and the point is an important one. For, while it is certainly the case that, when once established, expanding chiefdoms or kingdoms might conquer neighbors (or be conquered by them), there remains the very basic question of the ways chiefdoms may come into being in the first place.

The patron-client relation appears between the band and the chiefdom levels of integration. It is the principal process whereby individuals began to concentrate power independent of the allocated power granted to them by their fellows. It first appears in obtaining women, who provide both food and children, but later

[32] Mair 1962, Ch. 4.

increasingly becomes focused on obtaining other needed goods. As it evolves, the patron-client relation is structurally a combination of already-existent relational modes. Since reciprocity is already an established basis of exchange in band-level polities, it now becomes a relationship that further differentiates persons of higher and lower rank. The mere reciprocal granting of power or exchange between two individuals can produce nothing more than a coordinated unit; with a superordinate, the pattern now shifts such that there is a reciprocity between allocated power and delegated power. The individuals of lower rank seek the client position and thereby become multiple with respect to a particular patron; and the higher-ranked patron responds reciprocally, but to a multiplicity of clients. Thus clients allocate power or goods to the patron, and the patron, in reciprocating, actually becomes involved in what becomes a process of delegating power and goods. The successful patron is he who succeeds in accumulating more so that he may give more away and thereby gain more clients. It is the size of the total client body that is the fundamental basis of power, since the basic source of power for the ranking individual is still allocation. Since the patron-client pattern evolves for ranking individuals as a part of competition with others aspiring to elevated rank, it contributes not to solidarity but rather to complementary segmentation. In itself, therefore, it leads not to social stratification but rather to the fluctuating multiplicity of ranked domains of Big Men and of affluent and charismatic chiefs.[33]

An important area for comparison is New Guinea and Melanesia, where a good many agriculturally based societies are semicentralized between the tribe and the chiefdom. The components here are villages, and the basic organization combines kinship coordinate dependence with the emergence of two clear political levels of integration. H. A. Powell has described this situation for the Trobriand Islanders, a stable horticultural society at what might be characterized as an advanced tribal level of integration:

Perhaps the best way shortly to describe indigenous Trobriand political organizations is as a variant of the systems of competitive individual leadership by "Big Men" common in adjacent parts of Melanesia, which is modified in the Trobriands, at least in Northern Kiriwina Is-

[33] See Sahlins 1963 and 1968 for discussion of Big Men.

land, by the system of rank. This restricts eligibility to compete for political leadership in any given locality to the members of the highest ranking matrilineal descent group or sub-clan (*dala*) associated with it, and at the same time tends to ensure that amongst them one man is always singled out as at least the potential leader of the locality. Upon him the population's economic and political relationships tend to focus so that it becomes organized as his following, and tends to co-operate as a unit in competition with similarly led and organized populations of other localities. Trobriand political activity thus consists in a continuing process of creation, expansion, and contraction of followings and area of influence by men qualified to compete for leadership. . . . The attribute of rank confers on those who possess it certain advantages which provide them with the nucleus of a following as well as with the right to aspire to expand it at least to the extent commensurate with their rank.[34]

The Kapauku, cited earlier, provide another instance of this system, with the levels and the client system both explicit. Of the political levels (see Table 1) only three are not subdivisions of the kinship system: the household, the village, and the confederation. For reasons already adduced, we would not include the household, or domestic unit, as a viable level on its own; so we would accept the statement that the Kapauku clearly had a band organization but had also semicentralized into forming clearly coordinated sets of Big Men. The maximal unit of the Kapauku is the confederation, but the headship of the confederation depends upon obtaining many supporters, and this, in turn, is achieved principally through eloquence and generosity, the latter being dependent upon wealth—and that, in turn, is dependent upon gaining supporters. Supporters attach themselves so long as it is to their benefit; if a more promising Big Man comes along, the likelihood is that many will switch their allegiance. Leadership of the confederacy, therefore, depends constantly on personal success, and a man aging or down in his luck will be displaced.

Contrast this with the East African cases, and it is clear that with inherited ritual power a Kapauku Big Man would have had a device to fix the locus of his competence in himself and his descendants. J. A. Barnes, with less attention to the ritual side of the

[34] Powell 1960, p. 118. Reprinted from the *Journal of the Royal Anthropological Institute*, vol. 90, no. 1.

matter, observed that the New Guinea highlands simply did not provide the "dogma of descent" that was so common in Africa.[35] Descent was only one of a variety of personal linkages that might be used by a Big Man to gain supporters; indeed, they were not even limited (in the Kapauku case) to the particular confederacy he was heading. Essentially the same picture has been reported by various Melanesian and New Guinea observers, and it returns us to the question of the possible importance of sacred elements, both in the sense of religion and ritual and in the Redfieldian sense of *sacred*, that is, matters of dogma that are not to be questioned.[36]

Before proceeding further, let us examine for a moment the kinds of power exercise with which we are now dealing. In the band, it will be recalled, the total basis of centralized power was allocation. Since the tribe consists of little more than a coordination of bands, it does require some increase in resources but is even more contingent on an increase in numbers. The chiefdoms, however, introduce a new element into the power scene. The building of support from a range of supporters means getting tribute in kind, accumulating this, and then providing periodic redistributional feasts. The Big Man depends upon the allocated power of individuals (including those of villages besides his own) who become his supporters because he is successful in obtaining and distributing wealth, successful as a war leader, and convincing as a talker. The Big Man is a surgent band headman; he does not have overwhelming power authority; but, instead of depending upon the general consensus of band members, he has established a series of reciprocal relations with individuals. He uses the power allocated

[35] Barnes also suggests, ". . . despite these qualifications I think that it may still be hypothesized that the disorder and irregularity of social life in the Highlands, as compared with, say, Tiv, is due in part to the high value placed on killing" (1962, p. 9). Violence and killing for its own sake, while of uncertain efficacy in the long run in keeping the population down, would certainly be a cause of a kind of disorder; it might have been contained by an appropriate "dogma."

[36] R. Redfield finds Durkheim's notion of the sacred to be too categorical and proposes that "an object is sacred to the extent that there is reluctance, emotionally supported, to call the thing rationally or practically into question" (1941, p. 353). Reluctance to call into question is the central issue here; for this, I prefer the term *dogma*, as it does not imply any supernatural concomitants and also does not deny that it may rest within a rational framework.

to him to gain more wealth and more power; and the agricultural and livestock (pigs) base allows him to accumulate this material so that his very success gives him some basis of independent power. This independent power, however, is unstable or, better said, undependable. Ideally, if a Big Man wanted to secure his position as the central figure in the tribe, he would, as Peter Worsley has pointed out, have to dissociate himself from a narrow allegiance to any of the segments or individual supporters on whom he is dependent. "To unite them, he must stand above them; he cannot afford to be identified with any one village or one clan. One of the most effective ways of doing this is to project his message on to the supernatural plane. He brings a message from God or the ancestors, and appeals to the people to join the movement on the basis of a common allegiance to a religion and an organization which stands above them all and unites them all."[37] The advantage the African Alur had over their neighbors was the widely shared common belief in the ritual effectiveness of their chiefs; and the success of the millenarian movements that Worsley studied was due to a common receptivity to the efficacy of the leader.

## C. The Regional Level and the Centralizing Role of Dogma

One prehistoric thesis on which there seems to be a high degree of consensus is that the early centralized societies beyond the band level were probably theocratic.[38] Citing Julian Steward, V. Gordon Childe, Robert Adams, and A. Leo Oppenheim, together with material on prehistoric evolution in the Andes, Richard P. Schaedel has argued that the "first public architecture is represented by the religious shrine." According to Schaedel, "The developments which were documented for Mesopotamia between 2,500 and 1,700 B.C. (Oppenheim) appear to correspond to the developments . . . in coastal Peru 500–1,250 A.D. Two ingredients of the situation underscored by both Adams and Oppenheim were . . . the coexistence for a time in the ceremonial center of political segments with religious segments, followed by a predominance of the former over the

[37] Worsley 1957, p. 27; cited in Netting 1972, p. 234.
[38] Flannery 1972, p. 413: "All the data at our disposal suggest that in the 'pristine' first-generational states, rulers were recruited from sanctified royal lineages."

latter . . ."[39] Then, of central importance, ". . . the point to be made is that a theocratic polity is functionally conceivable only while the redistributive factor is essentially cyclical. The integrative force of the religious function rests upon this principle of participation. The mechanism of secular coercion which characterizes functional urbanism is inimical to the system."[40]

Schaedel has linked two important elements: what he calls a cyclical redistributional system (of the type practiced among contemporary Meso-American Indians and the Big Man societies of Melanesia) and the appearance of theocratic polities as the first evidence of supralocal centralization. Robert Netting has recently argued the ethnographic parallel from materials in West Africa (and again the Alur): when societies are expanding in population so that resources are becoming circumscribed, and the problems of managing the society cannot be handled on terms of coordinate relations, then "the mastery of socially inclusive religious rituals and embodiment of sacred forces [are] viewed as crucial attributes of emerging institutionalized leadership in localized politics. . . . Where organized coercive mechanisms are weakly developed, these ends may be achieved most effectively by the concentration of magical potency in a leader, the expansion of his religious authority, and the crystallization of a more inclusive moral community."[41] If we ask how this religious, sacred, or dogmatic element comes into being, one possibility is that it was a part of an earlier coordinate relational system; that is, not only language, or kin, or trade, but also common manipulatable beliefs may have been

[39] Schaedel, n.d.*b*, pp. 3–4, 6. Used by permission of the author.

[40] Ibid., p. 14.

[41] Robert Netting 1972, pp. 240, 242. Reprinted from *Population Growth: Anthropological Implications*, ed. Brian Spooner, by permission of MIT Press. An earlier proponent of a more general argument along this same line was Robert Lowie: "With frankly evolutionary aim I shall assemble some data from the simpler American tribes in order to show that religious beliefs were used to attain political influence there and I suggest that the awe which surrounded the protege of supernatural powers formed the psychological basis for more complex political developments. It is possible for a titular chief to add to his standing by combining spiritual blessings with civil eminence, or he may enter an alliance with the religious functionary, thus foreshadowing the familiar spectacle of State and Church joined in the support of the established order" (Lowie 1967, p. 84).

involved in the basic coordination. Another alternative is that stresses of the kind cited by Netting or encountered by Worsley in post–World War II Melanesia made the population willing to allocate power to some religiously framed activity or object.

Fundamentally, however, the importance of what we may think of as "religion" lay in the fact that pristine chiefdoms were societies that were still heavily dependent on allocated power. Every Big Man in surgence toward chiefdom and many so-called African kings were dependent on the same allocated sources of power that provided them with their basic power at the outset, that is, other people. And, when the system achieved that level, allocated power continued important. No one has described this better than Gluckman for the Barotse of Africa: The "wealthy and powerful do not form what might be called a separate 'class,' cut off from the poor by a quite different style of life. . . . In fact, the powerful and wealthy use the land and goods they control to attract followers, and a man's prestige is determined by the number of dependents or subjects he has, much more than by mere possession and use of goods. Prestige and power are important in all these societies and enable a man to control the action of others; but he gains that control through establishing relationships of personal dependence with as many others as he can."[42] Later Gluckman made it clear that this dependence on allocated power still rested on the level of production: "With the goods and technologies available to the Barotse economy, the rich and powerful could not live in much finer houses, surrounded by relatively luxurious furnishings, or bedeck themselves with fine clothes; there was therefore no point in attempting to exercise their power to profit from sweating the labor or to expropriate the goods of underlings."[43] In short, the wealthy Barotse took their tribute but rewarded tribute with gifts.

[42] Gluckman 1965*b*, p. 46. Goody confirms this general picture for West Africa as well, but suggests that both the relative primitiveness of African agriculture, where neither the plough nor the wheel was used, and the relatively bad soils meant that the larger groupings could not depend so much on independent power aggregated by a chief. West African chiefdoms, even large ones, continued until the introduction of the horse, firearms, and other trade resources well into the nineteenth century to look to allocated power as a crucial foundation of the power structure. (See Goody 1971, pp. 30–32.)

[43] Gluckman 1965*b*, p. 46.

There is no necessary energetic connection between allocated power and religion, but there is a very crucial mentalistic one. Allocated power is essentially the granting of power; but it is more; for, in granting, the allocator accepts the fact that the grantee is capable of certain things. In the ethnographic literature, this is referred to often in terms of the grantee "having power." The mana complex of Melanesia and Polynesia and individual power holding among North American Indians have this kind of granted power. The power holders are inherently capable in certain directions, and at the same time that capability is recognized when others grant to them the fact that they have such capabilities, such powers. It is but a small psychological step, of which any man is capable, to project this granted power as in fact having been granted to an individual, as existing apart from him and given him in some mysterious way. Thus supernaturalism is not intrinsic to allocated power but can be readily associated to it.[44]

Recourse to supernatural powers by people who regard themselves as essentially insufficiently strong probably predates chiefdoms. Rivière, in the paper earlier cited, notes among the Akwe-Shavante that "Accusations of sorcery are made by the more powerful against the less powerful, while sorcery itself is made by the weaker against the stronger . . . For the Shavante, physical force is associated with superiority, mystical sanctions with inferiority."[45] Nor is this kind of allocated (religious) power limited to chiefdoms, as is illustrated by the emphasis placed by the contemporary North American black on "soul," or by the North American Indian on the power that resides in adherence to old tribal-law ways.[46] And Goody notes specifically among the West African groups that "the autochthones, weaker in military might, were stronger in supernatural power, which served as some counterweight to their political inferiority."[47]

Religion must be seen fundamentally as a device that enhances and extends allocative power. The allocation of power to a head-

[44] Lane 1974.

[45] Peter Rivière 1970, p. 252. Reprinted from *Witchcraft Confessions and Accusations*, ed. Mary Douglas, published by Tavistock Publications Limited, by permission of Associated Book Publishers Limited.

[46] Stanley 1974.

[47] Goody 1971, p. 65.

man or Big Man on the basis of skill authority will stop if the individual persistently fails to carry out his obligations satisfactorily. If power can be "allocated" to a nonhuman object or act, that is, a drum, a ritual behavior, a presumptive descent relationship (that is, a set of people), then the persons who stand to control the acts or objects in question have many of the advantages of allocated power but without always having all of the responsibilities. Indeed, in the case of the Divine King of the Shilluk, the king himself had no effective administrative powers. Power based on dogma, belief, religion, etc., is allocated power of the believer, not independent power of the figure to whom it is allocated. Thus, if anything happens to weaken the dogma, and no substitute controls are available, the entire system resting on the dogma can crumble. The importance of ceremonial redistribution was that it gave the priests some independent power. The importance of isolation to these systems is to keep competitive beliefs out of the picture. Once dissipated, dogma-based allocated power can seldom be reassembled.

In a more general way, Roy Rappaport has observed that "Sanctity . . . is a functional equivalent of political power among some of the world's peoples. We can distinguish among past and present human societies on a continuum from those governed largely by sacred conventions in the absence or near absence of human authorities . . . to those of the contemporary west, in which authorities stand much more heavily on power than they do upon sanctity."[48] Rappaport continues by arguing that, as technological competence increased, direct coercive ability displaced the need for this kind of sanctity. Noting that the "archaic states were, at least at the outset, theocratic," he then proposes that "sanctity, before power, provided a foundation for the regulatory prerogative of discrete authorities. Indeed, sanctity may have permitted the emergence of discrete authorities."[49]

---

[48] Rappaport 1971*b*, p. 37. Reprinted, with permission, from "The Sacred in Human Evolution," *Annual Review of Ecology and Systematics*, Volume 2, page 37. Copyright © 1971 by Annual Reviews, Inc. All rights reserved.

[49] Ibid., p. 39. Rappaport here uses a rather limited definition of *sanctity*, but it is more or less equivalent to my use of the term *dogma*. For Rappaport sanctity is "the quality of unquestioned truthfulness imputed by the faithful to unverifiable propositions" (ibid., p. 29). This definition seems to have an ele-

Wallace has suggested a typology of religions that correlates with the present argument. While bands and tribal organizations have religions of an "individualistic" or "shamanistic" nature, chiefdoms and kingdoms have what he refers to as "olympian" religions, religions that come from some larger, more distant, more encompassing wellspring of "power." Whatever religion evolved, it presumably had to be one that claimed larger scope than the local deities and spirits that satisfied the needs of separate bands and villages.[50] I will not try here to trace the evolving interrelations between the sacred and the secular. The emergence of theism as a dominant Western religion, the evolution of other varieties in the East, and the continuing coherence of these with secular developments warrant serious research. We know that the relation between the religious and the political continued in varying degrees of intimacy at the state level until the seventeenth-century English Revolution and the eighteenth-century American Revolution. It is probably not too far from the truth to suggest that, while religion was displaced as the major basis of power much earlier, its importance as the vehicle of dogma in governing activities only began to be displaced by nontheistic dogma with the secular success of the mercantilist and technological preconditioning of the Industrial Revolution and was in fact seriously threatened only after the Industrial Revolution was well underway. Certainly the Spanish, English, Dutch, and French killed off native peoples as well as each other in the name of God; and well past the middle of the twentieth century the United States was waging war against the spread of "Godless Communism," while Arab chiefs of state seriously proposed a holy war against Israel.

The general correlation between religion and chiefdoms, on the one hand, and the correlation between chiefdoms and certain types of religions, on the other hand, will probably stand up under more careful scrutiny. Emphasis on this direct correlation, however, draws attention away from an additional variation in dogma that

---

ment of the inherent irrationality which characterized Redfield's use of the term but which I do not think is necessary for my own arguments. Also, the use of the term *the faithful* tends to make the statement somewhat tautological.

[50] Wallace 1966, p. 88.

relates to the shift from coordinate to centralizing processes. This will be clearer if we see charisma as being the close kin of dogma, but referring to the specific "powers" that may be attributed to individuals rather than ideas.

The resurgence at any period of coordinate linkages as opposed to centralized linkages will effect a disappearance of charisma from sheerly political roles. Since, allowing for cultural variations from one society to another in matters of style, charisma is in the eye of the beholder as well as in the quality of the man, it is likely to be found where there is a need for good leadership; that is to say, good leaders are in considerable part made by the followers.[51] Charisma will be particularly in evidence when a society is centralizing and people feel the need for confidence in leadership in the political realm. As such, it will tend to appear in various areas of life where individuals are incapable of action, of solving their problems, without some allocation or granting of power. Charisma is a way of power granting or allocating that is particularly dogmatic, that is, uncritical, in quality.

The allocation of power is fundamentally a centralizing process; it gives the right of making decisions to some unit or units and denies it to certain others. When members of a society, correctly or not, are convinced that their best interest lies in political centralization, charisma is likely to be allocated to the political leader. Political centralization, however, is distinct from centralization formulated in other idioms, since it relates to the definition of the maximal boundaries of the societies. It is often the case that societies of lesser scale, or lesser segments of larger societies, perceive their welfare to lie, not in strengthening the integrity of the maximal boundaries, but in the strengthening of some lesser portion, some specific network of relations that is defined differently from that of the whole; and this is done in part to more clearly define the relations that hold between that part and the other parts, and with the whole. This is a coordinating process, and charisma is likely to be attached to leaders in those lesser segments and networks. In large societies, however, direct allocation of power to a particular leader is not likely to be of extensive duration because of

[51] Cf. Worsley 1968, Introduction to Second Edition.

the impossibility of his being able to reciprocate with conduct that will work to the benefit of a very large number of people.

To illustrate the above, we can compare the charisma attached to such leaders as Hitler, Churchill, De Gaulle, and Roosevelt during such times of national crisis as the Second World War to that of their political successors during periods when the survival of the nation was not the primary question. In the latter instance, whatever charisma was allocated was destined for leaders in lesser networks of interest, such as trade, sports, religious cults, science, etc. We would expect charisma to attach itself to successful aboriginal Big Men because they are centralizing; by the same token, we would expect similar charisma to attach itself to contemporary millenaristic, messianistic, or nativistic leaders, who, in a very real sense, try to centralize around some idiom other than the political state and on a local or regional rather than a national scale.

Thus we would expect spiritualistic or theistic charisma in balanced chiefdoms and in the fragmented states of the early Christian era in the West. Political charisma we would expect to find in the West in the nineteenth and first half of the twentieth century, but disappearing today; in the mercantilistic expansion period of the sixteenth- and seventeenth-century Spanish colonial empire, but not in the period of the so-called depression. In short, political charisma goes with political centralization, whereas sectarian and parochial charisma appear when networks of lesser or greater scope are brought into play. The effort at "one-worldism" that followed the Second World War found its charisma attached to leaders in "moral rearmament" and other relational networks that specifically did not follow the boundaries of the nation-state. For these efforts, such criteria as race, religious cult, ethnic membership, occupational dedication, etc., mark the participant; or, merely being a believer may suffice.

This correlation between the formal features that characterize leadership and the kind of process that is at work at a given time allows us to identify regularities between social power (which in turn derives from energetic controls) and the nature of the culture at a point in time. Symbolic inversions, touched upon in Part Two, are very common elements of the shifts in emphasis from the centralizing to the coordinating processes; they reflect a change in the direction and target of the allocation of power. Similarly, specific ecological conditions may lead people to shift from one to another. Migrants will seek to identify their relations with a new environment, seek to clarify and strengthen their controls. In so doing, they will be establishing coordinate relations on the one hand and centralizing on the other. The leadership that arises will reflect the scale of the operation, and the cultural forms chosen will reflect the level of identification.

As a working hypothesis, I believe that it can be argued that what I have been calling *dogma*, the unchallenged acceptance of a decision-making process, will always be claimed for and to some degree will characterize the ideology of centralizing units at the highest level of integration. There is little question that in much of the Western world today dogma exists at that level, but it is not in a religious or, better said, theistic vehicle. The idiom has changed and, for example, in the United States it has been taken over by the Rule of Law, and its priests are lawyers, and its high priests are the justices of the Supreme Court. Further, if it exists at the highest centralized level, then it can also be argued that at the next highest level, which will of necessity be coordinated, there will be found the elements of a further protodogma that waits in the wings for the curtain to rise on its act. This is tangential to the train of our exposition, however; so let us return to chiefdoms.

It seems likely, then, that tribes could have been centralized in at least the manner just described. How, then, about conquest, warfare? I confess that I find it difficult to see a chiefship emerging from tribal war that involved no chief. Fried has justly pointed out that "warfare increases in frequency as societies become more complex,"[52] and I do not know any evidence that contradicts this. Indeed, an extensive recent study of power among modern nations concludes that those nations that tend to hold more power in general are those that are likely to be busier in war: "The more powerful nations, where power is derived from average demographic, industrial, and military resources, go to war more often, spend

[52] Fried 1967, p. 214. This is further confirmed by Otterbein's cross-cultural study of war (1970). He finds that military sophistication improves with higher degrees of political centralization (p. 75), and the greater the military sophistication, the "more likely that communities of a cultural unit will engage in frequent or continual offensive external war" (p. 88).

more months in war, and lose more lives (both in sheer numbers and as percentages of their populations and armed forces) than do the less powerful nations. In addition, they have tended more often than the less powerful nations to be the initiating actor, and the international wars they do initiate tend to be more bloody than those initiated by nations less powerful."[53]

The question, however, concerns not how much warfare there was but whether it was used to centralize, and it is about this that my observation about the antecedent presence of a chief was made. Even where there may have been chiefs, such as among the "barbarians" who sacked parts of Europe periodically over the first millennium A.D., the result was seldom the establishment of stable greater chiefdoms. Carneiro argues that with population growth incentives for war shifted from mere revenge or raids to a need to acquire land and that, under these circumstances, the conquered village faced four alternatives: (*a*) expulsion; (*b*) extermination; (*c*) subordination by being required to pay tribute or tax; (*d*) subordination by political incorporation. Clearly the first two of these would not account for greater centralization, since they simply eliminated people; and the last two obviously presume an existing system that knows about tribute or tax or that has the mechanisms available for incorporation—and thus would presuppose a chiefdom (at least). When we seek Carneiro's explanation as to *how* centralization would take place, we are told that "Through the recurrence of warfare of this type, we see arising in coastal Peru integrated territorial units transcending the village in size and in degree of organization. Political evolution was attaining the level of chiefdom."[54] In other words, in spite of its not being able to happen, it did, in fact, just happen. I cite this, not to argue against Carneiro's broader and much more convincing thesis that involves social and environmental circumscription as a prerequisite, but rather to argue that chiefdoms would have arisen as a response not to nonchiefdom wars but to other factors related to circumscription. As to Carneiro's argument that there is a "demonstrated inability of autonomous political units to relinquish their

[53] Stuckey and Singer 1973, p. 39. Used by permission of the authors.

[54] Robert L. Carneiro 1970, p. 735. Reprinted with permission, from *Science*, Vol. 169 (21 August 1970). Copyright 1970 by the American Association for the Advancement of Science.

sovereignty in the absence of overriding external constraints,"[55] I
will have to argue that Mair's and Netting's proposals, coupled
with Schaedel's posited cyclical redistribution, make it quite possible to think that the original theocratic chiefdoms emerged as a
device that guaranteed economic security through the medium of
ritualistic performance. If power allocated in dogma pays off, that
is, if there are satisfactory economic returns, then it can work. An
economically successful Melanesian Big Man with dogma might
have become a chief; and it is precisely this element that the millenarian movements tried to introduce.[56]

The displacement of the sacred by the secular, or of the dogmatic
by the doubtful, is as important an aspect of the evolution of power
as is the original appearance of the sacred. The pattern seems generally to have been that the new technology provided rulers, or
challengers to rulers, with new elements of control that allowed
them independent power and permitted them to substitute the use
of force where allocated power seemed lacking. It seems likely that
the attempt to do this by Big Men in situations where in fact they
had not achieved this kind of independent power accounts for their
regular failure to further centralize.

Perhaps the most outstanding case of the shedding of dogma by
the very actors whose power had depended upon it occurred in
1819 when the king, or principal chief, of Hawaii and his entire nobility cast out the dogma and allocated power of mana and tabu
that had provided them with sacred protection and extraordinary
power over the population. The literature has posed this as an extraordinary event, but in fact it appears to have been a necessity
for the secular rulers to continue to rule. The condition of mana
and tabu had become so intensive that royalty was all but immo-

---

55 Ibid., p. 734.

56 Balandier has observed that "In every society, the political power is never
quite completely desacralized; and in the case of 'traditional' societies, the *relation with the sacred* is quite overt. But whether it is unobtrusive or apparent, the sacred is always present in political power" (1970, p. 38). This is
one of those statements that can be regarded as sound if we define the terms.
If *sacred* = *dogma*, then I would agree; but, if it means *religion* in the
traditional sense, then I would be less enthusiastic, since in the contemporary
world there are segments of humanity that use other than religious idioms for
their political dogma.

bilized. Coupled with this was the fact that European firearms had been introduced, and the actual independent power of the king was such that he could do without the excessive and crippling allocated power that so sanctified him. The solution was a massive symbolic inversion to reject the ritual of the religion as a whole. Of course, believing did not stop, and much of it continued until it was gradually supplanted by the competitive and politically stronger Protestantism that arrived shortly after the "cultural revolution."[57]

To summarize, then, chiefdoms are centralizations of tribes that rest heavily on allocated power, but coupled with a device to secure the allocated power from a number of different bands, a number of different "subcultures." Schaedel has argued that the early theocratic chiefdoms' success was due to the economic surplus that was centralized in a "ceremonial fund" for ceremonial redistribution. While surely some of this accumulation enhanced the ritual and its practitioners, by and large it was a device whereby the inequalities of the environment and the ecological process were corrected by a centralized power. Storage of food to cover bad years anywhere in the entire population also established further collateral bonds. The political order, however, was always unstable, because it depended on dogmatic allocation, a process that serves only for units of limited scale. Further expansion, which became necessary as technology improved, required that the dogmatic allocation be subordinated to independent power.

## D. *The State Level and Social Stratification*

The concern in the literature on the subject of the "state"[58] has been fruitful in that it has forced further thought on a number of important topics, such as the nature and causes of centralization, the nature of stratification, etc. It has an unfortunate side, however, since the concern too frequently has become that of the scholar who, having invented a category, spends the rest of his life vainly searching for substance to fill it. In the case of the Missing Origin of the State, we cannot even dignify our category with being

[57] Davenport 1969; my interpretation has been helped by a research paper by Stan Verhoeven (1974).

[58] See Fried 1968*b*; Carneiro 1970.

a "logical category": it is not derived from any particularly orderly mental process but rather has been shaped by the intellectual
"folk" usage of the Western tradition. It may be that we can
blame it all on Aristotle, who, in his early examination of society,
simply considered the city-state to be the society and the society to
be the state. In a different argument, Marx could also say that
"The *State* and the *structure of society* are not, from the standpoint of *politics, two* different things. The State is the structure of
society."[59]

Impressionistically, I suspect concern over the state continues
because its origin is felt to signify a turning point in human history when man had succeeded in taking so much power to himself
that he could readily subordinate his fellow man; the autonomy of
man was lost.[60] But in examining the sequence suggested in Figure
16 it is a little difficult to be convinced that the state appeared suddenly. The infrahuman primate who serves as the center of attention for other members of his "band" has already been allocated
power, even if he has not evolved the possibilities to exploit it as
man has. So I would have to agree with Aristotle and Marx in
some measure; insofar as power is inherent to human society, then
to that degree the society constitutes the state.

Marx has been seen by recent observers as a figure of Coperni-
can proportions because his theory located the individual or group
within the economic structure, identifying thereby two strata or
"classes" on the basis of their relative control over the means of
production. By the nineteenth century, industrialization had so expanded society that existing theories of social structure could not
handle it. Marx, with that too human ability, cut into the matter
with a simple binary differentiation, exposing hitherto-obscured
dynamics. But, as with all binary contrasts, even those that shatter
paradigms, the energetics were more complicated; subsequent
thinkers proceeded to detail the energetic varieties, to show simultaneously the remarkable theoretical value of the formulation and

[59] Bottomore and Rubel, eds. 1964, p. 216. From *Karl Marx: Selected Writings in Sociology and Philosophy*, ed. T. B. Bottomore and Maximilian Rubel.
Copyright © 1956 C. A. Watts and Co. Ltd., London. Used with permission
of McGraw-Hill Book Company.

[60] I am, obviously, not attempting here to account for all the usages of the
term *state* that abound in the literature.

the necessary further empirical problems it spawned among both "orthodox Marxist" and "anti-Marxist" thinkers.

Marx's theory was, of course, by no means as simple as a mere binary differentiation; but, in its influential outlines, it did what such contrasts must do: by dividing the universe in two it pointed out common features of certain things that had earlier been thought to be separate and distinct entities. Among the most important bunchings of concepts that accompanied Marx's argument was the claim that the "state," long conceived as an entity that referred to a variety of things, from rulers, ruling elite, or class, on the one hand, to the totality of the sovereign people, on the other, was misidentified; that the state lay at neither of these extremes but emerged as a particular kind of society which bifurcated the ownership of productive means from the productive process and left the determination of events to evolve from a necessary internal confrontation. Thus did Marx argue not only that a state society was bifurcated but also that it was inherently incompatible and ultimately self-destructive.

It was a century before Western scholarship collectively focused on the ramifications of Marx's theory, although it provided the germinal bed for "Marxist theorists" from the start. And collective attention was finally drawn to the issues in part because the very conditions that Marx tried to clarify by his dichotomy had so grown energetically that they could not be avoided. In a sense, scholars who did not come to it with the commitment of praxis (the belief that the very study of the events should be designed to further their path toward the ultimate "stateless society") found Marx's argument threatening to their own delicately balanced social-power positions and were reluctant to admit publicly that it could have utility. Only when the course of events permitted them to argue that Marx's reasoning had been a product of his age was it possible for them to accept the wisdom he offered and proceed to enlighten their own thinking with his insights.

Within the more limited traditions of anthropology, perhaps the most influential recent work in this area has, once again, been that of Morton Fried, who, in his evolutionary model of political matters, proposed that the appearance of stratification and the appearance of the state were closely related, but that stratification somehow emerged first and then was, in some manner, overtaken or captured by the state.[61] This permitted him to argue that no pre-state stratified societies could have survived, since, following Marx, stratification would have produced the state.

In brief, Fried holds that a "stratified society is one in which members of the same sex and equivalent age status do not have equal access to the basic resources that sustain life."[62] The proposal, I believe, is inherently sound but too general to be helpful in the present analysis. Also this says what the power base of stratification was (and is), but it does not really define stratification. It tells us that there are societies with unequal access to resources, but how do we know empirically when we have stratification? In his search for origins, Fried answers this by arguing that "the blocking of access to enlarged labor groups is derived from an earlier process of blockage from basic resources. . . . the question of the origins of stratification revolves about the process by which basic resources were converted from communal to private property."[63] And this, he generally concludes, is in response to population pressures, in some instances aided by a shift in residence rules. Fried's "origins" may seem anticlimactic, until we remember that such societies do not exist anyway; no sooner had they appeared than they were converted into states, and no pristine cases could survive. Without abandoning the substance of Fried's "definition," I think we can move further than this.[64]

If social organization operates through mentalistic structures as well as energetic structures, and Fried has chosen the energetic, let us then have a look at the mentalistic side. Stratification is basically a ranking phenomenon, but it is not the ranking of individuals, or of larger parallel segments or operating units, such as

[61] Fried's exposition of his general position is in his 1967 essay, Chs. 5–6. That his position represents something more than a parochial anthropology is suggested by the fact that the editors of the *International Encyclopedia of the Social Sciences* sought him to prepare the article on "State: The Institution" (Fried 1968*b*). While it will be apparent that I am not in accord with portions of his thinking, his work has the quality, so rare in social science, of allowing one to see where problems lie and to seek further to correct them.

[62] Fried 1967, p. 52; see also Ch. 5.

[63] Ibid., p. 191.

[64] Fried does not call it a "definition" in the text; it is so characterized in the index.

lineages, villages, or bands. Rather than a ranking of moderately unequal elements within a single set, it is a ranking of sets; and the sets are themselves distinguished by the fact that the members of one are extremely unequal, as a collectivity, to the members of the other. Thus a macroranking evolved out of what had first been mere individual rank differences. Energetic expansion both in numbers of people and in perceptible differences of equality led those with the greater controls and social power to form a separate identity unit (if Marx could invent it, so could they) and then a coordinate unit that ranked itself apart from and superior to those it did not count among its members. Given the inequality that would have been manifest in a society centralizing at the chiefdom level, such ranking of unequal sets would have been almost inevitable. Interstrata exclusivity would have been inherent in the fact that the superior unit was explicitly a coordinate unit (i.e., its internal organization was based on reciprocity) and, similarly, would have been outside the system of ranking.

Given this suppositional picture, let us now return to the question of how the energetic changes came about. Fried is very specific in holding that the conditions that forced the emergence of stratification were due first to population pressure, which, through a series of intermediate processes, resulted in the emergence of private property.[65] While private property surely came into the picture at some point, I am doubtful about using it as a historical factor in a model, since it requires that we make specific assumptions about the value systems in a series of archaic situations for which we have little evidence. Private property is, fundamentally, some set of objects or acts to which exclusive rights are given; more specifically, they pertain to some value class of relatively high priority. When we start exploring the details of these value classes and how they work in different societies, we quickly realize that forms of exclusion may be obvious or obscure and are not always readily recognizable. Thus, while I readily allow that private property is theoretically an important issue, I believe it can better be used where we know just what kind of energetic objects are involved and where they may have stood in the larger control and power situation of the society. Thus, I can recognize the general importance

[65] Fried 1967, pp. 191–226.

of land; but I am also impressed that land in Africa has not played the role that it has in Europe.

There is another track that may offer an alternative to dependence on the concept of private property, without eliminating it from a place of importance in the larger picture. Prehistorians who have followed the Steward model have argued that the theocratic chiefdoms were historically followed by evidence of militarism or by the gradual displacement of sacred aspects by secular elements. If it is the case that chiefdoms came into being in part because of the population growth that simultaneously placed pressure on the environmental resources and found a solution to that pressure by centralization and ceremonial redistribution (presuming the presence or emergence of an adequate technology), it is logical that continuing population growth would lead to interchiefdom pressure, which would presumably be handled in some degree by war. The rise of the military would then be a necessary later stage of a successful ceremonial chiefdom in a region of expanding population. The rise of a military not only would involve external conquest but also would institute secular centralization, since it would give a central figure control over a major source of independent power, that is, the means of destruction. This would signal the fixing of two tendencies that I believe were closely interdependent: (*a*) conquest and subjugation of other societies, and their incorporation by various means; and (*b*) the fixing of social stratification, the internal ranking of an operating unit of those with power authority as against those without or with less.

The relation that I see between secular power, based principally on the military and on some economic controls, and the emergence of stratification is not a conquest theory of the state, wherein the conquerors constitute an upper class and the conquered, a destituted lower class. While private property is important, the more central issue is power in general. Private property tends to lead us to consider only the means of production, and not consumption or destruction. If chiefdoms did depend on allocated power, then their origins might be found in the differential accumulation of the products and in the manipulation of popular opinion. The ceremonial cycle of redistribution, insofar as it has continued to operate in contemporary peasant communities in Middle America, has operated not because the elders of the community "owned" all the landed property but because they controlled the consumption of much of it. Let me seek a parallel (and let me insist that it is presented as a parallel, not as "how it worked"). Goody differentiates West Africa in accord with three degrees of concentration of power on the basis of differences in the means of destruction: (*a*) acephalous societies, based mainly on the equalitarian bow and arrow; (*b*) grassland kingdoms, based principally on control of the war horse; (*c*) forest kingdoms based on control of firearms. "The dichotomy between the gun states of the forest (where the horse could not operate, partly for trees, partly for tsetse) and the horse states of the savannahs corresponds to significant differences in the social systems. In the grasslands, the ruling estates tended to be mass dynasties, within segments of which high office often circulated. In the forest, office tended to be more autocratic and to be retained within a narrower dynasty."[66] The intended thrust of Goody's argument is that it was control over these destructive implements that determined the relative power of the societies and their degree of concentration.

Now in more pristine conditions we are dealing, not with such great technological differentials as would be created by the introduction of the horse or firearms, but with control over consumption. This has been well witnessed in Big Man societies and, we have argued, could have moved with dogma into ceremonial funds controlled by groups of men rather than single Big Men. Indeed, if the land was in control of lineages or clans, as it has been in some instances, then the differential control of land would have emerged on a communal basis, with some "elite" operating unit handling it in the name of the community. The shift to private property may well have come later, when population pressure was even greater. So it appears that quite varying differentials in control of land preceded "private property." If such communal concentration was made first, then it seems likely that the control exercised over that land would have had the goal of increasing production so that adequate consumption could be guaranteed. The Big Man's first job was to assure consumption, as that was the basis of his power.

My argument is, first, that the origins of stratification lie in differentiation in power by levels and that initial power-base differ-

[66] Goody 1971, p. 55.

entials were more likely in control over consumption than in control over production.[67] Second, the emergence of the military, as observed by the prehistorians, shortly followed the ceremonial emphasis, and this would have resulted in control over means of destruction. Also, as argued earlier, this would have occurred in response to circumscription, to growth in population; and a failure to militarize would have resulted in the subjection of the society to another in which military skills were more successful.

Thus far I have treated stratification as if it were merely a ranked binary differentiation. There are problems here: What was the process by which the binary differentiation that recognized two nonequivalent operating units (or two sets) took place? And was the differentiation of nonequivalent operating units limited to two? Let us take up the second of these first.

As human populations grew and agricultural technology improved, there were not merely basic resources to control, but also many intermediate activities, including determining when it was wise to start planting, and directing an army to defend against raiding neighbors. "Societies are bundles of differentiated roles that are both functionally and evaluatively ranked," writes Harold A. Gould of the emergence of occupational specialization in early civilization.

Clearly hundreds of formally differentiated occupational roles could not be individually ranked. This exceeded even the classificatory skills of man! Just as clearly, the functions of individual occupational roles had to be viewed and judged according to their place in larger social structures whose overall functions made major contributions to the operation of the state system. . . . Some occupations had so much in common that making discriminations of rank among them was neither necessary nor feasible. Carpenters, potters, weavers, and glass-blowers all had in common the facts that they were artisans and that each received about the same remuneration for his work. Determining "worth" and therefore "rank" by monetary means . . . became a major

[67] It might be inserted here that this primal (but not primary) emphasis on consumption poses the possibility that the early controls were on what the ecologists call the "downstream" end of the energy flow process and that the gradual shift to control over production was steadily moving upstream. The later imperial efforts to gain natural resources were, of course, moves still further "upstream."

evaluation instrument because the market became the dominant mechanism for regulating the flow of goods and services in the state system and the primary basis for determining the worth of the products that a role produced.[68]

Gould concludes that preindustrial civilization came up with not simply a stratification based on access to basic resources, but rather strata that "reflected a subtle mixture of power and functions." Minimally, he proposes that there were three kinds of occupation roles: "power-elite roles, technical implementation roles, and menial roles."

Gould's proposal is important, not merely for its recognition that a simple binary differentiation would not have long held in an expanding civilization, but also for its proposal that the differentiation was based on different kinds of power. What he calls "power-elite roles" I would consider to be roles based on *power authority*, that is, based on some independent controls; his "technical implementation roles" I would consider to be roles based on *skill authority*; and "menial roles" I would see as roles with little power and *no authority* at the societal level. The emergence of a series of strata may not have become explicit until the appearance of kingdoms, but differentiation of occupation was surely already being recognized in chiefdoms and may well have seen nascent stratification in more highly developed situations.

The question of how the binary differentiation processes operated to separate a top, or elite, group from others is one that probably needs to be asked at various points in the evolutionary process.[69] Early as well as later history has seen the successive horizontal segmentation of operating units that took over the task of ruling the society. In the early stages, it may well have occurred after the manner that has been suggested by Don E. Dumond. He sees it as emerging in ranked societies through the expansion in population with the accompanying squeeze on basic resources and their increasing control by individuals of high rank.

Given, then, an increasingly large though unstable society made up of a number of segments, each with its few men accorded high status, it

[68] Gould 1971, pp. 5–6. Reprinted, with permission, from Gould, *Caste and Class: A Comparative View*, 1971, Addison-Wesley, Reading, Mass.
[69] See Keller 1963.

in time becomes possible for high status individuals to count themselves numerous enough to form a special social group. How many
would this require? It is tempting here to refer to Birdsell's report[70]
that dialectal tribes in Australia approach a statistical population of
500, a constant figure that tends to be preserved by fragmentation when
a tribe becomes too large or by integration with neighbors when a tribe
becomes too small. . . . I am suggesting that there is some numerical
threshold that the elite must pass before they are inclined to place
identification with each other above identification with their own
localized kin unit.[71]

What Dumond is suggesting is that at some point there was a sufficient differentiation of a large enough number of highly ranked
individuals, along with their presumably marriageable daughters
and inheritance-hungry sons, that they found it convenient to
make a binary differentiation between themselves as an operating
unit and the rest of the society as another operating unit, and that,
in so doing, they ranked their unit above the other unit(s).

Dumond, in a footnote that follows the quotation cited earlier,
asks, concerning Birdsell's number, five hundred, "Was it only an
accident that Mrs. Astor's ballroom held as many as *four* hundred?"[72] Without trying to answer this, it may be pointed out that
others have asked the same question. Frank Bonilla, in a report on
an extensive study of contemporary Venezuelan society, found
that 346 people were generally regarded as important in national
decision-making. "These 346 might be thought of as Venezuela's
'400.' The recurrence of this number in efforts to identify notables
in social systems of quite different magnitudes suggests that there
may be some natural limit on the number of persons mutually
aware of being involved at the upper reaches of power or status
systems of a given complexity."[73] Bonilla's speculation reintroduces
the limits of the human capacity, or collective capacity, to handle
quantity. Certainly there are "small communities" bigger than

[70] He refers to Birdsell 1968.

[71] Don E. Dumond 1972, p. 302. Reprinted from *Population Growth: Anthropological Implications*, ed. Brian Spooner, by permission of MIT Press.

[72] Ibid., p. 309.

[73] Frank Bonilla 1970, p. 18, n. 19. Reprinted from *The Failure of Elites* by
permission of MIT Press.

four or five hundred. But few reach a thousand without manifesting tendencies toward factionalism or some kind of fission.

There is little question that there is a threshold beyond which a human community, in the sense of Ferdinand Tönnies's *Gemeinschaft*[74] or Lévi-Strauss's *authentic culture*,[75] ceases to be a community. If the number becomes too great, then, as Dumond indicated, the problem may be resolved by fission, segmentation into two or more communities; this usually occurs by budding off of the more marginal elements, usually the young or less successful families, or along other existing segmented lines. Another way is for the community to be integrated within a larger domain, to become a residential locale with no exclusive territorial *Gemeinschaft*, the residents having their own community of relations elsewhere, usually deriving from their occupations and social class. It seems very likely that the early emergence of what Gould saw as a "power-elite" was first a "community" in itself and was only tentatively a distinctive social stratum. What I suspect brought the full bloom of a separate segment was the presence in other societies of similar processes, the threat of more effective neighbors becoming more powerful because they were achieving that kind of centralization.

Thus far I have discussed stratification in terms of the differentiation of levels, and the separation off of an elite—a power elite. Gould's analysis indicates that the elite separation is clearly not the only, or even the most significant, aspect of stratification. In more complex societies the horizontal segmentation that emerges clearly is something that is based on more refined recognition of the emerging differentials in power: relative amount of power; types of power bases; types of power exercise; degree of organization as an operating unit; etc. In working with the concepts that have grown up in this area we are involved in a differentiation of usage that stems not only from the conceptual and theoretical differences of different scholars, but also from the fact that the political significance of the strata and the stratification structure has led certain of the concepts to be grasped as being of especial importance in the contemporary world.

[74] Tönnies 1957.
[75] Lévi-Strauss 1963, pp. 366–367.

I believe that, if we wish to keep to an analytical scheme that will serve us through the entire course of the evolution of power, it is useful not to insist on specific terminology at this point, but to turn to the usage that seems most appropriate at any given point in history. For the earliest period, I suspect that *caste* may serve as well as any, since, if Gould is correct, the emergent differentiation at that time, which continued until the mercantilist expansion, was a somewhat ritualized stratification by occupation. *Occupation* here would refer to the work specialization in differential controls over elements of the environment. There is general accord that *social class* is most useful if restricted to a phenomenon that emerged as a part of the industrial revolutionary process, wherein restrictive caste usage broke up on the face of entrepreneurial success with the new sources of energy and diverse niches that were becoming available. Whether to favor Weber's emphasis on the issue of economically based life chances in a labor-commodity situation,[76] or Marx's differential control over the means of production, or "function in the organization of production"[77] must be a methodological question that depends more on the problem at hand than on any innate importance of the definition. In terms of the present analysis, Joseph Schumpeter's characterization of class structure as the "ranking of individual families by their social value in accordance with differing aptitudes"[78] is one which, if somewhat expanded, could be used at many points of history.[79]

Should stratification be conceptualized as a variable entirely independent of (although contributive to) the "state," as Fried assumes? Says Fried, ". . . a state is . . . the complex of institutions by means of which the power of the society is organized on a basis superior to kinship. . . . In the final analysis the power of a state can be manifested in a real physical force, an army, a militia, a police force, a constabulary, with specialized weaponry, drill, con-

[76] Gerth and Mills, eds. and trans. 1946.

[77] Bendix and Lipset 1966.

[78] Schumpeter 1966, p. 45. Note here that "aptitudes" must be judged by someone, and we might presume that it will be the judgment of the more powerful that will determine the outcome.

[79] I have elsewhere undertaken an analysis of the emergence of contemporary social classes in Latin America on the basis of the differentiation of new power bases and the crucial criteria (1973a). See Ossowski 1966 and Bendix and Lipset 1966 for reviews of class.

scription, a hierarchy of command, and the other paraphernalia of structured control."[80] If we accept the prehistorians' findings concerning the emergence of a military arm in the theocratic chiefdoms, and if my supposition is correct that such an arm could not have been exclusively for external aggression and defense, then whether we limit the chiefdom to the premilitary emergence or allow it to include that emergence depends on how we want to use the term. The emphasis on the "basis superior to kinship" also holds some definitional traps, because it is certainly the case that many early kingdoms as well as chiefdoms continued to use kinship as an important recruitment criterion into the *elite* group, and even the differentiation of the strata was not exclusive of a kin basis. But kinship also ceased to be the only issue in power in groups as primitive as the Kapauku Papuans, even before chiefdoms arose. So kinship is not a categorical element, and the presence of legitimately constituted force would allow a mature chiefdom to qualify as a "state" under these definitions.

Fried's proposition that stratification must have preceded the state is, similarly, a rather meaningless issue. He himself observed that the state "maintains an order of stratification,"[81] suggesting that stratification, even under his conception, could not have lasted long without the state. The issue is not whether one came first, but that they essentially emerged as part of a single complex of social differentiation, each answering to the call to control different areas of the emergent whole. Stratification was, as suggested earlier, a differentiation of the society as a whole into nonequivalent (we think of them as "horizontal") segments. Thus, unlike the earlier unstratified bands, villages, lineages, or clans, stratification emerged as the first differentiation of those with power as opposed very generally to those "without." Those with power, however, could quite conceivably separate off as a coordinated unit from the rest. Possibly, from the first signs of stratification, those destined to

[80] Fried 1967, pp. 229, 230. Elman Service does not consider the chiefdom to qualify as a "state" and poses a definition similar in some respects to Fried's: "A true state, however undeveloped, is distinguishable from chiefdoms in particular, and all lower levels in general, by the presence of that special form of control, the consistent threat of force by a body of persons legitimately constituted to use it" (1962, p. 171).

[81] Fried 1967, p. 235.

form the upper stratum not only found their own identity but did so through already being attached in some manner (e.g., through clients, kinsmen, etc.) to the leaders. Thus, in contemporary terminology, an upper stratum, leadership and elite, separated out as a part of the generalized whole, and, simultaneously, specialized tasks of governing (including religious activities) appeared.

In this connection, the question of governance has been reintroduced recently as being definitive of the state and possibly also in some manner explanatory of its emergence. Wright set forth the first of these points by arguing that "a state can be recognized as a society with specialized decision-making organizations receiving messages from many different sources, recoding these messages, supplementing them with previously stored data, making actual decisions, storing both the message and the decision, and conveying decisions back to other organizations." Information processing, he pointed out, makes demands on channel capacity, and therefore the "number of levels of administrative hierarchy in an organization was a function of the rate at which that organization would have to process information regarding the activities it conducted."[82] Johnson pushed this argument a step further, however, and argued that "primary state development involves overloading the decision making organization of a chiefdom. Since no single factor such as increasing irrigation, population, warfare, local exchange or whatever can be shown to have led to state development, it would appear that multiple sources of information input are required to force basic organizational changes at this level."[83]

These arguments are important but have to be handled carefully. Wright is careful to point out that "Information cannot exist by itself. It is conveyed in the form of materials or energy."[84] Thus the question of administrative "channel capacity" is one that has to do both with decision-making, on the one hand, and energetic information markers, on the other. To follow Johnson in arguing that such information input could "force basic organizational changes" presupposes that someone has already decided that the meaning attached to this new information is more important than the meaning attached to the existing organization. We can agree

[82] Wright, forthcoming.
[83] Johnson 1973, pp. 160–161.
[84] Wright, forthcoming.

with the position taken by both authors that the amount of energy input necessarily correlates with the complexity of the hierarchical structure; but the idea that increasing information "forces" structures to change (as I think Johnson is arguing) works only insofar as natural selection allows an out (in a number of senses) for those organizations that do not wish to accommodate the increase of information. So the information argument actually is reducible to a question of increased energy; it simply requires that we give due attention to changes in flow of information markers.

Whether we want to identify the "state" as something that emerged with specialized tasks during the theocratic chiefdoms, or later with the emergence of the military arm, or yet later with the recruitment of independent bureaucrats and the formalization of administrative levels—whether we choose one or another of a number of criteria seems to me to be totally dependent on what problem we may have at hand. Certainly there is nothing in Fried's work that would give any' evidence that stratification emerged free of other protoappurtenances of what we might wish to call the "state."

Between a set of coordinated "chiefdoms" and a well-centralized kingdom there are a variety of political conditions. Aiden Southall has distinguished "segmentary states" where "the exercise of central authority depends upon consensual delegation to it by the component units in each case, without any stable recognition of the right to enforce and maintain this by coercion."[85] The so-called "feudal" states or kingdoms comprise another instance of the semi-centralized variety. These are sufficiently different, and the "feudal" category is so varied that Goody, for one, feels that the term should not be used in a comparative context.[86] The reason for including them here as "semicentralized" is that they clearly

---

[85] Aiden Southall 1965, p. 126. Reprinted from *Political Systems and the Distribution of Power*, ed. Michael Banton, published by Tavistock Publications Limited, by permission of Associated Book Publishers Limited. Southall's analysis is actually arguing that most African states are "segmentary" but that it is important to distinguish those with this consensual base (which he characterizes as "pyramidal") from those where the enforcement is regarded as a right to be exercised by the central authority (a "hierarchical" system). Southall uses the terms *delegation* and *allocation* in precisely the opposite sense of that used in the present essay.

[86] Goody 1971.

are not examples of "noncentralization," such as competing Polynesian chiefdoms; nor have they achieved the degree of hierarchical
integration characterized by internal interdependencies that characterizes the kingdoms of the Buganda and Barotse, with their
"politics of the capital" and appointed rather than hereditary
council members, or the more complex West African states, with
differentiated economies, slave labor, external trade, landed mag-
nates, mercenaries—and even peasant revolts,[87] or the mercantilist
absolute monarchies of Europe in the seventeenth and eighteenth
centuries. It is not that the semicentralized kingdoms merely had
weaker kings, but that the very structure of their power system
was pluralistic in that the king was neutralized either by having no
secular power (as in the Shilluk "divine kingdom") or by being
dependent upon the allocated power of a series of immediate supporters, who themselves retain controls of the basic elements of
the environment.

The problem the kingdom faced in centralization paralleled that
of the chiefdoms in some respects but was different in others. Both
the king and his chiefs knew what independent power might mean.
Therefore there necessarily existed between the king and his immediate supporter-subordinates a delicate problem of the balance
between their allocated power to him (which they would give so
long as it was to their advantage) and his delegated power to them,
which he would presumably juggle and balance, using it to show
favor, play off one against another, etc. This semicentralized situation did not inhibit expansion. With the Bemba and Zulu, princes
and chiefs administered territories for the king but periodically
mobilized followers in support of their own bid for power.[88] Those
at the periphery of the kingdom would expand outward, but would
also turn occasionally toward the center to try to usurp the kingship itself.

These competitive processes reflect again on the emergence of
stratification. Recalling the earlier speculation on the size of an
emergent elite, we see that the central figure would have had little
more power than the other major successful figures. Centralization
within such a group must have been on the basis of allocated
power. The "immediate supporters" were the leading members

[87] Gluckman 1963, p. 1546.
[88] Ibid. See also Colson 1958, p. 45.

of the upper stratum; and all kings who fundamentally depended on the allocated power of their immediate group of supporters and who had little independent power of their own were necessarily weak.

An instance of the shift from the semicentralized condition to a centralized kingdom is to be seen in Joseph P. Smaldone's analysis of the effect of the appearance of firearms in the Central Sudan in the late nineteenth century. Prior to their appearance, the king was dependent for his military forces on his fief-holders, each of whom had his own supporters, and each of whom would mobilize his supporters to the aid of the king—if he wished. As in the case of feudal Europe, "The possession of war horses was monopolized by the ruling class, insuring the availability of a ready force of cavalry to meet the military requirements of the state. . . . Possession of the horse virtually entailed the military obligation."[89] The power of the king heavily depended upon these fief-holders, who really constituted the base of the military power. The introduction of firearms, controlled by the king, centralized power in his hands, because the new weapons were used by infantry and were particularly effective against cavalry. Not only did the infantry displace the aristocratic cavalry, but the armies were often placed under the command of slaves, as they were more responsive to the king's wishes than were his semi-independent fief-holders. "As slave officials gradually displaced the fief-holding nobility, the traditional feudal-bureaucratic conflict tended toward a resolution in favour of bureaucracy: government by feudal aristocracy yielded slowly to government by royal autocracy."[90]

An additional manner in which chiefdoms centralized toward kingdoms was through explicit confederation. The confederation of chiefdoms presumably happened when some set of chiefs saw a common threat, but their segmentary characteristic did not lead

[89] Joseph P. Smaldone 1972, p. 598. Reprinted from "Firearms in the Central Sudan: A Revolution," *Journal of African History*, vol. 13, no. 4, by permission of Cambridge University Press.

[90] Ibid., p. 605. It should not be thought that the introduction of firearms automatically resulted in a centralization of power; obviously it depended on who got hold of them. In West Africa and the Central Sudan, it was principally the central figures who succeeded in doing this. In Ethiopia, however, firearms were widely distributed and served to reinforce "the fragmentation of power long characteristic of the Ethiopian state" (Caulk 1972, p. 630).

them always to react in this manner. It is probably the case that the so-called Aztec "Empire" that was in expansion at the time of the conquest was, in present terms, basically an alliance of three chiefdoms, Tacuba, Texcoco, and Tenochtitlan, with the latter having become the dominant member following a subsequent period of external conquests.[91]

In moving to the kingdom, we again shift our emphasis from the process of coordination to that of centralization, and we find some disagreement as to whether kingdoms of this scale were stable in Africa. They reflect the shift to what Southall characterizes as "a political system . . . when authority is allocated from the centre in a *de iure* and a *de facto* sense. Of course, there is always the consent of the governed, but it is quite clear when right of allocation from the centre is regarded as legitimate by the majority in the sense that the enforcement of this right is also legitimate."[92] Max Gluckman, however, feels that "on the longest consideration there is an apparent instability deep-rooted in these states; though the unifying influence of the kingship may keep the segments united for many years, the state was likely in the end to break up . . . Since the Kingdom's segments were not dependent upon one another for specialized production of various goods, after a period whose limits I cannot fix, the state would fall apart, and there would be left many small chieftainships. Force at the centre, and ritual supremacy, seem to me insufficient to give permanent internal stability to such a state. Regions of Africa have probably displayed what can be called an oscillating equilibrium between a large state holding together a while and a number of smaller states."[93] If we can assume that the basis for this lack of stability was the inability to consolidate sufficient control to retain continuing power over the various segments of the kingdom, then Gluck-

[91] Gibson 1964. Robert McC. Adams observes, on other grounds than those used here, that "The term 'empire' is not an entirely suitable one for these patterns. . . . Many features we tend to associate with empires apparently were missing or at best very poorly developed" (1966, p. 153). Since the *calpulli*, a unit still based in some degree on both locality and kinship, seems to have been among the main components of the provincial unit, the *waman*, it is difficult to see the Aztec society as being more than an emerging kingdom that was embarked on the conquest of neighboring chiefdoms.

[92] Southall 1965, p. 126. (Southall's *allocate* = our *delegate*.)

[93] Gluckman 1965, p. 143.

man's next observation makes even better sense: "Only at salt and jade mines, and at important points on trade routes, do chiefs establish a more permanent authority. Similarly, I believe that wherever a state in Africa has had a longer and more permanent history it will be found that this is based on some special kind of external trade, or on the internal differentiation within the nation."[94]

Gluckman's observation receives support from societies of a comparable level of integration in Polynesia: "Advanced Polynesian political systems were overtaxed. In Hawaii and other islands cycles of centralization-decentralization appear in the traditional histories: periodic violent dissolution of larger into smaller chiefdoms and, by the same means, periodic reconstitution of the great society . . . The expansion of a chiefdom seems to have entailed a more-than-appropriate expansion of the administrative apparatus and its conspicuous consumption. The ensuing drain on the people's wealth and expectations was eventually expressed in an unrest that destroyed both the chief and chiefdom."[95]

If we follow Marx in seeing stratification to be inherent in the emergence of the state and the state to be, in essence, the workings of such an identification, it need not follow that either the one or the other is going to disappear. The fact that contradictions are inherent in the structure can mean that there will be constant stress, but not necessarily that there will be a higher level of resolution. When man perceives disjunctions, such as those that stem from such contradictions, he will change his acts to recognize the facts. But this does not mean that he will correctly interpret the energetic basis of the fact, and it does not mean, therefore, that his consequent behavior will in fact resolve or improve the condition; given the complexity of the energetic components themselves, and given their geometrically increased complexity when working through and in conjunction with systems of meanings, it is almost inevitable that attempts at correction will simply breed

[94] Ibid., pp. 143–144. Gluckman then cites the Lozi, who, occupying both a woodland and a floodplain area, were able to maintain a continuing stable kingship. The Lozi case would, on the surface, appear to support Carneiro's argument as to the importance of resource concentration to the formation of states.

[95] Sahlins 1968, pp. 92–93.

further problems. Not only does cultural structuring itself pose such problems, but the expanding nature of the human system means that whatever cultural elements are at work constantly have a greater energetic component to handle. Thus the state and stratification are inherently linked to the expanding process; what is less clear is whether the mere fact of increasing energy controlled per capita makes the Marxian contradictions and the power-structure confrontations inevitable.

I am less concerned with the "nature" of the state than with whether any society finds it possible to have dependable, excessive power that does not eventuate in its being used to exploit others. Whatever the complex reasons may be that Big Men of Melanesia fail to consolidate their clientage power into primitive chiefdoms, it is not because many Big Men do not want to. If we look again to the question of the consolidation of chiefdoms, we may see the germs of the problem more clearly spelled out.

This chiefdom marks a centralization over coordinate proto-organizations, be they collecting tribal organizations or surgent Big Men organizations. Analytically, the crux of the change is in the presence in the chiefdom of mechanisms that can either extend the controls, consolidate the controls, or, in some manner, permit certain individuals to retain controls to the exclusion of others; and this set of others forms the energetic base of the emergent lower class. It has long been accepted in a general way that it is "technology" that makes this possible. But the technology that operates in this phase of human history is not solely that of extra-somatic tools and weapons (i.e., independent power by the rulers), nor that of allocated power by the individual members of the population, but some combination of these.

What I believe may have happened is that those to whom decision-making was (in the first instance) allocated stood in a special position to benefit from their knowledge and control and to expand on it. Such knowledge had to do with matters directly affecting control or power, such as the prediction of when to plant and harvest, when to abandon one settlement and move to a new one, when to defuse or eliminate a tyrant, and so on.

If we start with the notion that any authority, that is, anyone who is holding allocated decision-making rights, by definition holds more power than those who have granted the power, then the question becomes one of how that authority can retain power when not all decisions will work to the benefit of the power grantors (i.e., the people). The answer probably lies in those situations where the authorities combine success (so as regularly to manifest that they have "superior" power) with events periodically contrived to meet specific confrontations to their continued exercise of power. Such successes may lie in military activities, in favorable opportunities to gain clients, in the unique control over some crucial juncture in a trading system, in a special ability for internal manipulations and eliminations of rival factions or leaders, or, indeed, in anything that makes people dependent upon the authorities for decisions. The origin of this dependence is not to be sought in the psychological dimension (although it is obviously manifest there) but in the power structure, where reinforcement is provided from above to new relational idioms and to the continuing but gradual expropriation of certain decision-making capabilities from the lower levels to the higher levels. Each decision removed and exercised at a higher level weakens not only the lower-level power but also the lower-level decision-making ability.

To bring into conjunction all these kinds of activities is without question difficult; and to continue to retain them also would be difficult. All this means that, over the long run, few chiefdoms had lengthy histories, and natural selection worked among them as it does among competitive populations seeking the same niche. The observation, made some years ago by Lowie, that religion lies at the bottom of political centralization, was on the right track. The issue, however, is that, while religion is one form that the process may take, it is only one. What necessarily happened is that some set of devices permitted the supplementation of allocated power by leaders who gained command of and tactically utilized independent power sources. Both excessive support of and objections to the thesis of early theocratic states[96] are somewhat misdirected.

[96] Fried makes the objection but also the correct supposition as to where the problem rests: "Because so many early states either were theocracies or conceived of the political rules as a god, there has been no shortage of theories attributing the origin of the state to the emergence of a powerful priesthood. Such theories tend to neglect or misinterpret the negative cases, such as ancient China, where the priesthood occupied an ancillary position. More importantly, however, such theorizing tends to miss the main question: Regard-

The issue was to keep allocated power; and, as our vantage on history now permits us to confirm, there are ways of doing this besides the use of "theism." If this is the crucial question in the "origin of the state," then we must re-examine cases to seek out evidence of this process. It is not necessarily "religion," nor can it be quantities of information, nor any other general class of phenomena defined by formal characteristics; rather, it was the specific conjunction of phenomena of different orders that started people on the road of first foregoing and then being deprived of their right to exercise their own independent power in their own best interest.

The expansion of chiefdoms led to conquest and the attendant problems of dealing with conquered peoples. The expansion pattern continued as kingdoms evolved, and the emergence of internal domination and stratification was paralleled by the extension of dominion over other societies and by the emergence of imperial stratification externally. External subjugation structurally replicated internal domination. Under tribal life, war might bring captives, but there was little space in tribal life for a sector of slaves. A few could be cared for and used, but for the most part they were handled like marginal tribal members. Chiefdoms, however, opened the way for handling larger numbers of such unfortunates; and expansion by kingdoms meant that too many people were involved to convert them into a slave status. The appearance of empires was therefore a natural extension of the state; it was in no way an "evolutionary advance" beyond the particular state form involved. It did not represent an additional level of integration; rather, it was a lateral extension that included more domains within the state domain.

The development of empires was in some respects a more overt manifestation of technological advance than was the growth of internal social power. Externally, the role of power tended at the outset to be secondary, because the first question in conquest was that of actual control, military might and ability. The Inca, in

---

less of the alternate roles occupied by those who filled leadership positions, what were the conditions that demanded or at least supported the development and concentration of such new and extreme forms of social power?" (1968*b*, p. 148).

their expansion, are said to have given their potential subjects the choice of joining the empire voluntarily to share in its benefits, or of being conquered and subjugated by force. But that was not the manner of all empires. In at least one respect the external relations of the imperial state tend to reverse the pattern of internal organization. In matters of control and power, the external pattern is to display control first and, once having established where the control lies, to proceed wherever possible on the basis of power. Internally, however, the state pattern has been to prefer reliance on power and, if that fails, to resort to force, that is, direct control. The reason for this is not complicated. In dealing with foreigners, the cultural differences may be such that it is necessary to demonstrate what the nature of one's controls are before one can expect a response to the use of power.

Since internal regulation and order depends much more on power, the advent of new technological devices has at times been historically more visible in the domination of other people than of the conqueror's own people. The advent of new transport forms, such as the domestication of riding animals, the bridle, saddle, and stirrup, or successively improved sea- and ocean-going vessels together with instruments of navigation obviously had internal consequences, but they also made possible vast continental and intercontinental empires. In these, the expansion of the species took an important new direction, for no longer was it merely a matter of the populations budding off due to their own natural increase; instead, the increase of levels of integration pointed to an incorporation of neighboring populations that was frankly predatory.

## E. The National Level and the Recent Historic Era

In shifting our attention from kingdoms to nations and from preindustrial and mercantilist empires to industrial empires, we move increasingly into the era of written history. The present essay, an effort at the construction of theoretical outlines to the structure of power, makes no pretense to be a treatise on the evolution of society or human history. In dealing with contemporary events there is often a desire to provide more specific answers; but I will continue here as in the preceding stages and merely explore some ways that the general theory may help to interpret some characteristics of contemporary history. In so doing, I will suggest regularities that I believe are a consequence of the nature of power and power structure.

One of the principal arguments of the present scheme is that the process of the evolution of power has led to the emergence of increasingly more powerful societal entities. While this can in some measure be indexed through the size in population or territory of the entities involved, neither of these in itself is a safe indicator. Evidence is clear that in the Valley of Mexico prior to the Spanish conquest there was a population of between one and three million persons, divided into entities that would be classed here as chiefdoms, coming gradually under the domination of the Aztec kingdom. By the seventeenth century, this population had dropped to some seventy thousand,[97] but the structure was that of a clearcut Spanish kingdom, of which the central Mexican portion was under a viceroy and administration that would be a level of integration below that of the Spanish emperor. The point here is that levels of integration continue to be the mentalistic constructs made around the energetic facts; while they provide a classification of those facts, they do not themselves necessarily allow a measure of them.

Since our independent variable is power, it is quite easy to accept the fact that chiefdoms and kingdoms manifesting a great variety of demographic and territorial extensions can exist concurrently within environmental conditions that allow each a special, if hardly permanent, niche. The contrast between the levels with which we are dealing here can much more readily be seen in terms, not of the absolute energy controlled by or population within the power of a domain, but of the relative number of domains in existence for some given population. A recent study by Charles Tilly estimates that Europe in 1500 had some five hundred formally autonomous governments; today, this has declined to about thirty-five.[98] The figure of five hundred represents kingdoms and possibly some residual chiefdoms (or rather entities that we would here regard as being on the chiefdom level); the figure of

[97] Gibson 1964, pp. 5–6.
[98] These estimates are contained in Tilly's forthcoming article; I am indebted to Professor Tilly for allowing me to make reference to them.

thirty-five refers to industrial nations, but, as Tilly points out, includes the ministates of Monaco and San Marino. It is in this kind of comparison that the importance of seeing the nation as a distinctive level of integration above the kingdom becomes perfectly clear. Although figures are not available so far as I can determine, it is equally clear that the comparison of numbers of autonomous African governments in 1800 and in 1970 would probably provide an even greater contrast.

In shifting our attention from kingdoms to nations, we bring ourselves into modern history, for the nation has evolved through the energy flow expansion impelled by capitalism and industrialism. These were the devices that provided the centralization of the collection of kingdoms that eventuated in nations. There existed prior to these the fact of coordination of kingdoms, entities which by the end of the sixteenth century were approaching the limits of the globe. This expansion obviously implied warfare, conquest, and trade; it also implied the appearance of what A. L. Kroeber has called the "world religions."[99] While chiefdoms and kingdoms came increasingly into contact, competition, and conflict that selected out many of the contestants, the events contributed to the growth of intersocietal cultures and cultural borrowing. The Divine King of the Shilluck helped to centralize something on the order of 100,000 people; Christianity, working through a weakly centralized elite of ecclesiastics, helped coordinate first Western and Eastern Europe, and later most of the New World. Islam similarly established a band of common custom from Spain to the Philippines. It is important to understand the coordinating function of these religions. In medieval Europe, the various feudal kingdoms may have had illiterate monarchs, but the knowledge of law and custom, of common belief, as well as court records, was maintained and advanced by the clergy. Control of these forms allowed them power that was sufficient at times to dominate the kings and even to succeed in launching the Crusades, a coordination of a series of consensus units of undependable allocated power. Just as the various gods of the Tahitian chiefdoms were known to each other,

---

[99] In the Kroeberian sense, that is, a religion that claimed to be for everyone, and not just for a single chiefdom or kingdom. See Kroeber 1948, p. 406. Wallace classifies these as monotheistic (1966, pp. 94–96).

so the God of Christianity and the God of Islam were historically derived from the same source.

In centralized empires, as in the African segmentary states, the king or emperor had relatively little real control over the more distant and peripheral areas. The famous Spanish colonial refrain of "I obey but do not comply" was an expression of the fact that the king was indeed many months away, and his orders could be shelved or ignored for extended periods. The "colony" had to produce certain things for the mother state, but slowness of communication and transport meant that the local delegated agents of the crown were locally more important than the crown itself. Karl W. Deutsch has observed that "The basis of empires is the political apathy of most of their population,"[100] an observation indicating that empires relied more on the weakness of the ruled than on the strength of the rulers. The preindustrial empires were based on independent power, but the amount of power they could exercise was extremely limited.

Humanity achieved empires on a technology that was still remarkably primitive; but it was adequate to reach the ends of the earth in a very brief period. It perhaps has not been enough noted that the fact of "one world" was already of importance in the first thousand years after Christ. The Vikings were simultaneously tearing up Europe and landing in the New World; Islam was at once battling in Western Europe and North Africa and reaching deep into South and Southeast Asia. China was trading intensively with Africa, and the Indian Ocean was the scene of a competition now long forgotten. What may have appeared as cycles to earlier scholars must be seen as expansive cycles; each rise and fall signaled the approach not merely of a successor, but of a successor in an ever more populated field, benefiting from an increasingly superior technological repertory.

The area for expansion of a society is determined by who currently occupies the environment and by the level of integration of the expanding society. That North America was well occupied by hunters and gatherers and primitive agriculturalists meant that it was open territory to the imperial expansion of the Europeans. That Middle America and the Andes housed expanding chiefdoms

[100] Deutsch 1968, p. 72.

and kingdoms might have proved more difficult had it not been for the telling presence of a few technological differences. Spain, Portugal, France, Holland, and England, all expanding mercantilistic empires and some coordinated under the articulating interests of the Roman church, moved west, and around Africa to the Far East. Back to back with Rome, the Eastern church emerged in Eastern Europe to meet in confrontation with expanding Islam. And the great expansive coordinate networks found themselves contained by each other.

The Christian kingdoms finally eliminated Islam from Europe and, with the technology of seafaring, gunpowder, and the war horse, began a series of competitive expansions. The Roman Catholic coordination could not contain the now rapidly differentiating whole, and first one and then another brand of Protestantism emerged so that, insofar as religion played a role at all, coordination rested solely in the recognition of a common God, not a common church. Protestantism essentially returned the control over the elements of religion to the growing kingdoms. As Weber later noted, mercantilist capitalism emerged as the new coordinating network for building states and empires that were increasingly independent of the compromises demanded by Rome. Empires were ranked in this great coordinating process. In general, the northern European states, England and to a much lesser degree Holland, expanded not only through the success of their own imperialist efforts over the tribal people of North America, but also by exploiting the wealth in precious metals brought back from Middle and South America by the Iberian empires.[101] England grew not only through direct colonialism but also through indirect capitalist exploitation of Iberian colonialism.

Within the western European kingdoms, irrespective of their success over technologically inferior peoples in the New World, there were still serious problems of local centralization. The seventeenth-century Spanish empire was, in some respects, sounder than the Spanish kingdom. But, of even greater importance, the secularizing tendency that began displacing the church as the vehicle of law and order with the rise of the military in the later

[101] Again, since I am attempting not a world history but the application of a model, I shall limit my discussion to the western world, an area with which I am familiar.

prehistoric chiefdoms reached its heights during Europe's mercantilist expansion. Jean Bodin argued in the sixteenth century that the notion of sovereignty must rest on a purely secular law, a law that depended for its ultimate authority on the state and was free from the church's influence. Furthermore, the insecurity of the individual king on his throne that marked all of medieval Europe reached a series of climaxes in the proclaimed "divine right" of James I, the fixed-succession law under Queen Anne, and the expressed notion of Louis XIV that "I am the state." Mercantilism and the technological and economic grumblings of an incipient industrial revolution were introducing too many new bases of power for secular absolutism to effectively contain, at the very moment that it was being proclaimed. The English Revolution of the seventeenth century and the French and American revolutions of the eighteenth rejected rule by an elite based on inheritance; its sacred sanction had become ambiguous through too many churches, and the dogma of descent was lost on the burghers who increasingly held the new energy forms out of which power grew.

The British Empire started as a mercantilist empire, but by the end of the eighteenth century England was midwiving the Industrial Revolution. Her basic control over the industrial process put an end to the cycles of preindustrial empires, and there emerged in the western world an entirely new growth sequence. World-wide coordination under the Christian and Islamic banners was displayed by world capitalism, and that was to be complemented (or displaced, if one were a Marxist) by world socialism. The kings running the kingdoms had already lost their divine right and now were increasingly challenged by republicanism of one form or another that accompanied the surge to nationhood. Mercantilist empires either converted to industrial empires or collapsed. England, France, and Russia converted; Spain and Portugal did not. By the end of the century Germany's sudden national emergence spread to a new industrial empire. The Italian petty states were trying to centralize beyond the control of the Austro-Hungarian Empire, and Japan, in her bid for membership among the industrial states, successfully confronted Russia. In the New World, the United States was creating her own industrial empire, spreading over tribal Indian domains, chopping off half of Mexico, buying Alaska, and finally spilling into a few remaining island niches left over by the final collapse of the Spanish overseas empire at the end of the nineteenth century. Some recent historians have labeled the widespread British success "a paper empire," and, indeed, it was. British expansion, once it successfully dealt with the Dutch and French, pushed to the end of the earth over technologically much inferior peoples.

The period from 1850 until approximately 1930 saw centralization at the world level under predominantly Euro-American management. Within this island full of Big Men, Great Britain was generally ranked the highest. Germany was already surpassing England when World War I destroyed both the German and the Austrian-Hungarian empires. Later, with Japan, Germany lost in her second attempt at empire, but succeeded in showing that the Industrial Empire was, in fact, made of paper. England, France, Holland, and Belgium shed themselves of their colonies.

But, as Christian coordination earlier expanded back to back with Islam's influence to the east, so world capitalism found its binary opposition in socialism. As Marx indicated in the nineteenth century, the great industrial empires were then a new coordinate unit, and he became the prophet of the counterorder. Whereas mercantilism had placed the energy forms and processes of commerce in the hands of the bourgeoisie with unskilled labor, so industrialization placed the process of production in the hands of industrialists, middle class, and urban proletariat. The rise of socialism as a significant political force was both in response to and inhibited by a signal occurrence: the world was full. There was no "other" place from which an army might be devised to attack, as one chiefdom, kingdom, or empire had attacked another. But, for socialism to succeed, it had to be more than a coordinating device; it had to centralize, and for this it needed a nation-state as a vehicle. Rebellion had always been an honorable way of displacing central figures, from the folk-level revolts of the *gumlao* Kachin against the *gumsa* system, to the beheading of Charles I and Louis XVI, the rejection of George III by the United States, and, perhaps more important, the Haitian revolt against the French whites. But socialism was nowhere a strong enough force; laborers, it was true, operated the means of production, but they did not control them; what was more important, they did not control the means of destruction.

Louis Althusser has pointed out that "Russia *was the weakest link in the chain of imperial states.*"[102] It was in Russia, broken by World War I, that socialism captured a huge centralized operating unit. In a way not unlike the Spanish Empire's harnessing of the lower sectors of Mexico and Peru, the Russian Communist government sought to harness all sectors of the population to the job of expanding the socialist state. A single state could later be overcome by the coordinated network of world capitalism—the job was also to institute a world-wide coordinate network of socialist states; and, for this, the Internationals were promulgated.

The Internationals did not win more states; that was accomplished by the *coup de grâce* of industrial imperialism, World War II.[103] The widespread world capitalist coordination continued, but now coupled in confrontation with world socialist coordination. The two were dedicated to a single purpose, that is, dominating externally and centralizing internally. Like the industrial empires before them, they were world-wide but did not command the world. Their means for this command could be gained only through their own increasing developmental success, and that success was dependent to some degree on their economically incorporating the Third World "new states"; so development became the crucial work of all nations; structural conflict evolved into structural escalation, Big Man against Big Man became supernation against supernation, and they called it "development."

In considering the expansion of bands, chiefdoms, and kingdoms, the most apparent aspect of the process is the geographical expansion of some at the expense and displacement of others. By the time of the mercantilist era, this was becoming less possible, because the kingdoms themselves were collectively filling the earth, and no one of them had sufficient controls to effect a conquest of all the others. As a result, the technological impact of industrialism did not bring the appearance of many new building blocks at higher

102 Cited in Godelier 1972, p. 100 (Althusser's italics).

103 It has been argued that, had Germany won World War II, all this would have been different. I doubt it; the process was clearly underway, and it is sometimes forgotten (because of their rush for development and the symbols of success) that the Nazis were socialists too. The world would have looked and sounded different, but it would not have differed fundamentally in the structure here being described.

levels of integration, but rather the higher levels emerged from within the existing kingdom-based (and usually imperial) states. While this may superficially appear as a significant change in the pattern of the evolution of power, I do not believe that it is anything more than the natural product of the constrictions attendant on the fact that the world is round and finite. The internal power structures were altered significantly by the integration of kingdoms, chiefdoms, and bands that accompanied the surges to new levels of integration.

The point has already been made that, when a new level of integration emerges, the particular idiom of relations that served as coordinating networks and those that served to centralize the component units becomes displaced as the new centralization takes place. Thus religion has served to coordinate kingdoms, but it has served neither as the centralizing device for kingdoms nor as the coordinating device for nations. The centralizing idiom of the pre-industrial kingdoms evolved around hereditary operating units, that is, units that promoted a dogma of descent. As industrialism pushed the emergence of nations from these kingdoms, the dogma of descent had to be broken or displaced, just as the dogma of sanctity had to be broken in the shift from chiefdoms to kingdoms. Two places where an earlier idiom was functionally displaced but preserved formally intact were the island states of Japan and England. In the former, the divinity of the emperor reached exaggerated manalike proportions in the first millennium after Christ, but the divinity was at some point separated from the aristocracy and left specifically to the emperor himself. Thus under the Shogunates, and most specifically the Tokugawa, the emperor was the divine symbol of Japan, but the actual rule was handled by nondivine courtiers. This displacement accompanied the emergence of a Japanese kingdom out of the earlier expanding chiefdom. England's monarchs, whose emergence from the chiefdom level was marked by the Norman Conquest, made latter-day claims to divine right but actually founded their rule in the dogma of descent, and the ruling nobility similarly argued their right to rule on that basis. With the emergence of the industrial nation, the House of Lords experienced a rapid decline. As in the Japanese case, the monarchy was not eliminated but displaced so that the actual rule was placed in the hands of individuals not constrained by descent, while the royal family continued to act as the symbol of centralization of the nation as a whole.

The contemporary world is clearly composed of nations, and these experience the problems of ranking very much as have Big Men, chiefdoms, and kingdoms. They clearly vary widely among themselves in the amount of control and power they can exercise, but the bases for control are constantly changing. Whereas the original industrial nations depended primarily on their own territorial resources to fuel their industrial development, the same industrial nations today are heavily dependent on the resources imported from other countries. Thus the flexing of Arab nationalist muscles in the 1970's is hardly surprising; the only question is whether the Arabs will find it possible to achieve a higher degree of coordination than they have classically manifested. This poses again the question of the idiom. Since Islam has been a principal bond of unity in the Middle East, there is reason to suspect that it will not effectively serve as a basis of centralization of power among those nations. As the so-called Third World nations find ways of more effectively coordinating their interests, they will create power organizations that will gradually change the general profile of the world at large.

If we accept the fact that the world can never be "one" in a politically centralized sense, then we should be more especially interested in the kinds of coordinating systems which may be in evidence or emerging today and which may not have been significant in the coordination of kingdoms or earlier forms. This would exclude networks that have already been long in existence, such as commercial and banking relations, religious affiliations, linguistic commonalities, and so forth. Among the kinds of coordination at the international level that are currently in evidence in a greater or lesser degree of development are the following:

(*a*) There is a set of regional blocs, generally determined by proximity and by certain diacritics of language, race, and culture: Black Africa, the Islamic Middle East, Latin America, Eastern Europe, Western Europe, etc. Members of each set rank themselves depending upon the particular set of coordinate relations with which they are most concerned. (*b*) There is also a coordinate unit of the high-ranking powers: the United States, Russia, China,

France, England, with claims for membership being made by India, Brazil, West Germany, Japan. Within this too there is ranking, especially among the giants. (*c*) There is the coordinate confrontation between the two major political economic domains, world capitalism and world socialism, each internally competitive and internally ranked in terms of relative power. (*d*) There are the United Nations and the other international organizations. And then there is a nascent organization of the subnational segments of powerless peoples, such as coordination of the North American Indian organizations with those of the still only slightly organized pan-Indian movements in Latin America. The last, of considerable ethnographic and intrinsic interest, is still poorly defined, and the criteria of centralization have yet to become clear because of the dominance of older coordinating relational idioms, such as ethnicity, race, or national origin.

Of the first four listed above, the last three operate in a normal coordinate manner, with the members among them being ranked and engaged in a variety of reciprocal relations. The last, of course, consists of a series of administrative agencies, but their membership of nations gives them a somewhat consensual quality. The first, the regional blocs, gives promise of being something more; my own suspicion is that it may turn out to be the next major centralizing unit to be built at a level above the nation. At this point, however, what is occurring is the appearance of one or a very few competitive states to dominate each regional area. The importance of China and Brazil lies not merely in their size, potential resources, and intent, but in the fact that each lies within a region fragmented by the break-up of the industrial empires. In East Asia, Japan and India may make claims, but it seems clearly to be China that will hold the dominant power of the area. In Latin America, nervous pretensions by Argentina or Mexico do not seriously threaten Brazil's future hegemony. Two of the world's regions are, within their own areas, in a condition of balanced confrontation: Africa and Oceania. In both there are so-called neocolonial nations, dominated by the residue of earlier European colonial population, and the indigenous nations. The two situations are not similar in that in Africa the neocolonial nations contain large Black African populations, whereas the Oceanic neocolonials are ethnically mixed. Within Black Africa itself there is a tentative coordination, but it is as yet weak, perhaps little more effective than an identity unit.

The industrially based empires that collapsed at the end of World War II are being replaced by these competitive regional blocs. They differ from the empires in a number of ways. They are similar in that the highest-ranking members form part of the exclusive world coordinate of high-ranking powers. They are different, however, in that they are not in competition for far-flung colonies but rather are in competition (*a*) among themselves for dominance *within* their domain and (*b*) with neighboring-domain nations for control of the peripheries. Where does Sudan belong, Black Africa or the Middle East? How will Mexico balance her cultural linkages with Latin America against her economic dependence on the United States? What happens to New Guinea (between Australia and Indonesia), to Korea? The regional blocs are also unlike empires in that they tend to be ethnically much more homogeneous.

It would not do to conclude this picture without some reference to the transnational conglomerates (TNCs), or multinational corporations. A good deal has been written about their strength, the amount of energy they control, and the fact that their annual budgets outrun those of most of the world's nations. This kind of comparison is telling for some purposes, but misleading in the framework of ranking nations. The TNCs and the nation are really not equivalents. The TNCs neither want nor claim political sovereignty or autonomy; they want and assume the protection of their home national government, because they assume that they are acting in the best interests of both. Their attitude toward the poorer countries within which they operate is that of treating, not with an equivalent entity, but rather with a field to be exploited, a market to be expanded, a bureaucracy to be manipulated. Their appearance during the mid-twentieth century reflected the growth and concomitant centralization of economic power within the United States and the appearance in poorer countries of a new set of energy forms to be controlled, that is, the new industries arising as a result of nationalism and import substitution policies, as well as of natural resources.

The modern national states themselves are ill-equipped to exploit foreign resources through their own governments, since such action would be overt political intervention and surely seen as a major international threat. Part of the dogma operating within a world-wide coordinate system of nations is that of sovereignty. Whether it is a question of a Jamaica or of a China, there is an endowment of equivalency in the recognition of sovereignty, and certain reciprocities are supposed to be observed between the governments of such sovereign nations. However, the highly ranked nations of the world have reached the position they occupy because of the controls they exercise, and it is of continuing importance to them to gain the benefits that the lesser nations have to provide by exercising and trying to retain power wherever possible. Getting supporters has been necessary ever since Big Men found that their power depended on the success in economic accumulation provided from that source. In point of time, governments have been behaving capitalistically since at least the seventeenth and eighteenth centuries. Republics and democracies (in the Western sense) found their most effective mechanisms for growth expressed in nineteenth-century Liberalism. The separation of enterprise from too much government control was central to this, although national recognition and protection were equally important; these customs continue today. Obviously the governments cannot be disconnected from the activities and successes (and failures) of these delegated economic enterprises, whether dealing with the British East India Company, the Hudson Bay Company, or the ITT in Chile.

Socialist states came into being after the demonstrated weakness of the empires in World War I and tried to keep direct control over their own economic enterprises. All foreign trade and technical assistance was done for the explicit benefit of the state policy. Following World War II, the expansion of enterprise became a major tool of capitalist development, and the United States was clearly far and away the leader in these efforts. The TNCs provide the capitalist states with a mechanism of economic enterprise abroad that was inherent in the organization of the socialist governments.

The argument that the TNCs are in some manner a threat to the full autonomous sovereignty of smaller nations is certainly true. But that they will replace the national state as the dominant societal control entity is surely an unwarranted extension of that argument. The easiest question that one may ask about the TNCs to identify their potential political role is the same question that Stalin asked of the Pope: How many divisions do they have? They are ultimately subject to the whims and policies of the national governments under which they operate; and they are particularly likely to be called to support the policies of their home government. That they exercise a degree of independent action does not differentiate them in any material way from their predecessors. They are the contemporary industrial counterpart of the great mercantilist trading companies, and their very extension over vast areas of the world is both a basis of their power and the source of their vulnerability.

It is always more difficult to see clearly the outlines of contemporary structural processes than to see those of the past. The value of a structural approach, however, is that it permits one to seek the repetitious, the replicative, to follow the outlines that effectively describe the past to see how they project on the future. The projection of the world blocs as the emerging coordinate sets is merely an argument that follows the growth sequence that seems to effectively characterize the evolution of power in the past. In contrast, the vast differences that are argued to mark the socialist from the capitalist nations make only a wrinkle on this fabric. The centralization of the nation and the oscillation of coordinate sets of nations toward and away from centralization seem to be the dominant power patterns in the immediate future as in the past.

## 11.  REPLICATIVE PROCESSES

### A. *Energetic Expansion and Mentalistic Reduction*

In Part Two of this essay we explored some aspects of two phases of our inquiry, the *energetic* and the *mentalistic*. I want now to examine one final manner in which these seem to be conjoined within the evolutionary and historical processes of the proposed model.

Whether seen deductively from Lotka's principle and the Second Law of Thermodynamics, or empirically by an overview of the entire range of the development of the human species, one fact that seems indisputable in human society and culture is that it has, in its totality, been expanding at some exponential rate ever since the time of the first evidence of that quality we regard as "humanness." This fact has been chronicled by prehistorians for the early phase and by historically inclined sociologists for the more recent period.[104] Among recent investigators, Carneiro has dedicated most serious attention to this process and has proposed, in terms of the cultural forms involved, a rule: "Other factors being constant, the number of new culture traits generated by a society is proportional to the number it already has."[105] He further likens this rule to the principle of mass action in chemistry, where the "speed of a chemical reaction is . . . proportional to the number of available units (molecules, ions, etc.) entering into the process at the given instance."[106]

In viewing this macroscopic expansion of the species, we are not focusing on any particular operating unit. It was earlier noted

[104] See Ogburn 1922; Hart 1959; Carneiro 1969.

[105] Carneiro 1969, p. 1022. Reprinted by permission of the New York Academy of Sciences and the author.

[106] Ibid., quoting Samuel Brody (*Bioenergetics and Growth* [New York: Reinhold Publishing Corporation, 1945], pp. 514–515, 516). The passage continues: "It is the principle of compound interest, with the 'interest added to the capital continuously from moment to moment,' rather than annually, semi annually, or quarterly. . . . The principle of mass action is applicable to the multiplication rate of any category of reproducing units whenever the reproduction rate tends to be directly proportional to the number of reproducing units." Hart earlier expressed the relation of rate to level of development as follows: "Human culture develops through a series of growth surges, in which the size of a given measurable variable at a given time tends to be a constant mathematical function (usually logistic; less often Gompertz) of the condition at the immediate preceding time" (1959, p. 217). Hart has provided a good many instances, as well as the formulation of a number of "laws" ("The law of cultural acceleration," the "law of logistic surges") to characterize the process involved. My only reluctance to follow Hart more closely is that I am never sure what kinds of units he is dealing with.

that, whereas man lives as a part of many operating units, each operating unit has its own life trajectory or career. The only thing we can say of all of them is that each must have a beginning and an end. So, in saying that there has been exponential expansion, we are saying that the totality has expanded, but that this happened precisely because many operating units exhaust themselves or disappear; at the same time others appear with better adaptation, or better control over the environment. With sheer random chance, over time it is inevitable that controls permitting survival at a higher population level would come into being; especially so if man was dedicating himself to inventing new technology. Since the response of improving technology is a response aimed at survival, expansion has had high selective value. When man "discovered" this fact, he linked the value of survival to the energetics of expansion, and structural escalation was invented. But this expansion has been entirely an expansion of the energy component, of the amount of energy processed and the amount of stock built up. Apparently, the human mind has not evolved in any signal way over this same period. The differences in Middle Paleolithic and modern human behavior, so far as we know, do not rest in remarkable differences in mentalistic structures, but in the cumulative cultural equipment upon which man could exercise these mental abilities.

Carneiro's formulation has much to recommend it for the materials with which he was dealing, that is, historical and protohistoric residual cultural forms. From the contemporary vantage point, however, and recalling the arguments set forth in Part Two, I believe that a more significant variable than "culture traits" is energy conversion, the process whereby energy is expended such that there is a loss to entropy. I choose to emphasize energy conversion rather than input as the independent variable because the process of input implicitly involves conversion, but the process of culture growth involves both conversion-through-consumption and conversion-through-production. It is possible for complex dissipative systems with great storage of energy to persist and develop for extended periods on the basis of stored sources, while input may be very low. Thus, viewed functionally, the immediate variable of consequence is the conversion. Seen in the longer term, obviously input ultimately determines what is available for further conversion. A formulation that presents the case in this manner, then, is the following: *The rate of cultural change is proportional to the rate of energy conversion carried out within the system.* This can be expanded if we wish to regard the rising exponential curve as being indicative of, in some sense, a level of cultural achievement, for the relative change going on at any two points on the curve will also be relative to the rate of conversion at those points.

If the evolution of human society directly responds to the amount of energy at work in the system, then the proposition presumably applies not only to primitive and archaic societies but also to contemporary and future societies. The literature on the last of these tends, however, to give little weight to energy as the dynamics behind the entire cultural system and sees it rather as necessary only for the Judeo-Christian image of the material portion of that system. If the argument of the present essay is correct, this is a severe error. For not only does the amount of energy in the system have a direct relation to the amount of energy that will be communicated and stored, but it also is subjected to the inevitable human-cultural device of reduction to size.

A significant aspect of the process of binary differentiation is that we do it constantly. While there is obviously great individual difference in the relative ability to project new cuts in the environment, we are nevertheless constantly imposing old bifurcate categories on new events, thereby reducing them and simplifying them —in a word, mentally classifying them. More important, there are regularly new formulations of such differentiations, new ways of cutting up the world, that are invented and tried out. Most of these, like the lethal mutants of the genetic process, serve to extinguish themselves (and in some cases their bearers). But, from time to time, one survives the social filtering process and becomes the foundation for a great new "discovery" or "invention." Westerners have tended to see this process of recutting the world as something of a hallmark of progress. It can, however, also be seen as man's way of reducing the world to size, to terms with which he can deal.

Looked at in this fashion, we can see mankind as a species confronting a regularly changing environment, one most specifically changing through demographic expansion; but the confrontations have been repeatedly made with a relatively fixed mental equipment. No matter how new the events perceived, they had to be reduced to a comprehensible scope and to familiar dimensions. The totality of the energetic component may have been beyond his control, but man could always cut a piece of it down to size and form it to fit the "order" demanded by his own mentalistic limitations. In this general theory of power evolution, it has not been necessary to propose very many such mentalistic structures— indeed, all that have been suggested can be seen as repeating binary differentiation and ranking. Binary differentiation produces things and operating units; *ranking* orders things, people, and units. If this were pursued so as to incorporate other basic processes for which universality might be claimed, it seems likely that more and better propositions could be devised. For the moment, the basic processes of binary differentiation and ranking are sufficient, and equally necessary, for both simple and complex societies. The repetitive *growth sequence* is in substance a process of creating new operating units composed of existing identity units. The levels of articulation and of integration obviously have their origin in binary differentiation. They appear as levels of social distance in coordinate circles; as power increases they became levels of articulation. But the human mind operating within a society is limited in the number of such taxonomic dimensions that it comfortably uses, so that, in spite of demonstrable increases in power and the possibility of increasing levels almost indefinitely, this does not happen. Levels of integration replace levels of articulation, reducing to a maximum of six or seven the number of levels that the human mind has to work with.

So, *while societies become increasingly complex in terms of their energetic structures, their organizational dimensions are constantly reintegrated to mentalistic structural dimensions that are comprehensible to the human mind.* Does it have to be this way? Will not the use of computers and other advances in communications and information processing overcome these mental limitations? Here we return to C. S. Lewis's observation: "Man's conquest of Nature turns out, in the moment of its consummation, to be Nature's conquest of Man."[107] If man succeeds in overcoming the limitations of his own mind to build machines that can create

[107] Lewis 1973, p. 327.

structures the mind is incapable of comprehending, then he will have created a Nature that is no longer human. Someone may ask, for whose survival is he working? his own? or the computer's?

The basic process of expanding humanity is that the energetic expansion is perceived and reduced to man's mental capacity. The expansion continues, however, and it is once again perceived and reduced to man's capacity; and the process continues. If the expansion should escape man's capacity and he should fail to reduce it to size, he would lose control. The reduction to man's capacity is man's secret adaptive weapon; he can handle something when he can "bring it down to size." If he fails to bring it down to size, it will handle him.

As in other species, man's biological composition is such that the species will expand demographically until it reaches natural constraints on that growth; and man in his earliest state apparently lived to some degree in accord with this principle. However, when his cultural ability permitted him to reconceptualize the world, to differentiate two parts of the environment so that he could recombine them in a different way, he effectively found increasing ways to set aside the constraints that would otherwise have continued to limit his expansion. So far as the survival of the species was concerned, this expansion was its own reward. The evolution of culture has been witness to this replicative interplay of man's mentalistic abilities with his increasingly changing environment.

It must be noted that I am explicitly not proposing a "cause and effect" relationship here; there is nothing inherent in the argument that permits us to argue that the energetic or the mentalistic has in some manner "caused" the other. Any such general proposition is meaningless theoretically because of the methodology. It will be remembered that, at the outset, I emphasized that the energetic-mentalistic distinction was a methodological convenience. My supposition was that what we deal with under the rubric of "mentalistic" is also energetic, but that we simply do not have adequate tools from investigations in those areas to permit us to handle the events in energetic terms. Consequently, the mentalistic and the energetic in any case are aspects or phases of a single chain or complex event in the external world; and it is meaningless, in general terms, to propose which of the two phases or aspects could stand in a "causal" relationship to the other.

## B. *The Phases of Expansion*

The fact of mentalistic reduction does not eventuate in reduction of expansion unless the intent is specifically in that direction, and even then the model built by the actors has to be sufficiently in accord with the facts that it does, indeed, result in a steady state. In Part Two of the essay I noted in passing that ecosystem theorists have laid special emphasis on seeing the ecosystem as a homeostatic phenomenon, and that such an emphasis seemed to be misplaced when dealing with human expansion. There is no question that the human species as a whole has not yet followed the decelerating phase of the familiar sigmoid curve of the maturing ecosystem (see Figure 8); so it is worth a moment to explore the relations here more.

Why is it that culture, unlike ecosystems or physiological forms, seems to manifest such a continuing expansion? Ecosystems tend to reach a climax, that is, a steady state of maturity; but it is not clear whether the human species will ever reach such a climax.[108] Particular societies at times achieve an apparent steady state, but it shows important differences from that of physiological systems. There is really very little reason to anticipate that the human cultural system will achieve a climax; rather, culture has provided man with the tools whereby what is a climax to an ecosystem has been a stage of growth to the human social system.

Gregory Bateson has observed that "all biological and evolving systems contain subsystems which are potentially regenerative, i.e., which would go into exponential 'runaway' if uncorrected . . . The regenerative potential of such subsystems are typically kept in check by various sorts of governing loops to achieve 'steady state.'" Given these dynamics, "the system as a whole tends to 'expand' into any area of unused freedom."[109] For a species whose behavior is fixed to rather slow adaptive changes through genetic mutation and random variation, there is not much chance to move rapidly into new ecological niches unless the reproduction rate is extremely rapid and the population great, such as is the case with

---

[108] I use *climax* here in the ecologist's sense of the steady state achieved by a mature ecosystem, not in the sense proposed by A. L. Kroeber of a "culture climax." (See Kroeber 1947, p. 4.)

[109] Bateson 1972, pp. 441, 501.

some insect species. For most species, an "area of unused freedom" necessarily means a habitat that is congenial to the species in its current form. For humanity, however, culture, with its inherent inventive and adaptive mechanisms, provides man with a device for breaking the tendency toward the steady state. By developing new technological capacities, new "areas of unused freedom" are brought into being, thereby opening new potentials of population expansion.

Carneiro, following Herbert Spencer, has differentiated a *quantitative* change in culture from a *qualitative* change. In examining the accumulation of culture traits in Anglo-Saxon England, Carneiro argues that the pattern of cultural expansion followed two separate curves. The first, running from 450 A.D. or before until 650 A.D., had a steep slant; the second, from 650 A.D. until the Norman Conquest, had a much flatter slant (see Fig. 18a).[110] Carneiro argues from this that the first period was one of *cultural development*, in which new culture traits were coming into being, or, to put it in our terms, new devices for controlling the environment were being invented, discovered, or borrowed from beyond the borders of the political unit. The second period was, for Carneiro, one of *culture growth*, during which the new available traits diffused over the geographical extent of Anglo-Saxon England.

Periods of cultural development are periods during which existing adaptative patterns are broken by new controls over the environment. They may be seen as periods during which previous steady-state adaptations are being set aside by the introduction of new ways of coping, and they are very likely periods that are opening, within the environment, new "areas of unused freedom." Periods of cultural growth are those in which these new areas are gradually adopting, and thereby extending, the new adaptation. Carneiro points out, for example, that the first water-driven grain mill was reported in 762 A.D., and by 1086 A.D. the number had risen to 5,600.[111]

We can now suggest that this pair of curves and their distinction as developmental and growth patterns have a further correlation

---

[110] Carneiro 1969, pp. 1018–1022. The equations for the two lines are, respectively: $y = .575x + 99.75$ and $y = .088x + 220.8$.

[111] Ibid., p. 1020.

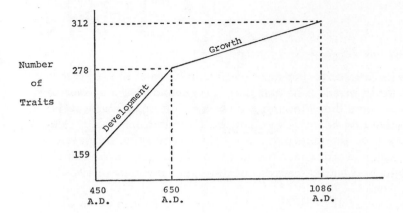

(a) Anglo-Saxon England, Development and Growth (after Carneiro 1969, Fig. 3)

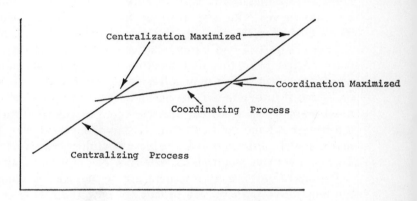

(b) Suggested Correlation with Expansion of Power Structure

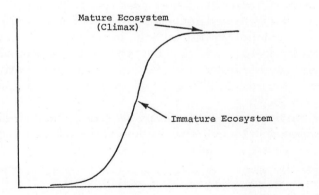

(c) Suggested Correlation with Pattern of Ecological Succession

Fig. 18. Hypothetical Correlations of Power Structure Expansion with Culture Trait Accumulation and Ecosystem Succession Pattern

within the power structure. The process whereby centralized units expand through a multiplication of their numbers is a coordinate process, but one that does not suggest any great change in the kind of technology; that is, it is a quantitative, not a qualitative, change. Centralization, however, marks a qualitative change, change in the amount of energy that is being brought under control within one part of the system. Figure 18*b* suggests that these phases are congruent. The process of development has as a parallel a process of power centralization, whereas the process of growth has as a parallel a process of coordination. What we have earlier referred to as a growth sequence then begins with the intersection of the two lines and proceeds through a process of coordination to a new phase of centralization.

If we now compare this suggested correlation with the curve usually assigned to the process of ecological succession (Fig. 18*c*), we will see that the period of development corresponds to the ecological expansion in production, and that of growth to the ecological period of maturity. The difference, however, is that in the ecosystem the constant energy input reaches a maximum productive possibility, and the system moves into a steady state. In the expansion of the human society and culture, we would argue that precisely this would occur, were it not that new inventions set aside this natural governing mechanism and permit an increase of energy input to press for a continued expansion.

The phase that Carneiro has characterized as "growth," which approximates an ecosystem's steady state, is not exactly replicated in sociocultural evolution. Rather than approximating a perfect steady state, the growth phase is characterized by oscillation and a gradual expansion. Oscillation is common to any steady-state condition of a complex dissipative system, since the different factors seldom operate so as to perfectly neutralize each other. This characteristic is common both to the ecosystem and to the coordinate, or growth, phase of the growth sequence. The fact that this coordination phase also is marked by a gradual expansion, however, does not parallel ecosystem successions, since the major source of input is determined by the energy available to the ecosystem through photosynthesis. There are limited ways in which new, additional inputs to the photosynthesis process allow a given ecosystem to suddenly move to a new period of advanced im-

maturity (if we may use that phrase) and to thereafter level off
into a new and higher steady state. In the evolution of the human
social system, the consistent application of new inputs is precisely
what does happen. In the first place the population tends to continue to grow, thus allowing some continued innovation; and in
the second place the circumscription created by the pressure of
this population tends to lead some social sector or component to
innovate technologically and achieve the possibility of an accelerating development to emerge out of an earlier period of slow
growth and coordination.

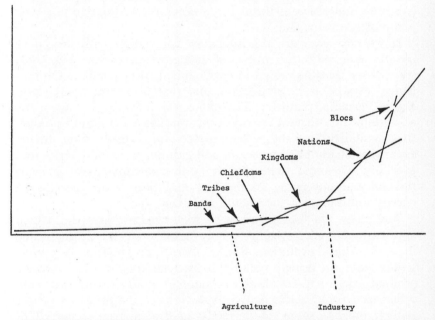

Fig. 19. Suggested Pattern of Emergence of Levels of Integration in General
Evolution

Figure 19 is an attempt to indicate schematically how this might
look if applied to the over-all evolution of human society. For
illustrative and possibly suggestive purposes, I have indicated how
this would appear if each of the major shifts from a centralizing
developmental to a coordinating growth phase were seen to achieve
a new level of integration based on a new centralization of co-

ordinated units. Of course, Figure 19 is schematic, just as is the paradigm of the levels of integration in evolution (Fig. 16). As real power structures are composed of specific levels of articulation, so real cases of specialized evolution are composed of specific periods of centralization and coordination.

The pattern that emerges is that which has already been shown to characterize the advance of technology in human history. Chauncey Starr and Richard Rudman have observed that "An historical survey of the performance growth of specific technical options reveals two predominant characteristics. First, when the performance of a given type of device or system is plotted against time it follows a sigmoid curve . . . The second . . . is that the over-all growth of a technological field is composed of a series of sigmoid curves. Each curve builds on the performance level of the previous generation device. . . . Thus the overall growth of a specific technological field often exhibits an exponential pattern."[112] There seems little question that the evolution of the energetic phases of human culture approximates both the characteristics suggested for technological advance. Both the replication of sigmoid curves and the exponential pattern of the over-all picture are as typical of the evolution of power, as manifested in the emergence of ever higher levels of integration, as they are of matters having to do directly with control over the energy forms that compose the environment. Thus (in Fig. 19) the coordinating (growth) line of collecting bands is flatter than that of chiefdoms, and that of chiefdoms flatter than that of kingdoms, etc. It seems likely that the rate of acceleration during the phases of centralization (development) will manifest an increasing slant, in accordance with the theory argued here and the observations of William E. Ogburn, Leslie White, Hornell Hart, and Robert Carneiro. This clearly poses a problem, since higher up the curve the phases of coordination tend to overlap those of centralization; and it is precisely this that we see occurring in the contemporary world and that causes so much confusion in the interpretation of current processes of the type under discussion here. For whenever variables

[112] Chauncey Starr and Richard Rudman 1973, p. 362. Reprinted, with permission, from *Science*, vol. 182, no. 4110 (26 October 1973). Copyright 1973 by the American Association for the Advancement of Science.

are seen to approach infinity, as the curve of energy utilization and cultural expansion seems to be doing, it necessarily means that they cannot long serve as meaningful variables and that the conditions that have produced them must soon be replaced by other conditions.

## C. *"Vertical" and "Horizontal" Oscillations*

The alternation of phases of coordination and centralization that can be seen in the macroview of societal and cultural evolution is equally useful in the examination of the processes that particular societies are undergoing at a given point in time. The literature of ethnography and history is replete with instances where societies seem to be undergoing some kind of oscillation, swinging from one kind of extreme to another; a well known case in anthropology is that of the Kachin extremes of *gumsa* and *gumlao* societies reported in Edmund Leach's classic study.[113] I believe that a great many of these cases can be analyzed by means of the same conceptual tools that I have been using in the description of this model.

First, it must be recalled that the model describes an expanding system. When we compare two societies at different phases, it is because we are saying that one is the result of an expanding process that has carried it further than the other in terms of power, in terms of the relative control it has over the environment. The coordination of a series of centralized elements and the centralization of a series of coordinated elements imply greater control and manifest greater power (cf. Fig. 18). If we treat man as a form of energy and his behavior, his control of stock, and the energy conversions in which he is involved as independent variables, then the dependent variable that concerns us is that occurring in the structure of power, with its consequences elsewhere in the system.

In low-energy societies the major surge toward expansion comes from population growth. This fundamental input continues, obviously, throughout the continuing multifarious history of man. Demographic expansion occurs in either of two circumstances: (*a*) the environment that can be handled under the existing technology

[113] Leach 1965.

is not limited, so that the population can expand without restriction; (*b*) the environment that can be handled under the existing technology is restricted. In the first case, the major process of growth is through simple segmentation, generational and/or collateral. This, if kept up regularly, would produce a continually expanding coordinate unit, along the peripheries of which the relations would probably decrease in intensity of interaction and, therefore, reciprocity; the ultimate periphery would shade off into identity relations and ultimately no relations whatsoever. Apparently, however, this kind of situation has not existed over most of the world for a long time; even though there are many unoccupied parts of the earth, it is not because they were never occupied, but rather because, for whatever reason, the peoples who formerly lived there moved out or their particular lines became extinct.

Restrictions on population expansion (either human or extra-human) apply to the specific technology and social relationships known to the people. The pressure resulting from expansion against restrictions can then be solved through technological and/or sociological innovation. Technological innovation may succeed in eliminating the restriction, or it may provide a substitute that permits the population to continue to expand, but with new, additional controls over the environment (power has also been increased). Sociological innovation similarly may produce an increase in control or power that permits pushing aside or eliminating the restriction; or it may lead to an intensification of the use of power within the group such that greater internal power permits greater density of population. There is an additional alternative (through technological and/or sociological innovation): control may be exercised over the demographic expansion. However, unless this is accomplished by all the contingent populations, the control by one will ultimately not resolve the problems, or pressure from other expanding populations will substitute for the local expansion pressure.

Given these alternatives, it is apparent that, if there is a restriction to population growth, it is almost inevitable in a universe of populations that at some point there will be innovation that will result in greater power or control over some segment of the environment. Population expansion over the long run, therefore, produces cultural expansion.[114] However, cultural expansion takes place, not just on one level, but rather on an increasing number of levels. The increase of control and power in a society eventually produces an intensification of relations that can only be resolved through coordination, first, and then centralization. When this happens, a new level of integration has been reached. If we begin with band expansion, we not only have the simple production of more bands, but also the inevitable consequence that tribal organization (coordination) will come into being, and subsequently chiefdoms (centralization). With two levels of integration now in existence, the expansion of which we have been speaking proceeds simultaneously on two levels. Not only do the bands continue to expand, seeking new forms of coordination and centralization, but the chiefdoms also expand, and they too proceed through the same growth sequence. Thus the expansion process leads to what *would appear to be* a continuing and simultaneous series of identity-coordination–centralization processes underway simultaneously at the domestic-unit level, the band/village level, the chiefdom level, and subsequently the kingdom or state level, and, indeed, continuing up to the expanding maximum level. While a given individual may be in the process of marrying (coordinating at the household level), his village may be centralizing against an infringing neighboring community, and his chiefdom may be engaged in a war with a neighboring chiefdom in an attempt to dominate and displace or subordinate the neighbor (centralization).

I have emphasized that these simultaneous processes would *appear* to be growth sequences. In fact, of course, the presence of restrictions, combined with the fact that every competitive success brings failure for another party, means that the processes are not indefinitely expansive, but rather show an oscillation between expansion and contraction. This oscillation may take place simultaneously in two phases or dimensions: (*a*) *horizontal*, that is, the shift from a fragmented (identity) unit to a coordinated unit and back (in other terms, fusion and fission, or recombination and segmentation); and (*b*) *vertical*, that is, the shift from a coordinated

[114] This problem area has been much reconsidered since the publication of Boserup's work; see Spooner 1972. Remember also that when we speak of "cultural expansion" we can only be referring to the energetic structure.

unit to a centralized unit and back (also described as integration and disintegration, centralization and decentralization, etc.). In Figure 15, the two processes are indicated by (*a*) the coordination of Centralized "A" units and (*b*) their centralization into "B" units. Both kinds of oscillation reflect intensification and fragmentation of relations.

Horizontal oscillation at the band level is familiar as a band's response to seasonal variation in availability of resources. The annual communal buffalo hunts of the Plains Indians is a classic case, but Lee summarizes that "The division of the year into two phases, a period of concentration and a period of dispersion, appears to be characteristic of . . . most of the world's hunter-gatherers as well."[115] In the case of !Kung Bushmen, Lee reports that the period of concentration (i.e., coordination) allows for the operation of boys' initiation camps, long trance dances that require more people for support than the ordinary dispersed family band could count, reciprocal trading between partners who see each other only at great intervals, and marriage contracting. However, the concentration periods also involve extra subsistence work and heightened tension; conflicts often break out and cause the camp to disperse.

The usual !Kung Bushman seasonal pattern is nine months dispersed and three concentrated. In a camp that had come to dwell next to a Herero cattle community, the pattern had been reversed so that seven different bands regularly concentrated for nine months. An increase in two kinds of power allowed this: (*a*) the Herero provided milk, meat, and agricultural produce to supplement the gathered and hunted food; (*b*) conflicts that otherwise would have broken up the concentrated camp were resolved by using the Herero as intervenors to maintain order. Quite literally the derivative power of the Herero had changed the oscillation pattern, permitting a greater period of sedentary living.[116]

A pulsating horizontal fluctuation at the tribal level is illustrated by the cases analyzed by Sahlins as the "predatory expansion" of "segmentary lineages."[117] This acephalous lineage organization ex-

[115] Richard B. Lee 1972*b*, p. 344. Reprinted from *Population Growth: Anthropological Implications*, ed. Brian Spooner, by permission of MIT Press. See also Birdsell 1973.
[116] Lee 1972*b*.
[117] Sahlins 1961.

pands into neighboring territory and, in doing so, undergoes some
degree of internal integration. Once a particular expansive phase
has been accomplished, however, this is relaxed and the system returns to a coordinated tribal collection of autonomous lineages.

The next vertical oscillations occur in two phases, the tribe–Big
Man phase and the Big Man–chiefdom phase. The classic example
of the first is the shift from the tribal to the Big Man situations described by Leach for the Kachin, the shift from *gumlao* to *gumsa*.[118]
*Gumlao* villages were small (ideally consisting of about ten families), totally autonomous communities that lived in a condition of
coordination with other such villages. "The *gumsa* ideal involves
the notion of a hierarchy of authority—*uma* chief–domain chief–
village cluster chief–village head–lineage head."[119] *Gumlao* villages
classically came into being through sheer rebellion against *gumsa*
chiefs within the *gumsa* situation. The reverse process takes place
through, among other things, influence of nearby clearly centralized Shan settlements. Leach explores many factors relative to this
oscillation and provides a number of reasons that a given community will move from one to the other condition, or return.

The Big Man position itself is one that is under a continuing
oscillatory process. The classic Big Men accumulate supporters and
food supplies, each seeking success and thereby concentrating increasing power in his own hands. Many observers of the Big Man
phenomenon have remarked on its oscillatory nature, although
they are not entirely agreed on the specific causes. M. J. Meggitt,
in describing the Mae-Enga of New Guinea, argues that there is a
cycle of peace and war.[120] Peace is a period of economic expansion
under a few Big Men. Their success leads to further population
growth and expansion and, thus, to war. There is a standing segmentary opposition among clans, and the war results in the success
of some Big Men, but in the failure and fragmentation of the clans
of the losers. The cycles then begin again. Sahlins's variant of this
is more parallel to Leach's description of the *gumlao-gumsa* oscillation: the successful Big Man derives his success from increasing
the flow of goods from his supporters; this inevitably becomes ex-

[118] Leach 1965.
[119] Ibid., p. 234.
[120] Meggitt 1967, pp. 30–32.

ploitative, and the result is a rebellion of the followers under other aspiring Big Men. In the more highly developed systems of Polynesia, the political evolution was also "eventually short-circuited by an overload on the relations between leaders and their people. The Polynesian tragedy, however, was somewhat the opposite of the Melanesian. In Polynesia, the evolutionary ceiling was set by extraction from the population at large in favor of the chiefly faction, in Melanesia by extraction from the bigman's faction in favor of distribution to the population at large."[121]

The oscillation from the semicentralized to the centralized condition is rather less fluid, since centralization implies the achievement of some degree of stability. However, the stability may well be short-lived. I am not familiar with a case of the transition from Big Man to chief, but Mair's description of the Gusii appears to show at least part of such a process.[122] There were six tribes of Gusii, each composed of clans, one of which was the "founders' " clan. There was a very strong identification with a specific clan territory, such that, when refugees from attacks of neighboring Masai or Nandi warriors sought refuge, they would be accepted only on a dependent-clientship basis. The Getutu "tribe" was less subject to foreign attack, and the leading men of the founders' clan received a disproportionate number of such refugees, thus expanding their wealth and power. The male clients became their supporters, and the women became their wives, thus multiplying the size of the clan in both generations. The male supporters became used as a source of independent force by the clan members against offenders. Mair notes that this appears to have been an emergent chiefdom, but it had no special myths that consecrated one clan above others, and she speculates whether one might have been invented had the process continued uninterrupted.

Oscillation between a collection of chiefdoms is illustrated by the history of the more advanced Polynesian chiefdoms, especially in Tahiti and Hawaii prior to the final centralization into kingdoms

[121] Marshall D. Sahlins 1963, p. 300. Reprinted from "Poor Man, Rich Man, Big Man, Chief: Political Types in Melanesia and Polynesia," *Comparative Studies in Society and History*, vol. 5, by permission of Cambridge University Press.

[122] Mair 1962, pp. 109–112; her source, unavailable to me, was P. Mayer, *The Lineage Principle in Gusii Society*, 1949.

early in the nineteenth century.[123] A similar pattern has been described for the relations holding between the lowland Mayan ceremonial centers, where power shifted from one to another of four regional centers over the years.[124] Within the Western tradition, Carneiro's description of the English chiefdoms prior to the Norman Conquest probably illustrates the process as well as any:

The states of the Heptarchy were frequently at war, with now one, and now another, increasing its power and enlarging its borders at the expense of its neighbors. But progress toward permanent aggregation of all the people and territory of England into a single cohesive state was slow, intermittent, and reversible. During the seventh century, for instance, Northumbria occupied the position of dominance, but was unable to retain it, losing it to Mercia during the following century. Then in the ninth century, power shifted once more, this time to Wessex, which under King Alfred and his successors succeeded in gaining control of virtually all of England. This control, however, was short lived. The Danish invasions of the tenth and eleventh centuries disrupted England once again, and prevented its consolidation into a single well-integrated state. The final unification and centralization of England was not achieved until after the Norman conquest. Thus, the period of English history running from 650 to 1066 may well have failed to provide the conditions required for continued development at the earlier rapid rate.[125]

The shifting alliances and confederations of chiefdoms have also been described in the fragmentation process that occurred in the segmentary states of East and South Africa. Gluckman describes the situation of coordination through rebellion and civil war in these states with

. . . technologies which force the people to spread widely for purposes of their husbandry. The wide and thin spread of the people over the land . . . necessitates that the ruler delegate power over territorial sections of his kingdom to subordinates. Delegated power is power given away. In many South African tribes . . . the territorial sections may participate in the circulation of tribute through the king. . . . [but] they are not held together by an integrating, differentiated economic system. The inhabitants . . . develop strong loyalties to their own

---

[123] See Davenport 1969; Hanson 1973.
[124] Marcus 1973, pp. 122–123.
[125] Carneiro 1969, p. 1020.

leaders, and also hostility toward other sections and the central government itself. Since weapons are simple . . . and owned by every man, each local authority has his private army to support his attempts at power. . . . The pressure of these forces produced a continuous segmentation of a number of African states and chiefdoms.[126]

Mair also notes that the "recent history of the Bito rulers is full on the one hand of rulers seeking to extend their authority by planting out clansmen on their borders, and on the other of princes rejecting superior authority when they were far enough away from the center of power to be able to disregard it."[127]

The phenomenon of oscillation is often so in evidence that it is forgotten that many such cases are actually part of longer-termed expansion or contraction processes. Even more important is the fact that the oscillations are visible manifestations of processes of power concentration that are in their base unidirectional. Oscillations are simply oscillations until someone introduces a new element of control into the scene. The !Kung Bushmen's change in seasonal schedule occurred with the derived power of the Herero; the Tahitian chieftain's competitive conflicts were raised to a new level by the availability of European derived power; the growth of population in the Late Feudal period, together with the complicated ramifications it entailed, gradually gave the kings an increased basis of independent power; and so on. Many oscillations mark real, although gradual, growth of control and power in the system, and its simultaneous concentration at higher levels. Queen Victoria may have had less power than did Queen Elizabeth; but the British government had inordinately greater power in the nineteenth century than it did in the sixteenth century. The value of understanding oscillations is that such an understanding draws one's attention to the fact of simultaneous changes within the power system.

[126] Gluckman 1963, p. 1531. Reprinted by permission of The Yale Law Journal Company and Fred B. Rothman and Company from *The Yale Law Journal*, Vol. 72, p. 1531. When Gluckman says that "Delegated power is power given away," he is referring to a situation in which the basic power is independent, and that held by the ruler is that which would be found in a majority unit.

[127] Mair 1962, p. 132. Reprinted from *Primitive Government* by permission of Penguin Books.

Among the more visible oscillations of history have been imperial ups and downs. As kingdoms extended to form empires, the human species for the first time began to reach the geographical limits of the continents. The ancient empires covered immense geographic territories, and the later mercantilist empires jumped the oceans and spanned the earth. The rise and fall of kingdoms and imperial centers, over a three-to-four-thousand-year period in the Old World and for at least a millennium before Columbus in the New World, were oscillations that prehistorians and historians have shown to reveal a gradual and inexorable increase of control and power. The apparent cycles of civilizations have fascinated historians and have brought out various hypotheses that have not always been entirely enlightened.

I think that we would have to argue that oscillations are inevitable parts of the evolutionary process; they are the ongoing trial-and-error of a unit, at whatever level, the coming into direct touch with the environment, the testing of the validity of mentalistic pictures and accumulated knowledge. It is the constant inherent structural push toward expansion that makes actors and the units they operate in try again. The oscillating pattern simply means some lack of success, which may be due to any of a wide variety of circumstances. But "success" is hardly the appropriate word, particularly when we recognize that consumption and destruction are both necessary parts of the scene. The fact that old people die will, in the long run, mean success for the young. Or what is successful centralization for one nation, state, chiefdom, or Big Man may spell disaster for another.

What is important about the oscillation process is that it cues the observer as to what he should be looking for. Every operating unit will be at some stage of oscillation at any point in time; to seek out its state and the factors that make it move is to understand how the power system is currently working.

## D. Power to the Top: The General Theory

A great deal has been said in the foregoing pages about the tendency of power to move toward the top of a system. It is perhaps worthwhile to restate the theoretical components of the process here, as it is unquestionably one of the most important of the replications in the total argument. It is not only to be observed in the over-all evolution of the human system but is also implicit in the fundamental energetics of the process as well as empirically determinable in the course of any microphase of history.

The argument can be summarized in aspects of the whole. At the base is the process of the expansion of energy in the system, due to the processes outlined by Lotka within the biosphere, and more specifically by structural escalation within the human social component. To ask whether this increase in energy in the system is "caused" by something or another is not helpful if one seeks a "prime mover"; the fact that it conforms to the widely observed principle of natural selection and the Second Law of Thermodynamics will have to stand as an "explanation" for the present. The concentration of energy within the life system follows the Second Law, and such a concentration will continue insofar as conditions of life may be met and the continuing supply of energy from the sun is available.

In human terms, this increase of energy forms and flows means an increase in control over the environment, and this in turn means an increase in the power within the human system. This process is inevitable, determinant, and without exception if one watches the system as a whole. This is to say, individual parts may cease to observe this, but those parts will be marginalized and/or eliminated as a result. Moreover, the fact that a given operating unit fails to grasp control over available energy processes simply means that another will when its technological competence permits. It is indeterminant and full of exceptions if one watches only a limited sector of the larger process. Other things being equal, it is quite impossible to predict the behavior of any particular unit within an aggregate or community of such units, unless one has special knowledge about the anterior history and condition of the individual units and the circumstances of the event.

The increase in control has as a power-structure consequence the determinant growth sequence of operating units. Centralization of decision-making must be preceded by coordination, and that in turn must be preceded by identity among units. The growth sequence as such constitutes the increase of levels in a system. Given any aggregate, new levels may be said to be emergent when they coordinate and to be fully constituted when they centralize. Since it is argued that centralization occurs permanently only when the units in question stand among a community of like units (and this only until higher levels extract the power, thereby possibly decentralizing them), it follows that the top level of any system must be composed of a coordinate set of centralized units. Centralization of the entire human system under the recognition of a common threat from the environment is conceivable, but difficult to imagine in view of the inherent lower-level fragmentation that occurs within complex systems.

The oscillations described earlier as occurring between the poles of identity and coordination, on the one hand, and coordination and centralization, on the other, are nothing more than the natural process of trial and error and natural selection as to which units shall centralize at the expense of others so long as energy increasingly enters the system. If energy input and output become equal and a steady state obtains, then such oscillations reflect the fluctuations of concentration within the coordinate sets as first one member and then another gains temporary advantage.

Finally, in observing historical events it may be argued that every change in a power structure will, irrespective of its superficial indications, constitute a move toward the concentration of power in the higher levels of a system if the amount of energy input to the larger system is increasing. Thus the much commented-on growth of power of the American president merely reflects an absolutely inevitable consequence of the expansion of the American system coupled with an expansion of the larger human system within which it is competing. This, it must be observed, is not to argue that such power has to be concentrated in the individual president; but it has to be invested at the presidential level; the particular kind of operating unit at that level will have to answer to the trial-and-error success in dealing with other like units (those in power in other equivalent units).

In summary, the increase of energy forms in a system means the creation of new controls; those controls will emerge wherever the energy forms may be, not necessarily where power is concentrated in the system. As controls continue to increase, the existent controls will tend to be concentrated. Thus new power foci will constantly serve as sources of power for the concentrations at higher levels—so long as energy inputs to the system continue to increase.

## 12. SOCIAL POWER AND THE FUTURE

The general thesis of this essay has been that man's particular relation to the environment is fundamentally similar to that of any other species, in that it is a continuing effort to exercise sufficient control to extract energy from the environment. Particularly typical of man, however, is his cultural mode of behavior, which leads him to seek this security of control through the constant redefinition of himself and his environment, permitting him to develop his society into an ever-expanding system. The argument suggests that this constant expansion is inherent in man's energy-using role within the thermodynamic system, that he is not doing anything particularly "unnatural" by virtue of this behavior.

The essay has been particularly concerned with the process of social power because it is in this that we can see especially clearly how man's cultural mode of behavior has enabled him, progressively, not merely to exploit other areas of the environment, but also to exploit himself. Furthermore, it is argued that this is typical of man since the earliest emergence of cultural behavior; it is not something peculiar to more recent agriculturally or industrially based systems. Man has always used the ability to manipulate his decision-making in order to improve his situation.

While the major burden of the essay has been on analysis and on projecting portions of this analysis to help in understanding the past, a few pages devoted to the future are not out of order. The purpose here is to suggest some of the effects that the things we have been calling control and social power may have. First we will try to set aside some things that cannot happen; and then we will explore a little among the remaining alternatives.

### A. Some Things That Cannot Happen

This essay has been concerned to relate man's society to energy. Our focus has not been on man's, particularly Western man's, headlong destruction of his environment; this is a matter of extraordinary importance, but it is outside the scope of our theoretical concern. It is probably the case that man as a species can live on earth for an indefinite period (indefinite in that it depends on the continuation of appropriate ecological conditions, and we cannot predict when these may eliminate man, quite apart from his abuse of them), but only if he (*a*) changes his choice of energy mix and (*b*) reduces the amount of energy conversion he exercises, so as to achieve something approaching a steady-state system. Social power and control obviously play a major role in each of these choices.

"Energy mix" refers to the particular selection among the variety of energy forms available to man, that is, the kinds of resources that man exploits for his own continuance. Foremost in the public eye at the time of writing is the question of some specific resources, such as oil and increasingly rare minerals, and what the prospects may be for their availability in the future. Just as important as their availability is the problem of their residue after use. This is, in the broadest sense, the problem of waste, the remaining compounds and conditions that remain after conversion is accomplished, and for which there is no further technology. The problem of material and gaseous pollution is well before us; somewhat less attention has been paid to the problem of heat in the atmosphere, a consequence that is contingent on the use of almost all kinds of energy forms except direct solar conversion and that available from direct solar radiation, gravity, and the earth's movement (which includes winds and tides). In a recent review, William R. Frisken estimates that "On the longer term (say, more than 100 years) we have the more serious problem of beginning to warm the climate directly with our own energy conversion. This will be with us (in slightly different degree at any one time) whether we derive our energy from coal fires, nuclear reactors, or from fusion generators as yet only imagined. . . . if we continue to double our energy conversion rate every 17.5 years, in about 250 years it will equal the rate at which we absorb solar radiation at the earth's surface at the present time."[128] Of more immediate possible concern in atmospheric change is the greenhouse effect of carbon di-

---

[128] Frisken 1973, p. 65. Reprinted from *The Atmospheric Environment* by permission of The Johns Hopkins University Press.

oxide increase, which raises the temperature, although the nature of this process seems quite uncertain. Claude M. Summers argues that there are energy collectors, specifically those turning to solar and wind energy, that "would add no heat load to the earth's biosphere; they can be called invariant energy systems." However, Summers's estimate for the time at which we would be releasing heat at the absorption rate of the sun's radiation is only 99 years from now, not 250.[129] If the problem of achieving the correct energy mix were merely a technical problem, the issue would be quite confounding in itself. It carries with it, however, an implicit and possibly even more difficult problem in the dimension of social power.

The relative mix of energy forms and sources available within any particular context will determine much about the amount and concentration of social power that we are likely to find there. The contemporary oil situation is as good an example as any. Oil has been contrived (with full intent by the industry) to be the major energetic resource of modern industrialism. From initial ownership of oil-bearing land to the ultimate consumer, oil engenders an incredibly complex power and control network that reaches deep into the government and economy of almost every nation in the world, as well as into a broad range of industries that are financially or technically dependent on the oil business. This is a vast coordinate operating unit that is bent both on retaining access to its own pluralistic resources and on utilizing the power it gains therefrom to the continued benefit of the unit. The problem that confronts man, very realistically, is how the species can effect sufficient countercontrols so as to exercise power over this complex coordinate system. If it were centralized, it might be somewhat easier, for then the center could be captured. But the great survival advantage of coordinate units is that they have no single brain, no vulnerable single nervous system.

Clearly the question of social power and its basis in control is central to this issue. If it were possible to make oil less important in the energy mix, then the coordinate unit would be less powerful; but it is specifically trying to avoid that eventuality. But there is one thing that we ultimately cannot have, and that is a system

[129] Summers 1971, pp. 105–106.

based on the present energy mix, and this means specifically that we must reduce our dependence on oil and other nonrenewable energy resources.

The amount of energy being converted, if we accept the theory proposed earlier in the essay, cannot continue to accelerate and must in fact be reduced and level off. Since the argument has been heavily made already, I will not repeat it in detail here, but will simply summarize it. The complexity, and therefore much of the form, of social and political organization is directly determined by the amount of energy that is being converted in the system. Since many of the particular forms of energy that we need are in terminal supply, we cannot indefinitely have an increase in the rate of conversion. This means that energy conversion and human society both have to level off into a steady-state condition. If the species does not devise some way to level off at its own rate, then it is quite simply the case that nature, of which it is a part, will level it off, if not all but eliminate it.

We might add here a point that was made earlier in the essay. At the maximal level of social organization of the species it may be possible to have one operating unit that is ranked clearly above others in terms of the controls and power that it exercises, but it is quite impossible to have this operating unit constitute an additional level of integration above its lesser peers. The species will never achieve a monolithic power structure, simply because it will always be composed of parts that will be contending for control, and this inevitably means they will be exercising power over each other and contending for better positions from which to do this. Structurally, the top will always remain multiple. There will never be a single "supranational agency, a state above states," that will be able to indefinitely exercise independent power either for the benefit or to the detriment of man the species.[130] Man can never be politically unified; he will ultimately find levels of living that will require less energy; and he will find that he has to change his energy mix. All these are safe, and not trivial, predictions; but they are also of very little immediate help. Can the theory of social power provide any clarification of the alternatives here?

[130] Cf. Fried 1968*b*, p. 150.

## B. What Level of Life?

Man is placing the environment out of control at a rate that is some function of the amount of energy converted. The more advanced the culture, the greater the consequent structuring of the environment. It is increasingly broadly recognized in scientific communities that man must reduce the amount of his energy conversion and that he must find a way of achieving a steady-state economy and ecology.[131] But there persists a nebulousness about the structure of this future. We tend to have dogmatic, but substantively indistinct, notions, such as Marx's "higher phase of communist society,"[132] or a kind of there-is-free-will-but-entropy-is-inevitable dualism. For example: "We could, for example, adopt as our cardinal philosophy the rule that no man or institution in our society may take any action that decreases the economic and social options of those who will live on the planet over the next 100 years. Perhaps only organized religion has the moral force to bring about acceptance of such a rule, but perhaps it could result also from an enlightened, widespread program of public education."[133] In suggesting religion, Jorgen Randers and Donella Meadows have resorted to a device that worked in the chiefdom stage of evolution; they then suggest public education, the cure-all that has marked the modern era, without recognizing that public education is a dependent variable of the system, not an independent variable that directs the system.

Harrison Brown foresees three future possibilities:

The first and by far the most likely pattern is a reversion to agrarian existence. This is the pattern which will almost certainly emerge unless man is able to abolish war, unless he is able to make the transition involving the utilization of new energy sources, and unless he is able to stabilize populations.

[131] See D. H. Meadows et al. 1972; Daly, ed. 1973.

[132] "In a higher phase of communist society, when the enslaving subordination of the individual to the division of labour, and with it the antithesis between mental and physical labour, has vanished; when labour is no longer merely a means of life but has become life's principal need; when the productive forces have also increased with the all-round development of the individual, and all the springs of co-operative wealth flow more abundantly . . ." (Bottomore and Rubel, eds. 1964, p. 258).

[133] Randers and Meadows 1973, p. 300.

In spite of the difficulties that confront industrial civilization, there is a possibility that stabilization can be achieved, that war can be avoided, and that the resource transition can be successfully negotiated. In that event, mankind will be confronted with a pattern which looms on the horizon of events as the second most likely possibility—the completely controlled, collectivized industrial society.

The third possibility confronting mankind is that of the worldwide free industrial society in which human beings can live in reasonable harmony with their environment. It is unlikely that such a pattern can ever exist for long. It certainly will be difficult to achieve, and it clearly will be difficult to maintain once it is established. Nevertheless, we have seen that man has it within his power to create such a society and to devise ways and means of perpetuating it on a stable basis. In view of the existence of this power, the possibility that the third pattern may eventually emerge cannot be ignored, although the probability of such an emergence, as judged by existing trends, may appear to be extremely low.

Brown then observes:

Indeed, it is amply clear that, if man wills it, a world community can be created in which human beings can live comfortably and in peace with each other.[134]

Like Randers and Meadows, Brown clearly sees the energy problems, but his first inclination is to be a little more realistic as to where this must ultimately lead. If nonrenewable resources cease to be available, then man must be reduced to an agrarian existence in which he can survive on renewable resources. But Brown, too, finds it hard to resist the culture in which he lives, and suggests that, if man could "abolish war," then this end might be avoided; and, further, that "if man wills it" a comfortable world community can be achieved. Perhaps Brown was not aware that war was a hallmark of neolithic societies, and that it has increased with the amount of power and energy in the system, not decreased. Man's will can have little to do with it unless expansion can be contained.

Gregory Bateson also seeks a solution, and, like the others, he is acutely aware of the energy component. His concern, however, is

---

[134] Brown 1954, pp. 264–265. From *The Challenge of Man's Future* by Harrison Brown. Copyright 1954 by Harrison Brown. Reprinted by permission of The Viking Press, Inc.

that we maintain a "high civilization." It is worthwhile to lay out his argument in some detail:

It becomes then necessary to work toward a definition of "high."

(a) It would not be wise even if possible to return to the innocence of the Australian aborigines, the Eskimo, and the Bushmen. Such a return would involve loss of the wisdom which prompted the return and would only start the whole process over.

This is an important and clever observation; and, as will be evident later, the possibility of starting "the whole process over" would seem likely. But Bateson's objection is phrased in terms of human mental—specifically, memory—capacity, and does not examine the inevitability even without that memory.

(b) A "high" civilization should therefore be presumed to have, on the technological side, whatever gadgets are necessary to promote, maintain (and even increase) wisdom of this general sort. This may well include computers and complex communication devices.

(c) A "high" civilization shall contain whatever is necessary (in education and religious institutions) to maintain the necessary wisdom in the human population and to give physical, aesthetic, and creative satisfaction to the people. There shall be a matching between the flexibility of people and that of the civilization. There shall be diversity in the civilization, not only to accommodate the genetic and experiential diversity of persons, but also to provide the flexibility and "preadaptation" necessary for unpredictable change.

Here Bateson proposes that "on the technological side" there will be available an establishment that is characteristic of a very high-energy civilization, including computers and "complex communication devices." He also proposes a "diversity" that would require a high cost of upkeep.

(d) A "high" civilization shall be limited in its transactions with environment. It shall consume unreplaceable natural resources only as a means to facilitate necessary change (as a chrysalis in metamorphosis must live on its fat). For the rest the metabolism of the civilization must depend upon the energy income which Spaceship Earth derives from the sun. In this connection, great technical advance is necessary. With present technology it is probable that the world could only maintain a small fraction of its present human population, using as energy sources only photosynthesis, wind, tide, and water power.[135]

[135] Bateson 1972, pp. 495–497.

Bateson evades some of the errors of the others. He does not directly invoke "will," education, or religion to solve the problem. He also realizes that for man to obtain the immense amount of energy input necessary he will have to become ecologically extraterrestrial (hopefully with greater success than Icarus). Yet elsewhere Bateson seems to make clear that this would be unlikely: "The unit of survival is *organism* plus *environment*. We are learning by bitter experience that the organism which destroys its environment destroys itself."[136] When Bateson argues that the organism can survive only in conjunction with its environment, but then holds that the future "high civilization shall be limited in its transactions with environment," we are left a little uncertain of his meaning of the terms. Clearly the sun can be little more than an energy resource; everything else currently comes from the terrestrial system, one way or another. I cannot help but suspect that Bateson's judgment has also been tilted by the magic notion of a high civilization based on little energy.

Whereas Brown, Randers, and Meadows share the implicit dualism that Bateson observed was fundamental in the Book of Genesis, Bateson and Marx seem to argue that such a dualism may be avoided and that man can have the world and heaven too. My limited familiarity with Marx leaves me unclear how he would achieve this, but Bateson suggests that we plug directly into the sun. In the present essay the argument is somewhat different. A mentalistic-materialistic dualism may be necessary for methodological reasons, but the components are not used as actors who confront, dominate, or lose. Rather, the mentalistic and the energetic are two aspects of a system that may be seen as conjunctive in every human act; every act is simultaneously a result of both components.

Basically, all these authors would probably agree that the species must achieve something akin to a steady state, but all to one degree or another seem to be drawn by what I have referred to as the magic of a high civilization with little energy.[137] So the question that faces us is a double one: not merely, how do we achieve a

---

136 Ibid., p. 483.

137 Among the most charming, if incredible, of these magic formulations may be found Shepard's argument that we may anticipate a return to hunting and gathering, but with underground computers (1973).

steady state? but also, at what level should we aim to settle? Bateson argues that to return to a hunting and collecting existence would be to forego the great wisdom that humanity has achieved to date. Roy Rappaport goes further than this and does not even feel comfortable with Harrison Brown's suggestion that the agrarian existence is a solution:

We may ask if a worldwide human organization can persist and elaborate itself indefinitely at the expense of decreasing the stability of its own ecological foundations. We cannot and would not want to return to a world of autonomous ecosystems such as the Tsembaga's [a New Guinea agricultural society]; in such systems all men and women are (and must be) farmers. We may ask, however, if the chances for human survival might not be enhanced by reversing the modern trend of successions in order to increase the diversity and stability of local, regional and national ecosystems, even if need be, at the expense of the complexity and interdependence of worldwide economic organization.[138]

Anthropologists have often treated peasant or primitive societies as if they were in a steady state, only to find later that they were not. Nevertheless, there is some reason to assume that many societies have lived for extended periods in at least an oscillating or quasi-steady state. Certainly Australian hunting and collecting bands that survived into the last century must have achieved some kind of steady state, since they had been in approximately that state for a good many millennia. Population was kept similarly in such a condition, presumably with fluctuations of the type mentioned in the last section. We are also reminded that they achieved limitation of births because a mother with more than one infant in arms would have had trouble keeping up with the band movements. A shift to sedentary life, however, "triggered population growth since women may have children frequently without . . . reducing their ability to provide for each one."[139]

Once into the sedentary life, local conditions may have restricted growth and expansion, but I suspect that we must regard the invention of agriculture and sedentary life as the real opening of

[138] Roy A. Rappaport 1971*a*, p. 80. Reprinted from "The Flow of Energy in an Agricultural Society," originally published in *Scientific American*, September 1971, by permission of W. H. Freeman and Co.

[139] Lee 1972*a*, p. 342.

Pandora's box. If one looks to the total sociocultural systems within which people were working and on the basis of which they were surviving, there has been little let-up in population and cultural expansion since that time. Arguments that urban populations do not reproduce themselves and that birth rates decline with education are small backwashes in a picture that is otherwise flooded with growth. There have been many particular cases where population growth has declined for various reasons; but they have not been sufficient to change the over-all expansion.

Besides the collectors, the only other type of society that might claim credit for establishing a steady state is the peasant. There is a literature in recent years that holds that these "part-societies" have devised a way to restrain advancement or expansion. Foster's theory of the "limited good" represents the ethic,[140] while Wolf's thesis concerning the "ceremonial fund" (that proved so useful in Schaedel's analysis of the organization of pristine chiefdomships)[141] and Ruben Reina's description of community pressure[142] suggest some of the societal processes that may operate. While it is hard to argue that peasant populations characteristically are a steady state demographically, it probably is reasonable to argue that there are various devices that have been instituted over the centuries to restrict cultural expansion. Peasants, however, are necessarily sub-sectors (in Kroeber's terms, "half-societies"), and often fairly marginalized ones, of complex macrosocieties. They are subject to many kinds of pressures, not the least of which are rent, tax, tribute payments, and market disadvantages, which can only increase if the superordinates become aware that the peasants are finding their art lucrative. Even without a "ceremonial-fund" hypothesis, it is quite reasonable to anticipate a reticence on the part of peasants to display excessive success. But the question of peasants in the context of the steady-state issue is misleading, because the crucial issue is not whether the peasants expand, but whether the society as a whole is expanding. Where peasant society manifests a cultural homeostasis, it may simply be that upper sectors are expanding their cultural activities at the cost of peasant rents and

140 Foster 1967, Ch. 6.
141 Wolf 1966, pp. 7–9.
142 Reina 1963.

taxes. If that is the case, then the society is, in fact, expanding.[143]

The problem that confronts us is that human society has always been an expanding system, and there are implicit reasons for this in the nature of biology and culture. Yet it is clear that it cannot continue for much longer as an expanding system, that it will have to move to some other kind of state or states. Harrison Brown's suggested agrarian existence may be workable if it is principally the question of energy that concerns us. Most writers, however, Brown included, prefer to opt for a society with many of the advantages of a high-energy system, but to have it based on less use of energy. This poses a dilemma that is insoluble.

The question then boils down to whether Brown's agrarian proposal can stand up or whether even it faces serious problems. Since human society, like other societies, achieves survival at the ultimate cost of overproducing, it may be assumed that the continuing success of an agrarian adventure will also depend upon the society's constant push toward expansion, either cultural or demographic[144] or both. Agrarian societies are already at such a high rate of energy expenditure that their rate of evolutionary change is relatively high, and they will necessarily manifest a tendency to move toward the limits of their environment, with the inevitable consequences in attempted cultural advance and demographic circumscription. Thus agrarian existence eventually implies an increased rate of conflict and an increased likelihood of again moving to chiefdomlike or kingdomlike levels of integration. Presumably the advance would be hindered or stopped at some point due to the ab-

---

[143] Our concern with an energetic steady state should not be confused by Bateson's analysis, "Bali: The Value System of a Steady State" (1972, pp. 107–127). Bateson is not explicitly concerned with an energy system, but rather with a value system; and, as such, the "steady state" is somewhat metaphorical. The Balinese situation he describes does, however, have elements of a possible energetic steady state. Lack of population information and allusions to earlier and other Balinese expansive activities suggest that the apparent condition described by Bateson may have been due to a combination of colonial control and an economy of abundance. Other work suggests that population growth was going on apace during Bateson's visit to Bali and that cultural expansion is certainly underway in some areas now. See Geertz 1963, pp. 21–22.

[144] "Any species that does not, potentially, produce more young than the number of the population of the parental generation is out" (Bateson 1972, p. 430).

sence of suitable energy forms, e.g., lack of adequate iron or other minerals. Thus man would presumably be contained at a steady state that would maximally be agrarian and empirically would probably consist of a rather wide variety of agrarian adaptations, contending and competing with each other depending upon the local circumstances. What would inevitably happen would be the repeated experiencing of adaptational catastrophe as the population grew beyond the limits of potential ecological production.[145]

Catastrophe within living memory or some reminder within the environment that provides a signal of danger seems to be important. Bateson has observed that, "In principle, the homeostatic controls of biological systems must be activated by variables which are not themselves harmful."[146] Within cultural systems too, it is not viable to wait until there is a series of catastrophes that make further signaling unnecessary. Rather, there must be some cultural meanings in the system that attach to variables to warn of impending danger so that the homeostatic mechanism may go into effect.

An additional feature of agrarian and higher-ordered societies is that their members are inevitably going to increasingly promote the exploitation of their fellow men for their own survival and benefit. Margalef, it will be remembered, argued this as a principle for ecosystems in general,[147] and, as such, his argument is a detailing of the more general principle that Lotka set forth some years earlier. The dependency created by higher levels among the lower ones subordinate to them, with the inevitable marginalization that follows, is inherent in agrarian cultures as well as others. (One must be careful here not to confuse rank peers with superordinate-subordinates at different levels.)[148]

Although hunting and gathering societies did not appeal to Bateson as a potential way of life, given the ancestry of man, they have something to recommend them. The only approximately steady-state society that man has ever achieved is the hunting and gather-

---

[145] "I am rather inclined to think that for many years to come human populations will alternate between scares of overpopulation and scares (as in the 1930's) of dying out altogether through underfertility" (Medawar 1973).

[146] Bateson 1972, p. 443.

[147] Margalef 1968, p. 16.

[148] Adams 1974a.

ing society. His tenure on earth has been principally in that condition, and the Australian aborigines and Bushmen of Africa give evidence that they have survived fairly successfully, at least until they were brought within the advantages of mercantilistic and industrial civilization.

The nomadic aspect is important, since that serves to keep the birth rate down, and the collecting level is important, since the rate of energy use is so low that the rate of cultural advance would be equivalently low. This alternative has certain other features to recommend it. The mentalistic structures of man proved eminently qualified to handle the kinds of problems that were presented at that level. Also, the governing mechanisms of these societies are totally allocative; there simply is not enough environment controlled to permit a concentration of power. It would, incidentally, also fit the democratic idea and the Marxist ideals. All men would have equality before the law, a thing patently impossible in a complex system. "From each according to his ability, to each according to his needs" would be a reality. It would achieve what Marx described as that "definitive resolution of the antagonism between man and Nature, and between man and man."[149]

I am not entirely sure what Marx may have had in mind by the ultimate socialism; but, without entering a realm of mysticism that is quite foreign to me, I cannot see what other kind of steady state would meet most democratically and socialistically oriented political philosophies. Hinduism has, in the caste system, built a model of energy flow with the entire society stratified so as to purify and allow those who are purest to live reasonably well. An outsider or the impure might find the system somewhat discouraging; but Indians seem to have adjusted to it for many centuries.[150] It may be that the steady-state demography in India in earlier years depended on periodic famines, a method that is certainly one of nature's favorites, if not generally regarded as the most desirable among human beings. An economist has suggested that "Buddhist economics" has much to recommend it: "The ownership and the consumption of goods is a means to an end, and Buddhist econom-

---

[149] Bottomore and Rubel, eds. 1964, p. 244.

[150] Gould 1971. Douglas, summarizing for some Brahmin castes, shows that they too may suffer intense restrictions to retain their purity (1970*a*, p. 171).

ics is the systematic study of how to attain given ends with the minimum means." Although he makes a convincing case that the ideal of Buddhism could conform with the needs for a steady state, he does not show how a full-scale Buddhist society, based on agriculture, could evade for a thousand years or more the likely possibility of population expansion that would force an eventual concentration of power.[151]

If the rate of culture change, as well as the level of evolution achieved, is hinged directly to the amount of energy being converted, then we presumably must think about the future of human society with that in mind. The present work, concerned as it is with human social power, would further argue that the political and social organizations will find themselves shackled to this variable quite as much as the technology, communication system, nutritional production, or any other aspect of the adaptive process. Liberty may be had, but not with a high-energy-level society; only collecting societies have offered this to man in previous eras, and even they cannot guarantee that such characteristics will flourish.

The problem of governance hinges on the fact that the kind of government we can anticipate depends upon the amount of energy in the system quite as much as do the kind of art, the kind of housing, the kind of recreation, and so forth. Just as a highly developed cinematography is impossible without the energy necessary for the diverse electrical, chemical, and developmental processes required, so it is difficult to have a centralized government without the available independent power that must come from reasonably well developed sources of food, shelter, and implements. The reason tribal organizations were prevalent during much of man's tenure and still visible widely during the past three hundred years was that it was not easy to get that extra power necessary to centralize.

By the same token, to assume that a "religion" or "widespread education" will produce an "ethic" can be meaningful only if the level of energy of the society and the level of power in the system are appropriate for those devices. Supernaturally oriented religions worked during chiefdoms, in lower-powered societies, because the governments were unable to support the bureaucracy and the num-

[151] Schumacher 1973, p. 235.

ber of nonproducers required. Proposals for utopian futures need to consider not only the energy sources but also the power structure that will necessarily come into being from any such energy base and the administration and communication systems that can be supported by that level of energy conversion. It is, perhaps, a little much to ask of man that, in order to survive, he cease to be human.

If we are curious about the shape of the future, some familiar alternatives are suggested in Figure 8. For the Wall Street oil investor, the first two would appeal; for the fancier of ecosystems, the steady state of that model will be attractive; for the doomsday addict, the human life provides as good a model as any; but, for the present writer, it appears that the models of the domestic unit or the empire may most closely fit the possibilities, although the horizontal portions of the decline would probably be much more broken, much more extended, to the point where the decline of man might in some manner mirror his rise: the rate of his conversion of energy would mark his place on the scale.

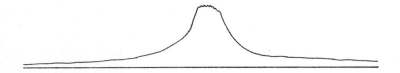

# WORKS CITED

Adams, Richard N.
  1962 "Changing Dietary and Health Practices." In *Agriculture*, pp. 86–96. Science, Technology and Development: United States Papers Prepared for the United Nations Conference on the Application of Science and Technology for the Benefit of the Less Developed Areas, vol. 3. Washington, D.C.: Government Printing Office.
  1966 "Power and Power Domains." *América Latina* 9(2):3–22.
  1967 *The Second Sowing: Power and Secondary Development in Latin America*. San Francisco: Chandler Publishing Co.
  1970a *Crucifixion by Power: Essays on Guatemalan National Social Structure, 1944–1966*. Austin: University of Texas Press.
  1970b "Brokers and Career Mobility Systems in the Structure of Complex Societies." *Southwestern Journal of Anthropology* 26(4): 315–327.
  1973a "Power Concentration, Social Class, and Human Survival: Thoughts on the Energetics of Expanding Society." To be published in Spanish by the Instituto Nacional de Antropología e Historia, Mexico City.
  1973b "El poder: Sus condiciones, evolución y estrategia." In *Estudios sociales centroamericanos*, no. 4 (January–April), pp. 64–141. San José, Costa Rica: Editorial Universitaria Centroamericana (EDUCA).
  1974a "Harnessing Technological Development." In *Rethinking Modernization: Anthropological Perspectives*, edited by John S. Poggie, Jr., and Robert N. Lynch. Westport, Conn.: Greenwood Press.
  1974b "Structure, Entropy and a Steady State Economy." *Reviews in Anthropology* 1(1):5–17.
  1974c "Correlativos de poder de cambio en los símbolos." In *Homenaje a Gonzalo Aguirre Beltrán*, II, 153–165. Mexico City: Universidad Veracruzana and Instituto Indigenista Interamericano.

by Robert Manners and David Kaplan, pp. 465–472. Chicago: Aldine Publishing Co.

Blair, Peter M.
  1964   *Exchange and Power in Social Life.* New York: John Wiley and Sons.

Bonilla, Frank
  1970   *The Failure of Elites.* Vol. 2 of *Politics of Change in Venezuela.* Cambridge: MIT Press.

Boserup, Esther
  1965   *The Conditions of Agricultural Growth: The Economics of Agrarian Change Under Population Pressure.* Chicago: Aldine Publishing Co.

Bottomore, T. B.
  1966   *Elites and Society.* Harmondsworth, Eng.: Penguin Books. First published by Messrs. C. A. Watts, 1964.

Bottomore, T. B., and Maximilian Rubel, eds.
  1964   *Karl Marx: Selected Writings in Sociology and Philosophy.* New York: McGraw-Hill Book Co.

Boulding, Kenneth E.
  1968   *Beyond Economics.* Ann Arbor: University of Michigan Press.

Bowers, Nancy
  1971   "Demographic Problems in Montane New Guinea." In *Culture and Population: A Collection of Current Studies,* edited by Steven Polgar, pp. 11–31. Cambridge, Mass.: Schenkman Publishing Co.

Brookfield, H. C., and Paula Brown
  1963   *Struggle for Land.* Melbourne: Oxford University Press.

Brown, Harrison
  1954   *The Challenge of Man's Future.* New York: Viking Press.

Brown, Paula
  1951   "Patterns of Authority in West Africa." *Africa* 21:261–278.

Buchler, Ira R., and Henry A. Selby
  1968   *Kinship and Social Organization: An Introduction to Theory and Method.* New York: The Macmillan Co.

Bunge, Mario
  1963   *The Myth of Simplicity.* Englewood Cliffs, N.J.: Prentice-Hall.

Burgers, J. M.
  1963   "On the Emergence of Patterns of Order." *Bulletin of the American Mathematics Society* 69:1–25. (Cited in J. A. Miller 1965, p. 201.)

Burns, Tom, and Matthew Cooper

1971  *Value, Social Power, and Economic Exchange.* Stockholm: Sämhallsvetave-forlagt.

Calhoun, John B.
1973  "R(x)evolution, Tribalism, and the Cheshire Cat: Three Paths from Now." *Technological Forecasting and Social Change* 4(3): 263–282.

Carneiro, Robert L.
1969  "The Measurement of Cultural Development in the Ancient Near East and in Anglo Saxon England." *Transactions of the New York Academy of Sciences,* 2d ser. 31(8):1013–1023.
1970  "A Theory of the Origin of the State." *Science* 169(3947): 733–738.
1972  "From Autonomous Villages to the State: A Numerical Expansion." In *Population Growth: Anthropological Implications,* edited by Brian Spooner, pp. 64–77. Cambridge: MIT Press.

Caulk, R. A.
1972  "Firearms and Princely Power in Ethiopia in the Nineteenth Century." *Journal of African History* 13(4):609–630.

Chance, M. R. A.
1967  "Attention Structure as the Basis of Primate Rank Order." *Man* 2(4):503–518.

Chapple, Eliot
1940  "Measuring Human Relations." *Genetic Psychology Monographs* 23:3–147.

Childe, V. Gordon
1948  *Man Makes Himself.* London: Watts and Co. (First published, 1936.)

Cohen, Abner
1969  "Political Anthropology: The Analysis of the Symbolism of Power Relations." *Man,* n.s. 4:215–235.

Cohen, Benjamin J.
1973  *The Question of Imperialism: Political Economy of Dominance and Dependence.* New York: Basic Books.

Cohen, Ronald
1972  Review. *American Anthropologist* 74(6):1427.

Cohen, Ronald, and John Middleton, eds.
1967  *Comparative Political Systems.* Garden City, N.Y.: The Natural History Press.

Cohen, Ronald, and Alice Schlegel
1968  "The Tribe as a Socio-Political Unit: A Cross-Cultural Examination." In *Essays on the Problem of Tribe,* edited by June Helm, pp. 120–149. Seattle: University of Washington Press.

Coleman, James S.
    1973   "The Loss of Power." *American Sociological Review* 38(1):
        1–17.
Colson, Elizabeth
    1958   "The Role of the Bureaucratic Norms in African Political
        Structures." In *Systems of Political Control and Bureaucracy in
        Human Societies*, edited by Verne Ray, pp. 42–48. Proceedings of
        the 1958 Annual Spring Meeting of the American Ethnological
        Society. Seattle.
Cotler, Julio
    1969   "Actuales pautas de cambio en la sociedad rural del Peru." In
        *Dominación y cambios en el Peru*, by José Matos Mar et al., pp.
        60–80. Lima: Instituto de Estudios Peruanos.
Cottrell, Fred
    1955   *Energy and Society*. New York: McGraw-Hill Book Co.
Dahl, Robert
    1957   "The Concept of Power." *Behavioral Science* 2(July):201–215.
    1968   "Power." In *International Encyclopedia of the Social Sciences*,
        XII, 405–415. New York: Crowell, Collier and Macmillan.
Dahrendorf, Ralf
    1959   *Class and Class Conflict in Industrial Society*. Stanford: Stan-
        ford University Press.
Daly, Herman E., ed.
    1973   *Toward a Steady-State Economy*. San Francisco: W. H. Free-
        man and Co.
Davenport, William
    1969   "The 'Hawaiian Cultural Revolution': Some Political and
        Economic Considerations." *American Anthropologist* 71(1):1–20.
Deevey, Edward S.
    1960   "The Human Population." *Scientific American* 203:195–203.
Deutsch, Karl W.
    1968   *The Analysis of International Relations*. Englewood Cliffs,
        N.J.: Prentice-Hall.
Dobzhansky, Theodosius
    1967   *Mankind Evolving: The Evolution of the Human Species*.
        New Haven: Yale University Press.
Douglas, Mary
    1970a   *Purity and Danger: An Analysis of Concepts of Pollution
        and Taboo*. London: Pelican Books.
Douglas, Mary, ed.
    1970b   *Witchcraft Confessions and Accusations*. ASA Monograph
        9. London: Tavistock Publications.
Dumond, Don E.

1972 "Population Growth and Political Centralization." In *Population Growth: Anthropological Implications*, edited by Brian Spooner, pp. 286–310. Cambridge: MIT Press.

Dumont, Louis
1970 *Homo Hierarchicus: An Essay on the Caste System*. Chicago: University of Chicago Press.

Dyson, Freeman J.
1971 "Energy in the Universe." In *Energy and Power*, pp. 19–27. A Scientific American Book. San Francisco: W. H. Freeman and Co.

Earls, John
1973 "La organización de poder en la mitología quechua." In *Ideología mesiánica del mundo andino*, edited by Juan Ossio, pp. 393–414. Lima: Ignacio Prado Pastor.

Easton, David
1953 *The Political System*. New York: Alfred A. Knopf.

Edel, Abraham
1959 "The Concept of Levels in Social Theory." In *Symposium on Sociological Theory*, edited by Llewellyn Gross, pp. 167–195. Evanston, Ill.: Row, Peterson and Co.

Etzioni, Amitai
1961 *A Comparative Analysis of Complex Organizations*. New York: The Free Press.

Field, G. Lowell, and John Higley
1973 *Elites and Non-Elites: The Possibilities and Their Side Effects*. Warner Modular Publications, Module 13, 40 pp. Andover, Mass.

Flannery, Kent
1972 "The Cultural Evolution of Civilizations." *Annual Review of Ecology and Systematics* 3:399–426.

Forde, C. Daryll
1967 "The Governmental Roles of Associations among the Yakö." In *Comparative Political Systems*, edited by Ronald Cohen and John Middleton, pp. 121–141. Garden City, N.Y.: The Natural History Press. Also in *Africa* 31, no. 4(1961):309–323.

Fortes, Meyer, and E. E. Evans-Pritchard, eds.
1940 *African Political Systems*. London: Oxford University Press.

Foster, George
1967 *Tzintzuntzan: Mexican Peasants in a Changing World*. Boston: Little, Brown and Co.

Fried, Morton H.
1967 *The Evolution of Political Society: An Essay in Political Anthropology*. New York: Random House.

1968*a* "On the Concepts of 'Tribe' and 'Tribal Society.'" In *Essays on the Problem of Tribe*, edited by June Helm, pp. 3–20. Seattle: University of Washington Press.

1968*b* "State: The Institution." *International Encyclopedia of the Social Sciences*, XV, 143–150. New York: Macmillan and the Free Press.

Fried, Morton, Marvin Harris, and Robert Murphy, eds.
1967 *War: The Anthropology of Armed Conflict and Aggression.* New York: Natural History Press.

Friedrich, Carl J.
1950 *Constitutional Government and Democracy.* Lexington, Mass.: Xerox College Publishing.

Frisken, William R.
1973 *The Atmospheric Environment.* Published for Resources for the Future. Baltimore and London: The Johns Hopkins University Press.

Gates, David M.
1962 *Energy Exchange in the Biosphere.* New York: Harper and Row.

Geertz, Clifford
1963 *Peddlers and Princes.* Chicago: University of Chicago Press.

Georgescu-Roegen, Nicolas
1973 "The Entropy Law and the Economic Problem." In *Toward a Steady-State Economy*, edited by Herman E. Daly, pp. 37–49. San Francisco: W. H. Freeman and Co.

Gerth, H. H., and C. Wright Mills, eds. and trans.
1946 *Max Weber: Essays in Sociology.* New York: Oxford University Press.

Gibbs, Jack
1972 *Sociological Theory Construction.* Hinsdale, Ill.: The Dryden Press.

Gibson, Charles
1964 *The Aztecs under Spanish Rule.* Stanford: Stanford University Press.

1971 "Structure of the Aztec Empire." In *Archaeology of Northern Mesoamerica: Part One*, edited by Gordon F. Ekholm and Ignacio Bernal, pp. 376–394. Handbook of Middle American Indians, edited by Robert Wauchope, vol. 10. Austin: University of Texas Press.

Gluckman, Max
1963 "Civil War and Theories of Power in Barotseland: African and Medieval Analogies." *Yale Law Journal* 72(8):1515–1546.

1965*a* *Politics, Law and Ritual in Tribal Society*. Chicago: Aldine Publishing Co.

1965*b* *The Ideas in Barotse Jurisprudence*. New Haven: Yale University Press.

1968 "Inter-hierarchical Roles: Professional and Party Ethics in Tribal Areas in South and Central Africa." In *Local Level Politics*, edited by Marc J. Swartz, pp. 69–94. Chicago: Aldine Publishing Co.

1971 "Tribalism, Ruralism and Urbanism in South and Central Africa." In *Profiles of Change: African Society and Colonial Rule*, edited by Victor Turner, pp. 127–166. Vol. 3 of *Colonialism in Africa, 1870–1960*, edited by Peter Duignan and L. H. Gann. Cambridge: Cambridge University Press.

Godelier, Maurice

1972 *Rationality and Irrationality in Economics*. Translated by Brian Pearce. London: NLB.

Goldhammer, H., and E. Shils

1939 "Types of Power and Status." *American Journal of Sociology* 54(2):171–178.

González, Nancie L.

1972 "Patron-Client Relationships at the International Level." In *Structure and Process in Latin America: Patronage, Clientage and Power Systems*, edited by Arnold Strickon and Sidney M. Greenfield, pp. 179–209. Albuquerque: University of New Mexico Press.

Goodenough, Ward

1956 "Residence Rules." *Southwestern Journal of Anthropology* 12(1):22–37.

Goody, Jack

1971 *Technology, Tradition and the State in Africa*. New York and London: Oxford University Press.

Gould, Harold A.

1971 *Caste and Class: A Comparative View*. Addison-Wesley Modular Publications, Module 11, 24 pp. Reading, Mass.

Gross, Llewellyn

1959 *Symposium on Sociological Theory*. Evanston, Ill.: Row, Peterson and Co.

Gulick, John

1955 *Social Structure and Culture Change in a Lebanese Village*. Viking Fund Publications in Anthropology, no. 21. New York: Wenner-Gren Foundation for Anthropological Research.

Guyol, Nathaniel B.

1971 *Energy in the Perspective of Geography.* Englewood Cliffs, N.J.: Prentice-Hall.

Hanson, F. Allan
1973 "Political Changes in Tahiti and Samoa: An Exercise in Experimental Anthropology." *Ethnology* 12(1):1–14.

Harner, Michael J.
1970 "Population Pressure and the Social Evolution of Agriculturalists." *Southwestern Journal of Anthropology* 26(1):67–86.

Harris, Marvin
1971 *Culture, Man and Nature.* New York: Thomas Y. Crowell Co.

Hart, C. W. M., and Arnold Pilling
1960 *The Tiwi of North Australia.* New York: Holt, Rinehart.

Hart, Hornell
1959 "Social Theory and Social Change." In *Symposium on Sociological Theory*, edited by Llewellyn Gross, pp. 196–238. New York: Row, Peterson, and Co.

Hass, Hans
1972 *La evolución y la energía: El oculto común denominador.* Barcelona: Plaza & Janes. (Originally published as *Energon*, Wien-München-Zurich: Verlag Fritz Molden, 1970.)

Heath, Dwight
1972 "New Patrons for Old: Changing Patron-Client Relationships in the Bolivian Yungas." In *Structure and Process in Latin America: Patronage, Clientage and Power Systems*, edited by Arnold Strickon and Sidney M. Greenfield, pp. 101–138. Albuquerque: University of New Mexico Press.

Helm, June, ed.
1968 *Essays on the Problem of Tribe.* Proceedings of the Annual Spring Meeting of the American Ethnological Society. Seattle: University of Washington Press.

Hickel, Walter J.
1971 *Who Owns America?* New York: Prentice-Hall.

Hofstadter, Richard
1955 *Social Darwinism in America.* Boston: Beacon Press.

Homans, George
1961 *Social Behavior.* New York: Harcourt Brace Jovanovich.

Horowitz, Irving Louis
1969 "The Norm of Illegitimacy: The Political Sociology of Latin America." In *Latin American Radicalism*, edited by idem, J. de Castro, and J. Gerassi, pp. 3–28. New York: Random House, Vintage Books.

Houthakker, H. S.

1968 "Engel, Ernst." *International Encyclopedia of the Social Sciences*, V, 63–64. New York: Macmillan and the Free Press.

Howard, Alan
1972 Review of I. Goldman's *Ancient Polynesian Society*. *American Anthropologist* 74(4):811–823.

Hymes, Dell
1968 "Linguistic Problems in Defining the Concept of 'Tribe.'" In *Essays on the Problem of Tribe*, edited by June Helm. Proceedings of the Annual Spring Meeting of the American Ethnological Society. Seattle: University of Washington Press.

Johnson, Gregory Alan
1973 *Local Exchange and Early State Development in Southwestern Iran*. Anthropological Papers, no. 51. Ann Arbor: Museum of Anthropology, University of Michigan.

Jowett, B., trans.
1937 *The Dialogues of Plato*. 2 vols. New York: Random House.

Keller, Suzanne
1963 *Beyond the Ruling Class*. New York: Random House.

Kluckhohn, Clyde
1951 "Values and Value Orientation in the Theory of Action." In *Toward a Theory of Action*, edited by Talcott Parsons and E. Shils, pp. 388–433. Cambridge: Harvard University Press.

Kroeber, A. L.
1947 *Cultural and Natural Areas of Native North America*. Berkeley and Los Angeles: University of California Press.
1948 *Anthropology*. New York: Harcourt, Brace and Co.

Kropotkin, P'etr
1904 *Mutual Aid: A Factor of Evolution*. London: William Heinemann.

Lane, Robert
1974 "Power Concepts in Melanesia and Northwest North America." Paper read at the American Association for the Advancement of Science Meetings on the Ethnography of Power, 28 February, San Francisco.

Lasswell, Harold, and Abraham Kaplan
1950 *Power and Society*. New Haven: Yale University Press.

Laughlin, William S.
1968 "Hunting: An Integrated Biobehavior System and Its Evolutionary Importance." In *Man the Hunter*, edited by Richard Lee and Irven De Vore, pp. 304–320. Chicago: Aldine Publishing Co.

Leach, Edmund R.
1965 *Political Systems of Highland Burma*. Boston: Beacon Press.

Lee, Richard B.
1968 "What Hunters Do for a Living, or, How to Make Out on Scarce Resources." In *Man the Hunter*, edited by idem and Irven De Vore, pp. 30–48. Chicago: Aldine Publishing Co.

1972a "Population Growth and the Beginnings of Sedentary Life Among the !Kung Bushmen." In *Population Growth: Anthropological Implications*, edited by Brian Spooner, pp. 329–342. Cambridge: MIT Press.

1972b "The Intensification of Social Life among the !Kung Bushmen." In *Population Growth: Anthropological Implications*, edited by Brian Spooner, pp. 343–350. Cambridge: MIT Press.

Lee, Richard, and Irven De Vore, eds.
1968 *Man the Hunter*. Chicago: Aldine Publishing Co.

Lenski, Gerhard
1966 *Power and Privilege*. New York: McGraw-Hill.

Leontief, Wassily
1968 "Input-Output Analysis." *International Encyclopedia of the Social Sciences*, VII, 345–354. New York: Macmillan and the Free Press.

Lévi-Strauss, Claude
1963 *Structural Anthropology*. Translated by Claire Jacobson and Brooke Grundfest Schoepf. New York: Basic Books.

1966 *The Savage Mind*. Chicago: University of Chicago Press.

1967 "The Social and Psychological Aspects of Chieftainship in a Primitive Tribe: The Nambikuara of Northwestern Mato Grosso." In *Comparative Political Systems*, edited by Ronald Cohen and John Middleton, pp. 45–62. Garden City, N.Y.: The Natural History Press. Originally in *Transactions of the New York Academy of Sciences* 7(1944):16–32.

1972 "Structuralism and Ecology." *Social Science Information* 12(1):7–23.

Lewis, C. S.
1973 "The Abolition of Man." In *Toward a Steady-State Economy*, edited by Herman E. Daly, pp. 321–332. San Francisco: W. H. Freeman and Co.

Lotka, Alfred
1921 "Note on the Economic Conversion Factors of Energy." *Proceedings of the National Academy of Sciences* 7:192–197.

1922a "Contribution to the Energetics of Evolution." *Proceedings of the National Academy of Sciences* 8:147–151.

1922b "Natural Selection as a Physical Principle." *Proceedings of the National Academy of Sciences* 8:151–154.

1925 *Elements of Physical Biology*. Baltimore: Williams and Wilkins.

1945 "The Law of Evolution as a Maximal Principle." *Human Biology* 17:167–194.

Lowie, Robert H.

1927 *The Origin of the State*. New York: Harcourt, Brace and Co.

1967 "Some Aspects of Political Organization Among the American Aborigines." In *Comparative Political Systems*, edited by Ronald Cohen and John Middleton, pp. 63–87. Garden City, N.Y.: The Natural History Press. Also in *Journal of the Royal Anthropological Institute* 78, nos. 1–2(1948):11–24.

McKeon, Richard, ed.

1941 *The Basic Works of Aristotle*. New York: Random House.

MacPherson, C. B.

1962 *The Political Theory of Possessive Individualism: Hobbes to Locke*. Oxford: Clarendon Press.

Mair, Lucy

1962 *Primitive Government*. London: Penguin.

Maranda, Pierre

1972 "Structuralism in Cultural Anthropology." In *Annual Review of Anthropology*, edited by Bernard J. Siegel, 1:329–348. Palo Alto: Annual Reviews.

Marcus, Joyce

1973 "Territorial Organization of the Lowland Classic Maya." *Science* 180(4089):911–916.

Margalef, R.

1968 *Perspectives in Ecological Theory*. Chicago: University of Chicago Press.

Martin, John F.

1973 "On the Estimation of the Sizes of Local Groups in a Hunting-Gathering Environment." *American Anthropologist* 75(5):1448–1468.

Maruyama, Magoroh

1968 "The Second Cybernetics: Deviation-Amplifying Mutual Causal Processes." In *Modern Systems Research for the Behavioral Scientist*, edited by W. Buckley, pp. 304–313. Chicago: Aldine Publishing Co.

Marx, Karl

1964 SEE Bottomore and Rubel, eds.

1971 *The Grundrisse*. Edited and translated by David McLellan. New York: Harper and Row.

Maybury-Lewis, David

1969   Review of *Mythologiques: Du miel aux cendres. American Anthropologist* 71:114–121.

Meadows, D. H., D. L. Meadows, J. Randers, and W. W. Behrens
1972   *The Limits of Growth.* New York: Universe Books.

Medawar, P. B.
1973   Review. *New York Review of Books,* 8 March.

Meggitt, M. J.
1967   "The Pattern of Leadership among the Mae-Enga of New Guinea." *Anthropological Forum* 2(1):20–35. Bobbs-Merrill Reprint No. A-441.

Merriam, Charles Edward
1934   *Political Power: Its Composition and Incidence.* New York: McGraw-Hill Book Co., Whittlesey House.
1950   *Political Power.* Glencoe, Ill.: The Free Press.

Miller, George
1956   "The Magical Number 7, Plus or Minus 2: Some Limits on Our Capacity of Processing Information." *Psychological Review* 63:81–97.

Miller, James G.
1965   "Living System: Basic Concepts." *Behavioral Science* 10(3): 193–257; 10(4):337–379.

Moore, Alexander
1973   *Life Cycles in Atchalan.* New York: Teachers College Press.

Mosca, Gaetano
1939   *The Ruling Class.* New York: McGraw-Hill.

Murdock, George Peter
1949   *Social Structure.* New York: Macmillan.

Netting, Robert McC.
1971   *The Ecological Approach in Cultural Study.* Addison-Wesley Modular Publications. Reading, Mass.
1972   "Sacred Power and Centralization: Aspects of Political Adaptation in Africa." In *Population Growth: Anthropological Implications,* edited by Brian Spooner, pp. 219–244. Cambridge: MIT Press.

Nicholas, Ralph
1966   "Segmentary Factional Political Systems." In *Political Anthropology,* edited by Marc J. Swartz, Victor W. Turner, and Arthur Tuden. Chicago: Aldine Publishing Co.

Odum, Howard
1971   *Environment, Power, and Society.* New York: Wiley-Interscience.

Ogburn, William E.
1922   *Social Change.* New York: B. W. Huebsch.

Oliver, Symmes C.
1962   *Ecology and Cultural Continuity as Contribution Factors in the Social Organization of the Plains Indians.* University of California Publications in American Archaeology and Ethnology, vol. 48, no. 1, pp. 1–90. Berkeley and Los Angeles: University of California Press.

Ossowski, Stanislaw
1966   "Different Conceptions of Social Class." In *Class, Status and Power*, edited by Reinhard Bendix and Seymour Martin Lipset, 2d ed., pp. 86–96. New York: The Free Press.

Otterbein, Keith F.
1970   *The Evolution of War: A Cross Cultural Study.* New Haven: HRAF Press.

Parkinson, C. Northcote
1957   *Parkinson's Law and Other Studies in Administration.* Boston: Houghton Mifflin Co.
1971   *The Law of Delay.* Boston: Houghton Mifflin Co.

Parsons, Talcott
1954   *Essays in Sociological Theory.* Glencoe, Ill.: The Free Press.
1963   "On the Concept of Political Power." *Proceedings of the American Philosophical Society* 107(3):232–262. Also in *Class, Status and Power*, edited by Reinhard Bendix and Seymour Martin Lipset, 2d ed., pp. 240–265. New York: The Free Press, 1966.

Piaget, Jean
1969   "Génesis y estructura en psicología." In *Las nociones de estructura y génesis*, by Maurice de Gandillac et al., pp. 241–266. Buenos Aires: Editorial Proteo. (Translated from 1966 French edition.)
1972   *The Principles of Genetic Epistemology.* New York: Basic Books.

Pilling, Arnold
1968   "Southern Australia: Levels of Social Organization." In *Man the Hunter*, edited by Richard Lee and Irven De Vore, pp. 138–145. Chicago: Aldine Publishing Co.

Plato. SEE Jowitt, B., trans. 1937

Polgar, Steven
1972   "Population History and Population Policies from Anthropological Perspective." *Current Anthropology* 13(2):203–211.

Polgar, Steven, ed.
1971   *Culture and Population: A Collection of Current Studies.* Cambridge, Mass.: Schenkman Publishing Co.

Pospisil, Leopold
1958a   "Kapauku Papuan Political Structure." In *Systems of Politi-*

*cal Control and Bureaucracy in Human Societies*, edited by Verne Ray, pp. 9–22. Proceedings of the 1958 Annual Spring Meeting of the American Ethnological Society, Seattle.

1958*b*    *Kapauku Papuans and Their Law*. Yale University Publications in Anthropology, no. 54. New Haven: Yale University.

1963*a*    *Kapauku Papuan Economy*. Yale University Publications in Anthropology, no. 67. New Haven: Yale University.

1963*b*    *The Kapauku Papuans of West New Guinea*. New York: Holt, Rinehart and Winston.

Powell, H. A.

1960    "Competitive Leadership in Trobriand Political Organization." *Journal of the Royal Anthropological Institute* 90(1): 118–145. Also in *Comparative Political Systems*, edited by Ronald Cohen and John Middleton, pp. 155–192. Garden City, N.Y.: The Natural History Press, 1967.

Randers, Jorgen, and Donella Meadows

1973    "The Carrying Capacity of Our Global Environment: A Look at the Ethical Alternatives." In *Toward a Steady-State Economy*, edited by Herman E. Daly, pp. 283–306. San Francisco: W. H. Freeman and Co.

Rapoport, Anatol

1968    "The Promise and Pitfalls of Information Theory." In *Modern Systems Research for the Behavioral Scientist*, edited by W. Buckley, pp. 137–142. Chicago: Aldine Publishing Co.

Rappaport, Roy A.

1968    *Pigs for the Ancestors*. New Haven: Yale University Press.

1969    "Some Suggestions Concerning Concept and Method in Ecological Anthropology." In *Contributions to Anthropology: Ecological Essays*, edited by David Damas, p. 184. National Museum of Canada Bulletin 230, Anthropological Series, no. 86. Ottawa.

1971*a*    "The Flow of Energy in an Agricultural Society." In *Energy and Power*, pp. 69–80. A Scientific American Book. San Francisco: W. H. Freeman and Co.

1971*b*    "The Sacred in Human Evolution." In *Annual Review of Ecology and Systematics* 2:23–44.

Ray, Verne, ed.

1958    *Systems of Political Control and Bureaucracy in Human Societies*. Proceedings of the 1958 Annual Spring Meeting of the American Ethnological Society. Seattle.

Redfield, Margaret Park, ed.

1962    *Human Nature and the Study of Society: The Papers of Robert Redfield*. Chicago: University of Chicago Press.

Redfield, Robert

1941 *The Folk Cultures of Yucatan.* Chicago: University of Chicago Press.

1942 Introduction to *Levels of Integration in Biological and Social Systems.* Vol. 18 of *Biological Symposia*, edited by Jacques Cattell. Lancaster, Pa.: Jacques Cattell Press.

Reina, Ruben

1963 "The Potter and the Farmer: The Fate of Two Innovators in a Maya Village." *Expedition* 5(4):18–30. Philadelphia: University of Pennsylvania Museum.

Ribeiro, Darcy

1968 *The Civilizational Process.* Washington, D.C.: The Smithsonian Press.

1970 *Os indios e a civilização.* Rio de Janeiro: Editora Civilição Brasileira S.A.

Rivière, Peter

1970 "Factions and Exclusions in Two South American Village Systems." In *Witchcraft Confessions and Accusations*, edited by Mary Douglas, pp. 245–256. ASA Monograph 9. London: Tavistock Publications.

Rodgers, William B., and Richard E. Gardner

1969 "Linked Changes in Values and Behavior in the Out Island Bahamas." *American Anthropologist* 71(1):21–35.

Roethlisberger, F. H., and W. Dickson

1939 *Management and the Worker.* Cambridge: Harvard University Press.

Rossi, Ino

1973 "The Unconscious in the Anthropology of Claude Levi-Strauss." *American Anthropologist* 75(1):20–48.

Russell, Bertrand

1938 *Power: A New Social Analysis.* New York: W. W. Norton.

Sahlins, Marshall D.

1958 *Social Stratification in Polynesia.* Seattle: University of Washington Press.

1960 "Evolution: Specific and General." In *Evolution and Culture*, edited by idem and Elman Service, pp. 12–44. Ann Arbor: University of Michigan Press.

1961 "Segmentary Lineage: An Organization of Predatory Expansion." *American Anthropologist* 63:322–345.

1963 "Poor Man, Rich Man, Big Man, Chief: Political Types in Melanesia and Polynesia." *Comparative Studies in Society and History* 5:285–303. Bobbs-Merrill Reprint No. A-339.

1965 "On the Sociology of Primitive Exchange." In *The Relevance of Models for Social Anthropology*, edited by Michael Banton. Association for Social Anthropologists Monograph No. 1. New York: Praeger.

1968  *Tribesmen.* Englewood Cliffs, N.J.: Prentice-Hall.

1972  *Stone Age Economics.* Chicago: Aldine-Atherton.

Sanders, William T.

1972  "Population, Agricultural History, and Societal Evolution in Mesoamerica." In *Population Growth: Anthropological Implications,* edited by Brian Spooner, pp. 101–153. Cambridge: MIT Press.

Schaedel, Richard P.

n.d.*a*  "The City and the Origin of the State in America." Unpublished.

n.d.*b*  "The Commonality in Processual Trends in the Urbanization Process: Urbanization and the Redistributive Function in the Central Andes." Unpublished.

Schrödinger, Erwin

1967  *What Is Life?* Cambridge: Cambridge University Press.

Schumacher, E. F.

1973  "Buddhist Economics." In *Toward a Steady-State Economy,* edited by Herman E. Daly, pp. 231–239. San Francisco: W. H. Freeman and Co.

Schumpeter, Joseph

1966  "The Problem of Classes." In *Class, Status and Power,* edited by Reinhard Bendix and Seymour Martin Lipset, 2d ed., pp. 42–46. New York: The Free Press.

Schwartz, Richard D., and Miller, James C.

1964  "Legal Evolution and Social Complexity." *American Journal of Sociology* 70:159–169.

Service, Elman R.

1962  *Primitive Social Organization.* New York: Random House.

1966  *The Hunters.* Englewood Cliffs, N.J.: Prentice-Hall.

1971  *Cultural Evolutionism: Theory in Practice.* New York: Holt, Rinehart and Winston.

Sharp, R. Lauriston

1958  "People Without Politics." In *Systems of Political Control and Bureaucracy in Human Societies,* edited by Verne Ray, pp. 1–8. Proceedings of the 1958 Annual Spring Meeting of the American Ethnological Society. Seattle.

Shepard, Paul

1973  *The Tender Carnivore and the Sacred Game.* New York: Charles Scribner's Sons.

Sherzer, Joel

1972  Personal communication. 15 February 1972.

Simon, Herbert
    1957   *Models of Man.* New York.
    1965   "The Architecture of Complexity." *General Systems* 10.

Skinner, G. W.
    1959   "The Nature of Loyalties in Rural Indonesia." In *Local, Ethnic, and National Loyalties in Village Indonesia,* edited by idem. New York: Institute of Pacific Relations; New Haven: Yale University, Southeast Asia Studies.

Slobodkin, L. B.
    1968   "Toward a Predictive Theory of Evolution." In *Population Biology and Evolution,* edited by Richard O. Lewontin, pp. 187–205. Syracuse: Syracuse University Press.

Smaldone, Joseph P.
    1972   "Firearms in the Central Sudan: A Revolution." *Journal of African History* 13(4):591–607.

Sorensen, Arthur R., Jr.
    1967   "Multi-Lingualism in the Northwest Amazon." *American Anthropologist* 69(6):670–685.

Sorenson, E. Richard
    1972   "Socio-ecological Change among the Fore of New Guinea." *Current Anthropology* 13(3–4):349–372.

Southall, Aiden
    1965   "A Critique of the Typology of States and Political Systems." In *Political Systems and the Distribution of Power,* edited by Michael Banton, pp. 113–140. London: Tavistock Publications.

Spengler, Joseph J.
    1959   "Economics and Demography." In *The Study of Population,* edited by Philip M. Hauser and Otis Dudley Duncan, pp. 791–831. Chicago: University of Chicago Press.

Spicer, Edward
    1971   "Persistent Cultural Systems." *Science* 174(19 November):795–800.

Spooner, Brian, ed.
    1972   *Population Growth: Anthropological Implications.* Cambridge: MIT Press.

Stanley, Sam
    1974   "American Indian Power and Powerlessness." Paper read at the American Association for the Advancement of Science Meetings on the Ethnography of Power, 26 February, San Francisco.

Starr, Betty
    1954   "Levels of Community Relations." *American Journal of Sociology* 60(2):125–135.

Starr, Chauncey, and Richard Rudman

1973 "Parameters of Technological Growth." *Science* 182(4110): 358–364.

Stavenhagen, Rodolfo
1967 "Las relaciones entre la estratificación social y la dinámica de clases." In *Estructura, estratificación y mobilidad social,* edited by Anthony Leeds, pp. 126–151. Estudios y Monografías 20; Studies and Monographs 7. Washington, D.C.: Pan-American Union.

Steinhart, John S., and Carol E. Steinhart
1974 "Energy Use in the U.S. Food System." *Science* 184(4134): 307–316.

Stevenson, R. F.
1968 *Population and Political Systems in Tropical Africa.* New York: Columbia University Press.

Steward, Julian
1955 *Theory of Culture Change.* Urbana: University of Illinois Press.

Strickon, Arnold, and Sidney M. Greenfield, eds.
1972 *Structure and Process in Latin America: Patronage, Clientage and Power Systems.* Albuquerque: University of New Mexico Press.

Stuart, William T.
1972 "The Explanation of Patron-Client Systems: Some Structural and Ecological Perspectives." In *Structure and Process in Latin America: Patronage, Clientage and Power Systems,* edited by Arnold Strickon and Sidney M. Greenfield, pp. 19–42. Albuquerque: University of New Mexico Press.

Stuckey, John, and J. David Singer
1973 "The Powerful and the War-Prone: Ranking the Nations by Relative Capability and War Experience, 1820–1964." Paper read at American Association for the Advancement of Science meeting, June, Mexico City. To be published in Spanish by the Instituto Nacional de Antropología e Historia, Mexico City.

Summers, Claude M.
1971 "The Conversion of Energy." In *Energy and Power,* pp. 95–106. A Scientific American Book. San Francisco: W. H. Freeman and Co.

Sumner, William Graham
1906 *Folkways.* New York: Ginn and Co.

Swanson, Guy
1960 *The Birth of the Gods.* Ann Arbor: University of Michigan Press.

Swartz, Marc J., Victor W. Turner, and Arthur Tuden, eds.
1966 *Political Anthropology.* Chicago: Aldine Publishing Co.

Taagepera, Rein
1968 "Growth Curves of Empires." *General Systems* 13:171–175.
Tawney, R. H.
1931 *Equality.* New York: Harcourt, Brace and Co.
Thompson, Warren S.
1956 "The Spiral of Population." In *Man's Role in Changing the Face of the Earth,* edited by W. L. Thomas, Jr., pp. 970–986. Chicago: University of Chicago Press.
Tilly, Charles
Forthcoming "Reflections on European Statemaking." In *The Formation of National States in Western Europe,* edited by idem. Princeton: Princeton University Press.
Tönnies, Ferdinand
1957 *Community and Society, Gemeinschaft and Gesellschaft.* Translated by Charles P. Loomis. East Lansing: Michigan State University Press.
Tribus, Myron
1961 "Information Theory as the Basis for Thermostatics and Thermodynamics." *Transactions of the American Society of Mechanical Engineers,* series 5. *Journal of Applied Mechanics* 83 (March):1–8.
Tribus, Myron, and Edward C. McIrvine
1971 "Energy and Information." In *Energy and Power,* pp. 121–128. A Scientific American Book. San Francisco: W. H. Freeman and Co.
Tullis, F. LaMond
1970 *Lord and Peasant in Peru: A Paradigm of Political and Social Change.* Cambridge: Harvard University Press.
Ubbelohde, A. R.
1955 *Man and Energy.* New York: George Braziller.
Vansina, Jan
1962 "A Comparison of African Kingdoms." *Africa* 32:324–334.
Verhoeven, Stan
1974 "The Overflow of Hawaiian Religion: Revolution or Evolution?" Manuscript in possession of the author.
Wallace, Anthony F. C.
1966 *Religion: An Anthropological View.* New York: Random House.
1970 *Culture and Personality.* 2d ed. New York: Random House.
Watkins, Frederick M.
1968 "State: The Concept." *International Encyclopedia of the Social Sciences,* XV, 150–156. New York: Macmillan and the Free Press.

Weber, Max
   [1946]  SEE Gerth, H. H., and C. Wright Mills, eds. and trans. 1946
   1964  *The Theory of Social and Economic Organization.* Translated
     by A. M. Henderson and Talcott Parsons. Glencoe, Ill.: The Free
     Press.
White, Leslie A.
   1943  "Energy and the Evolution of Culture." *American Anthro-
     pologist* 45:335–356.
   1949  *The Science of Culture.* New York: Farrar and Straus.
   1959  *The Evolution of Culture.* New York: McGraw-Hill.
Whyte, William F.
   1974  "Rural Peru—Peasants as Activists." In *Contemporary Cul-
     tures and Societies of Latin America,* edited by Dwight Heath, 2d
     ed., pp. 526–541. New York: Random House.
Winckler, Edwin A.
   1970  "Political Anthropology." In *Biennial Review of Anthropolo-
     gy, 1969,* edited by B. Siegel. Stanford: Stanford University Press.
Wolf, Eric
   1966  *Peasants.* Englewood Cliffs, N.J.: Prentice-Hall Publishing Co.
   1967  "Levels of Communal Relations." In *Social Anthropology,*
     edited by Manning Nash, pp. 299–316. Handbook of Middle Amer-
     ican Indians, edited by Robert Wauchope, vol. 6. Austin: Univer-
     sity of Texas Press.
Wolf, Eric, and Edward C. Hansen
   1972  *The Human Condition in Latin America.* New York: Oxford
     University Press.
Worsley, Peter
   1957  "Millenarian Movements in Melanesia." *Rhodes-Livingston
     Institute Journal* 21:18–31.
   1968  *The Trumpet Shall Sound: A Study of "Cargo" Cults in
     Melanesia.* 2d, augmented ed. New York: Schocken Books.
Wright, Henry T.
   Forthcoming  "An Explanation of the Origin of the State." To be
     published in a volume edited by James Hill. Santa Fe: School of
     American Research.

# INDEX

Access to power, 68

Adams, Robert McC., 232, 260 n

Adaptation: as capacity to change, 200; as capacity to respond, 187–188; common, 56; and consistency of experience, 187; and control of energy, 201; and control of environment, 200; and cultural growth, 285; and experience, 191; and input and output, 140; levels of, 188–189; limits of, 187; of man to environment, 152; of operating units, 54–56; and ranking, 223; of society to environment, 187; symbiotic processes and, 201; by use of goals, 120; and value changes, 177. *See also* Evolution

Administered unit, 57, 67

Africa, 87, 101–102, 224, 231, 234, 248, 260, 268, 275, 296. *See also* Alur; Bito; Buganda; Bushmen; East Africa; Gusii; Herero; Mandari; Masai; Nandi; Nigeria; Nuer; Plateau Tonga; Shilluk; West African society; Zulu

Aggregate units, 56–60

Agrarian existence, 311; future, 306

Agrarian societies, 311–312

Agricultural revolution, 146

Agriculture, invention of, 309–310; technology of, 193–194

Akwe-Shavante, 224, 235

Allocated power, 42, 43–47, 81; and centralization, 238; and delegated power, 44; extension of, 49; and multiple granting of power, 44; in primitive societies, 45–46; and ranking, 172–173; and religion, 236; and social complexity, 45–47; and super-

naturalism, 235–236

Althusser, Louis, 272

Alur, 228, 233

American Revolution, 237, 270

Anglo-Saxon England, 285, 296

Anne, Queen, 270

"Antagonistic cooperation," 84

Arabs, 45, 237, 274

Archaic society, 207

Argentina, 93, 275

Aristotle, 29, 191 n, 244

Aron, Raymond, 21 n

Articulation. *See* Levels of articulation

Ashby, W. Ross, 128 n

Atchalan, 48 n

Australia, 276

Australian aboriginal society, 60, 144, 156, 223, 224. *See also* Tiwi; Yir Yoront

Austro-Hungarian Empire, 270

Authentic culture, 253

Authority, 236; decision-making, 262–263; definition of, 30–31; kinds of, 34, 223; "lack" of, 223; and legitimacy, 30–36; recognition of, 24; stratification of, 248. *See also* Skill authority; Power authority

Aztecs, 35, 260, 266

Bailey, F. G., 6, 77, 171

Balandier, Georges, 6–7, 28–29, 242 n

Bali, 311 n

Bands, 61, 218; centralized nature of, 222; and chiefdom relations, 228–229; conflicts between, 224–225; co-ordination between, 224; evolution of, 204, 207, 208; expansion of, 223, 225, 292; in growth sequence, 223; and horizontal oscillation, 293; and